Essentials of Applied Mathematics

J. R. Irwin

Head of Mathematics
Harrow Weald Sixth Form College

Edward Arnold

© R Irwin 1979

First Published 1979
by Edward Arnold (Publishers) Ltd.
41 Bedford Square, London WC1B 3DQ

Reprinted 1981, 1983

ISBN 0 7131 0306 X

British Library Cataloguing in Publication Data

Irwin, J R
  Mathematics, applied.
  1. Mathematics
  I. Title
  510   QA36

  ISBN 0–7131–0306–X

Filmset in 'Monophoto' Times 10 on 11 pt. and
printed in Hong Kong by
Wing King Tong Co. Ltd.

Preface

The purpose of this book is to cover in a single volume the applied mathematics content of the single subject 'Mathematics' offered at Advanced level by many examining boards. A comprehensive chapter on basic probability is included and considerable use is made of the style of vector work currently being examined.

The main difference between this and other textbooks is one of approach. Firstly it is hoped that by sacrificing rigour the text has been kept clear enough to be comprehended by the average student and concise enough to serve as a useful revision text immediately prior to examination. Secondly, the book as a whole is designed to help both student and teacher by breaking each chapter down into relatively short teaching units each with an accompanying set of exercises. This is especially true of the early chapters in which the introductory ideas are approached in easy stages and the various types of force are introduced one by one, as needed, instead of all together which can often lead to confusion.

The book should be particularly helpful to those students embarking on sixth form mathematics courses who have difficulty acquiring the basic principles of applied mathematics. At the same time, however, the teacher should find that there is plenty of material to occupy the more gifted students.

It is intended that, in the main, the work of each section will form the subject matter for a single teaching session and that further sessions will be used for students to complete the accompanying exercises satisfactorily. Exercises constitute the most important part of a mathematics text and every effort has been made to make the questions, the vast majority of which are original, both varied in content and sufficient in number. Most exercises finish with some more difficult questions.

My thanks are due to all those who have encouraged me in this work and, in particular, to my mother for her painstaking care with the typescript.

Note to the Reader

Questions marked * introduce ideas or techniques which are not specifically mentioned in the text. Many of these questions will need discussion after the group has attempted them.

Questions marked † require techniques of pure mathematics which are not necessarily familiar to the student at this stage in his course. As a general guideline here it is assumed that the basic calculus results will be known in time for chapters 5 and 6 (the calculus work of chapter 1 being deferred if necessary) and the trigonometric addition formulae in time for the later sections of chapters 9 and 10.

Contents

1

Velocity and Acceleration

1.1 Uniform Acceleration Equations

To many people **velocity** is just an alternative word for **speed**; in other words it measures how fast a body is moving – how many metres it travels in a second or how many kilometres per hour. We shall see later that there is far more to the concept of velocity than this, but for the work of this first section we shall nevertheless use only the everyday meaning of the word.

When the velocity of a body is changing it is said to undergo **acceleration**. For the moment we may define acceleration as the rate at which velocity *increases*. A negative acceleration according to this definition will mean that the velocity is decreasing. This is called **retardation**. In the next section 1.2 we will be more precise about these terms but we shall not define them strictly until section 5.8.

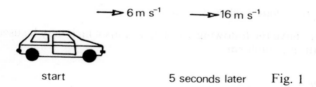

start   5 seconds later   Fig. 1

Consider the car shown in Fig. 1. If the car is gaining velocity at a steady rate we say that the acceleration is *uniform*. If this is the case, the velocity must be increasing by

$$10 \text{ m s}^{-1} \text{ every 5 s}$$
$$\text{or by } 2 \text{ m s}^{-1} \text{ every second}$$

i.e the acceleration is 2 m s^{-2}.

Suppose we denote the initial and final velocities of the car by u and v respectively and the time interval by t. (Fig. 2)

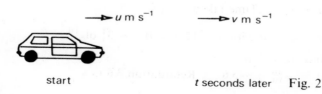

start t seconds later   Fig. 2

Comparing with the first example we see that if the acceleration is uniform then

$$\text{acceleration } a = \frac{\text{increase in velocity}}{\text{time}} = \frac{v - u}{t} \tag{1}$$

$$\Rightarrow v - u = at \qquad \text{or} \quad v = u + at \tag{2}$$

Notice that if the car is slowing down, so that $v < u$, then equation 1 will give us a negative acceleration as expected.

What about the distance travelled by the car? We shall see in section 1.5(ii) that for a uniform acceleration it is true to say that

distance covered = average velocity × time

Thus in our original example, where the average velocity was 11 m s^{-1}, the distance travelled during the 5 seconds would be $11 \times 5 = 55$ metres, whilst in symbols we obtain the formula

$$\text{distance } s = \tfrac{1}{2}(u + v).t \tag{3}$$

Two further formulae may now be obtained. Substituting 2 into 3

$$s = \tfrac{1}{2}(2u + at)t = ut + \tfrac{1}{2}at^2$$

Multiplying 1 by 3

$$as = \frac{(v - u)}{t} \cdot \frac{(u + v)}{2} \cdot t$$

$$\Rightarrow 2as = (v - u)(u + v) = v^2 - u^2$$

We therefore have the following set of equations which may be used whenever acceleration is uniform

$$\begin{aligned}
v &= u + at \\
s &= \tfrac{1}{2}(u + v).t \\
s &= ut + \tfrac{1}{2}at^2 \\
v^2 - u^2 &= 2as
\end{aligned}$$

Example 1

A body moving initially at 12 m s^{-1} slows down uniformly to rest over a distance of 20 metres. Find the retardation and the time taken.

using $\quad s = \tfrac{1}{2}(u + v).t$ with $u = 12, v = 0, s = 20$

$$20 = 6t$$

$$t = 3\tfrac{1}{3} \qquad \text{Time taken} = 3\tfrac{1}{3} \text{ s}$$

using $\quad v = u + at$ with $u = 12, v = 0, t = 3\tfrac{1}{3}$ or $\tfrac{10}{3}$

$$0 = 12 + \tfrac{10}{3}a$$

$$a = -\tfrac{36}{10} = -3.6 \qquad \text{Retardation } 3.6 \text{ m s}^{-2}$$

Example 2

A train accelerates uniformly from 25 km h^{-1} to 45 km h^{-1} over a distance of $3\frac{1}{2}$ kilometres. Find (i) the acceleration, (ii) the time taken to cover the first $1\frac{1}{2}$ kilometres.

This example demonstrates that any set of units may be used providing they are *consistent*. This means that we may use km h^{-1} as our unit of velocity providing that all distances are measured in km and all times in hours. On this system acceleration would have to be measured in km h^{-2}.

(i) Using $\qquad v^2 - u^2 = 2as$

or $(v + u)(v - u) = 2as \qquad\qquad$ with $u = 25$, $v = 45$, $s = 3\frac{1}{2}$

$\qquad\qquad 70 \times 20 = 7a$

$\qquad\qquad\qquad a = 200 \qquad\qquad$ acceleration $= 200$ km h^{-2}

(ii) Using $\;\; s = ut + \frac{1}{2}at^2 \qquad\qquad$ with $u = 25$, $s = 1\frac{1}{2}$, $a = 200$

$\qquad\quad 1\frac{1}{2} = 25t + 100t^2$

$\qquad\qquad \Rightarrow 200t^2 + 50t - 3 = 0$

$\qquad\qquad (10t + 3)(20t - 1) = 0$

$\qquad\qquad$ ignoring the negative answer we have time $= 1/20$ h or 3 min

Note: Many questions may be done very conveniently, without writing down any formulae, simply by using the idea that distance $=$ average velocity $\times$ time. In example 2 (i) for instance, we have an average velocity of 35 km h^{-1} so that the time taken for 3.5 km must be $1/10$ h (or 6 minutes). Hence the acceleration is 20 km h^{-1} in $1/10$ h or 200 km h^{-2}.

Exercise 1 (a)

1. A car travelling initially at 15 m s^{-1} begins to accelerate uniformly at 3 m s^{-2}. What will be its speed 4 s later and how far will it have travelled in this time?

2. A train travelling at 40 m s^{-1} begins to climb an incline and loses speed uniformly at $1/2$ m s^{-2}. After how long will its speed have fallen to 30 m s^{-1} and how far up the incline will it have travelled in this time?

3. A car accelerating uniformly away from rest at traffic lights reaches a speed of 20 m s^{-1} in 12 s. How far has it travelled and what is the acceleration?

4. How far does a tube train travel in accelerating uniformly from 10 km h^{-1} to 80 km h^{-1} in 2 minutes and what is the acceleration? How fast is the train moving at the half-way point?

5. A pistol shot accelerated uniformly from rest along a 25 cm barrel reaches a speed of 200 m s^{-1}. For how long is it in the barrel?

6. A cyclist coasting downhill accelerates uniformly at $1\frac{1}{2}$ m s^{-2}. If his initial speed is 5 m s^{-1}, find (i) how far he travels in 4 s (ii) how long he takes to travel 8 m.

7. A train driver slightly misjudges his arrival at a terminus, his train striking the buffers at 1.6 m s^{-1} and depressing them by 40 cm. What retardation is caused by the buffers and how far would they be depressed by a train travelling at 1.2 m s^{-1}, assuming the retardation to be the same?

8. A four-man bobsleigh starting down a run at 8 m s^{-1} accelerates uniformly at 2.4 m s^{-2} over the first 40 m. How long does this take? Find also the speed after 30 m.

9. A train travels two-thirds of a kilometre whilst accelerating uniformly from 70 km h^{-1} to 90 km h^{-1}. Find its acceleration and the time taken. How fast is the train travelling at the half-way point?

10. A train travelling at 80 km h^{-1} starts braking uniformly 2 km before a station at which it stops. How long does the train take to reach the station? If the train started braking only $1\frac{1}{2}$ km in advance, at what speed would it reach the station, assuming the retardation to be the same?

11. A stone sliding across ice slows down from 14 m s^{-1} to 10 m s^{-1} in travelling 30 m. What is the retardation? What will be the speed after a further 30 m? Find also the times taken over each of these distances.

12. The front of a train 60 m long passes a signal at 54 km h^{-1}. The rear of the train passes the signal 5 s later. Is the train accelerating or braking and at what rate? At what speed does the rear of the train pass the signal?

13. A boy in a train times the intervals between kilometre posts beside the track. Two successive kilometres take 40 s and 30 s respectively. Find the speed of the train in km h^{-1} at the start of the first kilometre, and also the acceleration (assumed uniform).

14. A plane is accelerating uniformly down a runway. The times over two successive sections of runway equal in length are in the ratio 2 : 1. Show that the initial and final velocities over this complete period are in the ratio 1 : 7.

1.2 Stricter Use of Symbols

In problems where motion takes place in both directions along a line we must be more precise in the way we use the symbols of the uniform acceleration equations.

s **measures displacement from a fixed origin O.** The value of *s* is most simply thought of as defining the *position* of the body on an axis measured through the origin O. (Fig. 3).

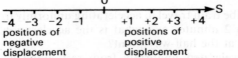

Fig. 3

Distance travelled must be found from *change in displacement*. Thus a body moving from displacement -3 to displacement $+2$ covers a distance of 5 units (providing its direction of motion does not change during this time).

The average velocity result of the previous section should more correctly be stated as change in displacement = average velocity × time.

Velocity. We give all velocities a sign according to whether they are in the direction of positive displacement or negative displacement (Fig. 4).

negative
velocity

positive
velocity

Fig. 4

Thus a velocity of -3 m s^{-1} indicates a body moving towards the negative end of the displacement scale with a *speed* of 3 m s^{-1}. (When we talk of speed we shall not be concerned with the direction of movement.)

Acceleration. This may also be positive or negative and is best explained by simple examples.

An acceleration of $+2$ m s^{-2} will mean that the velocity is changing by $+2$ m s^{-1} each second. Thus we could have sequences of velocities at 1 second intervals like

(a) Initial velocity $+15$ m s^{-1} succeeding values $+17, +19, +21$ m s^{-1}
or
(b) Initial velocity -12 m s^{-1} succeeding values $-10, -8, -6$ m s^{-1}

i.e. a positive acceleration gives motion in the positive direction speeding up (case a) or motion in the negative direction slowing down (case b).

An acceleration of -2 m s^{-2}, however, if applied to the same initial velocities as before would lead to the following sequences

(c) Initial velocity $+15$ m s^{-1} succeeding values $+13, +11, +9$ m s^{-1}
(d) Initial velocity -12 m s^{-1} succeeding values $-14, -16, -18$ m s^{-1}

Thus a negative acceleration gives motion in the positive direction slowing down (case c) or in the negative direction speeding up (case d).

It is important to realise that a uniform acceleration in the opposite sense to the velocity of a body will ultimately cause the body to change direction, e.g case (b), if continued, runs $-10, -8, -6, -4, -2, 0$, then $+2, +4$ m s^{-1} etc. The change of sign indicates that the velocity is now in the opposite direction.

Providing we adhere carefully to these sign conventions, the equations of section 1.1 are still applicable.

Example 3

Investigate the first 6 s of motion of a body starting from a fixed point O with initial velocity $+8$ m s^{-1} and subject to a uniform acceleration of -3 m s^{-2}.

As the acceleration is -3 m s^{-2} the sequence of velocities at one second intervals will be $+8, +5, +2, -1, -4$ m s^{-1} etc. Thus the body moves initially in the positive direction but subsequently changes direction and moves back the other way, presumably returning through its starting position O. We could therefore investigate (i) the time and displacement at which the body changes direction (ii) the time at which it returns through its starting position (iii) its displacement at the end of the 6 seconds considered.

$v = u + at$ with $u = 8$ and $a = -3$

$\Rightarrow v = 8 - 3t$ (1)

$s = ut + \frac{1}{2}at^2$ with $u = 8$ and $a = -3$

$\Rightarrow s = 8t - \frac{3}{2}t^2$ (2)

Equations (1) and (2) are the general formulae for the velocity and the displacement at time t. They may be used as follows.

(i) When changing direction there must be an instant when the body is at rest, i.e. $v = 0$. From (1) $v = 0$ when $t = 8/3$ or $2\frac{2}{3}$ s. The displacement at time $t = 8/3$ is then found from equation (2)

$$s = \frac{64}{3} - \frac{3}{2} \cdot \frac{64}{9} = +\frac{32}{3} \text{ m}$$

Thus the body moves to displacement $+10\frac{2}{3}$ m before stopping instantaneously and changing direction.

(ii) At the instant of its return through O the body has displacement zero. (This does not mean it has covered no distance.) Putting $s = 0$ into (2) we obtain

$$0 = 8t - \frac{3t^2}{2}$$

$$\Rightarrow 0 = 16t - 3t^2 = t(16 - 3t) \quad t = 0 \text{ or } 5\frac{1}{3} \text{ s}$$

So the body returns to its starting position at time $5\frac{1}{3}$ s. ($t = 0$ is the starting instant when it also has zero displacement.)

(iii) The displacement at time $t = 6$ is also found from (2)

$$s = 48 - \frac{3.36}{2} = -6 \text{ m}$$

Exercise 1(b)

1. In which of the following situations will a particle change direction and return to its starting point? (No calculation needed.)
   (i) initial velocity -15 m s^{-1} acceleration $+4$ m s^{-2}
   (ii) initial velocity -4 m s^{-1} acceleration -6 m s^{-2}
   (iii) initial velocity 80 m s^{-1} acceleration -2 m s^{-2}
2. In question 1 (i) at what time and at what displacement does the particle come instantaneously to rest?
3. In question 1 (ii) how long does the particle take to reach a displacement of -15 m and what is its velocity at this point?
4. In question 1 (iii) at what times is the particle at displacement $+1200$ m? Why are there two answers?
5. A body starts from a fixed point O with initial velocity -10 m s^{-1} and uniform acceleration $+4$ m s^{-2}. Write down the general formulae for displacement and for velocity at time t seconds and hence find
   (i) the displacement at times 2, 4, 6 s
   (ii) the velocities at these times
   (iii) the greatest negative displacement reached during the motion.
6. A particle moving initially east at 15 m s^{-1} is subject to an acceleration of 4 m s^{-2} westwards. Find the times at which it is 7 m east of its starting point. Find also its displacement at the instant when its velocity is 5 m s^{-1} due west.
7. The displacements of a body moving with uniform acceleration are 0, 10 and 14 m at times 0, 1, 2 s respectively. Find the acceleration and the initial velocity of the particle. At what time is the displacement again zero?

1.3 Vertical Motion Under Gravity

We know that due to the 'gravitational pull' of the earth a freely falling body accelerates. The magnitude of this acceleration, which we call the **acceleration due to gravity** (g), varies slightly between different parts of the earth's surface but is always close to the value of 9.8 m s^{-2}, which is the value we shall work with in this book. This means that if we neglect the effect of air-resistance the speed of a falling body will increase by 9.8 m s^{-1} during each second of fall.

In fact, as we shall see in section 17.4, the magnitude of the acceleration due to gravity does decrease significantly at large distances from the earth but in problems where we are working in close proximity to the earth's surface (that is at distances small in comparison with the radius of the earth) we are justified in considering this acceleration to be uniform.

In problems on falling bodies, or on bodies projected vertically upwards, we use a vertical axis of displacement and may choose to measure positive displacement either upwards or downwards according to convenience.

Example 4

A stone is thrown vertically upwards at 21 m s^{-1}. (i) How high is it after 2 seconds? (ii) What is the maximum height reached? (iii) If the stone is thrown from the edge of a cliff 17.5 metres high, after how long will it strike the ground at the foot of the cliff?

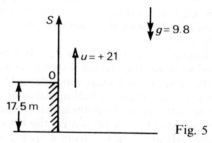

Fig. 5

We shall choose to measure positive displacement upwards from the starting position. (See Fig. 5.) On this basis the initial velocity is positive and g is negative.

(i) height after 2 s
$$s = ut + \tfrac{1}{2}at^2$$
$$= 42 + \tfrac{1}{2}(-9.8)4$$
$$= 42 - 19.6$$
$$\text{height} = 22.4 \text{ m}$$

(ii) at maximum height velocity is zero
$$v^2 - u^2 = 2as$$
$$0^2 - 21^2 = 2 \times (-9.8) \times s$$
$$-441 = -19.6s$$
$$\text{height} = \frac{441}{19.6} = 22.5 \text{ m}$$

(iii) When the stone hits the ground its displacement on our axis is -17.5 m

$$s = ut + \tfrac{1}{2}at^2$$
$$-17.5 = 21t - 4.9t^2$$
$$\Rightarrow 49t^2 - 210t - 175 = 0$$
$$7t^2 - 30t - 25 = 0$$
$$(7t + 5)(t - 5) = 0$$

Ignoring the negative answer we have time = 5 sec

Note that in solving part (iii) it is not necessary to consider the upward and downward parts of the motion separately.

Exercise 1 (c)

For this exercise take g as 9.8 m s^{-2}

1. A stone falls vertically from rest. How far does it travel in each of the first three seconds?
2. A pellet is catapulted upwards at 40 m s^{-1}. Find its velocity after 3 seconds and after 5 seconds. How high up is it at each of these times?
3. A pistol shot is fired vertically upwards at 200 m s^{-1}. How long does it take to reach its highest point, and how high is this?
4. A football kicked vertically upwards is in the air for 5 seconds. How high does it reach and with what speed was it kicked?
5. A rock is dropped down a disused mine shaft 65 m deep. For how long does it fall and with what speed does it strike the bottom?
6. A body thrown vertically downwards covers 60 m in 3 seconds. With what speed was it thrown?
7. A hot air balloon is falling vertically at 2 m s^{-1}. A ballast bag is allowed to fall and is observed to strike the ground 4 seconds later. How high up was the balloon at the instant the ballast was released?
8. A boy standing beside a wall throws a ball upwards at 10.5 m s^{-1}. The top of the wall is 5.6 m higher than the point at which the ball is released. For how long is the ball visible to a person on the far side of the wall?
9. A diver is thrown upwards at 6.8 m s^{-1} from a springboard 6 m above the water. How long is he in the air and with what speed does he enter the water?
10. A stone is dropped from the top of a tower. One second later a second stone is thrown downwards at 12.25 m s^{-1}. If both stones hit the ground simultaneously, what is the height of the tower?
11. A stone is let fall from the top of a cliff 18 m high. At the same instant another stone is projected vertically upwards at 15 m s^{-1} from the foot of the cliff and in the same vertical line. Where and when will they collide?
12. Two particles are projected vertically upwards from the same point with speed u but at times t apart. Prove that they will meet at a height

$$(4u^2 - g^2t^2)/8g$$

It must be emphasised that the formulae used in sections 1.1–1.3 hold only for uniform acceleration. When, as is more usual, the acceleration is non-uniform, then other methods must be employed. In the next two sections 1.4 and 1.5 we consider the graphical treatment of general acceleration. Further methods will be dealt with in chapter 17.

1.4 Properties of the Displacement–Time Graph

(i) A straight line represents uniform velocity

In Fig. 6 line 1 shows displacement increasing by 10 m each second and therefore represents a velocity of $+10 \text{ m s}^{-1}$

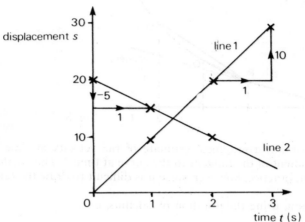

Fig. 6

Line 2 shows displacement decreasing by 5 m each second so that motion is in the negative direction. This line corresponds to a velocity of -5 m s^{-1}. Note that in each case the velocity is given by the gradient of the line.

(ii) A curved line represents acceleration

The graph of Fig. 7 shows a motion in which the velocity is increasing since the distances covered in successive seconds are 4, 6 and 10 m.

The dotted line represents a motion in which the velocity is decreasing.

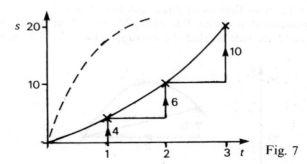

Fig. 7

(iii) Velocity at an instant is given by the gradient of the curve

Fig. 8 shows an enlarged portion of Fig. 7. The gradient of the line PQ gives the average velocity (10 m s^{-1}) between $t = 2$ and $t = 3$.

The gradient of the line PQ_1 gives the average velocity between $t = 2$ and $t = 2\frac{1}{2}$.

By moving Q progressively closer to P in order to find the average velocity between $t = 2$ and $t = 2.2$ and then between $t = 2$ and $t = 2.1$ etc. we obtain answers which must be getting closer to the instantaneous velocity at time 2. But as Q moves very close to P, the line PQ becomes almost indistinguishable from the tangent at P.

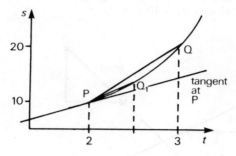

Fig. 8

Thus we may obtain a graphical estimate of the velocity at time 2 by measuring the gradient of the tangent to the curve at time 2. This method is not very reliable in practice, however, since it is difficult to draw the tangent correctly.

The exact relation, using the notation of calculus, is

$$v = \frac{ds}{dt} \quad \text{or} \quad s \underset{\text{diff}}{\longrightarrow} v$$

(iv) Distinction between average speed and average velocity

Velocity may be defined as rate of change of displacement and speed as rate of change of distance travelled. Consider the motion represented by Fig. 9 in which a body moves from displacement $+15$ to displacement $+20$ and then returns to displacement $+10$.

During the 2 seconds from $t = 1$ to $t = 3$ the particle covers a total distance of 15 m so that its average speed is $7\frac{1}{2}$ m s^{-1}.

Its displacement however has changed by -5 m (from $+15$ to $+10$) during these 2 seconds so that the average velocity is $-2\frac{1}{2}$ m s^{-1}.

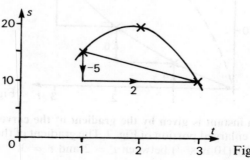

Fig. 9

1.5 Properties of the Velocity–Time Graph

(i) Gradient gives acceleration

A similar argument to that used in section 1.4 (iii) may be used to establish that the gradient of a velocity-time graph gives us acceleration at an instant.

Using calculus notation the result may be written

$$a = \frac{dv}{dt} \quad \text{or} \quad v \xrightarrow[\text{diff}]{} a$$

Bearing this in mind we can interpret the following types of velocity-time graph

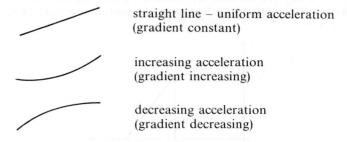

straight line – uniform acceleration (gradient constant)

increasing acceleration (gradient increasing)

decreasing acceleration (gradient decreasing)

(ii) Area under graph gives change in displacement

The inverse relation to $s \xrightarrow[\text{diff}]{} v$ is $s \xleftarrow[\text{int}]{} v$ or $s = \int v \,.\, dt$

Students familiar with calculus will know that $\int y \, dx$ gives the area under a graph drawn on conventional y/x axes. $\int v \, dt$ is thus the area under the velocity-time graph (which is drawn on v/t axes). We therefore have the result that

$$\text{Change in displacement} = \text{area under } v/t \text{ graph}$$

A particular case worthy of note is that of uniform acceleration from initial velocity u to final velocity v. This will be a straight line graph. (Fig. 10.)

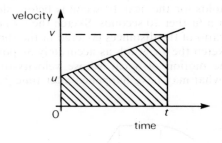

Fig. 10

$s = $ area under v/t graph
$\quad = \frac{1}{2}(u + v)t$

(using the standard area method for a trapezium)

Exercise 1(d)

1. Describe the motion represented by this displacement-time graph, distinguishing carefully between the sections a, b and c.

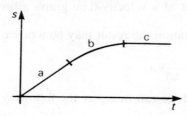

2. Describe briefly the motion represented by this velocity-time graph. If the distances covered in the 2 parts of the motion are equal, what is the ratio $t_1 : t_2$?

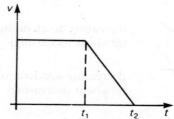

3. Describe briefly the motion represented by this displacement-time graph and sketch the corresponding velocity-time graph. Is this motion a realistic one?

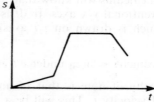

4. In the first 10 seconds of its motion a particle accelerates uniformly up to top speed, which it holds for the next 10 seconds before slowing down uniformly to rest over a further 20 seconds. Sketch the v/t graph for this motion. What is the ratio of the distances covered in the three phases of the motion? Hence sketch the s/t graph as accurately as possible.

5. Describe carefully the motion of a car whose velocity-time graph is shown here. Suggest what may have happened after time T.

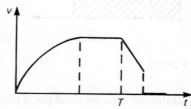

6. Two bodies A and B both accelerate from initial velocity u to final velocity v in the same time t, but, whereas A's acceleration is uniform, that of B is decreasing. Sketch the two velocity-time graphs on the same axes and hence decide which body covers the greater distance.

7. Find the displacement at times 1, 2, 4 and 7 seconds of the motion represented by this v/t graph. Draw the corresponding s/t graph labelling the points which correspond to A, B, C and D.

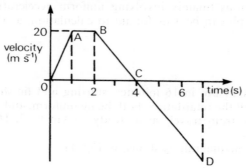

8. A truck is shunted 50 m forward, 30 m back then finally 40 m forward, the times for the three phases being 10 s, 6 s, 8 s respectively. Find (i) the average speed (ii) the average velocity.

9. The velocity of a train between two stations is given by the following table

time (min)	0	1	2	3	4	5	6	7
velocity (km h^{-1})	0	32	64	80	80	80	40	0

Both acceleration and retardation are uniform and there is a period of steady velocity in between. Plot a velocity-time graph and hence find
   (i) the time at which top speed is reached
   (ii) the distance between the stations in km.

10. Plot the following values of s and t

s(m)	0	14	22	27	29	30	31	29	23	14
t (s)	0	2	4	6	8	10	12	14	16	18

From your graph find
   (i) the period of time for which the displacement exceeds 25 m.
   (ii) the velocity at times 5 s, 10 s, 17 s.
   (iii) the average velocity during the first 3 seconds.

11. A recording device notes the velocity of an aircraft at 5 second intervals. During take-off the instrument records the following values

time (s)	0	5	10	15	20	25	30	35	40
velocity (m s^{-1})	3	23	37	45	52	56	59	62	64

Plot a velocity-time graph and hence estimate
   (i) the acceleration at times 8 s and 20 s
   (ii) the distance covered before take-off if the plane leaves the ground when moving at 60 m s^{-1}.

12. A body moves in a straight line in such a way that its velocity v m s^{-1} at time t s is given by the table

t	0	1	2	3	4	5	6
v	0	1.5	2.45	3.1	3.55	3.9	4.2

Plot a velocity-time graph and use it to estimate
(i) the velocity at $t = 3.3$
(ii) the acceleration at $t = 2$
(iii) the average speed during the 6 seconds

1.6 Use of Sketched Velocity–Time Graph

In some questions (mainly involving uniform acceleration) a sketched velocity-time graph can be a useful aid to calculation, as the following example shows.

Example 5

A train travels 14 km in 16 minutes, starting and finishing at rest. The acceleration is half the retardation, both being uniform, and there is a period during which the train travels at a steady 75 km h^{-1}. How long is this period?

The velocity-time diagram is shown in Fig. 11.

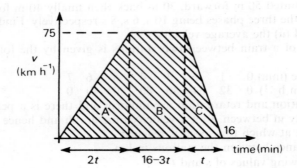

Fig. 11

If retardation takes t min then the acceleration, being half as rapid, will take $2t$ min. Thus steady speed is maintained for $16 - 3t$ min. We now use the fact that the area under the graph will represent a distance of 14 km.

$$\text{Area B} = 75 \text{ km h}^{-1} \times \frac{16 - 3t}{60} \text{ h} = \frac{5(16 - 3t)}{4} \text{ km}$$

Areas A and C (which are conveniently combined as a single triangle)

$$= \tfrac{1}{2} \times 75 \text{ km h}^{-1} \times \frac{3t}{60} \text{ h} = \frac{15t}{8} \text{ km}$$

hence
$$\frac{5(16 - 3t)}{4} + \frac{15t}{8} = 14$$
$$10(16 - 3t) + 15t = 112$$
$$160 - 30t + 15t = 112$$
$$\Rightarrow 15t = 48 \quad \text{or} \quad t = 3.2 \text{ min}$$
Steady speed is maintained for $16 - 3t = 6.4$ min.

Note that some care with units is needed when writing down the areas under the graph.

Exercise 1 (e)

1. A car accelerates uniformly to a speed of 20 m s⁻¹ and then continues at this steady speed, taking a total of 29 seconds to cover the first 1/2 km from rest. Find the rate of acceleration and the distance covered whilst accelerating.
2. A train takes 15 minutes to travel between two stations 27 km apart. It accelerates uniformly for 2 minutes, maintains a steady speed and then brakes uniformly for the last 1 minute. Find the maximum speed reached.
3. The average speed of a cyclist on a 10 km journey is 25 km h⁻¹. For 20 minutes the journey is flat and he maintains a steady speed but on the last section, which is downhill, he gains speed uniformly. If he finishes the journey with a speed of 36 km h⁻¹ find his earlier steady speed and also the length of the downhill section.
4. A firework rocket rises vertically with uniform acceleration 4 m s⁻² while its chemicals burn. After this it is retarded at 9.8 m s⁻² by gravity. Sketch the v/t graph of the motion up to the highest point. If this is 35 m up, find the greatest velocity reached during the ascent.
5. A driver starts his car from rest, changes into second gear at 8 m s⁻¹, into third gear at 15 m s⁻¹ and into top gear at 20 m s⁻¹, by which time he has travelled 100 m. He spends the same interval of time in each of the first three gears and acceleration in each is uniform. How long does the 100 m take and what is the average speed over this distance?
6. A train starts from rest with constant acceleration a, then travels with uniform speed and finally slows down to rest with constant retardation a. If the total distance travelled is d and the total time taken is T, show that

the train travels at uniform speed for a time $= \sqrt{T^2 - \dfrac{4d}{a}}$.

1.7 Calculus Methods

We have seen earlier in this chapter that

$$v = \frac{ds}{dt} \quad \text{and} \quad a = \frac{dv}{dt}$$

These and the corresponding integration results are best summed up in a simple chart.

$$\text{displacement} \underset{\text{int}}{\overset{\text{diff}}{\rightleftarrows}} \text{velocity} \underset{\text{int}}{\overset{\text{diff}}{\rightleftarrows}} \text{acceleration}$$
$$s \qquad\qquad v \qquad\qquad a$$

Using these results we can handle quite easily problems in which motion is governed by a simple function of time. When integrating, however, we must be careful not to overlook 'constants of integration'.

Example 6

A particle starts from O with initial velocity 16 m s^{-1} and thereafter moves in a straight line with variable acceleration $12 - 8t$ m s^{-2} where t is the time in seconds. Show (i) that the particle comes to rest after 4 s and find (ii) the distance covered during the third second of motion.

(i) We have . . . . $a = 12 - 8t$

Integrating $v = 12t - 4t^2 + c$ (c is the constant of integration)

$v = 16$ at $t = 0 \Rightarrow c = 16$

Thus $v = 12t - 4t^2 + 16$ (1)

(Notice that the constant of integration corresponds to the initial value of the variable v we are trying to find.) From formula (1) we may easily verify by substitution that the velocity is zero when $t = 4$.

(ii) We could obtain by integrating (1) a formula for the displacement s at time t, the constant of integration this time being found from the initial displacement (zero in this question). A more convenient approach, however, is

change in displacement during third second

$= $ area under v/t graph from $t = 2$ to $t = 3$

$= \int_2^3 v \, dt$ or $\int_2^3 12t - 4t^2 + 16 \, dt$

In evaluating this definite integral we need not concern ourselves with a constant of integration. Continuing, we obtain

$$\left[6t^2 - \frac{4t^3}{3} \times 16t \right]_2^3$$

$$= (54 - 36 + 48) - (24 - \frac{32}{3} + 32)$$

$$= 20\tfrac{2}{3} \text{ m}$$

Exercise 1(f)

1. The displacement s m of a body is given at time t s by the formula $s = 2t^3 - 9t^2 + 12t + 6$. Find when its acceleration is zero and also its velocity at this instant.
2. The velocity v m s^{-1} of a body is given by $v = 16t - 4t^2$. Find how far it travels during the third second. Find also its average speed from $t = 1$ to $t = 3$.
3. A body starts from O with velocity 20 m s^{-1} and moves in a straight line with acceleration $a = 3 + 2t$ m s^{-2}. Find its velocity after 3 s and the distance covered in this time.
4. A bus moves from rest in a straight line with velocity $v = \frac{1}{2}t(12 - t)$ m s^{-1}. Calculate the distance travelled by the bus before it is again at rest and also the maximum speed attained during this period.
5. The displacement s metres of a particle from a fixed point O is given by: $s = 6t^2 - t^3$ where t is the time in seconds. Find
    (i)   the initial velocity and acceleration of the body
    (ii) the distance covered before it is instantaneously at rest

(iii) the total distance covered in the first 6 seconds

(iv) the average speed and the average velocity over the first 6 seconds.

6. The velocity of a body falling vertically through a resisting fluid is given by $v = 3 + 4t$ m s^{-1}. At what speed did the body start to fall and what is its acceleration? How long does it take to fall 20 m and what velocity has it then achieved?

2
Forces

2.1 Newton's First Law

Force is a word in common usage and most people have an intuitive idea of its meaning. When I push a piano or some other object across the floor I do so by exerting a force on the piano. A falling body does so because of the gravitational force exerted on it by the earth. This is often called the **weight** of the body (Fig. 2a). A force then is something which tends to make a body move.

Early mathematicians believed that all moving bodies had to have forces pushing or pulling them along. Newton, however, revolutionised thought with his first law which contradicted this idea,

> EVERY BODY REMAINS STATIONARY OR IN UNIFORM STRAIGHT LINE MOTION UNLESS ACTED ON BY SOME OVERALL EXTERNAL FORCE.

This law has several implications.

(i) A force is needed to *start* an object moving (and to stop it) but once moving it may continue at steady speed without any force being needed.

(ii) When a body is at rest or in uniform straight-line motion, then any forces acting must exactly balance.

(iii) When motion is changing (i.e in speed or in direction) then the forces cannot balance – in fact some overall force must be acting.

In apparent contradiction to (i) above, we know that bodies left to move freely, e.g. a stone skimming across a playground, do not continue at steady speed but gradually slow down to a standstill. However, in all situations of this kind there *is* a force acting; the force of **friction** which results from bodies catching on one another due to the slight roughness of their surfaces.

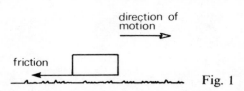

direction of motion

friction

Fig. 1

A simple example of implication (ii) is that of a body suspended on a string (Fig. 2b). Since the body is at rest we infer that the **weight** of the body is exactly balanced by a force of support in the string. This force is called the **tension** in the string.

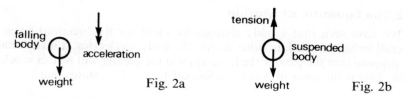

falling body · acceleration · weight — Fig. 2a

tension · suspended body · weight — Fig. 2b

A more difficult example to understand but one which illustrates implication (iii) is that of a car travelling at steady speed around a corner (Fig. 3). If no forces acted the car would continue along a straight line path in accordance with Newton's First Law. In order to corner, an external force is needed to pull the car continually away from a straight line path. This force comes from friction between the tyres and the road. If the road is wet and the tyres are bald then cornering can be difficult!

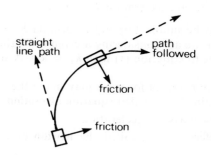

straight line path · path followed · friction · friction

Fig. 3

Notice that, contrary to popular belief, the force is *inward*. To turn a car to the right as in this diagram there is no point in applying a force to the left. This will be dealt with in more detail, however, in chapter 15.

Exercise 2(a)

Discuss the following situations, and the forces acting, in the light of Newton's first law.

1. A body falling vertically.
2. A trunk being dragged at constant speed across the floor.
3. A packing case resting on the ground.
4. The packing case at the instant it is lifted from the ground by a crane.
5. A stone sliding across ice.
6. A parachutist descending at constant speed.
7. The rope of a tug-of-war being pulled by teams of equal strength.
8. A man pushing hard against a solidly built wall.
9. A space-ship drifting in space.
10. A satellite in orbit around the earth.
11. The motion of a billiard ball striking a cushion.
12. A plane flying horizontally at steady speed.
13. A ball thrown horizontally over a cliff.
14. A stone suspended from the roof of an accelerating train.

2.2 The Equation of Motion

We have seen that a body changes its speed (or its direction) when an overall force is applied. In other words, the body accelerates. It is reasonable to suppose that the greater the force applied the greater will be this acceleration. This is the basis of Newton's Second Law, which states that

> ACCELERATION IS PROPORTIONAL TO THE OVERALL FORCE ACTING AND IS IN THE SAME DIRECTION.

That is for a given body $F = k_1 a$ (k_1 is a constant)   (1)

There is, however, another consideration – that of **mass** (how much matter there is in the body). A body of large mass, e.g a furniture van, will require a larger force to accelerate it than a suitcase or a chair

That is to produce a given acceleration $F = k_2 m$ (2)

Both these effects may be summed up in the formula $F = kma$ (where k is a third constant), since if we are considering a given body then m is constant and the formula reduces to equation (1) with $k_1 = km$. A similar argument holds for equation (2).

By suitably defining our unit of force we may make the constant k equal to unity and hence obtain the so-called **equation of motion**

$F = ma$ 'force = mass × acceleration'

The unit of force referred to is called the **newton** and it is defined as follows

> ONE NEWTON IS THAT FORCE WHICH GIVES A MASS OF 1 KILOGRAM AN ACCELERATION OF 1 M S^{-2}.

It follows from this definition that in using the equation of motion $F = ma$ we must be careful to use units of kilograms for mass and m s^{-2} for acceleration.

Example 7

What force is needed to give a body of mass 25 g an acceleration of 12 m s^{-2}?

This is a straightforward application of the formula $F = ma$. Remembering that the mass should be put in kilograms, we obtain

$$F = \frac{25}{1000} \times 12 = 0.3 \text{ N}$$

Example 8

A trunk of mass 15 kg is pulled by a horizontal force of 40 N and covers a distance of 3 m in 2 s, starting from rest. Find the magnitude of the friction force (assumed constant) which opposes the motion.

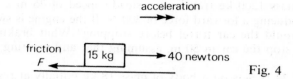

Fig. 4

Since the forces are constant the acceleration will be uniform. We may therefore use the uniform acceleration equations

$$s = ut + \tfrac{1}{2}at^2 \quad \text{with } s = 3 \quad u = 0 \quad t = 2$$
$$\Rightarrow 3 = 0 + 2a$$
$$\text{acceleration } a = 1\tfrac{1}{2} \text{ m s}^{-2}$$

The force needed to produce this acceleration may now be found using $F = ma$.

force needed $= 15 \times 1.5 = 22.5$ N

But this is the overall force required in the direction of the acceleration. Hence, from Fig.4, we see that

$$40 - F = 22.5$$
$$\text{friction} = 17.5 \text{ N}$$

Exercise 2(b)

1. What force is needed to give a car of mass 2 tonnes (2000 kg) an acceleration of 1.3 m s^{-2}?
2. A stone of mass 15 g is acted on by a force of 0.6 N. What will be its acceleration?
3. An electron of mass 9.1×10^{-31} kg has a momentary acceleration of 4.6×10^{15} m s^{-2}. What force is acting?
4. A body of mass 4 kg is accelerated uniformly from rest by a force of 5 N. What speed will it acquire in 3 s?
5. When pushing a large object like a wardrobe, the force needed seems to decrease immediately the wardrobe begins to move. Explain.
6. A cyclist free-wheeling loses speed at the rate of 0.4 m s^{-2}. If the total mass of the cyclist and his machine is 75 kg, find the total resisting force.
7. A trunk of mass 24 kg is pushed at steady speed by a force of 150 N. How large is the friction force opposing motion?
8. What force would be needed in question 7 to give the trunk an acceleration of 1.5 m s^{-2}, the frictional resistance remaining the same?
9. A power-boat accelerating uniformly from rest covers 60 m in 8 s. The engine is producing a forward thrust of 900 N and the resistance provided by the water is 225 N. Find the mass of the power-boat.
10. A rifle barrel is 80 cm long. If the muzzle velocity of a 20 g bullet is 400 m s^{-1} find the explosive force, assumed uniform, which accelerates the bullet along the barrel.
11. An ice-hockey puck of mass 150 g loses speed from 25 m s^{-1} to 24 m s^{-1} over a distance of 35 m. Find the frictional force, which may be assumed to be uniform. How much further could the puck travel (space permitting) before stopping?

12. A car of mass 1200 kg travels at a steady speed of 25 m s⁻¹ with its engine producing a forward force of 300 N. If the engine is switched off, how far would the car travel before stopping? What braking force is needed to stop the car in 50 m, assuming that any resisting forces still operate?
13. A force of 24 N acts on a body of mass 18 kg initially at rest. After 1½ seconds the force ceases to act. If there is no resisting force, how far does the body travel in the first 5 seconds of its motion?
14. If, in question 13, there is a frictional resistance of 9 N, for how long will the body travel before coming to rest? What distance will it have covered?
15. A four-engined aircraft can produce a maximum thrust of *D* N in each engine. At a certain speed it can achieve three-fifths of maximum acceleration if one of the engines fails. Find an expression for the air-resistance at this speed and deduce what fraction of maximum acceleration is possible with two engines out of action.

2.3 Mass and Weight

Mass is not a force. It is simply a measure of how much material a body contains. This is fixed in value so the mass of a body cannot change.

Weight, however, *is* a force: the gravitational force with which the earth attracts the body. As this differs slightly from place to place, it follows that the weight of a body will in fact vary at different parts of the earth's surface.

Consider now a body falling freely. We know that the single force we call the 'weight' of the body causes a downward acceleration *g* (Fig. 5).

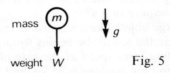

Fig. 5

Thus using force = mass × acceleration we obtain the important result

$$W = mg$$

This simple formula enables us to calculate in newtons the magnitude of the weight of a given body.

A body of mass 10 kg has weight $W = 10 \times 9.8 = 98$ N
A body of mass 2 kg has weight $W = 2 \times 9.8 = 19.6$ N

In many questions, however, we will find it convenient to leave the weights of these two bodies as 10*g* and 2*g* N respectively.

Notice that the weights of these bodies on the moon, where $g = 1.62$ m s⁻², would be considerably less; in fact 16.2 N and 3.24 N respectively.

Example 9

A load of 200 kg is being raised on a cable. Find the tension in the cable (i) when the load is lifted at a steady speed of 2 m s^{-1} (ii) when the load is lifted with upward acceleration 0.5 m s^{-2}.

The weight of the load is $200g$ or 1960 N.

(i) When the load is lifted at steady speed no overall force is needed. Newton's first law tells us that the forces involved must balance so the tension is 1960 N.

(ii) Here, since there is an upward acceleration there must be an overall force upwards. It follows that the tension must this time exceed 1960 N. (See Fig. 6.)

$$\text{Using overall force } F = ma$$
$$T - 1960 = 200 \times 0.5$$
$$T = 2060 \text{ N}$$

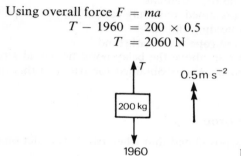

Fig. 6

Note that the load is accelerating at 0.5 m s^{-2} not $(9.8 + 0.5)$ m s^{-2}, which is a commonly held misconception.

Exercise 2(c)

1. Find the weight in newtons of the following bodies:
   (i) A 3 kg bag of potatoes
   (ii) A tractor of mass $2\frac{1}{2}$ tonnes (1 tonne = 1000 kg)
   (iii) A tennis ball of mass 60 g.
2. What would be the weights of the bodies in question 1 on Mars, where the acceleration due to gravity is only 3.8 m s^{-2}?
3. A 25 kg punch bag is suspended on a rope. What is the tension in the rope?
4. A crane lowers a 3 tonne crate into a hold at steady speed. What is the tension in the cable?
5. If, in question 4, the crane lifts the crate with upward acceleration 0.22 m s^{-2}, what would be the tension in the cable?
6. A parachutist of mass 75 kg whose parachute only partly opens accelerates downwards at 1.8 m s^{-2}. What upward force must his parachute be providing?
7. A lift is ascending. Is the cable more likely to break at the top or the bottom of the ascent? Justify your answer. Is the same result true when the lift descends?
8. A body of mass 30 kg is being lowered by a cable. If the tension in the cable is 330 N, what can be deduced about the motion of the body?

9. A stone of mass 40 g is falling through a viscous fluid. In the first second of motion the stone falls 35 cm from rest. What force is the fluid exerting on the stone?
10. A balloon, together with occupants, has mass 160 kg. It is descending at a steady speed of 3 m s^{-1} when 8 kg of ballast are thrown out. How many seconds will pass before the balloon starts to rise?
11. What size mass would be accelerated upwards at 0.7 m s^{-2} by a vertical force of 84 N?
12. (a) A rock climber of mass 65 kg falls when 4 m vertically above the 'belay-point' at which his rope is held securely. Find
    (i)   his speed when the rope tightens
    (ii) the retardation (assumed uniform) caused by the rope if it stretches 20% in holding the fall
    (iii) the tension that the rope must withstand.
   (b) If the climber fell from 6 m above the belay-point he would stretch the rope by 25%. What answer is obtained for part (iii) this time? What do you notice?

2.4 The Normal Contact Force

Newton's famous Third Law postulated that when two bodies act on one another then

ACTION AND REACTION ARE EQUAL AND OPPOSITE

That is, the force exerted by the first body on the second is exactly equal and opposite to that exerted by the second body on the first.

Everyday life is full of examples of 'action and reaction'. If, unfortunately, you drive your car into the back of somebody else's you will find that your car is dented as well as his. When a hammer is used to drive home a nail, it is not just the nail that receives a blow on impact – as you will readily perceive if you attempt to drive it in with your own fist. According to Newton's third law the 'forces of interaction' which occur in these situations are always equal and opposite.

Consider first a 5 kg block resting on a horizontal support. The weight of the block is 5 × 9.8 = 49 N. Since the block is at rest it follows that the ground must be exerting an upward pressure[1] of 49 N on the bottom surface

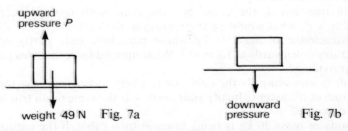

upward pressure *P*

weight 49 N   Fig. 7a

downward pressure   Fig. 7b

[1] Throughout this book the word pressure is used in its loosest sense i.e. that of a force due to one body pressing on another, *not* in its exact scientific sense of force per unit area.

of the block (see Fig. 7a). At the same time it is clear that the block must be exerting a downward pressure on the ground (see Fig. 7b). These two pressure forces are often called **normal contact forces** (or normal reactions) – forces caused by the contact of two bodies and which are normal to the surfaces in contact.

This is a typical example of 'action and reaction' between two bodies and, by Newton's third law, the two normal contact forces are equal and opposite. Thus the downward pressure on the ground is also 49 N.

This result is not, of course, unexpected, but it is a mistake to assume that the force on the supporting surface is always equal to the weight of the body. Suppose, for example, that the supporting surface is accelerated upwards at 3 m s^{-2}. The block must necessarily accelerate upwards also, but in order for this to happen there must be an overall force upwards on the block. Considering again Fig. 7a, we see that the only way in which this can happen is for the upward pressure force now to exceed the weight of 49 N.

Using overall force $F = ma$
$$P - 49 = 5 \times 3$$
$\Rightarrow$ upward pressure $= 64 \text{ N}$

It now follows that the downward pressure on the supporting surface is also 64 N, no longer the same as the weight of the body. A commonsense explanation of this result is that the upward acceleration of the support drives it harder into the block and increases the pressure or normal contact force between them.

Example 10

The contact force between a 60 kg man and the floor of a lift in which he is ascending is 450 N. What can you deduce about the motion of the lift?

We need consider only the forces acting on the man, which are shown in Fig. 8. (There is in any case no future in considering the lift, as we are not told its mass.)

450 N

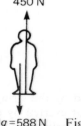

$60g = 588 \text{ N}$ Fig. 8

We see there is an overall force of 138 N *downwards* on the man. Hence he must accelerate downwards.

$$F = ma \Rightarrow \text{acceleration} = \frac{138}{60} = 2.3 \text{ m s}^{-2}$$

So the lift, although ascending, is subject to a downward acceleration of 2.3 m s^{-2}, i.e it is being retarded at 2.3 m s^{-2}.

Exercise 2(d)

1. A 12 kg block rests on horizontal ground. What is the normal contact force on the block?
2. A cord is attached to the block of question 1 and an upward vertical force is applied. Describe what happens to the block and write down the magnitude of the normal reaction when the vertical force is
    (i) 50 N   (ii) 100 N   (iii) 150 N
3. What vertical force will just lift the block of question 1 off the ground? What is the magnitude of the normal reaction at the instant the block leaves the ground?
4. A man of mass 70 kg is ascending in a lift. What is the normal contact force between the man and the floor when the lift is ascending:
    (i) at steady speed 1.3 m s^{-1}.
    (ii) with upward acceleration 1.3 m s^{-2}?
5. An astronaut, who, together with his spacesuit, has mass 90 kg, experiences an upward acceleration of 6 g (i.e. 6×9.8 m s^{-2}) at blast off. What contact force does he experience from his seat? Explain why the seat needs to be constructed more strongly than, for example, the seat of a car.
6. A helicopter pilot of mass 80 kg experiences a contact force of 1040 N from his seat on take-off. What is the acceleration of the helicopter?
7. An aeroplane accelerates down a runway at 1.6 m s^{-2}. What pressure force does a passenger of mass 72 kg feel in his back?
8. Two rectangular blocks of mass 5 kg rest one on top of the other on a horizontal surface. Find the contact forces between each pair of surfaces in contact
    (i) when the system is at rest
    (ii) when the system accelerates upwards at 2 m s^{-2}

2.5 Tension and Thrust

Consider a body of weight W supported (i) by a string (ii) by a rod or strut. Fig. 9 shows the forces acting *on the body* in each case.

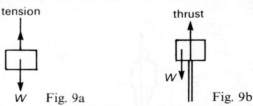

tension	thrust
W Fig. 9a	Fig. 9b

The supporting force exerted by the string is called a **tension**, as has already been mentioned, but that exerted by the strut is called a **thrust**. The difference, essentially, is that the string is pulled outwards or *stretched* by the body, whereas the strut is pushed inwards or *compressed* (see Fig. 10).

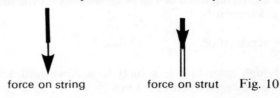

force on string   force on strut   Fig. 10

Notice that although the body pulls outwards on the string (see Fig. 10) the string pulls inwards on the body, and it is this inward force which we have called the **tension** in Fig. 9a. This is really another case of action and re-action being equal and opposite. Similarly the body presses inwards on the strut but the strut pushes back outwards on the body (the **thrust**).

Clearly a string cannot be used to support a body in the manner of Fig. 9b. It is impossible, therefore, for a string to provide a force of thrust.

What can we deduce about the tension in a string which supports two weights W_1 and W_2 over a pulley (Fig. 11) where $W_1 > W_2$? Both parts of the string are in tension.

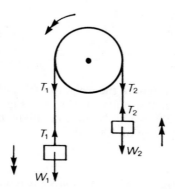

Fig. 11

Consider now the forces on the pulley. If it is a large pulley, or if there is friction in the bearings, it will require a force to turn it so that $T_1 > T_2$. If, however, the pulley has negligible mass (when compared with that of the weights) and there is no friction, then no significant force is needed to turn it. Such a pulley is called a 'smooth light pulley' and in this case the tensions on either side may be assumed equal. A similar result applies when a rope runs over a 'smooth' beam, which offers no friction to hinder the movement of the rope. (In practice this is almost impossible to achieve.)

Example 11

A string supports masses of 300 g and 500 g on either side of a smooth light pulley. Find (i) the acceleration of the masses, (ii) the tension in the string and (iii) the vertical force required to support the pulley.

We need consider only the forces on the masses (see Fig. 12). Here it is more convenient to call their weights 0.5 g and 0.3 g rather than evaluating them as 4.9 N and 2.94 N respectively.

Let the acceleration be a m s^{-2} and write down the equations of motion for each mass separately ... (i.e. overall force = mass × acceleration.)

for 500 g mass	$0.5g - T = 0.5a$	(1)
for 300 g mass	$T - 0.3g = 0.3a$	(2)
add (1) and (2)	$0.2g = 0.8a$	
$\Rightarrow$	acceleration $\frac{1}{4}g$ (or 2.45 m s^{-2})	

Substitute in (1) $4.9 - T = 1.225$
$$\Rightarrow \text{tension} = 3.675 \text{ N}$$

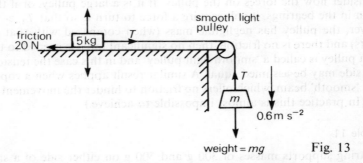

Fig. 12

In answering part (iii) we can ignore the weight of the pulley itself as it is 'light'. The downward pull on the pulley is $2T$ (see Fig. 11). Hence the supporting force required is $2T = 7.35$ N (not, as might be expected, the sum of the two weights $0.5g + 0.3g$ or 7.84 N).

Example 12

In the situation shown in Fig. 13, what mass m kg is required in order to give the system an acceleration of 0.6 m s^{-2}?

smooth light pulley

friction 20 N

5 kg

T

T

m

0.6 m s^{-2}

weight = mg Fig. 13

The weight of the mass m is mg N. The equations of motion are

mass m $mg - T = 0.6m$ (1)
5 kg mass $T - 20 = 5 \times 0.6$ (2)

adding $mg - 20 = 0.6m + 3$
$$9.8m - 0.6m = 23$$
$$\Rightarrow m = \frac{23}{9.2} = 2.5 \text{ kg}$$

Notice that the weight of the 5 kg mass does not hinder its motion, being balanced in fact by an upward contact force. This is why it is possible for a smaller mass to provide the acceleration.

Exercise 2(e)

1. Masses of $1\frac{1}{2}$ kg and 2 kg are supported by a cord passing over a smooth light pulley. Find the acceleration of the masses and the tension in the cord. How long will the heavier mass take to descend 35 cm from rest?

2. A rope over a smooth beam supports two equal buckets, each of mass 1.4 kg. A stone of mass 400 g is placed in one of the buckets. Find
   (i) the acceleration of the system
   (ii) the tension in the rope
   (iii) the normal contact force between the stone and its bucket.

3. In Fig. 13 what mass m would give the system an acceleration of 1.4 m s^{-2}? What would then be the tension in the string?

4. In Fig. 13 what is the largest mass m which will hang in equilibrium?

5. A mass of 700 g lies on a table 80 cm from the edge. It is connected by a light string running over the edge of the table to a mass of 50 g hanging freely. If there are no frictional forces, find how long the 700 g mass takes to reach the edge of the table, starting from rest. (The string is perpendicular to the edge of the table.)

6. Two children cling to the ends of a rope passing over a smooth beam. The lighter child, who has mass 30 kg is pulled upwards with acceleration 0.8 m s^{-2}. Find the mass of the second child and also the total downward force on the beam.

7. Masses of 18 kg and 15 kg are connected by a rope over a large pulley which requires a difference in tension of 3 N between the two sides of the rope in order to turn it. What is the acceleration of the masses?

8. Masses of 200 g and 300 g are attached to a string passing over a smooth light pulley. Motion starts from rest with the larger mass 50 cm above a horizontal surface. Find
   (i) The speed with which the 300 g mass strikes the horizontal surface
   (ii) The time that the 300 g mass rests on the surface before being jerked into motion again (assuming that it does not rebound on impact).

9. Two masses M and m are supported by a string over a smooth light pulley. Motion is allowed to take place. What upward force is needed to support the pulley? Check that your answer is correct for the case $M = m$.

2.6 Connected Bodies

A lorry towing a trailer is accelerating forward. What forces are responsible for the acceleration of each of the two bodies? Fig. 14 shows an 'exploded force diagram'. Only horizontal forces are considered, as this is the direction of the acceleration.

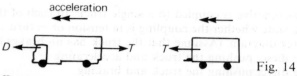

Fig. 14

The trailer. Common sense tells us that the trailer must experience a forward force T due to the pull of the lorry. It is this force which accelerates the trailer.

The lorry. If the lorry pulls forward on the trailer with force T, then by Newton's third law, the trailer must pull back on the lorry with an opposite force T. This is the 'drag' of the trailer, which we would in any case expect the lorry to experience. The effect of this is to eat away some of the driving force D created by the engine, so that acceleration will be lower than normally achieved by the lorry alone.

The two forces T would in practice be provided by tension forces in the tow bar or coupling, which is clearly being stretched in this situation. Notice that the magnitude of T must be less than that of D, otherwise there would be no overall force forward to accelerate the lorry.

Example 13

The lorry and trailer considered above have masses 2.8 and 3.2 tonnes respectively. The maximum braking force the lorry can achieve is 9000 N. The brakes of the trailer are out of action. What is the maximum retardation possible and what then is the force in the coupling?

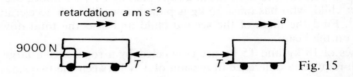

Fig. 15

Since the trailer cannot brake, it will push forward on the lorry, so that the coupling will be compressed. The two forces T in Fig. 15 are therefore thrust forces pushing outwards.

The two equations of motion are

lorry	$9000 - T = 2800a$	(1)
trailer	$T = 3200a$	(2)
adding (1) and (2)	$9000 = 6000a$	(3)
	$\Rightarrow$ retardation $= 1.5 \text{ m s}^{-2}$	
substitute in (2)	thrust $= 4800$ N	

The equation (3) may be obtained by the argument that the 9000 N has to retard a total mass of $2.8 + 3.2 = 6$ tonnes. This method, however, does not enable us to find the thrust in the coupling.

Exercise 2(f)

1. A diesel locomotive is coupled to a single truck. In each of the following situations, state whether the coupling is in tension or in thrust and draw a simple force diagram. (Assume that the truck has no brakes.)
    (i)   The diesel pushing the truck and accelerating
    (ii) The diesel pushing the truck and braking
    (iii) The diesel pulling the truck and braking.
2. If, in question 1, the diesel and the truck have masses of 12 and 8 tonnes respectively, find

(a) the tractive force needed to produce an acceleration of 0.8 m s^{-2} in part (i)

(b) the braking force needed to produce a retardation of 1.3 m s^{-2} in part (ii).

In each case find also the force in the coupling.

3. A car of mass 1100 kg tows a caravan of mass 700 kg. The engine of the car is producing a tractive force of 2500 N and both car and caravan are subject to frictional resistances of 200 N. Find the acceleration and the tension in the coupling.

4. A 7 kg mass is being drawn upwards by a cord. It is connected by a second short cord to a mass of 5 kg vertically below. If both masses rise with acceleration 1.5 m s^{-2}, find the tensions in the two cords.

5. Two trucks, each of mass 3 tonnes, are free-wheeling together. Both are subject to frictional resistances of 500 N and to air-resistance, which is 450 N on the leading truck but only 150 N on the other. Find the retardation of the trucks and the thrust in the coupling.

6. A lift cage of mass 500 kg is designed to take 4 passengers of average mass 75 kg each. When stopping, the retardation of the lift is 2.7 m s^{-2}. Show that the lift cable must be strong enough to take a tension of at least 10 kN. What force must the floor of the lift be capable of withstanding?

3
Vectors

3.1 Vectors and Scalars

A **vector quantity** is one for which direction is of importance as well as magnitude. In 'displacing' a body to a new position the direction of the displacement may well be of as much importance as the actual distance through which the body is moved. When applying a force to a body the direction of the force influences the subsequent behaviour of the body as well as the size of the force, for varying this direction will cause the body to move off along different paths. Displacement and force are, therefore, vector quantities.

Quantities for which no idea of direction is involved are called **scalars**. Typical examples are the temperature of a fluid or the density of a solid. Mass is also a scalar but weight, being a force with a clearly defined direction, is a vector.

Another important distinction is that between speed and velocity. By the speed of a body we mean only how fast it is travelling, whereas in specifying velocity we always give a complete description of the motion, i.e. how fast and in which direction. In other words, we take speed as a scalar and velocity as a vector.

In this chapter the vector quantities we shall be concerned with are force, displacement and velocity. Others will be dealt with later in the book.

3.2 Triangle Addition

What would be the combined effect of:

(i)   Two forces acting on a body: one of 5 N west and the other of 2 N west?

(ii) A displacement of 4 m north followed by a second displacement of 3 m west?

(iii) A man walking with velocity 2 m s^{-1} south across the deck of a ship if the ship begins to move with velocity 10 m s^{-1} due east?

In each of these situations we are asked to find the combined effect or 'sum' of two vector quantities. Our method of 'addition', however, cannot be expected to resemble ordinary addition, since we have directions to take into account as well as numbers.

When the directions are along the same line as in (i) there is no problem. The answer to (i) is clearly that the two forces are equivalent to a single force of 7 N west.

We shall investigate (ii) and (iii) diagrammatically.

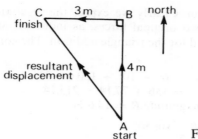

Fig. 1

Fig. 1 shows the effect of the 2 displacements in (ii), the body moving from A to B and then on to C. The final situation is equivalent to that obtained by a single straight line displacement from A to C. This is called the **resultant displacement** and it is readily shown to be 5 m in direction N 36° 52′ W.

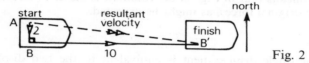

Fig. 2

Figure 2 shows the movement of the man and the ship across the surface of the Earth in 1 second. Imagine that the man starts at A. If the ship were stationary he would, after 1 second, be at point B. The effect of the ship's motion, however, is to move point B 10 m east to B′. The man has, therefore, travelled from A to B′: a distance of $\sqrt{4 + 100} = 10.2$ m in direction arctan 5 east of south.

The **resultant velocity** is, therefore, 10.2 m s^{-1} in direction S 79° E approximately. It is 'represented' on Fig. 2 by the line AB′, both in magnitude and in direction.

Examples (ii) and (iii) show us that if two vectors are 'represented' by two sides of a triangle then their sum or **resultant** is represented by the third side of the triangle. Notice carefully, however, the configuration of the arrows in these triangles.

This method of addition, '**triangle addition**', is the one used for all vector quantities. The triangles involved will not always be right-angled as in the two examples so far.

Example 14

Two forces, 6 N north and 10 N north 50° east, act on a particle. What single force would be equivalent to these two?

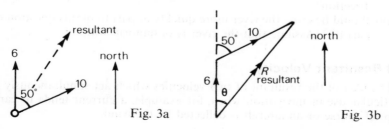

Fig. 3a

Fig. 3b

Fig. 3a shows the situation. Clearly we expect the resultant force to act somewhere between the two original forces, as indicated on Fig. 3a, but this diagram cannot be used for the triangle addition. The correct triangle is shown in Fig. 3b.

by the cosine rule $R^2 = 6^2 + 10^2 + 120 \cos 50°$
$$= 136 + 77.14 = 213.14$$
$$\Rightarrow \quad \text{magnitude } R \simeq 14.6 \text{ N}$$

by the sine rule $\dfrac{\sin \theta}{10} = \dfrac{\sin 50°}{R}$

$$\sin \theta = \frac{7.66}{14.59} = 0.525$$
$$\Rightarrow \quad \text{direction N } 31° \text{ } 40' \text{ E}$$

This answer means that in Fig. 3a the resultant is closer in direction to the larger of the original forces, as might be expected.

Exercise 3(a)

1. Find what single displacement is equivalent to the two displacements given in each of the following
   (i)   5 m west then 12 m east
   (ii) 5 m west then 12 m north
   (iii) 5 m S.W. then 12 m N.W.
2. What is the sum of displacements 10 km south and 10 km N 60° W? Does the order of addition make any difference to the answer?
3. (i) What single force would replace two forces of 15 N north 36° 52′ east and 7 N east which act at a point?
   (ii) What single force would exactly oppose the two forces given?
4. A boy sitting in a railway carriage throws a paper pellet at 3 m s^{-1} due west across his compartment. If the train is travelling due north at 12 m s^{-1} what is the resultant velocity of the pellet across the Earth's surface?
5. Two dogs pull a sledge, one with a force of 50 N due south and the other with 40 N south 35° east. Find the resultant force. If the sledge has mass 30 kg and a resistance of 35 N opposes any motion, what will be its acceleration?
6. (i)   A boy tries to swim due north at 4 km h^{-1} across a river flowing from west to east at 2 km h^{-1}. What is his resultant velocity?
   (ii) In which direction should he attempt to swim in order that his resultant velocity, after taking the current into account, is due north in direction?
   (iii) Would he cross the river more quickly in part (i) of this question or in part (ii)? (Assume that the river is of uniform width.)

3.3 Resultant Velocity

The idea of the resultant of two velocities which act simultaneously is of particular use in navigation when, for example, a current tends to carry a ship off course or an aircraft is deflected by the wind.

Example 15

A navigator thinks his ship is heading N 60° E at 12 knots but, unknown to him, there is a current of 4 knots flowing from the north-west. Which course is the ship actually sailing and at what speed?

Fig. 4 shows the triangle used to 'add' the two velocities affecting the ship.

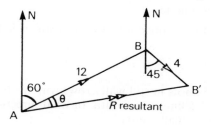

Fig. 4

(A justification of this triangle is as follows: if there were no current the ship would travel from A to B in 1 hour, but during this time the whole surface of the sea moves 4 nautical miles south-east, moving position B to B'.)

by the cosine rule we obtain $R = 13.6$ knots
by the sine rule we obtain $\theta = 16\frac{1}{2}°$

Thus the **true velocity** of the ship is 13.6 knots in direction N $76\frac{1}{2}°$ E.

Example 16

If the ship in example 15 must follow course N 60° E in order to reach a port, what course should the navigator set in order to allow for the current? If the port is 8 nautical miles away, how long will the journey take?

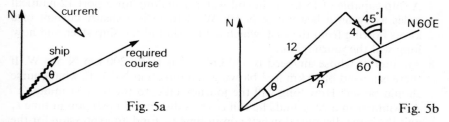

Fig. 5a   Fig. 5b

Fig. 5a illustrates the general idea behind solving problems of this sort. The ship must head somewhat north of the required course so that the current pulls the ship onto the correct course. The correct angle θ needed to achieve this is not at present known. The triangle of Fig. 5b, however, is constructed as follows (i) the ship 'heads' at 12 knots $\theta°$ north of the required course (ii) the current of 4 knots is added on so that (iii) the resultant velocity R lies on the required course

by the sine rule $\dfrac{\sin \theta}{4} = \dfrac{\sin 75}{12}$

$$\theta = 18° 47'$$

$\Rightarrow$ course to be set is approximately N 41° E

To find the time for the journey

$$R = 12 \cos \theta + 4 \cos 75*$$
$$= 12.4 \text{ knots}$$
$$\text{time} = \frac{\text{distance}}{\text{speed}} = \frac{8}{12.4}$$
$$= 0.645 \text{ h or } 39 \text{ minutes}$$

* This method of calculation is preferable to the cosine rule here.

Exercise 3(b)

1. A man who can row at 5 knots in still water rows with his boat pointing due west in a current of 1.5 knots due south. In what direction and with what speed will the boat actually move?
2. The man in question 1 points his boat in direction N 50° E. What will be the true speed and direction of the boat this time?
3. An aircraft whose speed in still air ('airspeed') is 700 km h^{-1} is heading south-west. If the aircraft encounters a wind of 60 km h^{-1} N 10° W, by how many degrees is it blown off course (the 'drift') and what is the new speed across the Earth's surface (the 'groundspeed')?
4. A boat heads N 20° E at 16 knots. After half an hour it is 9 nautical miles from its original position on a bearing of N 28° E. What is the speed and direction of the current?
5. A river flows at speed u. How long will a motor-boat whose speed in still water is v ($v > u$) take to complete a return journey to a point distance d upstream, i.e. there and back.
6. In which direction should the man in question 1 point his boat in order to follow a course of (i) due west (ii) N 50° E?
7. A ship capable of 15 knots in still water is making for a port 12 nautical miles away on a bearing of N 60° W. If there is a steady current of 6 knots flowing from the east, which course should the ship steer and how long will the journey take?
8. An aircraft whose airspeed is 350 km h^{-1} is to fly 200 km N 50° W. If there is a wind of 70 km h^{-1} blowing in a direction N 55° E, what course should be set? How long will the journey take, to the nearest minute?
9. A swimmer in a river finds he can cover a distance d upstream in time t_1 and the same distance downstream in time t_2. Find an expression for the speed with which he can swim in still water. If the width of the river is also d, show that, allowing for the current, the time it will take him to cross directly to a point exactly opposite on the far bank is $\sqrt{t_1 t_2}$.
10. (i) At noon a ship, whose speed in still water is 12 knots, is heading for a small island 16 nautical miles away to the south-east. She sets a course to compensate for a current of 3 knots due south. What is the estimated time of arrival?
    (ii) If, in fact, the current is 4 knots due south, how far from the island will the ship be at the estimated time of arrival? (Lengthy calculation unnecessary.)
11. (i) What is the least speed a bird must be capable of flying at if it is to

return due north to its nest, when a 60 km h^{-1} wind is blowing in direction N 54° W?

(ii) If the bird can only fly at 30 km h^{-1}, in which direction should it fly in order to get as close as possible to the nest?

3.4 Resultant Force

Strictly speaking there are two types of **triangle of force**. The first type we have already used. It is for finding the resultant of two forces acting at a point, and was illustrated in Example 14. The second type will be considered in the next section.

Consider again Example 14, in particular Figs. 3a and 3b, which show two forces acting at a point and the construction of the appropriate triangle of force for finding their resultant. This method may be extended to cases where there are more than two forces. We then use what is called a **polygon of forces**. The method is illustrated in Fig. 6.

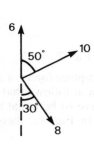
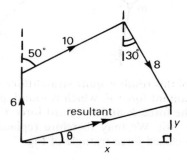

Fig. 6

In the polygon the three forces added form a 'chain' in which the arrows follow on. The resultant force goes from the beginning to the end of this chain. The simplest method of calculation is usually based on right-angled triangles. Thus in Fig. 6

$$x = 10 \sin 50 + 8 \sin 30°$$
$$y = 6 + 10 \cos 50 - 8 \cos 30°$$

whence
$$\text{resultant} = \sqrt{x^2 + y^2}$$

and
$$\tan \theta = \frac{y}{x}$$
completes the solution

Exercise 3(c)

1. Forces of 5 N north and 8 N north 60° east act at a point. What is the resultant force?
2. Forces of 15 N east and 12 N S 15° W act on a mass of 5 kg. With what acceleration does the mass move and in what direction?
3. A barge is being towed by two cables whose tensions are 3 kN N 50° W and 2.5 kN N 20° W. In which direction does the barge move?
4. Two forces with directions east and N 12° E have resultant exactly north-east in direction. If the first force has a magnitude 6 N, what is the magnitude of the second?

5. Forces of 4 N east, 3 N S 20° E and 5 N S 50° W act on a mass of 2 kg. Find the acceleration of the mass, both in magnitude and direction.

6. Show that the resultant of the following four forces is very nearly zero: 4 N north, 6 N west, 10 N S 20° W and 11 N north 60° east.

3.5 Three Forces in Equilibrium at a Point

A body whose mass may be considered to be concentrated at a single point is called a **point-mass** or **particle**. The second type of force-triangle is used when such a body is held in equilibrium under the action of three forces. In this situation it may be shown that the three forces may be represented by the sides of a closed triangle in which *the arrows follow round* (see Fig. 7). It is important to compare the configuration of the arrows in Fig. 7 with that of Fig. 3b.

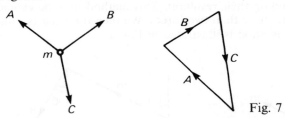

Fig. 7

The proof of this result is quite straightforward. If we replace forces A and B by their resultant force R, which is found as in Fig. 8a, it follows that for equilibrium the force R and the third force C would have to be equal and opposite (Fig. 8b). We may therefore replace R by C in Fig. 8a, thereby obtaining the closed force-triangle of Fig. 7.

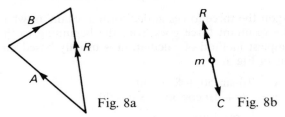

Fig. 8a   Fig. 8b

Example 17

A 200 g mass suspended on a string is pulled to one side by a force of 1 N acting at 20° above the horizontal. At what angle to the vertical will the string rest in equilibrium and what will be the tension in the string in this position?

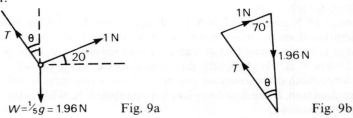

$W = \frac{1}{5}g = 1.96\,\text{N}$ Fig. 9a   Fig. 9b

Fig. 9a shows the forces acting on the mass and figure 9b the closed force triangle in which the directions of the sides must correspond exactly with the directions of the forces in Fig. 9a.

by the cosine rule we obtain $T = 1.87$ N

by the sine rule $\dfrac{\sin\theta}{1} = \dfrac{\sin 70}{T}$

$$\Rightarrow \theta = 30° \, 9' \quad \text{angle} \simeq 30°$$

Example 18

A light rod AB, 3 m long, is fixed to a vertical wall at A and supports a load of 30 kg at B. The end B is supported by a 5 m rope attached to a point C on the wall 6 m vertically above A. Find the forces in the rod AB and the rope BC.

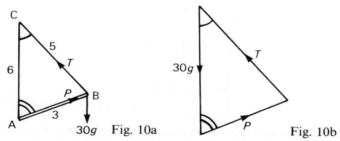

Fig. 10a   Fig. 10b

Fig. 10a shows the situation. The rod AB is being compressed by the effect of the tension T in the rope and the downward load of 30g N at B. It will therefore push outwards with a thrust force P.

We therefore have three forces acting at point B. For equilibrium they form a closed triangle (Fig. 10b). The solution is easily completed by noticing that the force triangle is similar to triangle ABC.

Thus $\dfrac{T}{5} = \dfrac{30g}{6} \Rightarrow$ tension $T = 25g$ or 245 N

$\dfrac{P}{3} = \dfrac{30g}{6} \Rightarrow$ thrust $P = 15g$ or 147 N

Note that the method of this section is frequently applied to bodies which are not strictly speaking point masses. This is generally satisfactory, however, providing the forces concerned act at, or very near, a point (see also section 9.3).

Exercise 3(d)

1. Suggest an alternative proof, based on Fig. 6, for the result that three forces in equilibrium at a point may be represented by the sides of a closed triangle.
2. A point-mass is in equilibrium under the action of three forces, two of which are 6 N west and 12 N north 30° east. What is the third force?

3. A mass of 500 g suspended on a string is pulled aside by a horizontal force of 2 N. In equilibrium what angle will the string make with the vertical and what will be its tension?

4. A 40 kg mass is suspended by two 5 m ropes which are attached to points 6 m apart at the same horizontal level. Find the tension in the ropes.

5. What force pulling at 10° below the horizontal will hold the mass of question 3 in equilibrium with the string inclined at 25° to the vertical?

6. A mountaineer of mass 80 kg falls through a crevasse. His fall is arrested by ropes held by two companions on either side of the crevasse. If the ropes make angles of 30° and 50° with the horizontal, find their tensions.

7. Fig. 11 shows a lamp L attached to a vertical wall by 2 rods AL and BL. The mass of the lamp is 1 kg. State the nature of the forces in the rods and find their magnitudes.

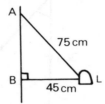

Fig. 11

8. A smooth circular wire of radius 25 cm is fixed in a vertical plane. A ring, of weight 1 N, threaded on the wire, is attached by a string of length 40 cm to the highest point of the wire. Find the tension in the string and the reaction of the wire on the ring.

9. A mass of 50 kg hangs from a derrick ABC in which AB = 3 m, AC = 1 m and angle CAB = 45°. (Fig. 12.) Show that the force triangle is similar to triangle ABC and hence find the forces in rods AB and BC.

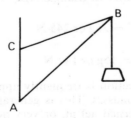

Fig. 12

*10. What is the least force needed to pull a 2 kg mass hanging on a string into a position in which the string rests at 20° to the vertical, and in which direction should it be applied?

11. A life-boat of mass 150 kg hangs on a fixed length of rope from an arm AB, which is hinged at A. The life-boat is lowered by feeding a second rope over a pulley P. (Fig. 13.) The lengths AB and AP are equal. Find the thrust in the arm AB and the tension in the rope BP when angle PAB is (i) 30°, (ii) 60°. What do you notice about the thrust? Is this result always true, even when B is lower than A?

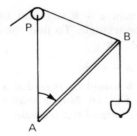

Fig. 13

12. A metal ring of mass 100 g is threaded onto a horizontal string. Explain why it is impossible for the string to remain exactly horizontal, no matter how tightly it is stretched. If each part of the string makes an angle of 1° with the horizontal, find the tension, to the nearest Newton.

*13. Prove Lami's theorem which states that if forces of magnitude A, B and C are in equilibrium at a point then

$$\frac{A}{\sin \alpha} = \frac{B}{\sin \beta} = \frac{C}{\sin \gamma}$$

where α, β and γ are the angles between the directions of B and C, C and A, A and B respectively. Try this theorem on questions 5 and 6.

3.6 General Vector Notation

If we wish to emphasise that we are treating a force F, a velocity V or a displacement S as a vector quantity then we write them

F V S

A vector quantity of unspecified type may be referred to as **a** or **b** or **x** etc. When forming vector triangles we represent these vectors by so-called **directed line segments**. Thus Fig. 14 shows the **representation** of two vectors **a** and **b** (taking north as up the page). We shall use these vectors **a** and **b** to illustrate the remainder of this section.

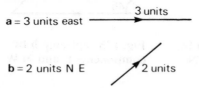

Fig. 14

Scalar multiplication and the minus sign. By 2**a** we mean a vector in the same direction as **a** but with twice the magnitude (see Fig. 15). By −**b** we mean a vector equal in magnitude to **b** but in the opposite direction. Hence −2**a** is opposite in direction to 2**a** and so on (see Fig. 15).

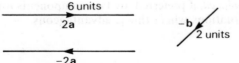

Fig. 15

Addition and subtraction. The sum **a** + **b** is found by adding the representations of **a** and **b** in a vector triangle. To find the difference **a** − **b** we add the representations of **a** and −**b**

That is we regard **a** − **b** = **a** + (−**b**)

An expression such as 2**a** − **b** would be regarded as the sum of 2**a** and −**b**. All of this is illustrated in Fig. 16. Notice that we normally put two arrows on the resultant, or third, side of the triangle.

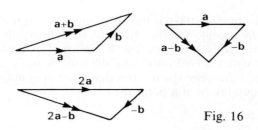

Fig. 16

Note questions 1 to 5 of exercise 3e may now be tackled.

3.7 Components

Any vector may be split into 2 (or more) parts by using triangle addition in reverse. These parts are called **components**. They are of particular importance in applied mathematics. Fig. 17 shows two ways in which the vector **b** (2 units N E) of the previous section may be split into components. Note that in each case the vector **b** is the sum of its two component vectors.

                                                          Fig. 17

Fig. 17a replacing **b** by   Fig. 17b replacing **b** by
components E and N   components E and N W

In Fig. 17a the components are **x** = 2 cos 45° east
                                  y = 2 sin 45° north
In Fig. 17b the components are **r** = 4 cos 45° east
                                  s =   2   N W

Any vector may be *replaced*, if preferred, by two components found in this way. There are many situations where this is advantageous.

Exercise 3(e)

1. (This question may be worked graphically on squared paper, if preferred.) Given that **r** = 4 units east and **s** = 3 units north, find

    3**s**, − ½**r**, **r** + **s**, **r** − **s**, **s** − ½**r**, 2**r** + 5**s**.

2. Given that **x** = 4 units north and **y** = 6 units S 60° W, find

    ⅓**y**, − 2**x**, **x** + **y**, **x** − **y**, ½(**x** − **y**), 3**x** + 2**y**.

*3. Is it true that **a** + **b** = **b** + **a** for any two vectors **a** and **b**? Justify your answer.

*4. Draw two vector triangles which illustrate **a** + **b** and 2**a** + 2**b**, where **a** and **b** are any two vectors. Is it true that 2**a** + 2**b** = 2(**a** + **b**)?

5. If **x** and **y** are vectors of equal magnitude, prove that the vectors **x** + **y** and **x** − **y** are perpendicular.

6. Split the vector **x** of question 2 into components in directions
    (i)   NW and NE
    (ii) NW and east
    (iii) N 30° E and N 30° W.

7. Split the vector **y** of question 2 into components in directions
    (i)   west and south
    (ii) SW and NW
    (iii) south and N 60° W.

8. Split a velocity of 6 knots N 30° E into components north and east. Hence show that in a current with this velocity a motor-boat must be capable of at least 3 knots if it is to keep on a course due north.

9. A swimmer in the sea is south of a straight coastline running east–west. The tide is going out and causes a current which has an average velocity of 2 m s⁻¹ S 14° W. Replace the vector representing this current by components along and perpendicular to the coastline and hence find the minimum speed that the swimmer must be capable of if he is to get back to the shore. (The exact point of landing is immaterial.)

4
Components of Force

4.1 Resolved Parts

A vector may be split into two components in any number of ways. The last few examples of exercise 3e, however, may have suggested to the reader that components which are at right-angles to one another are of particular use. This is certainly the case and such components are called **resolved parts** of the vector concerned. Thus, for example, a vector of 5 units N 30° E (see Fig. 1a) may be replaced by resolved parts of 4.33 units north and 2.5 units east (see Fig. 1b) in accordance with the vector triangle of Fig. 1c.

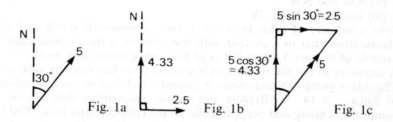

Fig. 1a   Fig. 1b   Fig. 1c

In this chapter we are concerned with the resolved parts of force vectors and their applications. Consider first a ring threaded on a horizontal wire. What happens to the ring if it is pulled by a force F at angle θ to the wire (see Fig. 2a)? It is clear that in this situation the ring cannot accelerate in the direction of the force F. We say that it is *constrained* to move along the wire.

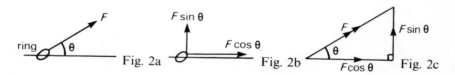

Fig. 2a   Fig. 2b   Fig. 2c

Fig. 2b shows the same force replaced by its resolved parts along and perpendicular to the wire. $F \sin \theta$, being perpendicular to the wire, cannot influence the motion so the effective force accelerating the ring is $F \cos \theta$ i.e. the resolved part along the wire. What happens, then, to the force $F \sin \theta$? The answer is that it pulls the ring against the wire and is opposed by a pressure or contact force from the wire.

Example 19

A bead of mass 50 g is threaded on a smooth (i.e. frictionless) vertical wire. If it is raised by a force of 2 N at an angle of 34° to the upward vertical, what will be its acceleration?

The resolved part of the force up the wire is

$$2 \cos 34° = 1.66 \text{ N}$$

The weight of the bead is

$$\frac{1}{20} \times 9.8 = 0.49 \text{ N}$$

Hence there is an overall upward force of 1.17 N, and from $F = ma$ we obtain

$$\text{acceleration} = 23.4 \text{ m s}^{-2}$$

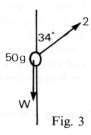

Fig. 3

Exercise 4(a)

1. In each of the following diagrams find the resolved parts of the given force in the directions of $0x$ and $0y$.

(i)

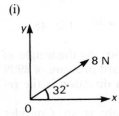

(ii)

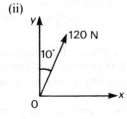

(iii)

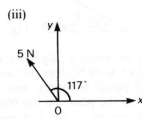

2. Find the resolved part of each force in the direction given
    (i)   5 N S 30° W in direction south-west
    (ii) 30 N north 22° east in direction N 48° E
3. A marble of mass 20 g is constrained to move along a groove in a horizontal surface. What will be its acceleration if subjected to a force of 0.3 N at 25° to the groove and in the same horizontal plane?
4. A bead of mass 150 g threaded on a smooth vertical wire is held in equilibrium by a string which makes an angle of 40° with the upward vertical. What is the tension in the string and what pressure does the bead exert on the wire?

5. A coal truck of mass 1400 kg is towed at steady speed along a straight horizontal track by two ponies, one on each side of the track. The tensions in the tow ropes are 350 N and 400 N and the angles they make with the track are 20° and 15° respectively. What resisting force is opposing the motion of the truck? Find also the contact force exerted by the rails on the truck.

6. A camera of mass 800 g is supported on a light symmetrical tripod in which each leg makes an angle of 27° with the vertical. What is the thrust in each leg?

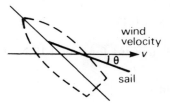

7. The diagram shows a sailing boat and indicates the direction of the wind velocity in relation to the sail. Copy the diagram carefully but replace the wind velocity by resolved parts along and perpendicular to the sail. In which direction is the force of the wind on the sail? Why? Hence explain how it is possible for a boat to sail into the wind. What feature of the boat's construction prevents it from being blown sideways?

4.2 More about the Normal Contact Force

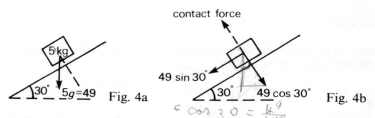

Fig. 4a shows a 5 kg block on a plane of inclination 30°. As the weight of the block is 49 N, does this mean that there is a downward pressure of 49 N on the plane? Secondly, and more important, in which direction is the reaction of the plane on the block?

The answer to the first question, perhaps surprisingly, is no. Consider Fig. 4b in which the weight of the block has been replaced by resolved parts along and perpendicular to the plane. It is the resolved part 49 cos 30° which measures the pressure exerted by the block on the plane. Since, by Newton's third law, the plane must exert an equal and opposite force, we can now answer the second question: the contact force on the block is again normal to the surfaces in contact, as in section 2.4. (Hence the origin of the name *normal contact force*.)

The other resolved part, 49 sin 30, exerts no pressure on the plane. It is this force, however, which will cause the block to slide down the incline – unless there is a sufficiently large friction force to oppose it. A plane on which no friction is possible is said to be **smooth**: in such a case motion would be inevitable.

Fig. 5, which in a sense is a summary of this section, shows the forces

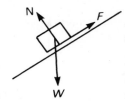

W   Fig. 5

acting on a block placed on a **rough** plane, i.e one on which friction is possible.

Example 20

Find the acceleration of the block in Fig. 4 down the incline if there is a friction force of 15 N opposing motion.

The resolved part of the weight down the plane

is 49 sin 30° = 24.5 N

Subtracting the friction we have an overall force down the incline

of 24.5 − 15 = 9.5 N

Hence, using $F = ma$, the acceleration is 1.9 m s^{-2}

Exercise 4(b)

1. (i) A block of mass 3 kg is placed on an incline of 15°. What is the magnitude of the normal contact force acting on the block? What friction force is needed to prevent the block sliding?
   (ii) If the maximum available friction is 5 N, what will be the motion of the block?
2. Show that the acceleration of a mass m down a smooth plane of inclination θ is $g \sin \theta$. How long is taken to slide a distance d starting from rest?
3. A 4 kg block is at rest on a rough inclined plane. If the normal reaction is 35.5 N, find the inclination of the plane. Find also the magnitude of the friction force acting.
4. A 50 kg trunk placed on a smooth loading ramp of inclination arctan 3/4 is supported by a rope running up the incline. What tension is needed:
   (i) to hold the trunk at rest
   (ii) to pull the trunk up at constant speed
   (iii) to pull the trunk up with acceleration 0.6 m s^{-2}?
5. What tractive force is needed to drive a car of mass 800 kg up an incline of 12° at steady speed? (Neglect any resistances.)
6. A skier of mass 85 kg, including equipment, accelerates at 2.4 m s^{-2} when pointing directly down a slope of angle 22°. What is the total resisting force opposing his motion?

4.3 Resultant of Forces at a Point

Using resolved parts we can improve on the **polygon of forces** method used in section 3.4, which is rather cumbersome when more than three forces are involved.

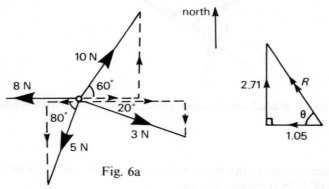

Fig. 6a   Fig. 6b

Fig. 6a demonstrates the idea of the method in a case where four forces, of magnitude 10 N, 3 N, 5 N and 8 N act at a point. The dotted lines indicate resolved parts. In practice these are *not* marked on the diagram, since the working is readily performed in the head. Combining resolved parts in the directions east and north, we obtain

$$R(\rightarrow) \text{ overall force east } = 10 \cos 60° + 3 \cos 20° - 5 \cos 80° - 8$$
$$= -1.05 \text{ N}$$
$$R(\uparrow) \text{ overall force north } = 10 \sin 60° - 3 \sin 20° - 5 \sin 80°$$
$$= 2.71 \text{ N}$$

We can now obtain the resultant force R from Fig. 6b.

$$\text{magnitude} \quad R = \sqrt{2.71^2 + 1.05^2} = 2.91 \text{ N}$$
$$\text{direction} \quad \tan \theta = \frac{2.71}{1.05} \Rightarrow \theta \simeq 69°$$

Thus resultant force is 2.91 N north 21° west

The symbols $R(\rightarrow)$ and $R(\uparrow)$ are used as a shorthand to indicate that resolved parts in the directions indicated are being combined.

Note that questions 1 to 3 of exercise 4c may now be tackled.

4.4 The Resolution Principle

The methods of the preceding sections lead us naturally to an important idea which is known as the **resolution principle**. This may be stated as follows

> THE SUM OF THE RESOLVED PARTS OF THE FORCES ACTING ON A BODY IN A GIVEN DIRECTION WILL DETERMINE THE ACCELERATION OF THE BODY IN THAT DIRECTION.

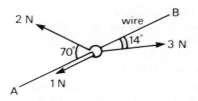

Fig. 7

Consider a bead threaded on a wire and subjected to forces in a horizontal plane as shown in Fig. 7. We can find the overall effective force along the wire by summing the resolved parts in this direction

R(AB) overall force in direction AB (i.e. from A to B)
$$= 3 \cos 14° - 2 \cos 70° - 1$$
$$= 1.23 \text{ N}$$

According to the resolution principle, this overall force will determine the acceleration of the bead along the wire. Thus if the bead has mass 100 g or 1/10 kg we obtain using $F = ma$

acceleration $= 12.3 \text{ m s}^{-2}$ (direction AB)

An important corollary of the resolution principle is the following

> IF THERE IS NO ACCELERATION IN A PARTICULAR DIRECTION THEN THE SUM OF THE RESOLVED PARTS IN THAT DIRECTION MUST BE ZERO.

The bead in Fig. 7, for example, would remain at rest if the resolved parts pulling one way along the wire were exactly balanced by those pulling the other way.

The following example illustrates the application of the resolution principle to a typical problem.

Example 21

A 5 kg body is pushed up an incline of 20° by a horizontal force of 30 N. If there is a frictional resistance of 8 N, find (i) the acceleration of the body (ii) the magnitude of the normal reaction N.

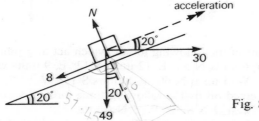

Fig. 8

In this type of question we must be careful to consider *all* the forces acting on the body. These are shown in Fig. 8.

(i) R(along plane) overall force up plane
$$= 30 \cos 20° - 49 \sin 20° - 8$$
$$= 3.43 \text{ N}$$
then, using $F = ma$, $3.43 = 5a$
$$\Rightarrow \text{acceleration} = 0.69 \text{ m s}^{-2}$$

(ii) To find the normal reaction we use the fact that there is no motion perpendicular to the plane. (See note below.) Thus

R($\perp$ plane) no overall force
$$\therefore N = 49 \cos 20 + 30 \sin 20°$$
$$= 56.3 \text{ N}$$

Important note: In the above example, the direction perpendicular to the plane is the *only* direction in which there is no acceleration and hence the *only* direction in which it is true to say there is no overall force.

As a general rule the following procedure should be observed with acceleration problems

direction of acceleration : sum of resolved parts
$$= \text{mass} \times \text{acceleration}$$
direction perpendicular: no overall force, so
to acceleration   resolved parts balance

With problems of equilibrium (or motion at constant velocity) the resolved parts must balance in all directions.

Exercise 4(c)

1. Find the resultant force in each of the following cases (units are Newtons).

(i)

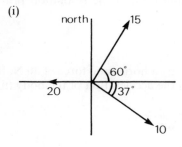

(ii)

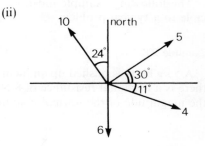

2. Find the resultant of the following forces, which act at a point
   (i) 5 units north, 6 units N 58° E, 12 units S 12° E, 9 units west
   (ii) 5 units N 25° W, 4 units N 60° E, 8 units S 15° W.

3. A point mass is acted on by the following three forces:
      3 N north 16° west, 2 N S 72° W, 5 N south.
   What fourth force is needed to hold the mass in equilibrium?

4. Find the overall effective force in the direction indicated by the double arrow, in the diagrams at the top of page 51.

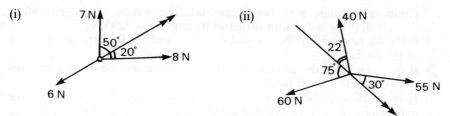

(i) 7 N 50° 20° →8 N 6 N

(ii) 40 N 22° 75° 30° 55 N 60 N

5. A 40 kg truck is pushed up a smooth incline of 30° by a horizontal force of 250 N. What is the acceleration of the truck?

6. Find the acceleration of a 5 kg block in each of the following situations. Find also the normal reaction in each case.

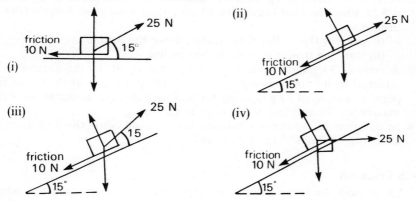

(i) friction 10 N   25 N   15°

(ii) friction 10 N   25 N   15°

(iii) friction 10 N   25 N   15   15°

(iv) friction 10 N   25 N   15°

7. In Fig. 9 a jeep is towing a glider at steady speed just prior to release. The mass of the glider is 200 kg. If the tension in the tow-rope is 1000 N find
   (i) the forces of air-resistance and lift acting on the glider
   (ii) the frictional resistance acting on the jeep if its engine is producing a tractive force of 1200 N.

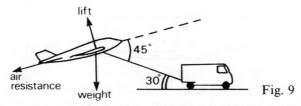

lift   45°   air resistance   weight   30°   Fig. 9

Questions 8–10 refer to Fig. 10, which shows the forces on an aircraft

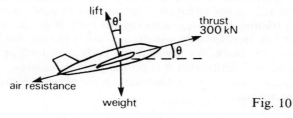

lift   θ   thrust 300 kN   θ   air resistance   weight   Fig. 10

climbing at angle θ to the horizontal. The weight of the aircraft is 750 kN and the maximum thrust of its engines is 300 kN.

8. If the air resistance is 70 kN and $\theta = 11°$, find the forward acceleration of the aircraft.

9. If $\theta = 16°$ and the aircraft is climbing at steady speed, find the air-resistance and the lift force.

10. If, in question 9, the pilot tries to increase the angle of ascent to 20°, the magnitudes of the forces remaining the same, investigate the overall force in the new direction of ascent. What would happen?

11. A car of mass 1200 kg is accelerating at 1.3 m s^{-2} up an incline of 18°. If the engine is developing a tractive force of 5.5 kN, find the total resistance opposing motion.

12. A trolley of mass 10 kg is on an incline of 14°. The resistance to motion is 8 N. Find the least force with which a man must push horizontally in order to

    (i) prevent the trolley from rolling down the incline

    (ii) start the trolley moving up the incline.

13. A mass of 3 kg on a smooth plane inclined at 30° to the horizontal is attached by a string passing over a smooth light pulley at the top of the plane to a mass of 2 kg hanging freely. Prove that the acceleration of the masses is $g/10$ and find the tension in the string.

14. In question 13, what mass hanging freely would cause the 3 kg mass to accelerate at 2 m s^{-2} up the incline?

4.5 Friction

All surfaces, however smooth in appearance, have irregularities which may be revealed under a microscope. When two bodies are in contact these irregularities of surface are pressed together and any tendency of the surfaces to slip over one another is opposed. This is the origin of the force we call friction and it explains, for example, why a heavy trunk can be pushed quite hard and yet not moved, (Fig. 11) or why a sliding body is gradually brought to rest.

applied force

friction   Fig. 11

In the case of the trunk we know from everyday experience that if the applied force is increased sufficiently there will come a point when the trunk starts to move. This tells us that there is a limit to the amount of friction which may act in a given situation. This maximum amount of friction is called **limiting friction**. When it is achieved the body is on the limit between equilibrium and motion, for only a slight increase in the applied force is now needed to move the body. We say that the body is in **limiting equilibrium** which means, paradoxically, that it is on the point of moving.

On what factors does the limiting friction between two given surfaces depend? There are two:

(i) **The pressure between the surfaces.** This will determine the degree of interlocking of surface irregularities and hence influence the friction available considerably. (As a simple demonstration, compare the force needed to push a book over a table top (a) unhindered, (b) when someone else presses the book downwards against the table.) The pressure with which the surfaces are forced together is measured by the normal contact force or normal reaction N. Experimentally it is found that the limiting friction is, to a good approximation, proportional to N. We can, therefore, write

limiting friction $= \mu N$

where μ is a constant of proportionality.

(ii) **The roughness of the surfaces.** In the above formula μ tells us what fraction, or proportion, of the normal reaction N may be achieved as limiting friction. This will depend on how rough, or irregular, the surfaces are; in fact the rougher the surfaces, the greater this fraction will be, i.e. the greater will be the value of μ.

μ is therefore a measure, in a sense, of how rough the surfaces are. It is called the **coefficient of friction**. The following examples give some idea of the sort of values taken by μ in different situations.

rubber tyre on dry road	approaching 1
two wooden surfaces	0.3 to 0.5
two metal surfaces	0.1 to 0.3
metal on ice	around 0.01

Dynamic friction. Experimentally it has been shown that once slipping occurs between two surfaces the friction force decreases slightly. In this book, however, we shall make no distinction between 'dynamic' friction, as this is called, and the limiting ('static') friction which is achieved just prior to equilibrium being broken.

Friction always acts so as to oppose the sliding of surfaces across one another. It is not widely appreciated, however, that in so doing friction may often *cause* motion. The following example is typical of this. Other situations of this type will be met in exercise 4(d).

Example 22

A large container rests on the back of a lorry. If the co-efficient of friction between the surfaces in contact is 0.35, what is the maximum rate at which the lorry may accelerate without the container sliding?

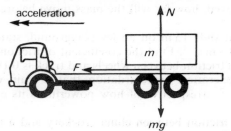

Fig. 12

Fig. 12 shows the forces acting on the container. The container has no engine to accelerate it forward: we in fact rely on friction to provide the forward force needed. Without friction the lorry would simply drive out from beneath the container. (Very similar to the feat which may sometimes be achieved with a tablecloth and crockery.) The friction force is forward in direction so as to oppose this tendency of the container to slide back relative to the lorry. If the mass of the container is m we have

$$\text{weight} = mg$$
$$\text{R($\uparrow$) normal reaction } N = mg \text{ (no vertical motion)}$$
$$\text{limiting friction } \mu N = \mu mg$$

This is the maximum forward force, so using $F = ma$

$$\mu mg = ma$$
$$\Rightarrow \text{maximum acceleration} = \mu g = 0.35 \times 9.8 = 3.43 \text{ m s}^{-2}$$

Notice that this result is independent of the mass of the container.

Exercise 4(d)

1. A 10 kg block rests on a horizontal surface. If the co-efficient of friction between the surfaces in contact is 0.35, find the limiting friction available in the following cases
   (i) the block rests undisturbed
   (ii) the block is pushed downwards by a force of 30 N
   (iii) an upward force of 30 N is applied to the block by means of a string.
2. The co-efficient of friction between a 20 kg sledge and the snow is 0.05. What horizontal force is just sufficient to move the sledge when it is
   (i) unladen
   (ii) carrying one child of mass 30 kg
   (iii) carrying two children of masses 30 kg and 35 kg?
3. A horizontal force of 175 N is just sufficient to move a cabinet of mass 40 kg. What is the co-efficient of friction between the cabinet and the ground?
4. A body of mass 5 kg at rest on a rough horizontal plane is pushed by a horizontal force of 20 N for 5 seconds. If $\mu = 0.3$, how far does the body travel in this time and how much further will it move after the force is removed?
5. A force of 2.5 N is applied to a 400 g mass at rest on a horizontal plane. After moving 1.8 m, the mass has acquired a speed of 3 m s^{-1}. Find μ. If the force is removed, how far will the mass move before its speed is reduced to 2 m s^{-1}?
6. A boy finds he can slide 15 m on an icy playground, starting from a running speed of 3.5 m s^{-1}. Find the co-efficient of friction.
7. If the co-efficient of friction between wheels and track is 0.14, show that the maximum acceleration or retardation that a train can achieve is about 1.37 m s^{-2}, irrespective of how powerful is its engine or its braking system.
8. The co-efficient of friction between china crockery and a tablecloth is

0.32. What is the least acceleration with which the tablecloth must be removed in order to leave the crockery on the table?

9. A container of mass 400 kg is on the back of a lorry accelerating at 1.8 m s^{-2}. What co-efficient of friction is necessary to prevent the container from slipping?

*10. If, in question 9, $\mu = 0.15$ only, what would be the maximum acceleration of the container? By using the idea of relative acceleration, or by finding separately the distances moved by the lorry and the parcel under their respective accelerations, find how far back the container will slip on the lorry during the first two seconds of motion.

11. A uniform chain of length 50 cm rests on the top of a table in a line perpendicular to one of the edges. If $\mu = 0.25$, find the greatest length of chain which may hang freely over the edge without disturbing equilibrium.

*12. A lump of coal of mass 1 kg drops vertically onto a horizontal conveyor belt moving at 0.7 m s^{-1}. If the co-efficient of friction is 0.5, find the acceleration of the coal and hence the time it takes to acquire the same speed as the belt. Deduce the distance that the coal slides along the belt before being carried without slipping.

13. At an airport a suitcase is dropped vertically onto a horizontal belt conveying luggage. Slipping is observed to occur for 0.2 second. If the belt is moving at 1 m s^{-1} find μ.

14. A van moving at 10 m s^{-1} is brought uniformly to rest in 3 s. If $\mu = 0.3$ find the retardation experienced by a package resting on the floor, in the rear of the van. Deduce the distance that the package slides across the floor before coming to rest.

4.6 Further Work on Resolution

Example 23

The co-efficient of friction between a 30 kg trunk and the floor is 1/3. Find what force is needed to move the trunk when (i) applied horizontally, and (ii) applied at 30° above the horizontal. (See Fig. 13.)

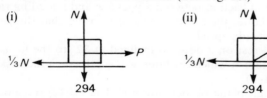

(i)   (ii)

Fig. 13

In both cases we consider the position of **limiting equilibrium**. The friction is therefore μN or $\frac{1}{3} N$.

Case (i)   R($\uparrow$) $N = 294$
            R($\rightarrow$) $P = \frac{1}{3} N = 98 \text{ N}$

Case (ii) –   It is important to realise that the normal reaction N will no longer be 294 N since the upward pull of the applied force P will reduce the pressure between the surfaces.
            R($\uparrow$) $N + P \sin 30 = 294$ (1)
            R($\rightarrow$) $P \cos 30 = \frac{1}{3} N$ (2)

Eliminating N we obtain

$$3 \, P \cos 30 + P \sin 30 = 294$$
$$2.598 \, P + 0.5 \, P = 294$$
$$\Rightarrow \quad P = 94.9 \text{ N}$$

Exercise 4(e)

1. What is the acceleration of a 500 g tile down a roof of inclination 30° if $\mu = 1/3$?

2. The co-efficient of friction between a laden sledge of mass 80 kg and horizontal ground is 0.2. Compare the least forces needed to move the sledge in the following situations
   (i) The force is applied by a rope pulling at arctan 3/4 above the horizontal
   (ii) The force is applied by pushing the rear of the sledge downwards at arctan 3/4 below the horizontal.
   Explain briefly why, in general, it is easier to pull an object rather than push it.

3. The sledge of question 2 is pulled by a rope at 30° above the horizontal with a force of 200 N. Find its acceleration.

4. A block of weight 60 N resting on a rough horizontal surface can just be moved by a horizontal force of 24 N. What force at 30° above the horizontal would just be sufficient to move the block?

5. Show that the acceleration of a particle down a rough plane of inclination θ is $g(\sin \theta - \mu \cos \theta)$. What happens if $\mu \cos \theta > \sin \theta$?

6. A boat of weight 1000 N is at rest on a slipway inclined at 14° to the horizontal. If $\mu = 0.3$, find the least force along the slipway needed to
   (i) drag the boat down at steady speed
   (ii) drag the boat up at steady speed.

*7. (i) A body of mass M rests on a rough surface whose inclination to the horizontal is slowly increased. Show that if the body is just about to slide when the inclination is θ, then $\mu = \tan \theta$. θ is called the **angle of friction**.
   (ii) If the co-efficient of friction between a package and a loading ramp is 1/3, at what angle should the ramp be placed in order that the package may slide down at steady speed?
   (iii) A book will just rest on a desk lid inclined at 22° to the horizontal. Find μ and also the rate at which the book will accelerate if the desk lid is lifted to an angle of 30°.

8. A body is on a rough plane of inclination θ. The least force along the plane needed to move the body upwards is three times that needed to prevent it sliding downwards. Show that $\mu = \frac{1}{2} \tan \theta$.

9. The roughness of a plane of inclination θ is not sufficient to prevent a mass M from accelerating down. What force up the plane would give the mass the same acceleration in the opposite direction?

10. By waxing his skis, a skier reduces μ by one-third of its usual value. On a slope of inclination θ this increases his acceleration down the slope by 20%. Show that $\mu = 3 \tan\theta/8$.

5
More Vectors

5.1 Displacement Vectors

We have seen in Chapter 3 that displacement is a vector quantity. The vector representing the displacement from point A to point B is written **AB** (see Fig. 1a). The order of the letters is of importance here: in writing **BA** we would mean the opposite displacement from B back to A (see Fig. 1b).

That is **BA** = −**AB**

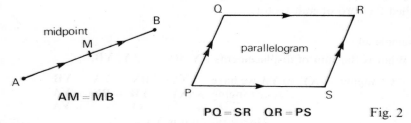

Fig. 1a   Fig. 1b

Two displacements are considered to be equal if they are of equal magnitude and in the same direction. They do not have to be between the same pair of points. Fig. 2 illustrates two typical examples of this.

midpoint

AM = **MB**

parallelogram

PQ = **SR**   **QR** = **PS**   Fig. 2

Triangle addition of displacements

Displacements **AB** and **BC** are equivalent to a single displacement **AC** (Fig. 3).

i.e. **AB** + **BC** = **AC**

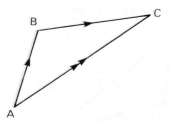

Fig. 3

It is important to notice the arrangement of the letters in this equation. Using a similar pattern we may split any displacement into two or more parts (or components)

e.g $\mathbf{RS} = \mathbf{R\overset{\frown}{Y}} + \mathbf{\overset{\frown}{Y}S}$
or $\mathbf{RS} = \mathbf{R\overset{\frown}{Y}} + \mathbf{\overset{\frown}{YZ}} + \mathbf{\overset{\frown}{Z}S}$ etc

where Y and Z are any other points. (What we are saying here is that the 'direct route' from R to S gives the same final displacement as the 'scenic tour' from R to S going via Y and Z.)

Closed loops

The sum $\mathbf{AB} + \mathbf{BC} + \mathbf{CD} + \mathbf{DE} + \mathbf{EA}$ is equivalent to $\mathbf{AA}$, which is a zero displacement. This is said to be a 'closed loop' of vectors (see Fig. 4). Such loops are of frequent use in solving problems.

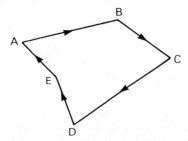

Fig. 4

We would normally write $\mathbf{AB} + \mathbf{BC} + \mathbf{CD} + \mathbf{DE} + \mathbf{EA} = \mathbf{0}$ where $\mathbf{0}$ is called the zero or null vector.

Example 24

What is the sum of displacements $\mathbf{XY}$, $\mathbf{BX}$, $- \mathbf{AY}$, $\mathbf{YB}$?

Changing $- \mathbf{AY}$ to $\mathbf{YA}$ we have $\quad \mathbf{XY} + \mathbf{BX} + \mathbf{YA} + \mathbf{YB}$
re-arranging $= (\mathbf{XY} + \mathbf{YB} + \mathbf{BX}) + \mathbf{YA}$
$= \qquad \mathbf{O} \qquad + \mathbf{YA}$

Hence the sum is $\mathbf{YA}$

Example 25

In a triangle ABC the midpoints of the sides AB, BC and CA are L, M and N respectively. If O is any point inside the triangle, prove that

$$\mathbf{OA} + \mathbf{OB} + \mathbf{OC} = \mathbf{OL} + \mathbf{OM} + \mathbf{ON}$$

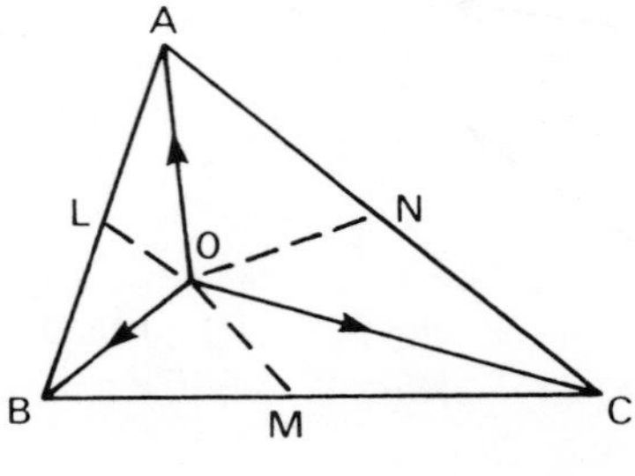

Fig. 5

$$\begin{aligned} \mathbf{OA} + \mathbf{OB} + \mathbf{OC} &= (\mathbf{OL} + \mathbf{LA}) + (\mathbf{OM} + \mathbf{MB}) + (\mathbf{ON} + \mathbf{NC}) \\ &= \mathbf{OL} + \mathbf{OM} + \mathbf{ON} + (\mathbf{LA} + \mathbf{MB} + \mathbf{NC}) \\ &= \mathbf{OL} + \mathbf{OM} + \mathbf{ON} + \tfrac{1}{2}(\mathbf{BA} + \mathbf{CB} + \mathbf{AC}) \end{aligned}$$

$(\mathbf{BA} + \mathbf{CB} + \mathbf{AC}) = \mathbf{0}$ since they may be re-arranged into a closed loop. The proof is therefore complete.

Exercise 5(a)

1. Find the sum of displacements:
   (i) **AB**, − **CB**, **CD**, **AD**
   (ii) 2**PQ**, **SR**, **RP**, − **PS**
2. ABC is a triangle and M is the midpoint of BC. Prove that
   $$\mathbf{AB} + \mathbf{AC} = 2\mathbf{AM}$$
3. PQRS is any quadrilateral. Prove that $\mathbf{SQ} + \mathbf{RP} = \mathbf{RQ} + \mathbf{SP}$
4. If A, B, C and D are any four points and M, N are the midpoints of AB and CD respectively, prove that $\mathbf{AD} + \mathbf{BC} = 2\mathbf{MN}$.
5. What can be deduced in each of the following cases?
   (i) $\mathbf{PQ} + \mathbf{QR} + \mathbf{RS} + \mathbf{ST} = \mathbf{O}$
   (ii) $\mathbf{PS} + \mathbf{TR} = \mathbf{PQ} + \mathbf{TS}$
6. E, F and G are the points of trisection of the sides BC, CA and AB of a triangle ABC which are nearest to B, C and A respectively. Show that $\mathbf{AG} + \mathbf{BE} + \mathbf{CF} = \mathbf{O}$. Hence prove that if O is any point inside the triangle

   $$\mathbf{OA} + \mathbf{OB} + \mathbf{OC} = \mathbf{OE} + \mathbf{OF} + \mathbf{OG}$$

7. ABCD is a parallelogram in which M and N are the midpoints of the sides BC and CD respectively. In each of the following, forces which may be represented by the vectors given act at a point. Find in each case the representation of the resultant
   (i) **AB** and **AD**
   (ii) **AM** and **AN**
   (iii) **AN** and 2**DM**
8. ABC is a triangle in which X and Y are the midpoints of BC and AX respectively. In each of the following cases find the resultant of forces at a point which are represented completely by the vectors given
   (i) **YB** and **AC**
   (ii) **AC**, **BA** and **XA**
   (iii) **YA**, **AC** and **XB**
9. (i) If the medians of a triangle ABC intersect at G, show that

   $$\mathbf{GA} + \mathbf{GB} + \mathbf{GC} = \mathbf{O}$$

   (ii) Hence show that if O is any point inside the triangle, the resultant of forces **OA**, **OB** and **OC** acting at a point is 3**OG**.

5.2 Base Vectors in Two Dimensions

Any vector whose magnitude is one unit is called a **unit vector**. Two unit vectors of particular use are those whose directions lie along the co-ordinate axes: they are given the special symbols **i** and **j** and may be defined as follows.

i is a unit vector in the direction of the *x*-axis (or east)
j is a unit vector in the direction of the *y*-axis (or north)

The two vectors **i** and **j** are sometimes called **base vectors** because they form a simple 'base' from which all vectors in 2 dimensions may be built. (They are not the only pair of vectors which form such a base – see exercise 5(b) No. 9 – but they are certainly the simplest.) Fig. 6 illustrates the way in which other vectors may be expressed in terms of **i** and **j**.

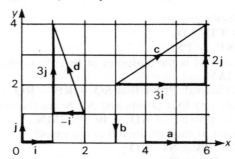

Fig. 6

Remembering the definition of scalar multiplication (section 3.6), we see that the vectors **a**, **b**, **c** and **d** may be written as follows:

$$\mathbf{a} = 2\mathbf{i} \qquad \mathbf{c} = 3\mathbf{i} + 2\mathbf{j}$$
$$\mathbf{b} = -\mathbf{j} \qquad \mathbf{d} = -\mathbf{i} + 3\mathbf{j}$$

Notice that we are effectively splitting each vector into components east and north.

Working with i/j components. One of the great advantages of expressing vectors in this form is the ease with which addition, subtraction and scalar multiplication may be performed. For example

$$\text{if} \quad \mathbf{c} = \quad 3\mathbf{i} + 2\mathbf{j}$$
$$\text{and } \mathbf{d} = -\mathbf{i} + 3\mathbf{j}$$

then

$$\mathbf{c} + \mathbf{d} = \quad 2\mathbf{i} + 5\mathbf{j} \quad \text{(add components)}$$
$$\mathbf{c} - \mathbf{d} = \quad 4\mathbf{i} - \mathbf{j} \quad \text{(subtract components)}$$
$$2\mathbf{c} = \quad 6\mathbf{i} + 4\mathbf{j} \quad \text{(multiply components)}$$
$$-\mathbf{c} = -3\mathbf{i} - 2\mathbf{j}$$

The reader should draw vector diagrams on squared paper to verify these results.

Magnitude of a vector. If $\mathbf{x} = a\mathbf{i} + b\mathbf{j}$ then the magnitude of **x** (denoted by $|\mathbf{x}|$ or x) is given by $|\mathbf{x}| = \sqrt{a^2 + b^2}$ in accordance with Pythagoras' Theorem.

Thus in the above examples

$$\mathbf{c} = \quad 3\mathbf{i} + 2\mathbf{j} \quad \Rightarrow \quad |\mathbf{c}| = \sqrt{13} \simeq 3.61 \text{ units}$$
$$\mathbf{d} = -\mathbf{i} + 3\mathbf{j} \qquad |\mathbf{d}| = \sqrt{10} \simeq 3.16 \text{ units}$$
$$\mathbf{c} + \mathbf{d} = \quad 2\mathbf{i} + 5\mathbf{j} \quad |\mathbf{c} + \mathbf{d}| = \sqrt{29} \simeq 5.38 \text{ units}$$

Notice that $|\mathbf{c} + \mathbf{d}| \neq |\mathbf{c}| + |\mathbf{d}|$.

In fact from the nature of triangle addition it is clear that in general $|\mathbf{x} + \mathbf{y}| \leqslant |\mathbf{x}| + |\mathbf{y}|$ (see Fig. 7) and that equality occurs only when the vectors $\mathbf{x}$ and $\mathbf{y}$ are in the same direction.

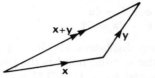

Fig. 7

Parallel vectors. Two vectors are in parallel directions if their components are in the same ratio, as is the case with the vectors

$$\mathbf{p} = 2\mathbf{i} - 4\mathbf{j} \qquad \mathbf{q} = 5\mathbf{i} - 10\mathbf{j}$$

When this occurs one vector may be written as a scalar multiple of the other; in this case $\mathbf{q} = 5\mathbf{p}/2$, which tells us that $\mathbf{q}$ is in the same direction as $\mathbf{p}$ but has $5/2$ times the magnitude.

Example 26

Forces $\mathbf{F}_1 = \mathbf{i} + 3\mathbf{j}$ and $\mathbf{F}_2 = 4\mathbf{i} - \mathbf{j}$ act on a point mass, $\mathbf{i}$ and $\mathbf{j}$ being in directions east and north respectively. Find the magnitude and direction of the resultant force. (Units are Newtons.)

The resultant force is $\mathbf{F}_1 + \mathbf{F}_2 = 5\mathbf{i} + 2\mathbf{j}$
The magnitude of this force is

$$|5\mathbf{i} + 2\mathbf{j}| = \sqrt{29} = 5.38 \text{ N}$$

Its direction is readily found from Fig. 8.

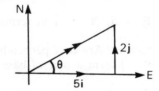

$$\tan \theta = 2/5 = 0.4$$
$$\theta = 21° 48'$$
Direction N 68° 12′ E

Fig. 8

Exercise 5(b)

(Take $\mathbf{i}$ as east and $\mathbf{j}$ as north where appropriate.)

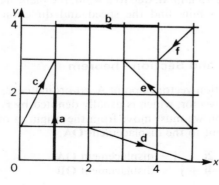

Fig. 9

1. (i) In Fig. 9 write the vectors **a**, **b**, **c**, **d**, **e**, **f** in terms of the vectors **i** and **j**.
   (ii) Write down the magnitudes of these vectors
   (iii) Use the answers of part (i) to show that

$$\mathbf{b} + \mathbf{c} = \mathbf{e} \qquad \mathbf{c} + \mathbf{f} = \tfrac{1}{2}\mathbf{a}$$
$$\mathbf{d} + \mathbf{e} + \mathbf{f} = \mathbf{0} \qquad \mathbf{e} - 2\mathbf{a} = 2\mathbf{f}$$

2. What is the sum of two displacements $3\mathbf{i} - \mathbf{j}$ metres and $2\mathbf{i} + 13\mathbf{j}$ metres? How far from the starting point is the final point reached?

3. Forces $\mathbf{F}_1 = 3\mathbf{i} + 6\mathbf{j}$ N and $\mathbf{F}_2 = \mathbf{i} - 7\mathbf{j}$ N act on a point mass.
   (i) Which force is the larger?
   (ii) What is the magnitude of the resultant force and in which direction does it act? (Give bearing.)

4. If $\mathbf{r} = \mathbf{i} - 4\mathbf{j}$ and $\mathbf{s} = 3\mathbf{i} + \mathbf{j}$, find
   (i) $|\mathbf{r} + \mathbf{s}|$ (ii) $|\mathbf{s} - \mathbf{r}|$ (iii) $|3\mathbf{r} - \mathbf{s}|$

5. In question 4,
   (i) find a scalar k such that $\mathbf{r} + k\mathbf{s}$ is parallel to the x axis
   (ii) find a scalar λ such that $\mathbf{r} + \lambda\mathbf{s}$ is parallel to the vector $2\mathbf{i} + \mathbf{j}$.

6. A ship has velocity vector $-3\mathbf{i} + 9\mathbf{j}$ knots. On what bearing is it travelling and at what speed? If it encounters a current of 5 knots due east, find its resultant velocity vector and hence the new bearing. By how many degrees is the ship carried off course?

7. Forces $2\mathbf{i} - 3\mathbf{j}$, $3\mathbf{i} + \mathbf{j}$, $-4\mathbf{i} - 2\mathbf{j}$ N act on a particle. What fourth force would hold the particle in equilibrium?

8. What are the magnitudes of the vectors $3\mathbf{i} - 4\mathbf{j}$, $7\mathbf{i} + 24\mathbf{j}$, $-9\mathbf{i} - 40\mathbf{j}$? By suitably reducing the magnitudes of these vectors, obtain unit vectors in the same directions.

*9. (i) Find scalars a and b such that the vector $3\mathbf{i} - \mathbf{j}$ may be written in the form $a(\mathbf{i} + \mathbf{j}) + b(\mathbf{i} - \mathbf{j})$.
   (ii) Express also the vectors $2\mathbf{i} + 4\mathbf{j}$, $-2\mathbf{i}$, $2\mathbf{i} - 2\mathbf{j}$ in terms of base vectors $(\mathbf{i} + \mathbf{j})$ and $(\mathbf{i} - \mathbf{j})$.
   (iii) Are these base vectors also unit vectors? Are they perpendicular?
   (iv) Would the vectors $\mathbf{i} - \mathbf{j}$ and $-\mathbf{i} + \mathbf{j}$ form a pair of base vectors? Justify your answer.

10. A plane has velocity 400 km hr^{-1} S $\theta°$ E where $\theta = \arctan 3/4$. Write down its velocity vector in terms of **i** and **j** components. If the plane's starting point is regarded as the origin, write down the co-ordinates of the point it reaches in 15 min. If, due to a wind, the plane actually arrives at $(65, -70)$ after 15 min, find the speed and direction of the wind (assumed constant).

5.3 Position Vectors and Section Theorem

Fig. 10 shows the position vector of point A, co-ordinates (2, 3), relative to the origin. This position vector, which is usually denoted by $\mathbf{r}_A$, tells us how far and in which direction we must move from the origin in order to arrive at point A. It is equivalent to the displacement **OA**.

thus $\qquad \mathbf{r}_A = 2\mathbf{i} + 3\mathbf{j} = $ displacement **OA**
similarly $\qquad \mathbf{r}_B = 4\mathbf{i} + \mathbf{j} \ = $ displacement **OB**

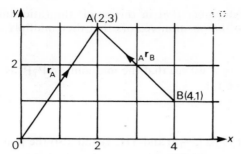

Fig. 10

Sometimes we may give the position of A in relation to a point other than the origin, e.g. B. This is called the position vector of A relative to B and is denoted by $_A\mathbf{r}_B$. From Fig. 10 we have

$$_A\mathbf{r}_B = -2\mathbf{i} + 2\mathbf{j} = \text{displacement } \mathbf{BA}$$

We notice immediately that

$$_A\mathbf{r}_B = \mathbf{r}_A - \mathbf{r}_B$$

i.e. the position vector of one point relative to another is obtained by subtracting the ordinary position vectors of the two points (in the correct order!).

Questions 1–8 of exercise 5(c) may be tackled now if wished.

Section theorem. This important result enables us to find the position vector of the point dividing a line in a given ratio. Its statement is as follows

> IF P_1 AND P_2 HAVE POSITION VECTORS $\mathbf{r}_1$ AND $\mathbf{r}_2$ THEN THE POSITION VECTOR OF THE POINT DIVIDING P_1P_2 IN THE RATIO $m:n$ is $\dfrac{n\mathbf{r}_1 + m\mathbf{r}_2}{m+n}$

Proof

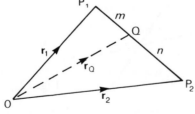

Fig. 11

Let the point concerned be Q. Then, from Fig. 11

$$\mathbf{r}_Q = \mathbf{r}_1 + \mathbf{P}_1\mathbf{Q}$$

$$= \mathbf{r}_1 + \frac{m}{m+n}\mathbf{P}_1\mathbf{P}_2$$

$$= \mathbf{r}_1 + \frac{m}{m+n}(\mathbf{r}_2 - \mathbf{r}_1)$$

$$= \frac{n\mathbf{r}_1 + m\mathbf{r}_2}{m+n}$$

It is important to remember that in this result the ratio numbers are 're-versed' in relation to the position vectors that they multiply.

Corollary

By putting $m = n = 1$ we see that the midpoint of $P_1 P_2$ is the point with position vector $\frac{1}{2}(\mathbf{r}_1 + \mathbf{r}_2)$.

Example 27

Find the midpoint of $X(5, -5)$ and $Y(1, 3)$ and also the point dividing XY in the ratio $3 : 5$.

The position vectors are $\mathbf{r}_X = 5\mathbf{i} - 5\mathbf{j}$, $\mathbf{r}_Y = \mathbf{i} + 3\mathbf{j}$
Midpoint $\frac{1}{2}(\mathbf{r}_X + \mathbf{r}_Y) = 3\mathbf{i} - \mathbf{j}$
Point dividing XY in ratio $3 : 5$
$$\frac{5\mathbf{r}_X + 3\mathbf{r}_Y}{8} = \frac{25\mathbf{i} - 25\mathbf{j} + 3\mathbf{i} + 9\mathbf{j}}{8}$$
$$= 3\tfrac{1}{2}\mathbf{i} - 2\mathbf{j}$$

The answers, in co-ordinates are therefore $(3, -1)$ and $(7/2, -2)$.

Example 28

What can be deduced about the points A, B, C and D if their position vectors: **a**, **b**, **c** and **d**, satisfy the relation $\frac{1}{2}(\mathbf{a} + \mathbf{c}) = \frac{1}{2}(\mathbf{b} + \mathbf{d})$?

$\frac{1}{2}(\mathbf{a} + \mathbf{c})$ is the position vector of the midpoint of AC
$\frac{1}{2}(\mathbf{b} + \mathbf{d})$ is the position vector of the midpoint of BD

As these two position vectors are equal, it follows that the midpoints of AC and BD coincide. The figure ABCD must, therefore, be a parallelogram, since its diagonals bisect one another. (Fig. 12.)

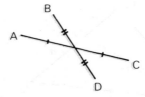

Fig. 12

Exercise 5(c)

1. Draw two perpendicular axes and mark the points A, B, C and D whose position vectors are $3\mathbf{i} + 5\mathbf{j}$, $-2\mathbf{i} + 7\mathbf{j} - 4\mathbf{j}$ and $-\mathbf{i} - 3\mathbf{j}$ respectively. Find the vectors representing **AB**, **DC**, $_A\mathbf{r}_C$ and $_D\mathbf{r}_B$.

2. A, B and C have co-ordinates $(2, 3)$ $(1, -3)$ and $(-5, 4)$ respectively. Find the position vectors of B and C relative to (i) the origin (ii) the point A. Show also that the sum of displacements **OA** and **OB** is parallel to the x-axis.

3. Prove that the points P, Q, R and S, with position vectors $4\mathbf{i} + 2\mathbf{j}$, $2\mathbf{i} - 4\mathbf{j}$, $-\mathbf{i} - \mathbf{j}$ and $\mathbf{i} + 5\mathbf{j}$ respectively, are the vertices of a parallelogram.

4. Prove that the points A, B, C and D, whose position vectors are $-i + 5j$, $5i + 7j$, $7i + 2j$ and $-2i - j$, form a trapezium. What is the ratio of the parallel sides?

5. Two forces may be represented by **OP** and **OQ** where P and Q have co-ordinates (10, 5) and (2, 11) respectively. If the resultant force is represented by **OR** find the co-ordinates of R. If the first force is reversed in direction, show that the magnitude of the resultant force is halved.

6. In a parallelogram ABCD the position vectors of A, B and C are **a**, **b** and **c** respectively. What is the position vector of D?

7. A ship with velocity $8i - 3j$ knots starts at a point with position vector $4i + 7j$ nautical miles relative to a fixed origin. What will be its position vector after 2 hours.
   (i) if there is no current
   (ii) if a current of $-i - j$ is flowing?
   What is the distance between these 2 positions?

8. In a regular hexagon OABCDE **OA** = **r**, and **AB** = **s**. Find the position vectors of A, B, C, D and E relative to O in terms of **r** and **s**.

9. The position vectors of P, Q and R are $5i - 4j$, $8i + 3j$ and $i + j$ respectively. Find the position vectors of M and N, the midpoints of PR and QR respectively, and verify that **PQ** = 2**MN**. Which geometrical theorem does this illustrate?

10. X and Y have position vectors $-2i + 3j$ and $6i + 5j$ respectively. Find the position vector of the points dividing XY in the ratios
    (i) $1 : 3$ (ii) $3 : 2$ (iii) $3 : 5$

11. What can be deduced about the points A, B and C, whose position vectors are **a**, **b** and **c** respectively, in each of the following cases.
    (i) $a = b = c$
    (ii) $|a| = |b| = |c|$
    (iii) $a = \frac{1}{2}(b + c)$
    (iv) $a = b - c$
    (v) $a - c = \lambda(b - c)$ where λ is a scalar.

*12. The vertices A, B and C of a triangle have position vectors **a**, **b** and **c** respectively. Find in terms of **a**, **b** and **c** the position vectors of
    (i)   the midpoints M and N of BC and CA
    (ii) the point dividing the median AM in the ratio $2 : 1$
    (iii) the point dividing the median BN in the ratio $2 : 1$
    Which geometrical result does this prove? Is all of this working necessary to establish the result?

13. OABC is a square of side 1 unit. M is the midpoint of BC. Find the position vector of P, the point dividing AM in ratio $2 : 1$, in terms of unit vectors **i** and **j** along OA and OC respectively. Hence prove that P is a point of trisection of OB.

14. The vertices A, B, C and D of a quadrilateral have position vectors **a**, **b**, **c**, **d** respectively. Write down the position vectors of the midpoints of all four sides of the quadrilateral. Hence obtain vectors representing the displacements
    (i) from the midpoint of AB to that of BC
    (ii) from the midpoint of AD to that of CD.
    What can be deduced?

5.4 Motion with Uniform Velocity

The velocity vector, **v**, of a body defines the displacement it undergoes each second, both in distance and in direction. If the velocity is uniform the

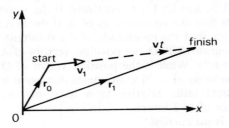

displacement after t seconds will be **v**t. Thus a body starting at position $\mathbf{r_O}$ will, at some subsequent time t, have position vector

$$\mathbf{r} = \mathbf{r_O} + \mathbf{v}t$$

Example 29

A particle P moving with uniform velocity $-2\mathbf{i} + 4\mathbf{j}$ is at position $6\mathbf{i} + \mathbf{j}$ at time O. Find an expression for its position at time t and hence find its closest distance from the point Q, which has position vector $3\mathbf{i} + 4\mathbf{j}$.

Using the above result we obtain P's position at time t

$$\mathbf{r_P} = 6\mathbf{i} + \mathbf{j} + (-2\mathbf{i} + 4\mathbf{j})t$$

Its position relative to point Q is

$$\begin{aligned}
{}_P\mathbf{r_Q} &= \mathbf{r_P} - \mathbf{r_Q} \\
&= 3\mathbf{i} - 3\mathbf{j} + (-2\mathbf{i} + 4\mathbf{j})t \\
&= (3 - 2t)\mathbf{i} + (4t - 3)\mathbf{j} \quad \text{(re-arranging)}
\end{aligned}$$

The distance PQ is least when the magnitude of ${}_P\mathbf{r_Q}$ is a minimum.

$$\begin{aligned}
|{}_P\mathbf{r_Q}|^2 &= (3 - 2t)^2 + (4t - 3)^2 \\
&= 20t^2 - 36t + 18
\end{aligned} \tag{1}$$

Differentiating, we have a minimum of $|{}_P\mathbf{r_Q}|^2$ and hence of $|{}_P\mathbf{r_Q}|$,

when $\qquad 40t - 36 = 0$

$$t = 0.9$$

Substituting back into equation (1), the least distance is

$$\sqrt{(1.2)^2 + (0.6)^2} = 1.34 \text{ units}$$

or, to be more precise

$$\sqrt{\left(\frac{12}{10}\right)^2 + \left(\frac{6}{10}\right)^2}$$

$$= \sqrt{\frac{180}{100}} = \frac{6\sqrt{5}}{10} \text{ i.e. } \frac{3\sqrt{5}}{5} \text{ units}$$

Exercise 5(d)

(Unless otherwise stated, units are metres and seconds.)

1. A body starts from position $3\mathbf{i} + 8\mathbf{j}$ and moves with velocity $2\mathbf{i} - 5\mathbf{j}$. Write down its position vector after (i) 1 s (ii) 2 s (iii) t s. How far from the origin is it after 3 seconds?

2. A body moves with velocity $4\mathbf{i} + 2\mathbf{j}$ starting from position $-3\mathbf{i} + 4\mathbf{j}$. Write down its position vector after (i) 1/2 s (ii) 5/2 s (iii) t s. When is it due north of the origin? How far from the point $(4, -2)$ is it after 3 seconds?

3. A ship leaves a port at noon and sails for 2 h 20 min with velocity $-9\mathbf{i} + 12\mathbf{j}$ knots. It then changes course and heads at the same speed for a small island with position vector $-14\mathbf{i} + 52\mathbf{j}$ nautical miles relative to the port. At what time will the ship reach the island? Find also the velocity vector on the second part of the journey.

4. A body starts from position $-4\mathbf{i} + 10\mathbf{j}$ and moves with velocity $3\mathbf{i} - \mathbf{j}$. Find an expression for the distance of the body from the origin at time t seconds. Hence find the times at which the body is 10 units of distance from the origin.

5. At noon a ship leaves a port at position $8\mathbf{i} + 10\mathbf{j}$ nautical miles. If the ship moves with velocity $-\mathbf{i} + 7\mathbf{j}$ knots, at what time will it be closest to a submerged rock at position $3\mathbf{i} + 40\mathbf{j}$ nautical miles? What is this closest distance?

6. Two ships A and B are at positions $-9\mathbf{i} + 6\mathbf{j}$ nautical miles and $12\mathbf{i} - 15\mathbf{j}$ nautical miles, moving with velocities $12\mathbf{i} + 4\mathbf{j}$ knots and $6\mathbf{i} + 10\mathbf{j}$ knots respectively. Write down the position vectors at time t hours for each ship and hence show that they will collide if their present velocities are maintained. What is the expected position of collision?

5.5 Acceleration as a Vector

A motion is said to be uniform only if both speed *and* direction remain constant. Thus the motion of a car cornering at steady speed is not considered to be uniform because the direction of the motion is changing. (See also section 2.1.) We would like to describe, by means of acceleration, *all* cases in which motion changes, but we have restricted ourselves so far to situations in which only the speed has changed.

In Chapter 1 where we considered cases of linear motion (motion along a single straight line) we obtained the following result for uniform acceleration

$$a = \frac{v - u}{t}$$

That is uniform acceleration $= \dfrac{\text{change in velocity}}{\text{time}}$

It is a comparatively simple matter to extend this result to cases where the direction of motion may be changing as well as the speed. Both these factors are reflected by changes in the velocity *vector* so it is logical to define

uniform acceleration $= \dfrac{\text{change in velocity vector}}{\text{time}}$

$$a = \frac{v - u}{t} \qquad (1)$$

Note that (a) Acceleration becomes a vector quantity under this definition since it is assigned both a magnitude and a direction (see examples 30 and 31).

(b) In cases where the acceleration is not uniform, equation (1) will determine the *average* acceleration over the time interval concerned.

(c) Re-arranging equation (1) we obtain the result $v = u + at$, for a uniform acceleration.

Example 30

Over a period of 5 s the velocity of a body changes from $3i - j$ to $5i + 9j$ m s^{-1}. What is the acceleration of the body, assumed uniform, and what will be its velocity after a further 2 s?

$$\text{acceleration} \quad a = \frac{v - u}{t}$$

$$= \frac{(5i + 9j) - (3i - j)}{5} = \frac{2i}{5} + 2j \text{ m s}^{-2}$$

Final velocity $v = u + at$

$$= 5i + 9j + 2\left(\frac{2i}{5} + 2j\right)$$

$$= \frac{29i}{5} + 13j \text{ m s}^{-1}$$

Example 31

In turning a corner, a car describes a 30° arc of radius 50 m. If the car's speed remains at 20 m s^{-1}, find its average acceleration.

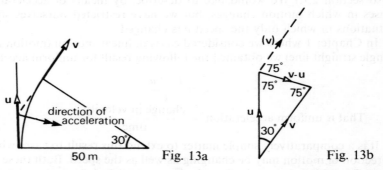

Fig. 13a   Fig. 13b

Fig. 13a shows the space diagram and Fig. 13b the velocity-triangle used for finding the change in velocity $v - u$.

The time taken on the corner (length of arc ÷ speed) is

$$\frac{1}{12} \times \frac{2\pi r}{20} = \frac{100\pi}{240} = 1.31 \text{ s}$$

Since $|\mathbf{u}| = |\mathbf{v}| = 20 \text{ m s}^{-1}$ we have
$$|\mathbf{v} - \mathbf{u}| = 2 \times 20 \sin 15° = 10.35 \text{ m s}^{-1}$$

So the magnitude of the acceleration is

$$\frac{10.35}{1.31} = 7.90 \text{ m s}^{-2}$$

The direction of the acceleration is that of the vector $\mathbf{v} - \mathbf{u}$. This may be seen from Fig. 13a to be inwards along the bisector of the angle between the two radii.

Exercise 5(e)

1. The velocity of a body changes uniformly from $3\mathbf{i} + \mathbf{j}$ to $5\mathbf{i} - 5\mathbf{j} \text{ m s}^{-1}$ in 8 seconds. Find the acceleration vector and the velocity at times 2 seconds and 6 seconds.
2. A body is undergoing a uniform acceleration of $4\mathbf{i} - 2\mathbf{j} \text{ m s}^{-2}$. If its initial velocity is $3\mathbf{i} + 7\mathbf{j} \text{ m s}^{-1}$, write down its velocity vector at times 1 s, 2 s and t s. At what time will it be moving (i) due east (ii) north-east?
3. A boat travelling initially at 6 m s^{-1} due north encounters a current. Five seconds later the velocity of the boat is 7 m s^{-1} N. 20°E. What is the average acceleration of the boat during this time?
4. A train travelling at 25 m s^{-1} comes to a bend in the track which is a 36° arc of radius 80 m. Find the average acceleration of the train whilst negotiating this bend, its speed remaining constant.
*5. In all cases where there is acceleration a force is required in order to produce that acceleration. How is this force produced in the situations of question 4 and example 31?

5.6 Uniform Acceleration Equations

Imagine that a body whose initial velocity is $\mathbf{u}$ moves with uniform acceleration $\mathbf{a}$. What will be the displacement of the body from its starting position after time t?

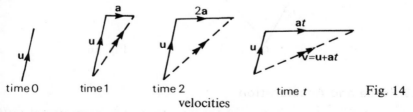

time 0   time 1   time 2   time t Fig. 14

velocities

Fig. 14 shows that the *velocity* of a body undergoing uniform acceleration may always be regarded as the sum of two components
 (i) the initial velocity $\mathbf{u}$
 (ii) a component due to the acceleration, which takes values $\mathbf{a}$, $2\mathbf{a}$, $3\mathbf{a}$ etc. after successive seconds of motion.

Since each component remains fixed in direction, we can consider each to define a straight line motion. Thus we have, simultaneously,

(i) A constant velocity $\mathbf{u}$ giving displacement $\mathbf{u}t$

(ii) A uniform acceleration from 0 to $\mathbf{a}t$ giving a displacement of average velocity × time = $(\frac{1}{2}\mathbf{a}t)t = \frac{1}{2}\mathbf{a}t^2$.

The total displacement $\mathbf{s}$ is therefore given by

$$\mathbf{s} = \mathbf{u}t + \tfrac{1}{2}\mathbf{a}t^2 \qquad\qquad \text{(see Fig. 15)}$$

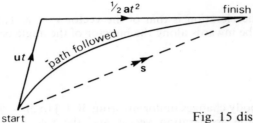

Fig. 15 displacements

The obvious analogy with the results of section 1.1 can be extended, by re-arranging this formula as follows

$$\begin{aligned}
\mathbf{s} &= \mathbf{u}t + \tfrac{1}{2}\mathbf{a}t^2 \\
&= \tfrac{1}{2}[2\mathbf{u} + \mathbf{a}t]t \\
&= \tfrac{1}{2}[\mathbf{u} + (\mathbf{u} + \mathbf{a}t)]t \\
&= \tfrac{1}{2}(\mathbf{u} + \mathbf{v})t
\end{aligned}$$

but, for the present, we cannot obtain a result corresponding to the formula $v^2 - u^2 = 2as$.

Note: It is important to remember that the vector $\mathbf{s}$ in these equations represents displacement from the initial position, not from the origin. Thus, if a body starts at position $\mathbf{r}_O$ it will finish at position $\mathbf{r}_O + \mathbf{s}$. (Fig. 16.)

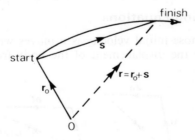

Fig. 16

5.7 Force and Acceleration

According to Newton's Second Law acceleration is proportional to the applied force and in the same direction. The Equation of Motion $F = ma$ does not reflect the direction aspect of this law. Using vectors we can remedy this by writing

$$\mathbf{F} = m\mathbf{a}$$

This formula always holds: a uniform force **F** will give a uniform acceleration **a**, a changing force will give a changing acceleration which may be determined at each instant in accordance with this result.

Example 32

A constant force of $4\mathbf{i} + 4\mathbf{j}$ N acts for 3 s on a body of mass 2 kg which is initially moving through the origin with velocity $3\mathbf{i} - 2\mathbf{j}$ m s^{-1}. Plot the path of the body and find the speed with which it is moving when the 3 s have elapsed.

Using $\mathbf{F} = m\mathbf{a}$ we have $4\mathbf{i} + 4\mathbf{j} = 2\mathbf{a}$
$\Rightarrow$ uniform acceleration $\mathbf{a} = 2\mathbf{i} + 2\mathbf{j}$

Using $\mathbf{s} = \mathbf{u}t + \frac{1}{2}\mathbf{a}t^2$ we obtain
$$\mathbf{s} = (3\mathbf{i} - 2\mathbf{j})t + (\mathbf{i} + \mathbf{j})t^2$$
i.e $\quad \mathbf{s} = (3t + t^2)\mathbf{i} + (t^2 - 2t)\mathbf{j}$

This displacement is from the origin, so we have

$$\mathbf{r} = (3t + t^2)\mathbf{i} + (t^2 - 2t)\mathbf{j}$$
hence   at $t = 1$ $\quad \mathbf{r} = \qquad 4\mathbf{i} - \mathbf{j}$
$\qquad t = 2 \qquad = \qquad 10\mathbf{i}$
$\qquad t = 2 \qquad = \qquad 18\mathbf{i} + 3\mathbf{j}$

The path followed for $0 \leqslant t \leqslant 3$ is shown in Fig. 17.

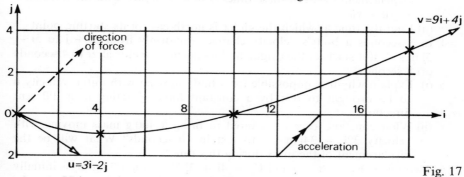

Fig. 17

Using $\mathbf{v} = \mathbf{u} + \mathbf{a}t$ the velocity after 3 s is
$$\mathbf{v} = 3\mathbf{i} - 2\mathbf{j} + 3(2\mathbf{i} + 2\mathbf{j}) = 9\mathbf{i} + 4\mathbf{j}$$
Hence the speed is $\sqrt{81 + 16} = 9.85$ m s^{-1}

Note: The velocity at time t is given by
$$\mathbf{v} = \mathbf{u} + \mathbf{a}t = 3\mathbf{i} - 2\mathbf{j} + t(2\mathbf{i} + 2\mathbf{j})$$
that is $\quad \mathbf{v} = (3 + 2t)\mathbf{i} + (2t - 2)\mathbf{j}$

In the motion considered this formula applies only for $0 \leqslant t \leqslant 3$. After time 3 s the body will continue with uniform velocity $9\mathbf{i} + 4\mathbf{j}$.

Exercise 5(f)

1. A body starts from the origin with velocity $6\mathbf{i} + 2\mathbf{j}$ and moves subject to an acceleration of $-2\mathbf{i}$. Find an expression for the position vector at time

t. Use this to plot the path followed by the body during the first 5 s of motion.

    (i) What is the shape of the path followed? In which direction associated with this shape is the acceleration?

    (ii) Find the velocities at times 1 and 3 and verify that they are in the directions of the tangents to the path at the appropriate points.

2. A ball is thrown upwards with velocity $10i + 21j$ m s^{-1} relative to horizontal and vertical axes through the point of projection. The acceleration is $-9.8j$ m s^{-2}. Find the position vector of the ball at time *t* seconds and use it to plot the motion of the ball during the first 5 seconds. From your graph, find the horizontal distance covered when the ball strikes horizontal ground through the point of projection. Write down also the velocity vector of the ball after 2 s and after 3 s and deduce in each case the angle at which it is travelling to the horizontal.

3. A model glider of mass 200 g is launched into the wind with initial velocity $-5i + 2j$ m s^{-1} relative to axes east and north in a horizontal plane through the launching point. If the wind exerts a constant force of $0.8 i + 0.2j$ N on the glider, find the position vector of the glider at time *t* seconds. (Ignore any vertical motion.) Plot the path of the glider during the first 5 seconds and mark on the directions of the initial velocity and the acceleration, as in Fig. 17.

    (i) Find the velocity vector at times 1 and 4 seconds and verify that the displacement between these times is in accordance with the formula $s = \frac{1}{2}(u + v)t$.

    (ii) Find the time at which the glider is north-east of its starting point.

4. In 8 seconds a body's velocity changes uniformly from $3i + j$ to $5i - 5j$ m s^{-1}. If it starts at the origin, find its position vector after (i) 4 seconds (ii) 8 seconds.

5. (i) Explain why it is impossible for a body moving with initial velocity **u** to be brought to rest by a constant force **F** acting in a different direction.

    (ii) What constant force is required to bring a 400 g mass moving with velocity $22i - 34j$ m s^{-1} to rest in 10 seconds? What will be the displacement of the mass during this time?

6. Two forces $F_1 = 2i - j$ and $F_2 = 4i + 3j$ N act on a 2 kg mass initially at rest at position $i - 3j$ metres. Find the position of the mass after 2 s and the speed with which it is then moving.

7. A body of mass 3 kg moving initially with velocity $2i + j$ m s^{-1} travels from position $5i + 8j$ to position $21i - 12j$ m in a time of 4 s. Find the constant force needed to produce this motion and the velocity of the body at the end of the 4 s.

8. A body of mass 5 kg leaves position $-8i + 10j$ m with velocity $7i + 2j$ m s^{-1}. For 4 s it travels under the influence of a force $F_1 = -10i - 5j$ N. Find its position and velocity when this time has elapsed. What force F_2 is now required to bring the body to rest in a further 4 s and what will be the position of rest? Plot the motion on rectangular axes, marking the positions at times 1, 2, 3, 4 and 8 s.

5.8 General Motion

Consider again the motion of example 32 in which the initial velocity was $3\mathbf{i} - 2\mathbf{j}$ m s^{-1}, the acceleration was $2\mathbf{i} + 2\mathbf{j}$ m s^{-2} and the following results were obtained for the position vector and velocity at time t

$$\mathbf{r} = (3t + t^2)\mathbf{i} + (t^2 - 2t)\mathbf{j}$$
$$\mathbf{v} = (3 + 2t)\mathbf{i} + (2t - 2)\mathbf{j}$$

It is apparent that if we differentiate each component of $\mathbf{r}$ we obtain the corresponding component of $\mathbf{v}$

i.e $\quad \mathbf{v} = \dfrac{d\mathbf{r}}{dt} \quad$ (or $\dot{\mathbf{r}}$)

Furthermore if we differentiate the components of velocity we get those of acceleration; $2\mathbf{i} + 2\mathbf{j}$

i.e $\quad \mathbf{a} = \dfrac{d\mathbf{v}}{dt} \quad$ (or $\ddot{\mathbf{r}}$)

Are these results always true? Consider Fig. 18 which may represent a part of any motion. Suppose that between times t and $t + \delta t$ a body moves from position $\mathbf{r}(t)$ to position $\mathbf{r}(t + \delta t)$. The change in position, $\delta\mathbf{r}$, is as shown.

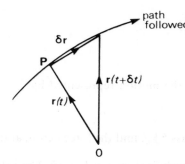

Fig. 18

For the interval of time considered, it should be clear from Fig. 18 that the average velocity of the body is given in both magnitude and direction by

$$\begin{array}{c}\text{average} \\ \text{velocity}\end{array} = \frac{\text{change in position vector}}{\text{time}} = \frac{\delta\mathbf{r}}{\delta t}$$

Similarly

$$\begin{array}{c}\text{average} \\ \text{acceleration}\end{array} = \frac{\text{change in velocity vector}}{\text{time}} = \frac{\delta\mathbf{v}}{\delta t}$$

As $\delta t \longrightarrow 0$ these results will approach more and more closely the instantaneous velocity and acceleration at the point P on the path

i.e $\quad \begin{array}{c}\text{velocity} \\ \text{at instant}\end{array} \quad \mathbf{v} = \displaystyle\lim_{\delta t \to 0} \frac{\delta\mathbf{r}}{\delta t} = \frac{d\mathbf{r}}{dt}$

$\quad\quad \begin{array}{c}\text{acceleration} \\ \text{at instant}\end{array} \quad \mathbf{a} = \displaystyle\lim_{\delta t \to 0} \frac{\delta\mathbf{v}}{\delta t} = \frac{d\mathbf{v}}{dt}$

We may now make the following precise definitions of velocity and acceleration

---

VELOCITY IS RATE OF CHANGE OF POSITION VECTOR ACCELERATION IS RATE OF CHANGE OF VELOCITY VECTOR

Mathematical note. We have not, as yet, proved that $\dfrac{d\mathbf{r}}{dt}$ is obtained in practice by differentiating each component in the normal way. This can be established as follows

$$\text{suppose } \mathbf{r}(t) = x(t)\mathbf{i} + y(t)\mathbf{j}$$

$$\text{where } x \text{ and } y \text{ are scalar functions of } t$$

$$\text{Then } \mathbf{r}(t + \delta t) = x(t + \delta t)\mathbf{i} + y(t + \delta t)\mathbf{j}$$

$$\frac{\delta \mathbf{r}}{\delta t} = \frac{\mathbf{r}(t + \delta t) - \mathbf{r}(t)}{\delta t}$$

$$= \left[\frac{x(t + \delta t) - x(t)}{\delta t}\right]\mathbf{i} + \left[\frac{y(t + \delta t) - y(t)}{\delta t}\right]\mathbf{j}$$

from which it follows that

$$\frac{d\mathbf{r}}{dt} = \lim \frac{\delta \mathbf{r}}{\delta t} = \frac{dx}{dt}\mathbf{i} + \frac{dy}{dt}\mathbf{j}$$

†Example 33

Plot the first 6 seconds of the motion represented by

$$\mathbf{r} = t\mathbf{i} + 3\cos\frac{\pi t}{6}\mathbf{j} \text{ m}$$

If the body concerned has mass 5 kg, find the force acting at times 0, 2, 4 and 6 seconds.

The path followed by the body is shown in Fig. 19. The values of **r** plotted were obtained as follows

$t = 0$	$\dfrac{\pi t}{6} = 0$ or $0°$	$\mathbf{r} = 0\mathbf{i} + 3\mathbf{j}$
$t = 1$	$\dfrac{\pi t}{6} = \pi/6$ or $30°$	$\mathbf{i} + 2.6\mathbf{j}$
2	$60°$	$2\mathbf{i} + 1.5\mathbf{j}$
3	$90°$	$3\mathbf{i} + 0\mathbf{j}$
4	$120°$	$4\mathbf{i} - 1.5\mathbf{j}$
5	$150°$	$5\mathbf{i} - 2.6\mathbf{j}$
6	$180°$	$6\mathbf{i} - 3\mathbf{j}$

To find the force, we need first the acceleration

$$\mathbf{v} = \frac{d\mathbf{r}}{dt} = \mathbf{i} - \frac{\pi}{2}\sin\frac{\pi t}{6}\mathbf{j}$$

$$\mathbf{a} = \frac{d\mathbf{v}}{dt} = -\frac{\pi^2}{12}\cos\frac{\pi t}{6}\mathbf{j} \text{ or } -0.82\cos\frac{\pi t}{6}\mathbf{j}$$

Thus $\mathbf{F} = m\mathbf{a} = -4.1 \cos \dfrac{\pi t}{6} \mathbf{j}$ N

At times 0, 2, 4 and 6 seconds we obtain forces of

$-4.1\,\mathbf{j}$, $-2.05\mathbf{j}$, $+2.05\mathbf{j}$, $+4.1\mathbf{j}$ N

It is instructive to draw representations of these values on the graph, as this illustrates how the changing force influences the shape of the path followed. (Fig. 19.)

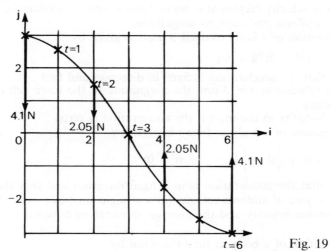

Fig. 19

Questions 1–6 of Exercise 5g may now be attempted.

Example 34

A body of mass 2 kg moving initially with velocity 4i m s^{-1} is acted on by two forces (i) a constant force of $-4\mathbf{i}$ N (ii) an increasing force of $t\mathbf{j}$ N. Find the velocity of the body after 3 seconds and also its position relative to the starting point.

The total force acting is $\mathbf{F} = -4\mathbf{i} + t\mathbf{j}$ N
Using $\mathbf{F} = m\mathbf{a}$ we have $\mathbf{a} = -2\mathbf{i} + \frac{1}{2}t\,\mathbf{j}$ m s^{-2}

We now integrate in order to obtain first the velocity and second the position of time t. Each time a particular component is integrated a constant of integration appears in that component.

Thus $\mathbf{v} = (A - 2t)\mathbf{i} + (\frac{1}{4}t^2 + B)\mathbf{j}$ (A, B constants)
Since $\mathbf{v} = 4\mathbf{i}$ when $t = 0$ we have $A = 4$ and $B = 0$
i.e. $\mathbf{v} = (4 - 2t)\mathbf{i} + \frac{1}{4}t^2\mathbf{j}$

integrating again

$$\mathbf{r} = (4t - t^2 + C)\mathbf{i} + \left(\dfrac{t^3}{12} + D\right)\mathbf{j} \quad (C, D\ \text{constants})$$

Since $\mathbf{r} = \mathbf{0}$ when $t = 0$ we obtain $C = 0$ and $D = 0$.

Hence at time $t = 3$

velocity $= -2\mathbf{i} + 2\frac{1}{4}\mathbf{j}$ m s^{-1}
position $= 3\mathbf{i} + 2\frac{1}{4}\mathbf{j}$ m

Exercise 5(g)

1. The position vector of a particle at time t is given by
$$\mathbf{r} = (3t^2 - 4t)\mathbf{i} + (5 - t^2)\mathbf{j}$$
Find the velocity vectors at times 0, 2 and 4. Show also that the acceleration is uniform and state its magnitude.

2. The position of a body of mass 3 units is given by
$$\mathbf{r} = (t^3 - 3t^2)\mathbf{i} + 6t\mathbf{j}$$
Show that the acceleration is fixed in direction and find
(i) the velocity at $t = 3$ and the magnitude of the force acting at this
instant
(ii) the velocity at the instant the acceleration is zero.

3. The position of a body at time t is given by
$$\mathbf{r} = (t + \frac{1}{t})\mathbf{i} + \frac{1}{t}\mathbf{j} \qquad (t > 0)$$
Show that the acceleration is in a fixed direction and that the motion
tends to one of uniform velocity (in a straight line) as $t \to \infty$. Find also
the average velocity and the average acceleration between $t = 1$ and t
$= 3$.

4. The position of a body at time t is given by
$$\mathbf{r} = (9t - t^2)\mathbf{i} + (3t^2 + 2)\mathbf{j}$$
Find the speed of the body at time $t = 2$ and the unit vector in the
direction of motion at this instant. Find also the least speed of the body
during the motion.

†5. Plot the first 6 s of the motion
$$\mathbf{r} = \tfrac{1}{2}t^2\mathbf{i} + 6\cos\frac{\pi t}{6}\mathbf{j} \text{ (metres)}$$
. . . remembering that the 'angle' $\pi t/6$ is in radians. If the mass of the body
is 2 kg, find the instantaneous force acting at times 0, 2, 4 and 6 and
mark representations of these on your graph (as in example 33).

†6. For 3 seconds a car moves in accordance with
$$\mathbf{r} = 10\sin\frac{\pi t}{6}\mathbf{i} + 10\cos\frac{\pi t}{6}\mathbf{j} \text{ (metres)}$$
Plot the path of the car during this time. Find the velocity and accelera-
tion vectors of the car at time t seconds and hence show that
(i)   The speed of the car is uniform
(ii) The magnitude of the acceleration is constant
(iii) The acceleration vector $\mathbf{a} = -k\mathbf{r}$ where k is a positive constant.
What does this tell you about the direction of the acceleration at
any instant?

Mark on your graph the direction of the force acting on the car at times 0, 1, 2 and 3 s. How is this force provided?

7. A body of mass 5 units has velocity $\mathbf{v} = 8t\mathbf{i} + 3t^2\mathbf{j}$ at time t. If the body starts at position $3\mathbf{i} - \mathbf{j}$, find its position at time $t = 4$ and the magnitude of the force acting at this instant.

8. A body of mass 4 kg moving initially through the origin with velocity $2\mathbf{i}$ m s^{-1} is acted on by a force $\mathbf{F} = 24t\mathbf{j}$ N where t is the time in seconds. Find the position vector of the body at time t and show that the path followed has equation $y = x^3/8$.

9. A body of mass 5 kg is acted on by a force

$$10\mathbf{i} + \frac{40}{t^3}\mathbf{j} \text{ N } \quad (t > 0)$$

The velocity of the body at time $t = 1$ is $-2\mathbf{i} - 3\mathbf{j}$ m s^{-1}. Show that the body is instantaneously at rest at time $t = 2$. Taking the position of rest as the origin, find an expression for the position vector of the body at time t seconds and plot the motion from $t = \frac{1}{2}$ to $t = 4$.

10. A particle of mass 250 g moving initially with velocity 10 m s^{-1} due south is acted on by two forces

    (i) 3 N due east, increasing steadily by 1 N each second

    (ii) 3 N due south, decreasing steadily by 1 Newton each second.

Find in terms of unit vectors east and north, the velocity of the particle 3 seconds later and also its position relative to the starting point.

6

Relative Velocity

6.1 Introduction

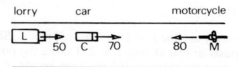

lorry   car   motorcycle

Fig. 1

Imagine that Fig. 1 shows a road running west–east. The speeds in km h^{-1} of a lorry L, a car C and a motorcycle M are as marked. If we take i to be a unit vector due east in direction then we can write the velocities of these vehicles as

$$v_L = 50i \quad v_C = 70i \quad v_M = -80i$$

To the driver of the lorry the car will appear to pull away to the east at 20 km h^{-1}. We say that the *velocity of the car relative to the lorry* is 20 km h^{-1} due east. We write this as

$$_C v_L = 20i$$

To the driver of the car the motorcyclist will appear to close at a speed of 150 km h^{-1}, i.e. the velocity of the motorcycle relative to the car is 150 km h^{-1} west.

$$_M v_C = -150i$$

It is clear that these results may be obtained as follows

$$_C v_L = v_C - v_L, \quad _M v_C = v_M - v_C$$

and we are naturally led to wonder whether such a result will always apply, i.e whether $_x v_y = v_x - v_y$ for the motion of any two bodies x and y. In the next section we shall investigate cases where the two bodies do not move along the same line. The following short exercise should first be worked.

Exercise 6(a)

1. A starts from the origin and moves with velocity $3i + j$. B starts from position $-2j$ and moves with velocity $3i - 2j$. Plot the paths followed on squared paper, marking the positions of A and B at times 0, 1, 2 and 3. Hence write down the position of B relative to A, $_B r_A$, at each of these times. How does B appear to move relative to an observer on A?

2. A moves as in question 1. C starts at position $4\mathbf{i} + 3\mathbf{j}$ and moves with velocity $-\mathbf{i} + 2\mathbf{j}$. Plot the paths and obtain $_C\mathbf{r}_A$ at times 0, 1 and 2. On a separate diagram imagine that A remains fixed in position, mark on the values of $_C\mathbf{r}_A$ obtained and hence show how C appears to move relative to an observer on A.

3. Repeat question 1 but with B starting from position $2\mathbf{i} - 3\mathbf{j}$. Show that $_B\mathbf{v}_A$ is still 3 units south in direction. (This demonstrates that the relative velocity of two bodies is independent of their starting positions.)

6.2 Introduction (Continued)

(i) In question 1 of exercise 6a it should be clear from the diagram obtained that B will always appear due south of A and that the distance of B from A increases by 3 units for every unit of time,

i.e. $_B\mathbf{v}_A = -3\mathbf{j}$ (where $\mathbf{j}$ is due north)

We notice that this result is in accordance with that predicted by

$_B\mathbf{v}_A = \mathbf{v}_B - \mathbf{v}_A.$

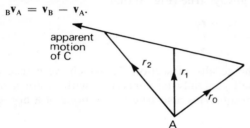

A   Fig. 2

(ii) Fig. 2 shows the second diagram which should be obtained in question 2 of exercise 6(a), the vectors $\mathbf{r}_0, \mathbf{r}_1$ and $\mathbf{r}_2$ being the positions of C relative to A at times 0, 1 and 2 respectively. From this diagram it can be seen that, relative to A, C appears to move with velocity $-4\mathbf{i} + \mathbf{j}$,

that is $_C\mathbf{v}_A = -4\mathbf{i} + \mathbf{j}$

This result could also have been predicted by $_C\mathbf{v}_A = \mathbf{v}_C - \mathbf{v}_A$

Definition of relative velocity. In both the above examples the relative velocity is given by the change in the relative position vector per unit time, i.e. by the rate at which the relative position vector is changing. This suggests a definition which is directly analogous to the definition of velocity given in Section 5.8, i.e.

THE VELOCITY OF X RELATIVE TO Y IS THE RATE AT WHICH THE POSITION VECTOR OF X RELATIVE TO Y IS CHANGING

---

i.e $_X\mathbf{v}_Y = {}_X\dot{\mathbf{r}}_Y$

In everyday terms we may describe it as the velocity with which X *appears* to move as seen from Y.

Determination of relative velocity. As a consequence of the above definition, we may now easily prove the general truth of the result

$$_X\mathbf{v}_Y = \mathbf{v}_X - \mathbf{v}_Y \tag{1}$$

which gives a simple method of determining relative velocity from the 'true velocities' (i.e. relative to Earth) of the bodies concerned.

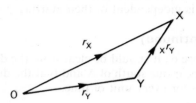

Fig. 3

Let X and Y be two moving bodies and let O be a fixed origin. No matter how X and Y move it is always true (Fig. 3) that

$$_X\mathbf{r}_Y = \mathbf{r}_X - \mathbf{r}_Y$$

differentiating $\quad _X\dot{\mathbf{r}}_Y = \dot{\mathbf{r}}_X - \dot{\mathbf{r}}_Y$

i.e. $\quad _X\mathbf{v}_Y = \mathbf{v}_X - \mathbf{v}_Y$

We have used here the results of section 5.8 which were true for any motion. Although we shall generally be concerned with uniform motions, this does mean that the result (1) is also true for motions of a non-uniform nature.

Exercise 6(b)

1. What can be said about $_X\mathbf{r}_Y$ and $_Y\mathbf{r}_X$? By differentiating, what can be deduced about $_X\mathbf{v}_Y$ and $_Y\mathbf{v}_X$? Satisfy yourself that this relation is correct for $_B\mathbf{v}_A$ and $_A\mathbf{v}_B$ in question 1 of exercise 6(a).
2. Prove the 'Relative Velocity Law' which states that if X, Y and Z are any 3 bodies then $_X\mathbf{v}_Z = {}_X\mathbf{v}_Y + {}_Y\mathbf{v}_Z$, by
   (i) expressing each of these relative velocities in terms of true velocities
   (ii) by a differentiation method based on a diagram similar to Fig. 3 section 6.2.
   Hence obtain $_C\mathbf{v}_B$ given that $_B\mathbf{v}_A = -3\mathbf{j}$ and $_C\mathbf{v}_A = -4\mathbf{i} + \mathbf{j}$. (Use also the result of question 1.)
3. 'All velocities are relative.' Explain briefly the truth of this statement. Hence show that the result $_X\mathbf{v}_Y = \mathbf{v}_X - \mathbf{v}_Y$ can be regarded as a particular case of the Relative Velocity Law (question 2).
4. If $\mathbf{v}_X = 3\mathbf{i} + \mathbf{j}$, $\mathbf{v}_Y = 4\mathbf{i} + 3\mathbf{j}$ and $\mathbf{v}_Z = -2\mathbf{i} + 3\mathbf{j}$,
   Find (i) $_Y\mathbf{v}_X$ (ii) $_X\mathbf{v}_Y$ (iii) $_X\mathbf{v}_Z$ (iv) $_Z\mathbf{v}_Y$
5. If, in question 4, the initial position of Y relative to X is $3\mathbf{i}$, what will it be after time (i) 1 unit (ii) 2 units (iii) t units? Hence find when the distance between X and Y is 6 units.
6. To a man in boat X an air-balloon B (which drifts horizontally with the wind) appears to have velocity $5\mathbf{i} - 8\mathbf{j}$. To a man in boat Y its velocity appears to be $-7\mathbf{i} - 3\mathbf{j}$. If boat Y has velocity $10\mathbf{i} + \mathbf{j}$, find $\mathbf{v}_X$, $\mathbf{v}_B$ and $_X\mathbf{v}_Y$.

7. Two ships, A and B, are moving with velocities $7\mathbf{i} - 3\mathbf{j}$ and $9\mathbf{i} - 2\mathbf{j}$ respectively. At time zero A is at position $10\mathbf{i} + 5\mathbf{j}$ relative to B.
   (i) Find the velocity of A relative to B.
   (ii) Find the position of A relative to B at times 1 and 2 units.
   (iii) Show that the ships must collide if their present velocities are maintained and determine the expected position of collision relative to the starting point of B.

8. The positions of A and B relative to a fixed origin are given by
   $$\mathbf{r}_A = (2t + t^2)\mathbf{i} + 3\mathbf{j} \text{ metres}$$
   $$\mathbf{r}_B = 3t\mathbf{i} - t\mathbf{j} \text{ metres}$$
   Find the values of $_A\mathbf{r}_B$ and $_A\mathbf{v}_B$ at times (i) 0 s. (ii) 2 s. (iii) t s.

9. The velocity of X relative to Y is $(3t^2 - 1)\mathbf{i} + 2t\mathbf{j}$, and Y is initially at position $3\mathbf{i} - \mathbf{j}$. If X is moving with uniform velocity $4\mathbf{i} + 3\mathbf{j}$, find the velocity of Y at time t, and also its position at time $t = 3$.

6.3 Further Examples

Example 35

A ship is moving at 7 m s^{-1} N 10° E. A bird flies over the ship at 10 m s^{-1} N 60° E. In which direction and at what speed does the bird appear to be moving relative to a passenger on the ship?

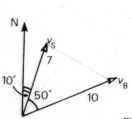

Fig. 4a

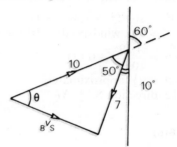

Fig.4b

Fig. 4a shows the true velocities $\mathbf{v}_S$ (ship) and (bird) $\mathbf{v}_B$. We require $_B\mathbf{v}_S$. This is given by the velocity triangle of Fig. 4b which has been drawn in accordance with the result

$$_B\mathbf{v}_S = \mathbf{v}_B - \mathbf{v}_S$$

By the cosine rule

$$|_B\mathbf{v}_S|^2 = 100 + 49 - 140 \cos 50°$$
$$= 59.01$$
$$\text{speed} = 7.68 \text{ m s}^{-1}$$

By the sine rule

$$\frac{\sin \theta}{7} = \frac{\sin 50°}{7.68}$$
$$\Rightarrow \theta = 44° \ 17'$$
$$\text{bearing} \simeq 104°$$

Example 36

To a cyclist travelling at 12 km h^{-1} due west, the wind appears to be blowing at 15 km h^{-1} from the north-west. What is the true velocity of the wind?

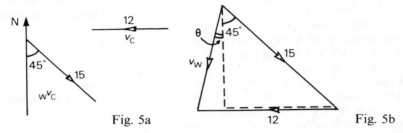

Fig. 5a   Fig. 5b

Denoting wind by W and cyclist by C we have the velocities shown in Fig. 5a. We require $\mathbf{v_w}$.

$$\text{Now } _w\mathbf{v_c} = \mathbf{v_w} - \mathbf{v_c}$$
$$\text{re-arranging } \mathbf{v_w} = {_w}\mathbf{v_c} + \mathbf{v_c}$$

We therefore draw the velocity-triangle of Fig. 5b. Dropping a perpendicular, which is of length 15 cos 45° = 10.61, we obtain

$$| \mathbf{v_w} |^2 = 10.61^2 + 1.39^2 = 114.5$$
$$\Rightarrow \quad \text{windspeed} = 10.7 \text{ m s}^{-1}$$
$$\tan \theta = \frac{1.39}{10.61} = 0.131$$
$$\Rightarrow \theta = 7\tfrac{1}{2}° \text{ approximately}$$
$$\text{i.e. direction S } 7\tfrac{1}{2}° \text{ W}$$

Exercise 6(c)

1. A man is walking north at 2 m s^{-1}. A bird flies over at 10 m s^{-1} N 60° W. In which direction does the bird appear to be travelling to the man?
2. What will be the apparent wind velocity to a cyclist travelling due west at 15 km h^{-1} in each of the following cases?
    (i)   wind velocity 10 km h^{-1} due east
    (ii) wind velocity 10 km h^{-1} due west
    (iii) no wind
    (iv) wind velocity 10 km h^{-1} south east.
3. A yacht is heading N 60° E at 12 knots and a ship S 80° E at 15 knots. What is the apparent velocity of the yacht as seen from the ship?
4. The pilot of an airliner travelling S 30° W at 600 km h^{-1} sees a fighter aircraft coming to intercept him. The fighter appears to be closing at a relative speed of 120 km h^{-1} from the north west. Find the true velocity of the fighter.
5. Two men are walking across a field. X is walking north at speed U, and it appears to him that the second man, Y, is coming to meet him from the north-east at the same speed. In which direction is Y actually walking and with what speed?

6. A plane's velocity is 250 km h⁻¹ due east. To a man in a train travelling along a straight section of track at 70 km h⁻¹, the plane appears to pass at right angles to the track. In which direction is the train moving? (Two possible answers.)

7. A keen meteorologist, who happens to know that the wind velocity is 20 km h⁻¹ from the south-west, notices that when the ship he is travelling on is heading due north the smoke trail from the funnel is at an angle of 60° with the forward direction of the ship. From this he is able to estimate the speed of the ship. What answer should he obtain?

8. To a man in a motor-boat travelling due east at 5 m s⁻¹ a yacht appears to be heading N 30° E. When he doubles his speed the yacht appears to head due north. Find the true velocity of the yacht.

9. A man in an open sports car travelling on a straight road at 40 km h⁻¹ notices that the wind has apparently changed direction by 90° when he returns by the same road at the same speed. If the true wind velocity is in fact unchanged, find the speed of the wind. Can the direction of the wind (relative to the road) be determined?

6.4 Closest Approach

There are many situations in which two bodies move on paths which involve a risk of collision. In assessing the safety of these situations one is clearly interested in the closest expected distance between the bodies. The next example shows a method by which this may be found.

Example 37

The positions of ships A and B at noon, and also their velocities are as shown in Fig. 6. Determine the closest subsequent distance between the ships and the time at which this occurs.

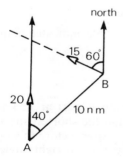

Fig. 6 motion relative to earth

Fig. 6 shows the situation as it would appear to a stationary observer looking down from above. If asked to judge when the ships are closest together he would have to watch two moving objects simultaneously and would find the task difficult.

A person in a better position to judge is someone on board one of the ships. He need only watch the other ship and decide when it stops getting closer to him and begins to move further away again. To solve this problem we therefore consider the motion of one ship relative to an observer on the second. The solution is as follows:

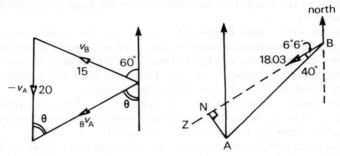

Fig. 7a velocity triangle   Fig. 7b motion of B relative to A

(i) Find the velocity of B relative to A.

$$_B v_A = v_B - v_A$$

From the velocity triangle of Fig. 7a we find by calculation that $|_B v_A| =$ 18.03 knots and that $\theta = 46° 6'$.

(ii) Draw a diagram showing how B moves relative to A. On this diagram (Fig. 7b), B moves at 18.03 knots on path BZ whose direction is identical to that of $_B v_A$ in the velocity triangle. Thus angle ABZ = 46° 6' − 40° = 6° 6'. Hence

closest approach AN = 10 sin 6° 6' = 1.06 nautical miles

$$\text{time taken} = \frac{\text{distance BN}}{\text{speed 18.03}} = \frac{10 \cos 6° 6' \text{ hrs}}{18.03}$$
$$= 0.546 \text{ h or 33 minutes}$$

so the ships are closest at 12.33 p.m.

Note: A unit vector method for closest approach is indicated in question 7 of exercise 6d.

Exercise 6(d)

1. Ship A steams north at 15 knots and ship B west at 12 knots. If B is initially 5 nautical miles N 30° E of A, find the shortest subsequent distance between them and the time which elapses before this occurs.
2. At a level crossing a road and a railway cross at right-angles. A car is approaching the crossing at 16 m s⁻¹ from the south. At the instant that the car is 100 m from the crossing, a locomotive is 150 m west of the crossing and approaching at 20 m s⁻¹. Find
   (i) which of the two gets to the crossing first and their distance apart at this moment
   (ii) the shortest distance between the two.
3. Two aircraft A and B are flying at the same horizontal level through cloud. At 9.00 a.m B is 10 km from A on bearing N 20° W. If the velo-

cities of A and B are 550 km h^{-1} N 30° E and 600 km h^{-1} east respectively, find the closest distance between the two aircraft and the time, to the nearest 5 seconds, at which this occurs.

4. Two straight roads running through a forest cross at 45°, their directions being east–west and N.E–S.W. A Frenchman, who only gives way to traffic on his right, is approaching the junction at 120 km h^{-1} from the south-west, while an Italian, who never gives way, approaches from the West at 80 km h^{-1}. At the instant that the Italian is 100 m from the junction he is exactly north of the Frenchman. By what distance do they miss collision?

5. Ship A steams north at 15 knots and ship B west at 8 knots. At midday B is $8\frac{1}{2}$ nautical miles due north of A. Find the closest distance between the ships and the time at which this occurs. If the limit of visibility is 5 nautical miles, show that A will be visible from B for about 21 minutes.

6. At noon a submarine is 4 nautical miles due east of a tanker which is heading north at 14 knots. The submarine sets a course on which it passes to the south of the tanker and on which the closest distance between the two is 1/2 km. If the time at which they are closest is 12.20, find the speed and course of the submarine.

*7. Two bodies X and Y are moving with velocities $-2\mathbf{i} + 9\mathbf{j}$ and $\mathbf{i} + 8\mathbf{j}$ respectively. Initially the position of X relative to Y is $12\mathbf{i} - 3\mathbf{j}$. Find the relative position at time t and obtain an expression for the square of the distance between X and Y at time t. Hence find the least distance between the bodies and the time at which it occurs.

8. Use the method of question 7 to find the least distance between bodies A and B whose velocities are $\mathbf{v}_A = 6\mathbf{i} - 3\mathbf{j}$ and $\mathbf{v}_B = 8\mathbf{i} + \mathbf{j}$, and whose initial positions relative to a fixed origin are $\mathbf{r}_A = 7\mathbf{i}$ and $\mathbf{r}_B = -12\mathbf{j}$. Find also the positions of A and B in which they are closest together.

6.5 Interception

The following example is typical of those in which the course required to intercept a moving body must be calculated.

Example 38

Ship A moves at 20 knots on bearing N 50° E. Ship B is initially 5 nautical miles east of A.

(i) If B has speed 15 knots, find the course that should be set in order to intercept A as quickly as possible, and find the time that this would take.

(ii) Find the least speed of B for which interception would be possible.

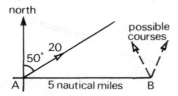

Fig. 8

(i) The idea behind the solution is quite simple. If B is going to intercept A then a person on board A must see B coming directly towards him. In view of the initial positions of the ships (Fig. 8), this means that the velocity of B relative to A must be due west in direction. We therefore attempt to draw a velocity triangle in which $_B\mathbf{v}_A$ has direction west. We have

$$_B\mathbf{v}_A = \mathbf{v}_B - \mathbf{v}_A$$

The direction of $\mathbf{v}_B$ is not known, so we begin by drawing the first side in our velocity triangle to represent $-\mathbf{v}_A$, which is known completely. (Fig. 9a.) Since $\mathbf{v}_B$ has magnitude 15, we now 'swing an arc' of length 15 about the point Q to determine the possible positions for $\mathbf{v}_B$. There are in fact two of these (see Fig. 9b).

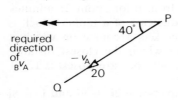

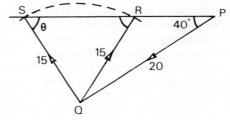

Fig. 9a position of $-\mathbf{v}_A$ Fig 9b possible positions for $\mathbf{v}_B$

B may, therefore, head in one of two directions – that of QS or that of QR. It is evident that QS would give the quicker interception: either by marking these directions onto Fig. 8 or by observing that QS gives the larger relative speed. (PS as opposed to PR.) The calculation is as follows:

$$\frac{\sin\theta}{20} = \frac{\sin 40°}{15} \Rightarrow \theta = 59°$$

hence course to be set is N 31° W (or N 31° E)

relative speed PS = 20 cos 40° + 15 cos 59° = 23.05 knots

time taken $= \dfrac{\text{relative distance } 5}{\text{relative speed } 23.05} = 0.217$ hours

or 13 minutes

(ii) If we consider Fig. 9a it is clear that the shortest possible length of $\mathbf{v}_B$ which would enable us to complete the triangle is the perpendicular from Q onto the required direction of $_B\mathbf{v}_A$.

least speed for interception = 20 sin 40° = 12.86 knots
(course due north)

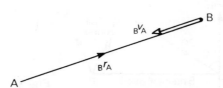

Fig. 10

Note: In terms of vectors, we may say that B will intercept A (or collide with A) if $_B\mathbf{v}_A$ is *opposite* in direction to $_B\mathbf{r}_A$. (Fig. 10.)

i.e if $_B\mathbf{v}_A = -\lambda_B\mathbf{r}_A$ (λ positive)

Exercise 6(e)

1. X is walking N 30° W at $5\,\text{m s}^{-1}$. Y is at a point 100 m north of X.
   (i) If Y walks at $4\,\text{m s}^{-1}$ in which direction should he walk in order to meet X as quickly as possible? How long would he take in doing so?
   (ii) What is the least speed with which Y may walk in order to intercept X? Which direction should he take in this case?
2. A bomber is flying N 15° E at $800\,\text{km h}^{-1}$. An enemy fighter, whose top speed is $1,100\,\text{km h}^{-1}$, is 15 km from the bomber on a bearing of N 70° E. How long will it take the fighter to intercept the bomber and which course should it follow in order to do so?
3. A cargo ship, steaming south at 15 knots, is 10 nautical miles N 50° E from a destroyer.
   (i) Find the minimum speed at which the destroyer must travel if it is to intercept the cargo ship.
   (ii) If the speed of the destroyer is in fact 13 knots, show that it may steer in either of two directions to reach the cargo ship. State both of these directions and calculate the earlier time of interception.
4. A smuggler fleeing north along a straight coastline running north/south sees a patrol boat 2 nautical miles off on a bearing of N 70° E. If the top speed of the patrol boat is 20 knots, find the least speed that the smuggler's boat must maintain if he is to avoid capture.
5. If the destroyer in Question 3 has a top speed of only 10 knots, what is the closest that it can get to the cargo ship and which course should be set to achieve this?
6. Investigate whether two bodies will collide in each of the following cases
   (i)   Initial positions: origin and $10\mathbf{i} - 5\mathbf{j}$
         initial velocities: $3\mathbf{i} - 5\mathbf{j}$ and $\mathbf{i} - 4\mathbf{j}$
   (ii) initial positions: $-4\mathbf{i} + 8\mathbf{j}$ and origin
         initial velocities: $2\mathbf{i} + 3\mathbf{j}$ and $-3\mathbf{i} + \mathbf{j}$
   (iii) initial positions: $-2\mathbf{i} + \mathbf{j}$ and $10\mathbf{i} + 9\mathbf{j}$
         initial velocities: $2\mathbf{i} - 3\mathbf{j}$ and $5\mathbf{i} - \mathbf{j}$

7
Moments

7.1 The Principle of Moments

So far we have been concerned with point-masses – or at least, bodies for which all forces may be considered to act at a point. With 'large bodies' forces may act in many different positions and we have to consider the possibility of rotation (Fig. 1).

↓10 N
↑10 N

↓10 N
↑10 N

Fig. 1

body in equilibrium   body will rotate

Experimentally it is a simple matter to demonstrate that the effect of a force in turning or rotating a body about a given point depends on the product.

magnitude of force × perpendicular distance from line of action to point

This we call the **moment** of the force. The unit used is the newton metre or N m. It is also necessary to specify the 'sense' of the moment, i.e. clockwise or anti-clockwise.

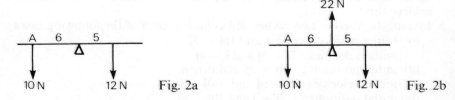

A   6   5
△

10 N   12 N   Fig. 2a

22 N
↑
A   6   5
△

10 N   12 N   Fig. 2b

A light balance arm loaded as in Fig. 2a would be expected to balance because the two forces acting have equal and opposite turning-moments about the pivot. This is a simple application of a general principle known as **the principle of moments** which states

> FOR A BODY IN EQUILIBRIUM THE SUM OF THE MOMENTS OF ALL THE FORCES ACTING MUST BE ZERO ABOUT ANY POINT.

i.e. sum of clockwise moments = sum of anti-clockwise moments

It is not immediately apparent that the moments must 'balance' about *any* point, as is stated here. Considering point A, for example, in Fig. 2a there would appear to be an overall clockwise moment of $12 \times 11 = 132$ units. But if we remember to include the supporting force at the pivot (Fig. 2b) then the problem is resolved, for we have

   clockwise $12 \times 11 = $ anti-clockwise 22×6

This simple example demonstrates the crucial importance of marking all forces acting onto the diagram.

Example 39

If the balance-arm in Fig. 3 is in equilibrium, find the unknown force F.

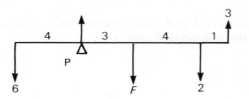

Fig. 3

In fact, there are two unknown forces in Fig. 3 – the second being the reaction at the pivot. To avoid introducing this force into our equation, we choose to 'take moments' about the pivot P – indicated by the abbreviation M(P).

   M(P)   clockwise moments = anticlockwise moments
   $(3 \times F) + (2 \times 7) = (6 \times 4) + (3 \times 8)$
   $3F + 14 = 24 + 24$
   $\Rightarrow$ force $F = 11\frac{1}{3}$ units

Example 40

   A uniform beam 6 m long and of mass 40 kg is supported on two trestles P and Q at points 1 m and $1\frac{1}{2}$ m from the ends of the beam.

(i) Find the reactions at the trestles when a man of mass 80 kg stands at a point 1 m in from Q.
(ii) How far past Q may the man walk before the beam overturns?

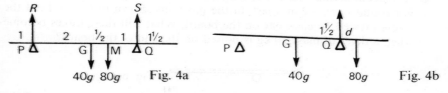

Fig. 4a   Fig. 4b

As we shall see in section 8.1, the weight of a large body may be considered to act at a single point (the 'centre of gravity'). For a uniform beam this point is at the centre. In Fig. 4a the centre of gravity and the man are denoted by G and M respectively.

(i) We have, R(↑) $R + S = 120g$ (1)

but to find the individual values of R and S it is necessary to use moments

$$M(P) \quad 3\tfrac{1}{2}S = (40g \times 2) + (80g \times 2\tfrac{1}{2})$$
$$3\tfrac{1}{2}S = 280g$$
$$\Rightarrow S = 80g \text{ or } 784 \text{ N}$$
$$\text{from 1} \quad R = 40g \text{ or } 293 \text{ N}$$

(ii) Fig. 4b shows the beam just starting to turn about Q. There is no re-action now at P, since contact at this point is broken. Thus

$$M(Q) \quad 80g \times d = 40g \times 1\tfrac{1}{2}$$
$$\Rightarrow d = 3/4 \text{ m}$$

Exercise 7(a)

1. Find the unknown force X and state the magnitude of the reaction at the pivot in each of the situations shown in Fig. 5.

(i)   (ii)

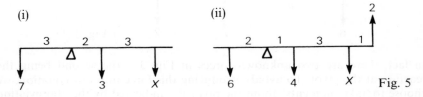

Fig. 5

2. A tree-trunk AB of mass 60 kg is 4 m long and has its centre of gravity 1.6 m from A. What vertical force is needed at B to lift this end off the ground? What will be the reaction at A when this happens?

3. The tree-trunk of question 2 is suspended by two ropes attached 40 cm from either end. Find the tension in each rope. If a boy of mass 40 kg hangs by his hands from end B, what will be the new tensions?

4. A uniform rod AB of length 40 cm and mass 200 g supports hanging masses of 600 g and 400 g at A and B respectively. At which point could it be supported by a single string, the rod AB resting horizontally?

5. A uniform gangplank of mass 15 kg and length 7 m is placed over the side of a ship with 5 m projecting, and is held in place by a boulder of mass 90 kg placed on the end on board. A man of mass 70 kg is ordered to walk the plank. How far does he get?

6. A uniform diving board 4 m long and of mass 9 kg is supported by two horizontal bars, 3/2 m apart, in the positions shown in Fig. 6. Find the forces exerted by each bar on the board. What will these forces become when a diver of mass 60 kg is poised on the end of the board?

Fig. 6

7. A force of 150 N is needed to lift one end of a non-uniform beam off the ground. To lift the other end requires a force of 200 N. What is the weight of the beam and in what ratio does it divide the length of the beam?

8. A uniform plank AB of length 6 m and mass 8 kg is supported on two trestles: one at A and the other 2 m from B. A boy of mass 32 kg walks slowly along the plank starting from A.
   (i)   Find the reactions at the trestles when he has walked 1 m.
   (ii) Find how far he has walked when the two reactions are equal.
   (iii) Find how far he walks before the plank tips.

9. (i) A laboratory balance has arms of equal length but the centre of gravity is not exactly at the pivot. This means that when measuring the mass of a body, different results, M_1 and M_2 are obtained, according to which scale pan the body is placed in. Prove that the correct mass of the body is $(M_1 + M_2)/2$.
   (ii) What would be the correct reading if the centre of gravity of the balance is at the pivot but the arms are of unequal lengths?

10. A table of width 80 cm has two hinged flaps each of which increases the width by 40 cm. The central part of the table top has mass 5 kg and the flaps are each 2 kg. The table is supported by four legs whose points of attachment are 15 cm from the lines of the hinges. Find the thrust in the legs
    (i)   when both flaps are hanging vertically
    (ii) when one flap is extended horizontally
    (iii) when both flaps are extended horizontally.
    Investigate whether a 4 kg mass may be placed anywhere on the table top in each of cases (ii) and (iii).

11. A merchant possesses a balance which has a uniform arm of length $2a$ and weight W. He pivots it a small distance x off-centre and then balances the arm by using scale pans of unequal weights w_1 and w_2 ($w_1 > w_2$). Write down, but do not simplify, an expression involving these symbols. Hence prove that if he places his 'weights' in the heavier of the two scale pans, he will always give short measure to his customers. If $a = 25$ cm, what value should he give x in order consistently to sell 4% short?

7.2 Forces at an Angle

What is the moment of force F about the point P in Fig. 7a? This is another situation in which it is helpful to replace the force by components. Fig. 7b shows that the answer to this question is $F \sin \theta \times d$ (since $F \cos \theta$

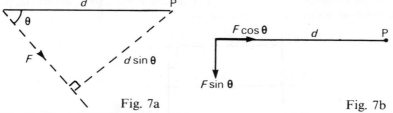

Fig. 7a   Fig. 7b

has no turning effect about P). This answer is equivalent to $F \times d \sin \theta$ which, in Fig. 7a, may be interpreted as

$$\text{magnitude of force} \times \text{perpendicular distance from}$$
$$\text{line of action to point}$$

i.e. the same result as in the previous section. In practice, however, it is frequently more convenient to use the resolved parts method of obtaining the moment.

Example 41

A uniform sun-blind of mass 8 kg, and 1.6 m in width, is hinged to a wall above a shop. The front edge of the blind is supported by two cords each attached to the wall at an angle of 40° and each lying in a vertical plane. Find the tension in the two cords when the sun-blind is held at 70° to the wall.

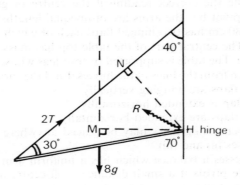

Fig. 8

Fig. 8 shows a side-on view of the sun-blind. The force at the hinge is unknown both in magnitude and direction. We therefore take moments about the hinge to exclude this unwanted force from our equation.

M(hinge) $2T \times HN = 8g \times HM$
$$2T \times 1.6 \sin 30° = 8g \times 0.8 \sin 70°$$
$$\Rightarrow \qquad T = 4g \sin 70° = 36.8 \text{ N}$$

Example 42

Find the moment of a force $3\mathbf{i} - \mathbf{j}$ N, acting at the origin, about the point with position vector $5\mathbf{i} + 2\mathbf{j}$ m (Fig. 9).

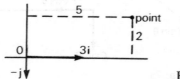

Fig. 9

Here is a case where it is easier to use components

The moment of $3\mathbf{i}$ is $3 \times 2 = 6$ Nm anti-clockwise
The moment of $- \mathbf{j}$ is $1 \times 5 = 5$ Nm anti-clockwise
$\Rightarrow$ Moment $= 11$ Nm anti-clockwise.

Exercise 7(b)

1. Find in each case the moment of the given force about the given point.
   (Units are newtons and metres.)
   - (i)   Force $4\mathbf{i} + 2\mathbf{j}$ acting at the origin, about the point $3\mathbf{i} + 4\mathbf{j}$
   - (ii) Force $-2\mathbf{i} + 3\mathbf{j}$ acting at the origin, about the point $\mathbf{i} + 5\mathbf{j}$
   - (iii) Force $-2\mathbf{i} + 3\mathbf{j}$ acting at $\mathbf{i} + 5\mathbf{j}$, about the origin
   - (iv) Force $5\mathbf{i} - 4\mathbf{j}$ acting at $-2\mathbf{i} + \mathbf{j}$, about the point $3\mathbf{i} + 2\mathbf{j}$

2. A uniform bar of mass 2 kg is hinged at its upper end. It is held at an
   angle of 30° with the downward vertical by a force perpendicular to the
   lower end of the rod. Find the magnitude of this force.

3. A light horizontal arm of length l, hinged to a wall, supports at its end
   an inn sign of weight W. The arm is supported by a chain joining a
   point distant $3l/4$ from the hinge to a point on the wall distance l
   vertically above the hinge. Find the tension in the chain.

4. Fig. 10 shows a uniform plank AB of length 3 m and weight 120 N
   resting on a smooth step 70 cm in height. If 50 cm of the plank are
   above the step, find
   - (i) the contact force at P. (Consider its direction carefully.)
   - (ii) the magnitude of the downward force needed at B to lift end A off
     the ground. (Assume the plank does not slip at P.)

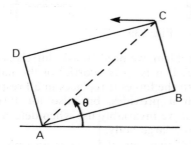

Fig. 10

5. A uniform rod of weight W is hinged at one end and supported in a
   horizontal position by a cord at the other end making an angle θ with
   the outward horizontal. Find an expression for the tension in the cord.

6. A packing case of weight W is to be turned on to its end by turning it
   about the horizontal edge through A (Fig. 11). Show that when the
   diagonal AC is at angle θ with the horizontal, the horizontal force
   needed at C is $\frac{1}{2} W \cot \theta$. What would be the least force required at C
   and in which direction should it be applied?

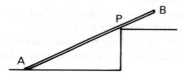

Fig. 11

7. A window frame of mass 2 kg, of symmetrical construction and of
   height 60 cm, opens outwards about a hinge H along its top edge and
   may be supported in an open position by a latch AB as shown in Fig.

12. Find the thrust in the latch when the window is opened through an angle of (i) 20° (ii) 40°

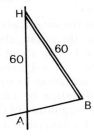

Fig. 12

8. A non-uniform tree trunk AB of length 6 m and mass 300 kg has its centre of gravity 2.6 m from B. It is dragged along, with the end B clear of the ground, by a cable attached at B. If AB is at 5° and the cable at 30° to the horizontal, find the tension in the cable. If the tree-trunk is being dragged at steady speed, deduce the frictional resistance at A.
9. A cylindrical drum of diameter 50 cm and mass 25 kg is to be rolled up a step of height 10 cm. What horizontal force applied at the top of the cylinder is just sufficient
    (i) to start the drum turning?
    (ii) to continue turning the drum when it is 5 cm clear of the ground?
(Assume that the drum does not slip on the step.)
†10. If the window of question 7 is of height h and weight W, prove that the thrust in the latch is $Wl/2h$, where l is the distance AB.

7.3 Resultant of Forces on a Large Body

If a heavy beam of length 2 metres is pulled by horizontal forces of 200 and 150 N, as in Fig. 13a, we would have little difficulty in deducing that the resultant force on the beam is 350 N. But at which point along the beam can this resultant be considered to act?

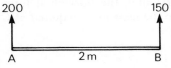
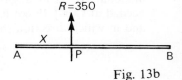

Fig. 13a   Fig. 13b

In order to tackle this problem, we need to ask ourselves exactly what is meant by a 'resultant force'. If it is to be worthy of the name, a resultant force should be equivalent to the forces it replaces in all respects – not only in the overall force which it provides, but also for turning effect (i.e. moment). It is moments that we invariably use when determining the point at which a resultant acts on a large body.

The idea of equivalence of two sets of forces is an important one. It is safest to draw two diagrams, one for each set of forces. Thus the set of forces in Fig. 13b (i.e. the resultant) must be equivalent to those in Fig. 13a in all respects.

M(A)   forces in Fig. 13a   forces in Fig. 13b
$$150 \times 2 = 350X$$
$$\Rightarrow X = \frac{300}{350} \text{ or } \frac{6}{7} \text{ m}$$

The exact point at which we take moments does not matter in this problem. Some people prefer in fact to take moments about the unknown position P.

M(P)   forces in Fig. 13a   forces in Fig. 13b
$$150(2 - X) - 200\,X = 0$$
$$300 - 350X = 0$$
$$\Rightarrow X = 6/7 \text{ m as before.}$$

In solving problems of this nature it is not uncommon to find that the resultant acts at a point outside the body. For example, in replacing the forces of Fig. 14a by the resultant of Fig. 14b, we have

M(A)   original forces   resultant
$$(6 \times 2) - (1 \times 1) = 2X$$
$$\Rightarrow X = 5\tfrac{1}{2}$$

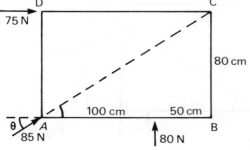

Fig. 14a $R=2$ Fig. 14b

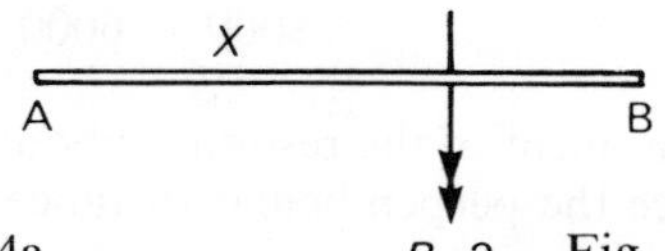

As X is measured from the fixed point A, it follows that the resultant acts $3\tfrac{1}{2}$ m beyond B. This is not a nonsensical result. A resultant force is only a convenient mathematical fiction – it does not exist as a real force. The forces actually applied (those of Fig. 14a), clearly have a strong turning effect on the body – to provide the same turning effect with a force of only 2 N, we would need to apply it on the end of a $3\tfrac{1}{2}$ m arm or lever.

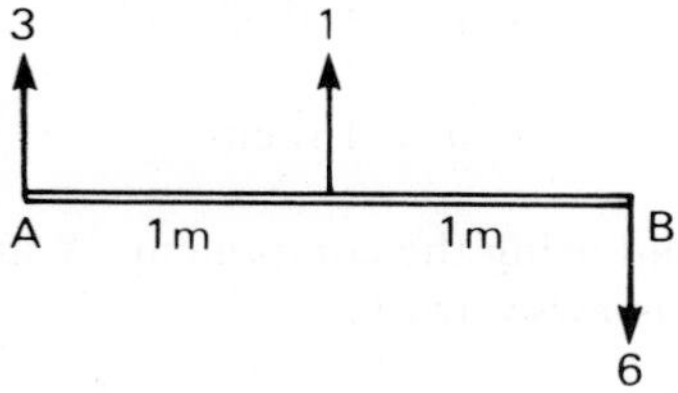

The two examples which follow illustrate further the replacement of a set of forces by its resultant, or (example 44) by an equivalent set of forces.

Example 43

Three people attempting to manoeuvre a large wardrobe with base measurements 150×80 cm push with forces as indicated in Fig. 15a. Find

Fig. 15a

the resultant of these forces on the wardrobe and the point on AB through which its line of action passes.

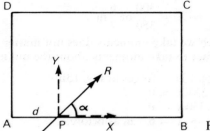

Fig. 15b

Let the resultant force R pass through the point P and let it have components X and Y as indicated in Fig. 15b. Before starting we notice that triangle ABC has 8–15–17 measurements, so that $\sin \theta = 8/17$ etc.

	original forces	resultant	
$R(\rightarrow)$	$75 + 85 \cos \theta = X$	$\Rightarrow X = 150$ N	
$R(\uparrow)$	$80 + 85 \sin \theta = Y$	$\Rightarrow Y = 120$ N	
$M(A)$	$(80 \times 100) - (75 \times 80) = Yd$		
	$8000 - 6000 = 120d$	$\Rightarrow d = 16\frac{2}{3}$ cm	

(The moment of the resultant about A is found using the components X and Y, since the perpendicular distance method is awkward here.)

Combining the results for X and Y we have

$$R = \sqrt{150^2 + 120^2}$$
$$= 30\sqrt{5^2 + 4^2} = 30\sqrt{41} \ (192) \text{ N}$$
$$\tan \alpha = \frac{Y}{X} = 0.8 \Rightarrow \text{direction } 38° \ 40' \text{ with AB at point } 16\frac{2}{3} \text{ cm from A.}$$

Example 44

How should two people push the wardrobe of example 43 in order to produce the same effect, if one pushes at the midpoint of AD in a direction parallel to AB, and the other pushes at the midpoint of AB?

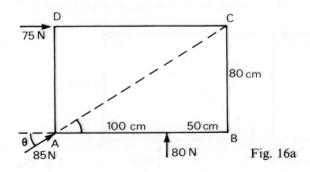

Fig. 16a

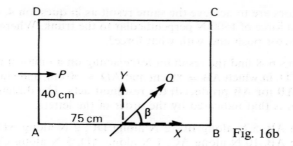

Fig. 16b

Let the two forces be P and Q respectively. The direction in which the second person pushes is not specified, so let this force (Q) have components X and Y as shown in Fig. 16b. The two sets of forces must be equivalent for resolving and for moments about any point

$$
\begin{array}{lll}
 & \text{original forces} & \text{resultant} \\
R(\rightarrow) & 75 + 85 \cos\theta = P + X & \Rightarrow P + X = 150 \\
R(\uparrow) & 80 + 85 \sin\theta = Y & \Rightarrow \qquad Y = 120 \text{ N} \\
M(A) \ (80 \times 100) - (75 \times 80) = 75Y - 40P & \\
\qquad 8000 - 6000 = 9000 - 40P & \\
\qquad\qquad\qquad 40P = 7000 & \Rightarrow P = 175 \text{ N} \\
\end{array}
$$

hence from the first equation $\quad X = -25$ N

Combining the results for X and Y we have

$$ Q = \sqrt{120^2 + 25^2} \qquad = 122.6 \text{ N} $$

direction arctan $\dfrac{120}{25}$ or $78°$ with BA (not AB)

Note: No further information can be obtained in these problems than that which is found from resolving twice and taking moments once. There is no advantage to be gained in writing down further equations – but when taking moments consider carefully which point will lead to the simplest expressions.

Exercise 7(c)

In questions 1–3 the forces given act on a 5 m beam AB, with mid-point M, which lies in an east–west direction (A west of B). Find, in each case, the resultant force and the point at which its line of action cuts AB.

1. 5 N north at A, 2 N north at M, 3 N north at B.
2. 1 N north at A, 3 N south at M, 6 N north at B.
3. 10 N north-east at A, 8 N north 60° east at M.
4. A large tree-trunk AB of length 10 m is being pulled by three tractors. Two pull on the same side of AB: one at A with a force of 1000 N at arctan 4/3 with AB, and the second at B with 1300 N at arctan 12/5 with AB produced. The third tractor is at the midpoint on the opposite side and pushes with a force of 1000 N perpendicular to the trunk. Where should a single tractor push, and with what force, in order that the same effect be achieved?

5. Two tractors are to achieve the same result as in question 4, one pulling at B with a force of 1500 N perpendicular to the trunk. Where should the second tractor push and with what force?

In questions 6–8 find the resultant force acting on a uniform rectangular plate ABCD, in which AB = 80 cm and AD = 60 cm, and state at which point on AB (or AB produced) the resultant acts. The direction of each force given is that indicated by the order of the letters.

6. 1 N along AB, 5 N along BC, 2 N along DC, 2 N along AD.
7. 2 N along AB, 10 N along AC, 4 N along AD, 5 N along CD.
8. 11 N along BC, 10 N along BD, 15 N along CA, 8 N along DC.
9. The set of forces in question 7 is to be replaced by two forces, one of 6 N along AD, and the other acting at a point on AB. Find the magnitude and direction of the second force and the point at which it should be applied.
10. The set of forces in question 8 is to be replaced by three forces acting along the sides of triangle ABC. Find the magnitudes of the forces and their directions.
11. A car, which may be considered to be of rectangular base 1.5 m × 3.6 m, is being push-started by three people. One pushes with 250 N directly forward at the middle of the boot. A second pushes at the rear right-hand corner with a force of 260 N along the diagonal. The third is at the midpoint of the left-hand side of the car, pushing with 200 N at 30° to the forward direction. Show that the resultant force on the car is exactly in the forward direction. Find its magnitude and the point on the rear of the car at which it may be considered to act.
12. Forces of 4, 5 and 6 N act along the sides AB, BC and CA of an equilateral triangle of side a. Show that the resultant force is perpendicular to BC and find where its line of action cuts BC.
13. A square plate OABC of side a is acted on by forces $-3\mathbf{i} - \mathbf{j}$, $2\mathbf{i} - \mathbf{j}$, $2\mathbf{i} + 3\mathbf{j}$ and $-2\mathbf{i}$ N at corners O, A, B and C respectively, where $\mathbf{i}$ and $\mathbf{j}$ are unit vectors along OA and OC. Find the resultant force and the position vector of the point at which its line of action cuts OA.

7.4 Couples

We have seen, in the opening chapters of this book, how overall force determines the linear motion or **translation** of a body. The theory of **rotation**, which is the other important aspect of a body's motion, is beyond the scope of this book but rotation clearly results when a system of forces has an overall turning moment.

In order to keep the study of rotation quite distinct from that of translation, we introduce the concept of a **couple**, which is defined as follows:

> ANY SET OF FORCES WITH ZERO RESULTANT BUT WHICH PROVIDES A TURNING MOMENT IS CALLED A COUPLE.

Since a couple is defined as having zero resultant it cannot produce translation. A couple, therefore, causes rotation only. We have a special way of marking a couple on force-diagrams (Fig. 17) which indicates that it provides a turning effect but nothing else. A body acted on by a couple will spin round but remain in the same spot.

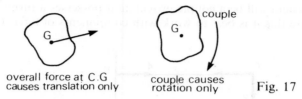

overall force at C.G causes translation only

couple causes rotation only

Fig. 17

The simplest, and most frequently encountered, type of couple is that shown in Fig. 18a – equal and opposite forces along different lines of action. Under our definition the set of forces in Fig. 18b would also constitute a couple – but that of Fig. 18c would not, since there is an overall force of 1 unit.

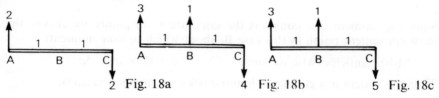

2 Fig. 18a   4 Fig. 18b   5 Fig. 18c

A couple is found to possess a rather interesting property. Considering moments about points A, B and C, we see that the set of forces in Fig. 18a has a clockwise moment of 4 units about all three points, and that of Fig. 18b a clockwise moment of 7 units about all three points. A similar result is *not* found in Fig. 18c.

> IF A SET OF FORCES CONSTITUTES A COUPLE THEN ITS TOTAL MOMENT IS THE SAME ABOUT ALL POINTS. THIS IS CALLED THE 'MOMENT OF THE COUPLE'.

Thus the systems of Figs. 18a and 18b are couples of moments 4 units clockwise and 7 units clockwise respectively. They could be replaced on the force diagram in the manner shown in Fig. 19.

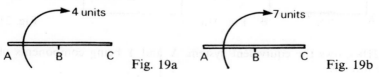

Fig. 19a   Fig. 19b

Example 45

A rectangle OABC in which OA $= 2a$ and OC $= a$, is acted on by forces $\mathbf{i} - 4\mathbf{j}$ at A, $-4\mathbf{i} + 6\mathbf{j}$ at B and $3\mathbf{i} - 2\mathbf{j}$ at C, where $\mathbf{i}$ and $\mathbf{j}$ are unit vectors in the directions of OA and OC respectively. Show that this system of forces is a couple and find its moment.

The resultant force is

$$(\mathbf{i} - 4\mathbf{j}) + (-4\mathbf{i} + 6\mathbf{j}) + (3\mathbf{i} - 2\mathbf{j}) = \mathbf{0}$$

Hence the system will be a couple providing it possesses a turning moment. To investigate this it is best to work with components of force. (Fig. 20.)

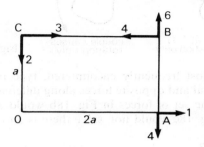

Fig. 20

Since the moment of a couple is the same about all points, we choose the most convenient point, in this case B, about which to take moments.

M(B)   anticlockwise moment $= (2 \times 2a) + (1 \times a) = 5a$

Thus the system is a couple with anti-clockwise moment $5a$ units.

Example 46

A square plate of side 40 cm is acted on by the forces shown in Fig. 21a. Find the single force at the centre of gravity and the couple which would together be equivalent to these forces.

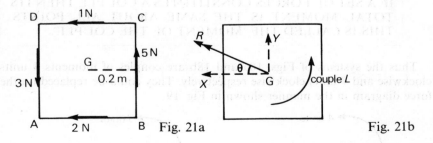

Fig. 21a   Fig. 21b

Fig. 21b shows the equivalent system, X and Y being components of the single force R.

	original system	new system	
$R(\leftarrow)$	$2 + 1$	$= X$	$\Rightarrow X = 3\,\text{N}$
$R(\uparrow)$	$5 - 3$	$= Y$	$\Rightarrow Y = 2\,\text{N}$
M(G)	$(5 + 1 + 3 - 2)0.2$	$= L$	$\Rightarrow L = 1.4\,\text{Nm}$

Combining the components X and Y

$$R = \sqrt{9 + 4} = 3.606 \text{ N}$$
$$\tan \theta = 2/3 \qquad \text{direction } 33° \ 42' \text{ with BA}$$
$$\text{couple} = 1.4 \text{ Nm anti-clockwise}$$

Notes: (i) A couple, having no overall force, does not enter resolving equations.

(ii) If moments are taken about any point other than G, then the moment of R would have to be considered.

Example 46 above illustrates the procedure in analysing the motion of a large body. The single force R acting at the centre of gravity can now be used to determine the translation of the body, and the couple to determine the rotation. Both types of motion would here occur simultaneously.

Exercise 7(d)

1. Which of the following sets of forces acting perpendicular to the x-axis would constitute a couple? Give the moment of the couple where appropriate.
    (i)   Forces 3, -4 and 2 units at $x = 0$, $x = 2$, $x = 5$
    (ii) Forces 2, -6 and 4 units at $x = 0$, $x = 4$, $x = 6$
    (iii) Forces -5, 6 and -1 units at $x = 0$, $x = 3$, $x = 4$.
2. In each case the forces given act on a square plate OABC of side a, and are in terms of unit vectors $\mathbf{i}$ and $\mathbf{j}$ along OA and OC respectively. Find the resultant force (you need not find where it acts) or, where there is no resultant, state the moment of the couple acting (if any).
    (i) $-3\mathbf{i} - 5\mathbf{j}$ at 0, $4\mathbf{j}$ at A, $3\mathbf{i} + \mathbf{j}$ at B
    (ii) $2\mathbf{i} - 6\mathbf{j}$ at 0, $5\mathbf{i} + 2\mathbf{j}$ at B, $-3\mathbf{i} + \mathbf{j}$ at C
    (iii) $-4\mathbf{i} + 2\mathbf{j}$ at A, $-2\mathbf{i} - 3\mathbf{j}$ at B, $6\mathbf{i} + \mathbf{j}$ at C.
3. A triangular plate ABC is acted on by forces represented completely by **AB**, **BC** and **CA**. Show that this system of forces is equivalent to a couple whose magnitude is given by twice the area of the triangle.
4. Which of the following sets of forces acting on a rectangular plate ABCD are couples? Give moments, where appropriate, in terms of the area of the rectangle.
    (i)   **AB, DA, CD, BC**
    (ii) **AC, CD, CB**
    (iii) **AC, BD, 2DA**
*5. (i) Explain how it is possible that a single force exerted on the end of a spanner does in fact provide a *couple* on the nut being turned.
    (ii) Show that the longer the spanner the less is the stress put upon the bolt mountings.
6. To open a jar one relies on friction between the rim of the lid and one's hand. If the lid has diameter 12 cm, $\mu = 2/3$ and a couple of 2 Nm is needed to turn the lid, what pressure must be exerted by the hand on the rim? (Assume that the pressure is concentrated at two diametrically opposed points.)

*7. A rough horizontal axle of radius 5 cm does not turn when a rope wound many times around it supports a mass of 6 kg hanging vertically.
  (i) Explain why the 6 kg mass causes a couple to act on the axle. Find the magnitude of this couple.
  (ii) What frictional couple opposes rotation?
  (iii) Would the 6 kg mass exert the same couple on the axle if it were accelerating downwards? Justify your answer.

8. In each of the following, replace the set of forces by a single force at the centre of gravity together with a couple.
  (i)   The forces of question 1 exercise 7(c)
  (ii) The forces of question 6 exercise 7(c)
  (iii) The forces of question 7 exercise 7(c)
  (iv) The forces of question 13 exercise 7(c)

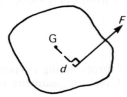

Fig. 22

*9. Fig. 22 shows a single force acting on a large body at a point other than the centre of gravity G. By adding two equal and opposite forces at G, show that an equivalent system is a force at G together with a couple. (State the magnitude and direction of the force and the moment and sense of the couple.) Hence describe briefly the motion of the body.

8

Centre of Gravity

8.1 Theory

The concept of centre of gravity has already been used a number of times in this book. It may be defined as the point at which the 'total weight' of the body may be considered to act.

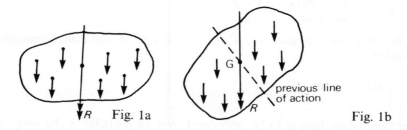

Fig. 1a   Fig. 1b

previous line of action

By the 'total weight' of a body we mean the resultant of the weights of all the individual particles which make up the body. For a given configuration of the body this resultant will act along a certain line (Fig. 1a). It may be shown, however, that no matter how the configuration of the body is changed, the line of action of this resultant force always passes through a certain point. This is the centre of gravity, G, (Fig. 1b).

How is the position of the centre of gravity to be found? We shall begin by building up a theory in terms of vectors. Consider first two particles m_1 and m_2 situated at positions $\mathbf{r}_1$ and $\mathbf{r}_2$ relative to a fixed origin O (Fig. 2). The centre of gravity[1] of these masses will lie on the line joining them and will

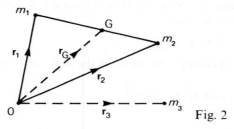

Fig. 2

---

[1] With systems of point masses the term 'centre of mass' might be preferred. For the purposes of this book, however, no distinction need be drawn between 'centre of mass' and 'centre of gravity'. We shall therefore use only the latter term.

divide this line in the opposite ratio $m_2 : m_1$. Using the section theorem (section 5.3) we therefore obtain

$$\mathbf{r}_G = \frac{m_1\mathbf{r}_1 + m_2\mathbf{r}_2}{m_1 + m_2}$$

If we now consider the total weight of m_1 and m_2 to act at G, and introduce a third particle m_3, the situation is identical for in effect we have two particles again ... $(m_1 + m_2)$ at $\mathbf{r}_G$ and m_3 at $\mathbf{r}_3$. The new centre of gravity, G^1, is therefore given by

$$\mathbf{r}_G{}^1 = \frac{(m_1 + m_2)\,\mathbf{r}_G + m_3\mathbf{r}_3}{(m_1 + m_2) + m_3} = \frac{m_1\mathbf{r}_1 + m_2\mathbf{r}_2 + m_3\mathbf{r}_3}{m_1 + m_2 + m_3}$$

This is the basis of a proof by induction from which we may obtain the general result

$$\mathbf{r}_G = \frac{m_1\mathbf{r}_1 + m_2\mathbf{r}_2 \ldots + m_n\mathbf{r}_n}{m_1 + m_2 \ldots + m_n}$$

or, denoting the total mass $(m_1 + m_2 \ldots + m_n)$ by M, and using summation notation:

$$\boxed{M\mathbf{r}_G = \Sigma\, m\mathbf{r}}$$

The summation here is to be performed over all particles in the body. At first sight the difficulties involved in performing such a summation may appear to be insuperable, since all bodies clearly contain an infinite number of particles. We shall see, however, in this chapter and in chapter 18, that by grouping the particles together suitably the summation may be achieved.

Two dimensional cartesian equations. The above result is valid in 3-dimensions (as was the proof of the section theorem given in section 5.3. We shall find, however, that even with solid bodies we are frequently able to reduce the working to a one- or two-dimensional nature. In these situations we may prefer to work with the corresponding equations in terms of cartesian co-ordinates (x, y). These may be obtained as follows:

The position vector $\mathbf{r}$ of each particle may be written as $\mathbf{r} = x\mathbf{i} + y\mathbf{j}$ where (x, y) are the co-ordinates of that particle's position. If the co-ordinates of G are denoted by $(\bar{x}, \bar{y})$ we have

$$M(\bar{x}\mathbf{i} + \bar{y}\mathbf{j}) = \Sigma m(x\mathbf{i} + y\mathbf{j})$$

and since the $\mathbf{i}$ and $\mathbf{j}$ components must be the same on both sides we obtain:

$$\boxed{M\bar{x} = \Sigma mx \text{ and } M\bar{y} = \Sigma my}$$

These results can be interpreted as moments equations. This is left to the reader as an exercise.

In the following example, and in exercise 8(a), we apply the theory to situations in which there are a finite number of particles only. In fact this proves to be the basis for more difficult problems.

Example 47

Find the centre of gravity of particles at the points $(4, -3)$, $(3, 0)$ and $(1, -1)$ given that their masses are in the ratio $2 : 1 : 3$.

We have mass $m_1 = 2$ units at $\mathbf{r}_1 = 4\mathbf{i} - 3\mathbf{j}$
$$m_2 = 1 \text{ unit} \quad \mathbf{r}_2 = 3\mathbf{i}$$
$$m_3 = 3 \text{ units} \quad \mathbf{r}_3 = \mathbf{i} - \mathbf{j}$$

hence, using $M\mathbf{r}_G = \Sigma m\mathbf{r}$
$$6\mathbf{r}_G = 2(4\mathbf{i} - 3\mathbf{j}) + 1(3\mathbf{i}) + 3(\mathbf{i} - \mathbf{j})$$
$$6\mathbf{r}_G = 14\mathbf{i} - 9\mathbf{j}$$
$$\mathbf{r}_G = 2\tfrac{1}{3}\mathbf{i} - 1\tfrac{1}{2}\mathbf{j}$$

so the centre of gravity has co-ordinates $(7/3, -3/2)$

Exercise 8(a)

1. Four equal point masses have position vectors $\mathbf{i} + 3\mathbf{j}$, $3\mathbf{i} - \mathbf{j}$, $-4\mathbf{i}$ and $2\mathbf{i} + 6\mathbf{j}$. Find their centre of gravity.
2. (i) Find the centre of gravity of point masses of 10, 30, 40 and 70 g at points $(5, 0)$ $(-3, 8)$ $(2, 7)$ and $(3, -1)$ respectively.
   (ii) If a mass of 50 g is added to the system at $(-7, 3)$, where will be the new centre of gravity?
3. (i) Point masses of 2, 4 and 6 units are at $x = 0$, $x = 3$ and $x = 5$ on the x-axis. Find their centre of gravity.
   (ii) What mass must be added at $x = 7$ to move the centre of gravity to $x = 5$?
4. Three point masses of 2, 3 and 5 units have position vectors $2\mathbf{i} - 5\mathbf{j}$, $-5\mathbf{i} + \mathbf{j}$ and $-\mathbf{i} + 3\mathbf{j}$ respectively. Together with a fourth point mass they have centre of gravity $-2\mathbf{i} + \mathbf{j}$. Find
   (i) the position of the 4th mass if its mass is 4 units
   (ii) the value of the mass and also its y-co-ordinate if its x-co-ordinate is -4.
5. If m equal particles have centre of gravity $\mathbf{x}$ and a distinct set of n similar particles has centre of gravity $\mathbf{y}$, where is the centre of gravity of all $(m + n)$ particles?
*6. Draw a diagram which shows how the result $M\bar{x} = \Sigma mx$ may be interpreted in terms of moments and resultant force.
7. Equal masses m are at the points A, B and C whose position vectors are $\mathbf{a}$, $\mathbf{b}$ and $\mathbf{c}$. Find the position vectors of
   (i) G_1 : the centre of gravity of the masses at B and C
   (ii) G_2 : the centre of gravity of the mass at A and a mass of $2m$ placed at G_1.
   Interpret these results geometrically, in relation to triangle ABC.
†8. Find the centre of gravity of point masses 1, 1/3, 1/9, 1/27 ... units, etc., placed at positions $x = 1, 2, 4, 8, 16 \ldots$ along the x-axis.

*9. In the result $M\mathbf{r}_G = \Sigma m\mathbf{r}$ all the position vectors are taken from some fixed origin. Prove that the position of G is not affected by the choice of origin.

8.2 Some Simple Applications

For certain symmetrical bodies the position of the centre of gravity is immediately apparent. The two simplest examples are those we have already used in chapter 7, i.e.

uniform rod   C.G at midpoint
rectangular lamina C.G at centre

(A **lamina** is a plane body of negligible thickness.)

The following examples illustrate how we may proceed from these simple results to the treatment of some commonly encountered types of body.

Example 48

Find the centre of gravity of a triangular framework constructed from uniform rods of lengths 5, 12 and 13 units.

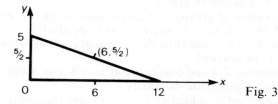

Fig. 3

With these measurements the triangle is right-angled and we may choose co-ordinate axes as in Fig. 3. The weights of the individual rods will be proportional to their lengths and act at their midpoints. The problem therefore reduces to that of three point masses i.e. 5, 12 and 13 units, at positions $2\frac{1}{2}\mathbf{j}$, $6\mathbf{i}$ and $6\mathbf{i} + 2\frac{1}{2}\mathbf{j}$.

Hence, using $M\mathbf{r}_G = \Sigma m\mathbf{r}$

$$30\,\mathbf{r}_G = 5(5\mathbf{j}/2) + 12(6\mathbf{i}) + 13(6\mathbf{i} + 5\mathbf{j}/2)$$
$$30\,\mathbf{r}_G = 150\mathbf{i} + 45\mathbf{j}$$
$$\mathbf{r}_G = 5\mathbf{i} + 3\mathbf{j}/2$$

Referred to the axes chosen the centre of gravity is (5, 3/2).

Example 49

Find the centre of gravity of the lamina shown in Fig. 4.

We may divide the lamina into three rectangles A, B and C whose areas are 12, 9 and 21 sq. units. Their weights are therefore in the ratio 4 : 3 : 7 and, for the purposes of this calculation, may be considered to act at the centres of the rectangles.

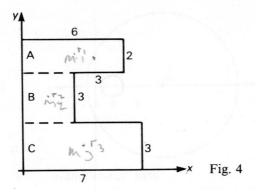

Fig. 4

Method 1

We have mass $m_1 = 4$ units at $\mathbf{r}_1 = 3\mathbf{i} + 7\mathbf{j}$
$$m_2 = 3 \text{ units at } \mathbf{r}_2 = 3\mathbf{i}/2 + 9\mathbf{j}/2$$
$$m_3 = 7 \text{ units at } \mathbf{r}_3 = 7\mathbf{i}/2 + 3\mathbf{j}/2$$

from which the centre of gravity is found as in example 48.

Method 2

Using the Cartesian equations the working may conveniently be set out in a table as follows. In general this method is preferable, as there is less chance of error.

		area	ratio mass	x	y
	rectangle A	12	4	3	7
+	B	9	3	3/2	9/2
+	C	21	7	7/2	3/2
=	lamina		14	$\bar{x}$	$\bar{y}$

$$M\bar{x} = \Sigma mx \qquad\qquad M\bar{y} = \Sigma my$$
$$14\bar{x} = 12 + 4\tfrac{1}{2} + 24\tfrac{1}{2} \qquad 14\bar{y} = 28 + 13\tfrac{1}{2} + 10\tfrac{1}{2}$$
$$\bar{x} = 41/14 \qquad\qquad \bar{y} = 52/14$$

Notice how the two calculations are easily taken from the columns of the table.

Example 50

Find the centre of gravity of a uniform disc of radius 10 cm through which has been drilled a circular hole of radius 2 cm, the centre of the hole being 4 cm from the edge of the disc.

Since this body has an axis of symmetry there is only one co-ordinate to find. We choose a single axis along the line of symmetry (see Fig. 5). The method used here is one of **subtraction**; from the mass of the complete disc we subtract the mass originally occupying the hole.

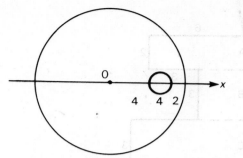

Fig. 5

	area	ratio mass	x
disc	$\pi(10^2)$	25	0
— hole	$\pi(2^2)$	1	6
= remainder		24	$\bar{x}$

$$M\bar{x} = \Sigma\, mx$$
$$24\bar{x} = (25 \times 0) - (1 \times 6) = -6$$
$$\bar{x} = -1/4$$

The negative result tells us that the centre of gravity is to the left of the origin, in fact by 1/4 cm.

Exercise 8(b)

1. A triangular framework with sides 15, 20 and 25 cm is made from three uniform rods of the same material. Find the position of the centre of gravity.
2. A framework is in the form of a trapezium OABC in which OC = CB = 40 cm, OA = 70 cm and angle O = angle C = 90°. Find the centre of gravity referred to axes along OA and OC.
3. Compare the positions of the centre of gravity of the L-shape shown in Fig. 6a when it is
    (i) cut from a sheet of cardboard
    (ii) made in outline by bending a uniform wire.

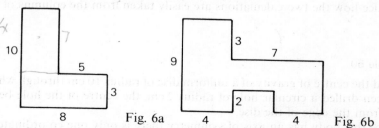

Fig. 6a   Fig. 6b

4. Find the position of the centre of gravity of the lamina shown in Fig. 6b.
5. Fig. 7a is an approximation to the cross-section of a length of railway track. Find the height of the centre of gravity, (units are cm).

6. A rectangular plate of dimensions a × b is divided into quarters by two lines – one parallel to each pair of sides. If one such quarter is cut away, what are the co-ordinates of the centre of gravity relative to the diagonally opposite corner? If the piece removed is glued over the diagonally opposite quarter of the rectangle, where will be the new position of the centre of gravity?

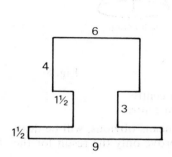

Fig. 7a

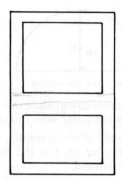

Fig. 7b

7. The surrounds of the 200 × 75 cm doorframe illustrated in Fig. 7b are everywhere $12\frac{1}{2}$ cm wide. The central bar is 25 cm wide. The upper opening which is 90 cm high is left vacant for a window and the lower opening is filled with panelling whose mass per unit area is one-third that of the main structure. Find the height of the C.G. (Only three masses need be considered.)

8. A crescent-shaped lamina is made by removing a circle of radius 3 cm from a uniform disc of radius 5 cm, the two circles touching internally. Find the position of the C.G.

9. A uniform disc, centre O, has radius 20 cm. Find the distance OG, where G is the centre of gravity, in each of the following cases:
   (i)   A single hole, radius 5 cm is drilled with centre 10 cm from O
   (ii) Two such holes, centres A and B, are cut so that AO = BO = 10 cm and angle AOB = 120°. (Use the axis of symmetry.)
   (iii) Three such holes are cut, symmetrically placed, and all with centres 10 cm from O.

10. If, in question 8, the original disc has radius R, what radius circle should be removed in order that the centre of gravity is exactly on the perimeter of the resulting crescent?

8.3 Standard Results

In this section we continue to deal with **compounded bodies**; that is bodies which are comprised of distinct parts for each of which the individual centre of gravity is known. We shall, however, be assuming certain standard results, some of which are illustrated in Fig. 8.

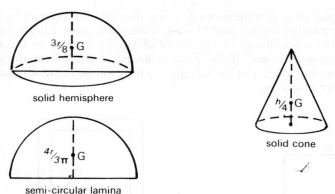

solid hemisphere

semi-circular lamina

solid cone

Fig. 8

Also   hemispherical shell (no base) $r/2$ from centre
         semi-circular wire (no diameter) $2r/\pi$ from centre

The proofs of these results, which are by no means obvious, will be dealt with in chapter 18. For the moment, we shall prove only the result for the triangular lamina.

Triangular Lamina. The centre of gravity is at the intersection of the medians, i.e. two thirds of the way along any one median, (see Fig. 9a).

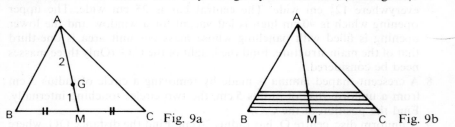

Fig. 9a

Fig. 9b

To prove this, consider the triangle divided first into narrow strips parallel to the side BC (Fig. 9b). If these are sufficiently narrow they may be regarded as rods. The centres of gravity of all these rods lie along the median AM and it therefore follows that the overall centre of gravity must be somewhere on this line. To complete the proof we need only repeat the argument taking strips parallel to one of the other sides of the triangle.

It is interesting to note in passing that if one-third of the mass of the lamina were to be concentrated at each vertex, then the centre of gravity would be in the same position. (See exercise 8(a), no. 7.)

Example 51

A solid consists of a cylinder 60 cm high and 20 cm in radius surmounted by a hemisphere of the same material and of equal radius. Find the distance of the centre of gravity from the plane face.

Since the centre of gravity must lie on the axis of symmetry, we need only a single axis as in Fig. 10. The centre of gravity of the cylinder is 30 cm from O

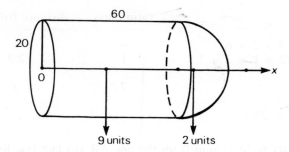

Fig. 10

and that of the hemisphere is $60 + (3/8 \times 20) = 67\frac{1}{2}$ cm from O. The masses may be taken as proportional to the volumes, but notice that it is *not* necessary actually to calculate these volumes.

	volume	ratio	masses	x
cylinder	$\pi r^2 h$	$3h$ or 9	9	30
+ hemisphere	$2\pi r^3/3$	$2r$	2	$67\frac{1}{2}$
= solid			11	$\bar{x}$

$$11\bar{x} = 270 + 135 = 405$$
$$\bar{x} = 36\tfrac{9}{11}$$

The centre of gravity is $36\frac{9}{11}$ cm from the plane face.

Example 52

Find the distance of the centre of gravity of the trapezium shown in Fig. 11 from the line AB.

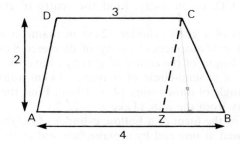

Fig. 11

Many methods are available here. Either (i) the sum of a parallelogram and a triangle – construction CZ or (ii) the sum of two triangles – construction AC or (iii) the difference of two similar triangles – extending lines AD and BC.

We shall use the first method. It is important to notice that the distance of the C.G. of the triangle from AB is $\frac{1}{3}$ of 2, even though the median from C is not necessarily perpendicular to AB.

	area	ratio mass	distance from AB
parallelogram	$3 \times 2 = 6$	6	1
+ triangle	$1/2 \times 1 \times 2 = 2$	1	2/3
= trapezium		7	$\bar{x}$

$$7\bar{x} = 6 + 2/3 = 20/3$$
$$\bar{x} = 20/21$$

The centre of gravity is 20/21 unit from the line **AB**. (In fact this fixes the position exactly, since it must also lie on the join of the midpoints of AB and CD – using the parallel rods argument again.)

Exercise 8(c)

1. A spherical lollipop of diameter 3 cm and mass 30 g is on a stick of length 10 cm and mass 5 g. If the stick penetrates the lollipop by 2 cm, find the distance of the centre of gravity from its free end. (Ignore the thickness of the stick.)
2. A hollow cylindrical can of height 10 cm and diameter 8 cm has a base but no lid. Find the distance of its centre of gravity from the base.
3. A trapezium has parallel sides of lengths $2a$ and $3a$ at a perpendicular distance d apart. Find the distance of the centre of gravity from the side of length $3a$.
4. Three wooden cubes of sides 6, 8 and 10 cm are placed on top of one another, the smallest on top and the largest at the bottom. Find the distance of the centre of gravity from the base. (The calculation is simplified by a suitable choice of origin.)
5. A uniform plate ABCD is in the form of a rhombus with side 10 cm and angle A = 60°. A triangular portion CMN, where M and N are the midpoints of CB and CD, is cut away. Find the centre of gravity of the remaining lamina.
6. An ashtray consists of a glass cylinder 12 cm in diameter and 6 cm in height from which a hemispherical cavity of diameter 8 cm has been removed. Find the height of the centre of gravity above the base.
7. A lamina consists of a semi-circle of diameter 14 cm adjoined by its diameter to a rectangle of dimensions 14×10 cm. Find the distance of the centre of gravity from the join. (Take $\pi = 22/7$.)
8. A gas container is in the form of a hollow cylinder of height 75 cm and diameter 30 cm closed at one end by a plane face and at the other by a hemispherical shell of equal diameter. If the material used is the same throughout, find the distance of the centre of gravity from the plane face.
9. A frustum of a cone has plane faces of radii a and $2a$ at a distance d apart. Find the distance of the centre of gravity from the larger plane face.
10. A lamina consists of a semi-circle of radius r attached by its diameter to the equal base of an isosceles triangle.

(i) If the height of the triangle is $2r$, find the distance of the centre of gravity from the join.

(ii) If the centre of gravity is to be exactly on the join, find the height of the triangle in terms of r.

11. A trough built from uniform metal sheeting is in the form of half the curved surface of a cylinder with two semi-circular ends. The length of the trough is 2 metres and its radius is 25 cm. Find the distance of the centre of gravity below the rectangular opening of the trough.

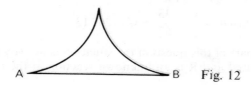

A   B   Fig. 12

12. The lamina shown in Fig. 12 is obtained by cutting two quadrants of radius a from a rectangle measuring $2a \times a$. Find the distance of the centre of gravity from AB.

8.4 Hanging Bodies and Toppling Bodies

Example 53

If the lamina shown in Fig. 13a is suspended from A, what angle will the edge AB make with the vertical when in equilibrium? If the weight of the lamina is W, find the horizontal force at C which would hold the edge AB vertical.

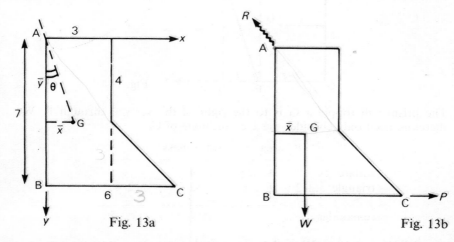

Fig. 13a   Fig. 13b

In equilibrium the line AG will be vertical so that the angle required is θ (Fig. 13a). If we take axes through A this angle can easily be determined from $\bar{x}$ and $\bar{y}$.

	area	ratio mass		x	y
rectangle	21	42 or 14		3/2	7/2
+ triangle	9/2	9	3	4	6
= lamina		17		$\bar{x}$	$\bar{y}$

we have $17\bar{x} = 21 + 12 = 33$
$17\bar{y} = 49 + 18 = 67$

from which $\tan \theta = \dfrac{\bar{x}}{\bar{y}} = \dfrac{33}{67} \Rightarrow \theta = 26° \ 13'$

For the second part of this question the situation is as shown in Fig. 13b. P is the force required and R is an unknown reaction at the point of suspension A.

M(A) gives $7P = W\bar{x} = 33W/17$

$\Rightarrow$ force required $= 33W/119$

Example 54

Fig. 14 shows the cross-section of a square prism of side 2 units from which a triangular section of base z units has been removed. Prove that the prism will topple when the face through OP is placed on a horizontal plane if $z > 3 - \sqrt{3}$.

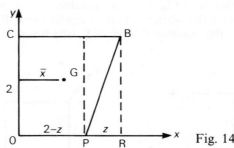

Fig. 14

The prism will topple if G is to the right of the vertical through P. We therefore need only consider the x co-ordinate of G.

	area	ratio mass	x
square	4	4	1
− triangle	$1/2 \times 2 \times z$	z	$2 - z/3$
= remainder		$4 - z$	$\bar{x}$

hence $(4 - z)\bar{x} = 4 - z(2 - z/3)$
in the limiting case $\bar{x} = 2 - z$ and we obtain
$(4 - z)(2 - z) = 4 - 2z + z^2/3$
$8 - 6z + z^2 = 4 - 2z + z^2/3$

This reduces to the quadratic equation

$$z^2 - 6z + 6 = 0$$
$$\Rightarrow z = \frac{6 \pm \sqrt{12}}{2} = 3 \pm \sqrt{3}$$

We can discount the solution $3 + \sqrt{3}$ since this is greater than the side of the original square. Hence the prism will topple if z exceeds $3 - \sqrt{3}$.

Exercise 8(d)

In this exercise it may be assumed that all inclines are sufficiently rough to prevent sliding.

1. An L-shaped lamina is formed by removing a rectangle 6×12 cm from the corner C of a rectangle ABCD in which AB $= 10$ and AD $= 16$ cm. If this lamina hangs in equilibrium from D, what angle will the edge AD make with the vertical?
2. A solid hemisphere is suspended from a point on its rim. What angle does the plane face make with the vertical? If the weight of the hemisphere is W, what horizontal force would be required at the lowest point of the rim in order to keep the plane face vertical?
3. (i) The height of a solid cylinder is three times its base radius. What is the steepest incline on which it may rest without toppling?
   (ii) Show that for a solid cone to topple on an incline of $30°$ its height must be nearly seven times its base radius.
4. A uniform prism has a triangular cross-section ABC in which AB $= 20$ cm, BC $= 10$ cm and angle B $= 90°$. What is the steepest incline on which the prism may rest without toppling when the face containing BC is in contact with the incline and (i) B is below C, (ii) C is below B? (In both cases BC lies along a line of greatest slope.)
5. A wire is bent into the form of a semicircle together with its diameter. When this shape is suspended from one end of the diameter, show that the angle between the diameter and the vertical is arctan $[2/(\pi + 2)]$.

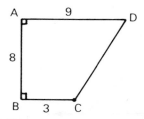

Fig. 15

6. Show that a uniform prism with the cross-section shown in Fig. 15 cannot rest with the face containing BC on a horizontal plane. If the weight of the prism is W, find the least force needed at the edge through D to prevent toppling and state the direction in which it should be applied.
*7. A top consists of a cylindrical shaft of radius r attached to the centre of the plane face of a hemispherical base of radius $4r$ and of the same

material. If the centre of gravity is below the join, draw a diagram showing the forces acting when the top is in a position slightly displaced from
the vertical, and explain why the top must right itself. Find in terms of r
the maximum length the shaft may have if the top is to right itself in this
way.

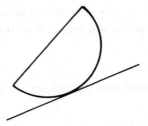

Fig. 16

8. Fig. 16 shows a solid hemisphere resting in equilibrium on a rough
incline of 15°. Find the angle that the plane face makes with the vertical.
9. A uniform prism has a cross-section in the form of a right-angled triangle
ABC in which AB = 6 cm and BC = 4 cm. The triangular section CPB
is removed. Find the maximum length of PB for which the prism will
remain in equilibrium as shown (see Fig. 17).

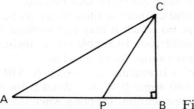

Fig. 17

10. The frustum of exercise 8(c) No. 9 is placed on its slant edge on a horizontal plane. Prove that it will topple if $d^2 < 28a^2/17$.

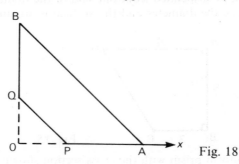

Fig. 18

11. Fig. 18 shows the cross-section OAB of a triangular prism. OA = OB =
a and angle BOA = 90°. The section OPQ is cut away where OP = OQ
= x. The face through PA rests on a horizontal plane. Show that

$$\bar{x} = \frac{a^2 + ax + x^2}{3(a + x)}$$

(i) Find in terms of the weight of the prism the horizontal force needed at B in order to prevent toppling when $x = a/2$.

(ii) Find the maximum value of x for which the prism will remain in equilibrium without toppling.

12. A walking stick consists of a semi-circular handle and a straight shaft made from wood of uniform thickness throughout. The length of the shaft is eight times the diameter of the handle. Taking the radius of the handle as unity, find the co-ordinates of the centre of gravity relative to axes through the join of the handle and the shaft. Hence find the angle between the shaft and the vertical when the stick is hung from a smooth horizontal rail.

9

Equilibrium of a Large Body

9.1 General Equilibrium Conditions

For a large body to remain in equilibrium the forces acting must satisfy two conditions:
  (i) No overall force (i.e. zero resultant) – otherwise the body will accelerate in the direction of such a force
  (ii) No overall turning moment – otherwise the body will rotate.

It follows that when a body is known to be in equilibrium we may write down equations which state that:

  (i) the sum of the resolved parts of the forces acting must be zero in any chosen direction
  (ii) the sum of the turning moments must be zero about any point. Examples 55 and 56 illustrate the method of approach in problems of this type.

Example 55

A hemisphere rests in limiting equilibrium with its curved surface in contact with rough horizontal ground and a rough vertical wall (Fig. 1). If $\mu = 1/4$ at both points of contact, find the inclination of the plane face to the vertical.

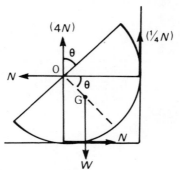

Fig. 1

In a problem of this nature a clear diagram is indispensable. The fact, for example, that both normal reactions pass through the centre O of the hemisphere is essential to the proof given. We also need the fact that OG $= 3r/8$.

In this particular problem (and in many others) we can make use of resolution equations as we mark the forces onto the diagram. The two horizontal forces must be equal and opposite. Marking these as N we may then mark the upward vertical forces (Fig. 1) as $4N$ and $\frac{1}{4}N$ since friction is limiting at both points of contact. We then proceed as follows

$$R(\uparrow) \qquad 4N + N/4 = W \qquad \Rightarrow N = 4W/17$$
$$M(O) \qquad W \times \text{OG} \cos\theta = Nr + Nr/4$$
$$W \times \frac{3}{8}r \cos\theta = \frac{5r}{4} \times \frac{4W}{17}$$
$$\Rightarrow \cos\theta = \frac{40}{51} \qquad \theta \simeq 38°$$

This is the steepest possible inclination of the plane face since, if we consider a steeper one, the moment of W about O is increased but that of the other forces is unchanged.

9.2 Reaction at a Hinge

It has already been mentioned that the force exerted by a body on the pivot of a hinge (or vice versa) may take any direction. This is because the pivot may be forced into contact with its circular surround at any point – depending on the effect of the other forces involved. The following example shows one method by which the direction and magnitude of the force at a hinge may be determined in a particular case.

Example 56

A uniform rod AB of weight W is hinged at its lower end A and carries at B a load of $4W$. It is supported at an angle of $60°$ to the vertical by a wire perpendicular to the rod and attached at a point dividing AB in the ratio $3 : 1$. Find the magnitude and direction of the force at the hinge.

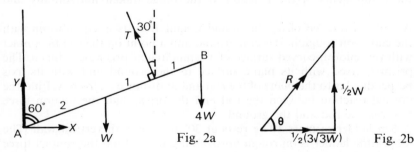

Fig. 2a

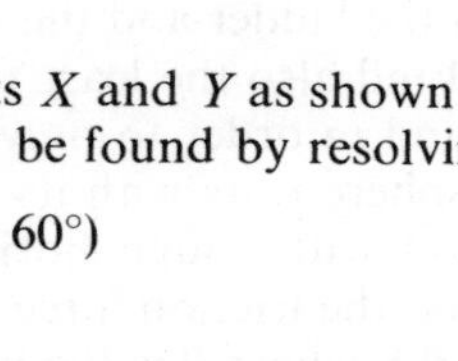

Fig. 2b

Let the reaction at the hinge have components X and Y as shown in Fig. 2a. If we first find the tension T, then these may be found by resolving

$$M(A) \qquad 3T = W(2\sin 60°) + 4W(4\sin 60°)$$
$$3T = 18W\sin 60° = 9\sqrt{3}\,W$$
$$\Rightarrow T = 3\sqrt{3}\,W$$
$$R(\rightarrow) \qquad X = T\sin 30° = \frac{3\sqrt{3}W}{2}$$

$$R(\uparrow) \qquad Y + T\cos 30° = 5W$$

$$Y + \frac{(3\sqrt{3W})\sqrt{3}}{2} = 5W$$

$$\Rightarrow Y = W/2$$

These two components are now easily combined to give the actual force acting at the hinge. (Fig. 2b.)

$$R = \frac{W\sqrt{(3\sqrt{3})^2 + 1^2}}{2}$$

$$R = \frac{W\sqrt{28}}{2} = \sqrt{7}W$$

$$\tan\theta = \frac{1}{3\sqrt{3}} \Rightarrow \theta \simeq 11°$$

The reaction is therefore $\sqrt{7}W$ at about 11° to the horizontal.

Note: In equilibrium problems of this type it is normal to use two resolution equations and one moments equation. In some cases, however, a problem may be solved by a single moments equation, if the point about which moments are taken is well chosen.

Exercise 9(a)

1. A uniform rod AB of weight W and of length 80 cm is hinged at B and rests horizontally with the end A supported by a string which is attached to a point 60 cm vertically above B. Find the tension in the string and the components of the reaction at the hinge (taken horizontally and vertically).

2. A uniform rod AB of length $2a$ and weight W rests in equilibrium with the end A on rough horizontal ground and a point on the rod in contact with the smooth curved surface of a semi-circular prism of radius a. The prism is fixed with its plane surface to the ground and with its axis perpendicular to the plane of the rod and at distance $2a$ from A. Find the normal reaction between the rod and the prism, and the friction force between the rod and the ground.

3. A 6 m ladder of mass 10 kg rests at 30° to a smooth vertical wall. The foot of the ladder is on rough horizontal ground. Find the contact force between the ladder and the wall when a man of mass 66 kg is 5 m up the ladder. Find also the least value of μ needed between the lower end and the ground in order to prevent the ladder from slipping.

4. A hemisphere rests with its plane face uppermost and its curved surface in contact with rough horizontal ground and a smooth vertical wall. Show that the friction force required at the ground to prevent slipping is $3W\cos\theta/8$ where θ is the inclination of the plane face to the vertical. If $\mu = 1/4$ show that θ may take any value greater than arccos 2/3 i.e. about 48°.

5. A triangular lamina **ABC** of weight W in which AB = AC is free to move

in a vertical plane about a hinge at its vertex A. It is held with the median AM at 45° to the vertical by a force applied along the edge BC. Find the magnitude and direction of the force at the hinge.

6. A 6 m uniform gangway of mass 120 kg is being used by passengers to board a ship whose deck is 5/2 m above the level of the quay. If the gangway is at 30° to the horizontal, find the normal contact force between the gangway and the edge of the ship when a laden passenger of mass 90 kg is 4 m up the gangway. If there is negligible friction at this point of contact, find the value of μ needed at the lower end to prevent the gangway sliding.

7. An opening bridge has two separate hinged sections which meet at the centre. Each section has length 10 m, mass 7 tonnes and is raised from the horizontal by a pair of cables running from the furthest end of the section to points 10 m above the hinges. If the cables can each take a load equal to the weight of 8.5 tonnes, what is the mass of the heaviest vehicle which may cross the bridge? When such a vehicle is just approaching the centre of the bridge, what is the reaction at the hinge on the load bearing side? (Consider the vehicle as a point mass.)

8. A semi-circular prism rests in limiting equilibrium with its plane face uppermost and its curved surface in contact with rough horizontal ground and a rough vertical wall. If $\mu = 1/8$ at both points of contact, find the steepest possible inclination of the plane face to the vertical.

9. A uniform beam of weight W rests at angle α to the horizontal with its lower end on smooth horizontal ground and its upper end on a smooth plane of inclination β. To prevent the beam slipping a horizontal force P is applied at the lower end. By resolving find the normal reaction at the lower end in terms of P and W. Hence show that $P = W/2(\tan \alpha + \cot \beta)$.

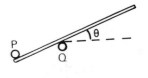

Fig. 3

10. Fig. 3 shows a uniform bar supported by two equally rough horizontal rails P and Q. If the total length of the bar is l and the distance PQ $= d$, show that to prevent the rod sliding $\mu \geqslant d \tan \theta/(l - d)$.

(Hint: resolve along the rod and take moments about both rails.) Hence show that if $\mu = 1/3$ and $\tan \theta = 1/2$ then the length of the rod must be at least $5d/2$ for equilibrium to be possible.

9.3 Three Force Equilibrium. Concurrency.

When a large body is in equilibrium under the action of three forces only, some special methods are available. The most important of these is the **principle of concurrency** which states that for equilibrium the lines of action of the three forces must either be concurrent or parallel.

This, essentially, is the condition for there to be no turning moment. Consider Fig. 4a in which the lines of action of forces *A* and *B* intersect at the point P. It is clear that the third force *C* must provide a turning moment about P, unless it too acts through this point i.e there will be a turning moment unless all three forces are concurrent. An obvious exception to this rule, however, is that the three forces may all be parallel – as in Fig. 4b.

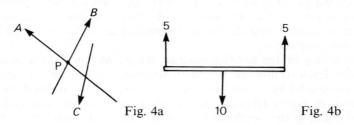

Fig. 4a   Fig. 4b

The other condition that must be satisfied for equilibrium is that of no overall force. When only three forces are involved it is often convenient to use the closed force triangle method of section 3.5 rather than resolution in two different directions.

Example 57

A uniform rod AB of weight *W* is hinged at the end A and held so that AB makes an angle θ with the downward vertical by a string connecting B to a point C vertically above the hinge A and such that CA = AB. Find the magnitude and direction of the reaction at the hinge.

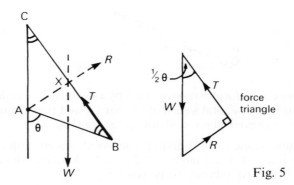

force triangle

Fig. 5

We need not use the method of the previous section for finding the reaction at the hinge, *R*. As the lines of the other two forces intersect at X (Fig. 5) we deduce by concurrency that *R* must act in the direction AX. Then

midpoint theorem $\Rightarrow$ X is midpoint of BC
triangle ABC isosceles $\Rightarrow$ angle B = angle C = $\theta/2$
and *R* and *T* perpendicular

From the force triangle of Fig. 5 we therefore have

$$R = W \sin \tfrac{1}{2}\theta$$

The direction of R is that of the bisector of angle CAB or, alternatively, $(180 - \theta)/2 = 90 - \theta/2$ with the vertical.

Example 58

(i) A string passing over a smooth peg is attached to the ends of a uniform rod AB. Prove that the rod cannot rest in an inclined position. (ii) If the length of the string is 3AB/2 and the end fastened to A is refastened to the point dividing AB in the ratio 1 : 3, at what angle to the vertical may the rod now rest in equilibrium?

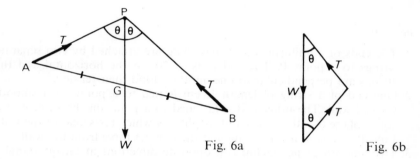

Fig. 6a   Fig. 6b

(i) Firstly we see, by concurrency, that G must rest vertically below the peg P. As the peg is smooth the tension is the same on both sides and the force triangle (see Fig. 6b) is therefore isosceles. This means that the two parts of the string must make equal angles, θ, with the vertical. But in Fig. 6a the angle bisector theorem then gives

$$\frac{AG}{GB} = \frac{AP}{PB} \Rightarrow AP = PB$$

Clearly this can only happen when the rod is horizontal. It may, therefore, rest only in a horizontal (or vertical) position.

(ii)

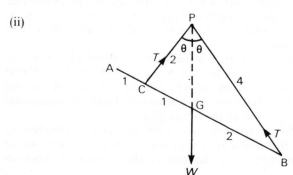

Fig. 7

The isosceles force triangle and the equal angles θ still apply. Taking AB = 4 units and the length of the string = 6 units, we obtain by the angle bisector theorem CP = 2 and BP = 4 (Fig. 7).

by the cosine rule $\qquad \cos 2\theta = \dfrac{16 + 4 - 9}{16} = \dfrac{11}{16}$

$$\Rightarrow 2\theta = 46° \, 34'$$

by the sine rule $\qquad \dfrac{\sin B}{2} = \dfrac{\sin 2\theta}{3}$

$$\Rightarrow B = 28° \, 57'$$

The angle made by the rod with the vertical is

$$\theta + B \simeq 52°$$

Exercise 9(b)

1. The ends of a uniform rod of mass 2 kg are attached by two separate strings to a point P. The rod rests at 20° to the horizontal and the strings are perpendicular to one another. Find their tensions.
2. One end of a string of length 18 cm is tied to a point on a smooth vertical wall. The other end is fastened to a point on the surface of a solid sphere of radius 7 cm and weight 6 N which rests against the wall. Find the tension in the string and the contact force from the wall.
3. Two smooth planes inclined in opposite directions at unequal angles meet in a horizontal line. Show that a semi-circular prism placed with its curved surface touching both planes can only rest with its plane surface horizontal. (The central axis of the prism is parallel to the line in which the planes meet.)
4. A uniform rod AB with its lower end A resting against a smooth verti-cal wall is supported at 30° to the horizontal by a smooth peg P in contact with a point on the rod. Show that AP = 3AB/8.
5. A solid hemisphere of weight W rests with its curved surface in contact with a smooth horizontal plane. It is held with its plane face at angle θ to the horizontal by a string attached to the lowest point of the rim and to a point on the plane. Find the direction of the string and its tension.
6. Two smooth planes which meet in a horizontal line are perpendicular to one another, the steeper of the two being at 50° to the horizontal. At what angle to the horizontal may a uniform beam rest with one end in contact with each plane?
7. A semi-circular lamina of weight W is free to move about a hinge at one end of its diameter A. Below the level of A is a smooth peg P such that AP is at angle θ with the horizontal. The lamina rests with its curved edge on the peg and its diameter AB horizontal. Find the magnitude and direction of the reaction at the hinge.
8. A string of length 64 cm passing over a smooth peg is attached to points on a uniform rod which are 15 cm and 25 cm from the centre of gravity. Find the inclination of the rod to the horizontal when in equilibrium.

9. A uniform rod AB rests in a vertical plane with end A in contact with a smooth vertical wall. The rod is held at 60° to the vertical, with B below A, by a string attached to B and to a point C on the wall vertically above A. Show that for equilibrium to be possible CA = AB/2.

10. A uniform rod AB of mass 1/2 kg is suspended from a smooth peg P by means of an 80 cm length of string tied at one end to A and fastened at the other end to a smooth light ring R, which may slide freely on the rod. In equilibrium the two parts of the string RP and AP are in ratio 3 : 5. Find
   (i)   the distance AR
   (ii) the length of the rod
   (iii) the inclination of the rod to the horizontal
   (iv) the tension in the string.

†11. A uniform rod of length $2l$ and weight W rests over the rim of a smooth hemispherical bowl of radius r, one end being in contact with the inner surface of the bowl. If the rod makes an angle θ with the horizontal, find the reaction of the bowl on the lower end of the rod and prove that $l \cos \theta = 2r \cos 2\theta$. Show also that $l \geqslant r \cos \theta$ and hence deduce that equilibrium is not possible unless the length of the rod is at least $\frac{2}{3}r\sqrt{6}$.

9.4 The Angle of Friction

The reader will already have encountered the term **angle of friction** in question 7 of exercise 4(e). It may be defined in the case of an object resting on a rough plane as the steepest angle at which the plane may be inclined without the object slipping. The importance of the angle of friction, which is usually denoted by λ, is largely due to the result that the tangent of this angle gives the co-efficient of friction between the surfaces concerned, i.e. $\tan \lambda = \mu$.

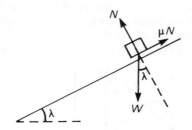

Fig. 8

This result may be proved as follows. When the inclination of the plane is λ the object is about to slip, so the friction is limiting. Resolving the forces in Fig. 8 we have

R (along plane) $\mu N = W \sin \lambda$
$R(\perp$ plane) $N = W \cos \lambda$

Dividing these $\mu = \dfrac{\sin \lambda}{\cos \lambda} = \tan \lambda$

9.5 The Total Reaction

There are two types of contact force between surfaces in contact – the normal reaction N and friction F (sometimes called the tangential contact force). In many situations it is useful to replace these two forces by a single force which is called the **total reaction** between the surfaces. It is generally denoted by the symbol R.

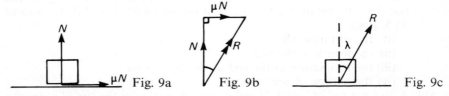

Fig. 9a

Fig. 9b

Fig. 9c

We need to know the direction in which this total reaction acts. If the friction is limiting, as in Fig. 9a, then the force triangle by which R may be found is that of Fig. 9b. We notice that the marked angle in this force triangle has tangent $\mu N/N = \mu$. This angle is therefore the angle of friction λ. It follows that when friction is limiting the total reaction R is at angle λ with the direction of the normal, (see Fig. 9c).

If friction is less than limiting then this angle will be smaller but such cases are not of great importance in practice.

The Total Reaction is of particular use in reducing equilibrium problems which involve four forces to problems of a three-force nature. The advantage of doing this is that concurrency may then be used as an aid to solution. Examples 59 and 60 are typical problems of this kind.

Example 59

A heavy uniform sphere of radius a has a light inextensible string attached to a point on its surface. The other end of the string is fixed to a point P on a rough vertical wall and the sphere rests in equilibrium touching the wall at a point distant h below P. If the point of contact of the sphere is about to slip downwards and the co-efficient of friction between wall and sphere is μ, show that the inclination of the string to the vertical is arctan $a/(h - a\mu)$.

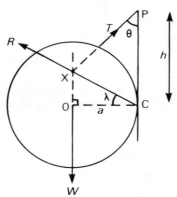

Fig. 10

In Fig. 10 the normal reaction and the limiting friction at C have been replaced by the total reaction R. The three forces R, W and T must be concurrent – let this be at point X. We then have

$$OX = a \tan \lambda = a\mu$$

$$\tan \theta = \frac{OC}{PC - OX} = \frac{a}{h - a\mu}$$

Example 60

A car has its centre of gravity at height h above horizontal ground and at horizontal distances a and b from the front and rear axles respectively. When parked facing uphill on an incline of angle θ, with only its rear wheels locked, find the co-efficient of friction necessary to prevent slipping.

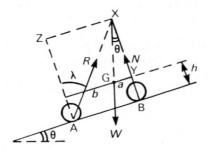

Fig. 11

There is no friction at the front wheels, B, which would simply roll downhill if allowed to do so. Locking the rear wheels, A, enables friction between the tyres and the road to be utilised. In Fig. 11 we consider the case where the limiting friction at A is just sufficient to hold the car from slipping. The total reaction at A is thus at angle λ to the normal AZ. Since the three forces must be concurrent, we obtain

$$\mu = \tan \lambda = \frac{XZ}{AZ} = \frac{XZ}{h + XY} = \frac{a + b}{h + a \cot \theta}$$

Exercise 9(c)

1. A non-uniform rod AB of length 30 cm has its centre of gravity 12 cm from B. It rests horizontally with the end A against a rough vertical wall and the end B supported by a string attached to a point on the wall 15 cm above A. Find the least value of μ which will prevent the end A from slipping.

2. The sphere of example 59 is placed against the wall in such a way that the point of contact is about to slip upwards. Find the inclination of the string to the vertical in this position.

3. A cylinder of mass 5 kg rests on a rough inclined plane with its axis horizontal and the midpoint of its highest generator attached by a horizontal string to a point on the incline. If $\lambda = 15°$ what is the steepest incline

on which the cylinder may rest in this position without slipping? Find also the tension in the string in this case.

4. A solid hemisphere of weight W rests with a point of its rim in contact with a rough horizontal surface and its plane face vertical. Find the horizontal force needed at the highest point of the rim to prevent the hemisphere from toppling. Find also the least value of μ which will prevent the point of contact from slipping.

5. A semi-circular wire AB of mass m is placed over a rough peg, the point of contact P being such that arc AP $= \frac{1}{3}$ arc AB. What mass must be attached to the end A in order that the wire may rest with its diameter horizontal and what co-efficient of friction is then needed to prevent the wire from slipping on the peg?

6. A uniform ladder of weight W rests in limiting equilibrium on rough horizontal ground, its upper end being in contact with a smooth vertical wall. If the ladder makes angle θ with the vertical, show that $\mu = \frac{1}{2} \tan \theta$ at the lower end and find the magnitude of the total reaction at this point.

7. Find the co-efficient of friction needed to prevent the car of example 60 from slipping when parked facing downhill on the same incline with only its rear wheels locked.

8. A solid sphere of radius a and weight W at rest against a rough vertical wall is supported by a string of length $a/5$ tied to the wall and to a point on the surface of the sphere. Show that it is possible for the sphere to rest with the string horizontal, provided that there is sufficient friction at the point of contact between the sphere and the wall. What is the least value of μ for which this may be achieved and find the tension in the string in this case.

9. A plank AB rests with end A in contact with a smooth horizontal plane and a point P in contact with the rough edge of a horizontal step of height h. If $\mu = 1/3$ show that the plank cannot rest in equilibrium unless AP $\geqslant \sqrt{10}\, h$.

†10. A uniform rod AB rests at angle θ to the horizontal with A on rough horizontal ground and a point P such that AP $= 3AB/4$ in contact with a fixed smooth peg. Show that for equilibrium to be possible the co-efficient of friction at the ground must be at least

$$\frac{\sin 2\theta}{2 - \cos 2\theta}$$

9.6 Least Force Needed to Move a Body

The use of a total reaction also provides us with a very convenient method for finding the least force needed to move a body at rest on a rough surface. This method is illustrated by the following example.

Example 61

What is the least force which will move a 15 kg mass up an incline of 14°, given that the co-efficient of friction is 0.35? In which direction should this force be applied?

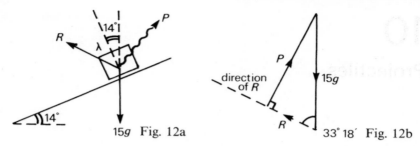

15g Fig. 12a

33° 18′ Fig. 12b

We consider the position of limiting equilibrium in which the friction force is limiting and down the incline. The total reaction is therefore as shown in Fig. 12a. Since $\mu = 0.35 = \tan \lambda$ we have from tables that $\lambda = 19°$ 18′. We now construct the force triangle so that the side representing the applied force P is as short as possible, (see Fig. 12b).

hence $P = 15g \sin 33° 18′ = 80.7$ N

From the force triangle we see that the direction in which the force P should be applied is $90° - 33° 18′ = 56° 42′$ with the vertical.

Exercise 9(d)

1. A trunk of mass 40 kg rests on a rough horizontal surface. If $\lambda = 20°$ what is the least force which will move the trunk and in which direction should it be applied?
2. Find the least force needed to move a 2 kg block (i) up, (ii) down a rough incline of 15° given that $\mu = 0.4$.
3. The magnitude of the least force which will move a crate of weight 200 N on a rough horizontal surface is 60 N. Find the co-efficient of friction.
†4. A block of weight W will just rest on a rough incline of arctan 1/3. What is the least force which will prevent it from sliding down an incline of arctan 1/2? Find also the least force which will move it up this incline.

10

Projectiles

10.1 Introductory Vector Work

By a projectile is meant any body moving freely, under the influence of gravity, in the absence of a driving force, e.g a ball thrown into the air or a rifle shot travelling through the air, but not a powered rocket or aircraft.

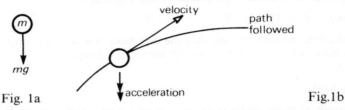

Fig. 1a   Fig.1b

There is only one force acting on a projectile – its weight (Fig. 1a). We shall ignore the effect of air resistance in the work of this chapter. This means that, irrespective of the direction in which the projectile is moving, it will always be subject to a *downward* acceleration of magnitude g. (Fig. 1b.) As was seen in chapter 5, the effect of an acceleration acting in a different direction to the velocity is to pull the body into a curved path.

It is usually convenient to consider the velocity of the projectile at any instant in terms of horizontal and vertical components. In this section we shall use the unit vectors **i** and **j** to do this. We may then apply the methods of sections 5.5 and 5.6.

Note: To simplify the working, we shall in many of the questions in this chapter take the value of g as 10 m s^{-2}. This will give answers whose accuracy is limited to 2 significant figures.

Example 62

A projectile is fired into the air with initial velocity $30\mathbf{i} + 27\mathbf{j} \text{ m s}^{-1}$ referred to horizontal and vertical axes through the point of projection. Taking g as 10 m s^{-2}, find the velocity of the projectile at times 1, 2, 3 and 4 s and plot graphically the path it follows during this time.

As **j** is in the direction of the upward vertical, we may write the acceleration due to gravity as $-10\mathbf{j} \text{ m s}^{-2}$. With the notation of chapter 5 we therefore have

$$\mathbf{u} = 30\mathbf{i} + 27\mathbf{j}$$
$$\mathbf{a} = \qquad -10\mathbf{j}$$

From the formula $\mathbf{v} = \mathbf{u} + \mathbf{a}t$, we obtain an expression for the velocity vector at time t s

$$\mathbf{v} = 30\mathbf{i} + 27\mathbf{j} - (10\mathbf{j})t$$
$$= 30\mathbf{i} + (27 - 10t)\mathbf{j}$$

The velocities at times 1, 2, 3 and 4 are therefore given by $30\mathbf{i} + 17\mathbf{j}$, $30\mathbf{i} + 7\mathbf{j}$, $30\mathbf{i} - 3\mathbf{j}$ and $30\mathbf{i} - 13\mathbf{j}$ respectively. Notice that the horizontal component remains constant while the vertical component is reduced by g each second.

We may obtain the position vector of the projectile at time t from the formula $\mathbf{s} = \mathbf{u}t + \frac{1}{2}\mathbf{a}t^2$

$$\mathbf{s} = (30\mathbf{i} + 27\mathbf{j})t - \frac{1}{2}(10\mathbf{j})t^2$$
$$= 30t\mathbf{i} + (27t - 5t^2)\mathbf{j}$$

From this the positions at times 1, 2, 3 and 4 are found to be $30\mathbf{i} + 22\mathbf{j}$, $60\mathbf{i} + 34\mathbf{j}$, $90\mathbf{i} + 36\mathbf{j}$ and $120\mathbf{i} + 28\mathbf{j}$. Notice that since the horizontal velocity remains constant, the projectile covers the same horizontal distance (30 m) each second. The path it follows is illustrated in Fig. 2.

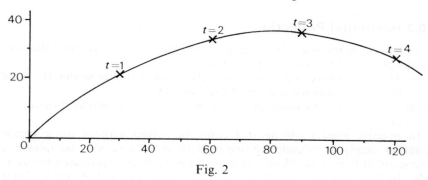

Fig. 2

Exercise 10(a)

In this exercise take g as 10 m s^{-2}, and $\mathbf{i}$ and $\mathbf{j}$ as unit vectors in horizontal and upward vertical directions respectively.

1. A stone is catapulted into the air with initial velocity $8\mathbf{i} + 32\mathbf{j} \text{ m s}^{-1}$. Find the position vector of the stone at time t s and plot the first 5 s of the motion. From your graph estimate the greatest height reached. Draw also the tangents to the path at times 2 and 4 seconds and verify that these are in the same directions as the velocity vectors at these instants.
2. A stone is thrown horizontally with speed 20 m s^{-1} from the edge of a vertical 50 m cliff. Find the position vector of the stone at time t s, taking the point of projection as origin. Plot the first 4 s of the motion and hence find the distance from the foot of the cliff at which the stone strikes the sea. Use the fact that the horizontal component of velocity is constant to estimate how long the stone is in the air.
3. Plot at half-second intervals the path followed by a ball thrown with initial velocity $12\mathbf{i} + 16\mathbf{j} \text{ m s}^{-1}$ and find from your graph:

(i) the height at which the ball strikes a vertical wall 27 m from the point of projection, and

(ii) the direction in which the ball is moving when it strikes the wall.

Verify your answer to part (ii) by calculating the time of impact and hence obtaining the velocity vector at this instant.

4. An aircraft releases a bomb with initial velocity $150i - 20j$ m s^{-1}. Write down the position vector of the bomb at time t s relative to the point of release. If the bomb strikes its target after 6 seconds, find the height of the aircraft at the instant of release and its horizontal distance from the target. Find also the speed of the bomb on impact.

5. A particle A is projected from the origin O with initial velocity $16i + 30j$ m s^{-1}. At the same instant a second particle B is projected with initial velocity $-8i + 20j$ from a point 60 m horizontally from O and 25 m higher. Find

(i) the position vectors of both A and B at time t s relative to O

(ii) the time at which both particles are the same horizontal distance from O.

Show that the particles collide.

10.2 Horizontal Projection

The work of the previous section should have established the following results about the motion of a projectile:

(i) The horizontal component of velocity does not change so that the same horizontal distance is covered each second.

(ii) The vertical component of velocity is subject to the acceleration due to gravity g.

In practice most problems can easily be solved without using vector notation simply by considering one or both of these velocity components. The simplest type of problem is that in which the body is projected horizontally. In the following example we consider how question 2 of exercise 10(a) could be solved by such means.

Example 63

Find where a stone thrown horizontally at 20 m s^{-1} from the top of a 50 m cliff enters the sea, and also its direction of motion at this instant. (Take $g = 10$ m s^{-2}.)

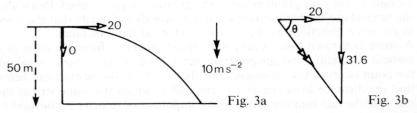

Fig. 3a   Fig. 3b

We consider first the vertical motion in order to find the time taken to descend by 50 m. With the usual notation, and taking the downward direction as positive, we have $u = 0$ and $a = +10$ (the initial vertical velocity being zero).

$$s = ut + \tfrac{1}{2}at^2$$
$$\Rightarrow 50 = 0 + 5t^2$$
$$t = \sqrt{10} = 3.16 \text{ s}$$

As the horizontal component of velocity does not change, the stone will have travelled a horizontal distance of $20 \times 3.162 = 63.2$ m during this time. In our answer, however, we are not justified in giving greater accuracy than 63 m, since we have taken g as 10 m s^{-2}.

Using $v = u + at$, the vertical component of velocity after 3.16 s is found to be 31.6 m s^{-1}. The direction of motion is then obtained from the velocity triangle of Fig. 3b.

$$\theta = \arctan \frac{31.6}{20} \simeq 58°$$

The stone is moving at approximately 58° below the horizontal.

Exercise 10(b)

Take g as 9.8 m s^{-2} unless otherwise indicated. Give answers to a suitable degree of accuracy.

1. A shell is fired horizontally at 200 m s^{-1} from a gun emplacement on top of a cliff 30 m high. How long is the shell in the air and how far out from the cliff does it strike the sea? (Take $g = 10$ m s^{-2}.)
2. A ball thrown horizontally at 15 m s^{-1} from the window of a tall building is observed to strike the ground after 5/2 s. Find the height of the window above ground level and the speed with which the ball hits the ground.
3. An aircraft travelling horizontally at 450 km h^{-1} is to release a bomb which initially will travel with the same velocity as the aircraft. If the altitude of the aircraft is 200 m, find how far in advance of the target the bomb must be released. (Take $g = 10$ m s^{-2}.)
4. In a game of cricket a bowler delivers the ball horizontally from a height of 2.2 m and it strikes the pitch 2 m from the batsman's wicket. Find the speed with which the ball was released and the angle at which it strikes the pitch. (Take g as 10 m s^{-2} and the length of the cricket pitch as 20 metres.)
5. A stunt motor-cyclist rides off a horizontal platform 5 m above ground level at 28 m s^{-1}. How many cars parked side by side may he safely clear if each car has width 1.7 m and height 1.4 m? How far past the last car does he land?
*6. A body is projected horizontally at 14 m s^{-1}. Write down expressions for x and y, the co-ordinates of the body at time t, referred to horizontal and vertical axes through the point of projection. By eliminating t, obtain the equation of the path followed by the body.
7. A stone thrown horizontally from the top of a tower of height h strikes the ground at a distance d from the foot of the tower.

    (i) Find the vertical height fallen when the stone has moved through a horizontal distance of $d/2$.

    (ii) Find the horizontal distance covered when the stone has fallen vertically through height $h/2$.

8. In a game of squash a ball struck horizontally at 10 m s^{-1} rebounds from a wall 3 m away and strikes the court 1 metre from the foot of the wall. If the ball rebounds from the wall with the same speed and at the same angle as when it strikes the wall, find the height at which the ball was struck and the height of its point of impact on the wall. (Take $g = 10 \text{ m s}^{-2}$.)

10.3 Projection at an Angle

The following examples illustrate how problems involving projection at an angle are tackled. The first example is a solution of question 3(i) of exercise 10(a).

Example 64

Find the height at which a ball thrown with initial velocity $12\mathbf{i} + 16\mathbf{j} \text{ m s}^{-1}$ strikes a vertical wall 27 metres away. (Take $g = 10 \text{ m s}^{-2}$.)

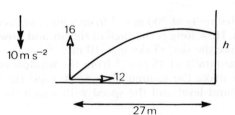

Fig. 4

Horizontal motion: As the horizontal velocity is constant, the time taken for the ball to reach the wall is 27 divided by $12 = 9/4$ s.

Vertical motion: With the usual notation we have, $u = 16$, $a = -10$, $t = 2\frac{1}{4}$. Using $s = ut + \frac{1}{2}at^2$ we obtain

$$h = 16 \times \frac{9}{4} - 5 \times \frac{81}{16}$$

$$= 36 - 25.3 \simeq 11 \text{ m}$$

Example 65

An airgun pellet is fired at 50 m s^{-1} in direction $30°$ above the horizontal. Find the 'range' of the shot on a horizontal plane and also the maximum height reached. (Take $g = 9.8 \text{ m s}^{-2}$.)

The horizontal and vertical components of the initial velocity are $50 \cos 30° = 43.3 \text{ m s}^{-1}$ and $50 \sin 30° = 25 \text{ m s}^{-1}$. We first obtain the 'time of flight'. This is found by considering the motion as far as the highest point at which the vertical velocity is zero. (Fig. 5.)

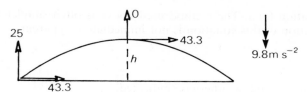

Fig. 5

Vertical motion: Time to reduce vertical velocity from 25 m s⁻¹ to zero =
25 ÷ 9.8 = 2.55 seconds.

As the motion is symmetrical (see exercise 10(c) question 11) the total time
of flight is 2 × 2.55 = 5.1 seconds.

Horizontal motion: range = 43.3 × 5.1 = 221 metres
Vertical motion: height = average velocity × time
= 12.5 × 2.55 = 31.9 metres

Example 66

A ball is thrown with speed 15 m s⁻¹ at arctan 4/3 above the horizontal
from a window 9 metres above the ground. Find (i) the speed with which the
ball hits the ground and (ii) the horizontal distance it has then travelled.
(Take $g = 10$ m s⁻².)

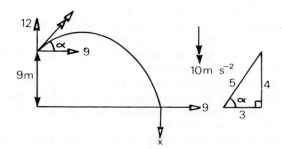

Fig. 6

The angle of projection (α in Fig. 6) is such that $\cos \alpha = 3/5$ and $\sin \alpha = 4/5$.
The initial components of velocity are therefore 9 and 12 m s⁻¹ as shown.

(i) Vertical motion: Letting the vertical velocity on impact be x m s⁻¹ and
using $v^2 - u^2 = 2as$, we have

$$x^2 - (-12)^2 = 2 \times 10 \times 9$$
$$x^2 = 180 + 144 \quad \Rightarrow x = 18$$

Since the horizontal component is still 9 m s⁻¹ the speed on impact is
$\sqrt{9^2 + 18^2} = 9\sqrt{5}$ m s⁻¹.

(ii) By considering the change in the vertical velocity (from 12 to -18) we
see that the ball is in the air for 3 s. Hence the horizontal distance covered is
9 × 3 = 27 metres.

Note: In problems of this type the time of flight may be found directly by
applying the formula $s = ut + \frac{1}{2}at^2$ to the vertical motion. This leads to a

quadratic equation for t. The method used above is often simpler in cases where the solution of this equation is not immediately apparent.

Exercise 10(c)

Take g as 9.8 m s^{-2} unless otherwise indicated.

1. A body is projected at an angle of arctan 3/4 to the horizontal with speed 75 ms^{-1}. Find how long it is in the air, the highest point reached and the horizontal range. (Take $g = 10$ m s^{-2}.)
2. A ball is thrown into the air at 40 m s^{-1} in a direction making 60° with the horizontal. Find the horizontal and vertical distances travelled after 2 seconds and also the direction of motion at this instant.
3. A golfer strikes a ball with initial velocity $30i + 24j$ m s^{-1}. For how long is the ball in the air and how far down the fairway does it land? At what height is the ball when one-third of this distance has been covered and what is its velocity vector at this instant? (Take $g = 10$ m s^{-2}.)
4. A fireman projects a jet of water at 40° to the horizontal with a speed of 20 m s^{-1}. At what height does the water strike a building 23 metres away? What angle does the jet make with the horizontal at this point?
5. Find the horizontal range of a mortar fired with speed 150 m s^{-1} at 58° to the horizontal. (Take $g = 10$ m s^{-2}.)
6. An aircraft releases a bomb which moves initially at 30° below the horizontal with speed 250 m s^{-1}. The bomb is observed to strike the ground 5 seconds later. At what altitude was the bomb released and in what direction is it moving on impact?
7. A batsman skies his shot and is caught 4 seconds after the ball is hit by a fieldsman 30 m away. With what speed was the ball struck and what is the greatest height it reaches? (Assume that the ball is caught at the same level as when it was struck.)
8. One and a half seconds after being thrown, a ball passes through an open window which is 9/2 metres above the point of projection and 9 m away horizontally. Find the speed and the direction of motion of the ball (i) when thrown (ii) when passing through the window. (Take $g = 10$ m s^{-2}.)
9. Suggest reasons why a jet of water tends to spread (i.e. in cross-section) as it travels through the air.
10. A high-jumper leaves the ground with velocity $2i + 6j$ m s^{-1}. The bar is 1 metre horizontally from his take-off point and he clears it by 5/2 cm. At what height is the bar? What would have been the highest bar he could have cleared with this jump and at what distance from the bar should his take-off point have been in order to achieve this?
*11. (i) Prove that if air-resistance is neglected, then the time taken by a projectile to reach its highest point and the time taken for it to fall again to its original level are equal.
   (ii) Explain why as a consequence of this result the path followed must be symmetrical about the highest point.
   (iii) If air-resistance is taken into consideration, which of the times of

part (i) would you expect to be the larger? Give reasons to justify your answer.

(iv) What effect would you expect air-resistance to have on the symmetry of the path?

12. A stone is thrown with speed 25 m s^{-1} at 30 above the horizontal from the top of a vertical cliff 30 m high. For how long is the stone in the air and how far from the foot of the cliff does it land? (Take $g = 10$ m s^{-2}.)

13. A ball thrown at 16 m s^{-1} from a school playground lands 2 seconds later on the horizontal roof of a building 8 m high and 11 m from the point of projection. Find the angle to the horizontal at which the ball was thrown and the distance from the edge of the roof at which it lands. (Assume that the motion takes place in a plane perpendicular to the edge of the roof.)

14. A stone thrown from the top of a tower strikes the ground 5/2 seconds later at a point 30 metres from the foot of the tower. If the speed on impact is 20 m s^{-1}, find the speed and direction with which the stone was thrown. Find also the height of the tower. (Take $g = 10$ m s^{-2}.)

15. A shot-putter releases the shot with velocity $9\mathbf{i} + 8\mathbf{j}$ m s^{-1} from a height of 1.8 m. Find the length of the throw, the greatest height reached and the speed of the shot on impact. (Take $g = 10$ m s^{-2}.)

*16. A projectile is fired at 50 m s^{-1} at arctan 3/4 to the horizontal. Write down expressions for the horizontal displacement x metres and the vertical displacement y metres at time t seconds, and hence obtain the equation of the trajectory referred to axes through the point of projection. If the point of projection is on an incline of arctan (1/20) and if the projectile is fired in the uphill direction, write down the equation of the incline referred to the same axes. Hence find the co-ordinates of the point at which the projectile lands. State also the time for which the projectile is in the air. (Take $g = 10$ m s^{-2}.)

17. In a game of cricket the bowler releases the ball at a point 2.1 m above the ground. The ball strikes the wicket at a point 18 m away horizontally, having risen on the way to a greatest height of 0.4 m above the bowler's hand. Find the speed and direction with which the ball was released. (Hint: consider the times to and from the highest point.)

18. A projectile fired at elevation θ has horizontal range R. Show that the time of flight is given by $\sqrt{2R \tan \theta/g}$.

19. A particle projected from point A at elevation α passes through point B when moving at angle β to the horizontal. If the line AB makes angle θ with the horizontal, prove that $2 \tan \theta = \tan \alpha + \tan \beta$.

20. A boy throws a stone with speed v at a bird passing above him with horizontal velocity u. At the instant the stone is released the bird is at height h vertically above the boy. Show that the angle of projection must be arccos (u/v) and that a hit is only possible if $v^2 \geqslant u^2 + 2gh$.

10.4 Maximum Horizontal Range

(i) We shall first establish a general formula for the horizontal range R of a projectile fired with speed v at elevation α. The initial components of velocity

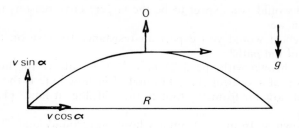

Fig. 7

are as shown in Fig. 7. Since the vertical component is reduced by g each second we have

$$\text{time to highest point} = \frac{v \sin \alpha}{g}$$

$$\text{total time of flight} = 2 \times \frac{v \sin \alpha}{g}$$

$$\text{horizontal range } R = v \cos \alpha \times \frac{2v \sin \alpha}{g}$$

$$\Rightarrow \qquad \boxed{R = \frac{v^2}{g} \sin 2\alpha} \tag{1}$$

(ii) For a given speed of projection v we now wish to know what elevation α will produce the greatest value of the range R. In equation (1) this is obtained when $\sin 2\alpha = 1$. Thus

$$\boxed{R_{max} = \frac{v^2}{g}} \tag{2}$$

To achieve maximum range, the projectile must be fired at elevation $45°$ (so that $2\alpha = 90°$).

All points on a horizontal plane which are closer to the point of projection than R_{max} may clearly be hit by the projectile, providing it is fired at a suitable elevation. The second part of example 67 shows that in general such points are accessible by 2 trajectories – a 'high' trajectory and a 'low' trajectory.

Example 67

The maximum range of a certain gun is 7 km. At what speed is the shot fired? Find also the elevations at which the barrel could be set in order to hit a target 6 km away.

(i) Using equation (2) we have

$$\frac{v^2}{g} = 7000$$

$$v^2 = 7000 \times 9.8 \Rightarrow v = 262 \text{ m s}^{-1}$$

(ii) From equation (1) it follows that to hit the target at distance 6 km we must satisfy the equation

$$\frac{v^2}{g} \sin 2\alpha = 6000$$

But from above we have $\dfrac{v^2}{g} = 7000$. The equation therefore reduces to

$$\sin 2\alpha = \frac{6000}{7000} = 0.857$$

From this $2\alpha = 59°$ (1st quadrant) *or* $121°$ (2nd quadrant)
$$\alpha = 29\tfrac{1}{2}° \text{ or } 60\tfrac{1}{2}°$$

Exercise 10(d)

Take $g = 9.8 \text{ m s}^{-2}$ unless otherwise stated

1. Find the maximum range of the mortar of exercise 10(c) question 5. (Take $g = 10 \text{ m s}^{-2}$.)
2. The maximum range of a certain rifle is 2 km. Find its muzzle velocity.
3. A shell fired at 220 m s^{-1} lands 4 km from its firing point. At what elevation was it fired? (Two answers.) Find also the maximum range that the shell could have achieved.
4. A golfer wishes to clear a bunker whose furthest edge is 150 m away. If he strikes the ball at 40 m s^{-1} between what limits must the elevation of the shot lie? (Take $g = 10 \text{ m s}^{-2}$.)
5. A particle is projected with speed v at elevation θ. Show that the greatest height reached, H, and the horizontal range, R, are given by

$$H = \frac{v^2}{2g} \sin^2 \theta, \qquad R = \frac{v^2}{g} \sin 2\theta$$

   Find the value of θ for which the horizontal range is three times the greatest height.
6. A boy returning a cricket ball to the wicket throws it with speed 20 m s^{-1} at elevation arctan $(4/3)$. What is the least speed with which he could have thrown the ball the same distance?
7. When the angle of elevation of a gun barrel is halved, the horizontal range is increased by 50%. Find the original elevation of the barrel.
*8. Show that if a gun whose maximum range is R is to strike a target at horizontal distance d ($d < R$), then it must be fired at an elevation α such that $\sin 2\alpha = d/R$. If θ is a solution of this equation, prove that $90° - \theta$ is also a solution. Show also that the greatest heights reached in the two cases are in the ratio $\tan^2 \theta : 1$.
†9. A tank fires with muzzle velocity 120 m s^{-1}. It fires a shot when moving with speed 20 m s^{-1} towards its target. If the barrel is inclined at angle θ to the horizontal, write down expressions for the initial horizontal and

vertical velocity components of the shot. Obtain a formula for the horizontal range and hence find the value of θ for which this is a maximum. (Note that this is not 45°.)

10.5 The Equation of the Trajectory

In this section we obtain the general equation for the trajectory (or path followed) of a projectile, referred to axes through the point of projection, and consider also some of its uses.

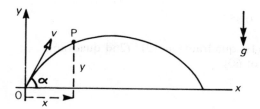

Fig. 8

In Fig. 8 let (x, y) be the co-ordinates of any point P on the trajectory. Let t be the time taken by the projectile to reach P. Then

$$\text{horizontal motion} \quad t = \frac{\text{distance}}{\text{speed}} = \frac{x}{v \cos \alpha}$$

vertical motion   using $s = ut + \frac{1}{2}at^2$ we obtain

$$y = v \sin \alpha t - \frac{1}{2}gt^2$$

$$= v \sin \alpha \left(\frac{x}{v \cos \alpha}\right) - \frac{1}{2}g\left(\frac{x}{v \cos \alpha}\right)^2$$

$$\boxed{y = x \tan \alpha - \frac{gx^2 \sec^2 \alpha}{2v^2}}$$

This is the equation of the trajectory referred to the axes shown. Although at first sight it is a rather complicated expression, it should be realised that in a particular case the values of v and α will be known. Thus, to take a simple example, if $\tan \alpha = 2$, $v = 20 \text{ m s}^{-1}$ and g is taken as 10 m s^{-2} we find (remembering the identity $\sec^2 \alpha = 1 + \tan^2 \alpha$) that the equation reduces to

$$y = 2x - \frac{10x^2 \times 5}{800}$$

i.e $y = 2x - \frac{x^2}{16}$

The equation of the trajectory is of most use in finding the elevations α for which a given projectile will hit a given point above or below the point of projection. The method is based really on the identity $\sec^2 \alpha = 1 + \tan^2 \alpha$ for this enables us to transform the equation into a quadratic in $\tan \alpha$. The versatility of the method is illustrated by the next two examples.

Example 68

A projectile is to be fired at 14 m s^{-1}.

(i) Find the two possible angles of projection for which it will pass through the point (8,2)

(ii) Show that the point (10, 8) is 'inaccessible'.

Substituting $v = 14$ and $g = 9.8$ into the equation of the trajectory, we obtain

$$y = x \tan \alpha - \frac{x^2(1 + \tan^2\alpha)}{40} \tag{1}$$

(i) If the trajectory passes through (8, 2) we must have

$$2 = 8 \tan \alpha - \frac{8(1 + \tan^2\alpha)}{5}$$

$$\Rightarrow 4 \tan^2\alpha - 20 \tan \alpha + 9 = 0$$
$$(2 \tan \alpha - 9)(2 \tan \alpha - 1) = 0$$
$$\tan \alpha = 9/2 \text{ or } 1/2$$

So the projectile should be fired at arctan (9/2) or arctan (1/2)

(ii) In this part of the question we follow the same general method but show that no solution for $\tan \alpha$ is possible. Substituting the co-ordinates (10, 8) into equation (1) we obtain

$$8 = 10 \tan \alpha - \frac{5(1 + \tan^2\alpha)}{2}$$
$$\Rightarrow 5 \tan^2\alpha - 20 \tan \alpha + 21 = 0$$

With the usual notation for a quadratic equation $b^2 - 4ac = 400 - 420 = -20$. There are therefore no (real) values of $\tan \alpha$ which satisfy this equation. This means that the point (10, 8) is inaccessible to the projectile.

Note: The astute reader will probably now have realised that in solving the quadratic equation in $\tan \alpha$ there are *three* possible outcomes.

$b^2 - 4ac > 0$ distinct roots – 2 possible trajectories
$b^2 - 4ac < 0$ imaginary roots – point inaccessible
$b^2 - 4ac = 0$ equal roots

and that the third situation must arise when the point concerned is on the limit of accessibility. When this is the case only one trajectory is possible, (Compare with the maximum horizontal range result) since the roots for $\tan \alpha$ are equal.

Example 69

Find the highest point that the projectile of example 68 may attain on a vertical wall 12 m from the point of projection.

We require the greatest possible value of y when $x = 12$. Equation (1) of example 68 becomes

$$y = 12 \tan \alpha - \frac{18(1 + \tan^2\alpha)}{5}$$

$$\Rightarrow 18 \tan^2\alpha - 60 \tan \alpha + (5y + 18) = 0$$

As the highest point is on the limit of accessibility the roots for tan α must be equal:

that is $b^2 - 4ac = 0$
hence $3600 = 72(5y + 18)$
$$50 = 5y + 18 \quad \Rightarrow y = 6.4 \text{ m}$$

As $b^2 - 4ac = 0$ the formula for the roots of a quadratic equation reduces to $-b/2a$.

$$\tan \alpha = \frac{-b}{2a} = \frac{60}{36} = \frac{5}{3}$$

the projectile must be fired at arctan (5/3)

Exercise 10(e)

Take g as 9.8 m s^{-2} unless otherwise stated.

*1. (i) For velocity of projection 14 m s^{-1} find the equations of the trajectories corresponding to angles of projection α such that tan α = 1, tan α = 2, tan α = 3, tan α = 7 (about 45°, 63°, 72° and 82° respectively).
(ii) Plot all of these trajectories on the same axes taking scales x : 0 to 25 and y : 0 to 15 units. (Only a few convenient points need be plotted in each case.)
(iii) Sketch in the 'envelope' of the curves plotted. This is called the 'bounding parabola'. What can be said about points outside the bounding parabola?
2. A body is projected at 20 m s^{-1}. Find the elevations at which it should be fired in order to pass through the points with co-ordinates (i) (30, 7$\frac{1}{2}$) (ii) (36, −6) referred to horizontal and vertical axes through the point of projection. Show also that the point (20, 30) is out of range. (Take g = 10 m s^{-2}.)
3. A boy throws a ball at elevation arctan (12/5). If the ball strikes a tall building 10 m away at a height of 14 m, with what speed was it thrown?
4. A stone thrown downwards at 21 m s^{-1} from the top of a tower 50 metres high strikes horizontal ground 30 metres from the foot of the tower. At what angle below the horizontal was it thrown?
5. An anti-aircraft gun has muzzle velocity 150 m s^{-1}. Find the height of the highest aircraft it can hit at a horizontal distance of 750 m. Find also the elevation at which it should fire. (Take g = 10 m s^{-2}.)
6. A particle is to be projected so as to pass through a point with co-ordinates $(d, d/18)$ referred to horizontal and vertical axes through the point of projection. If the maximum horizontal range of the particle is $2d$, find the two possible angles of projection. Show also that the distance between the points at which the two trajectories strike horizontal ground through the point of projection is $12d/65$.

7. A boy throws a ball with speed u at a vertical wall a distance d away. Use the method of example 69 to find the highest point he can hit. Find also the required angle of projection and prove that this is always greater than 45° (providing the wall is within horizontal range).

8. A gun emplacement is situated on top of a cliff of height h. If the shells are fired with muzzle velocity v, show that the maximum range out to sea, R, is given by

$$R = \frac{v}{g}\sqrt{v^2 + 2gh}$$

11
Momentum and Energy

11.1 Impulse and Momentum

There are many situations in which a force acts on a body for a definite interval of time and then ceases. In many cases the time interval concerned is very short, e.g. a ball being struck by a cricket bat, and the situation may well be described as a 'blow' or a 'jolt'. In other cases the force concerned may act for a longer period of time, e.g a car being pushed for a period of many seconds in order to be started.

The product, force × time, is called the **impulse** given by the force to the body concerned. Thus if a cricket bat exerts a force of 600 N on the ball and the two are in contact for 1/100 second, the impulse which the ball receives is

$$600 \times 0.01 = 6 \text{ newton seconds (or 6 N s)}$$

In a situation such as this the impulse has a clearly defined direction: that of the force which is acting. Impulse is therefore a vector quantity and may be defined as follows:

> IF A FORCE **F** ACTS ON A BODY FOR A TIME t THEN THE IMPULSE GIVEN BY THE FORCE TO THE BODY IS **F**t.

This definition is only meaningful when the force **F** remains constant, both in magnitude and in direction. We shall deal with cases in which the force changes in chapter 18.

Consider a uniform force **F** acting on a body of mass m for a time t. Since the force is uniform there will be a uniform acceleration **a** and we may write

$$\mathbf{F} = m\mathbf{a} = \frac{m(\mathbf{v} - \mathbf{u})}{t}$$

hence $\quad \mathbf{F}t = m\mathbf{v} - m\mathbf{u}$ \hfill (1)

This is the first of a number of results in which the product mass × velocity appears. This is called the **momentum** of a moving body. In terms of momentum we may interpret equation (1) as

$$\frac{\text{impulse}}{\text{of force}} = \frac{\text{final}}{\text{momentum}} - \frac{\text{initial}}{\text{momentum}}$$

that is $\quad$ | Impulse = Change in momentum |

Momentum is also a vector quantity. We may define it as follows

> ## A BODY OF MASS m MOVING WITH VELOCITY v IS SAID TO POSSESS MOMENTUM mv.

Since equation (1) tells us that an impulse is, in a sense, converted into a corresponding amount of momentum, it follows that momentum may be measured in the same units as those of impulse, i.e. newton seconds. In order to obtain a measurement of momentum in these units, however, it is important that both mass m and velocity v are measured in their standard units, i.e. kg and m s^{-1}.

Thus a mass of 4 kg moving at 5 m s^{-1} has momentum 20 N s
and a mass of 200 g moving at 5 cm s^{-1} has momentum $1/5 \times 1/20$
$= 0.01$ N s

Example 70

A body of mass 2 kg moving with velocity $8i + 3j$ m s^{-1} is subjected to a force of $2i - 6j$ N for a period of $5/2$ s. Find the velocity with which the body is moving after the force has ceased.

This is a simple application of the result 'impulse = change in momentum'. We may work from the equation (1).

$$Ft = mv - mu$$
$$2\tfrac{1}{2}(2i - 6j) = 2v - 2(8i + 3j)$$
$$2v = 5i - 15j + 16i + 6j$$
$$\Rightarrow v = 10\tfrac{1}{2}i - 4\tfrac{1}{2}j$$

Notice that the force $2i - 6j$ is not in the same direction as the initial velocity. We are in effect finding the final momentum by adding in a vector triangle (Fig. 1) the initial momentum and the impulse of the force (i.e. $mv = mu + Ft$)

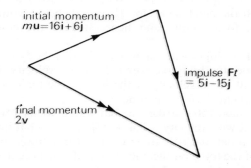

initial momentum
$mu = 16i + 6j$

impulse Ft
$= 5i - 15j$

final momentum
$2v$

Fig. 1

Example 71

A ball of mass 500 g moving at 20 m s^{-1} strikes a wall at right-angles and rebounds with speed 12 m s^{-1}. Find the impulse given to the ball by the wall and the force between them, given that contact lasts for 0.02 s.

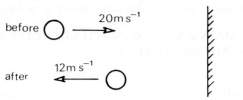

Fig. 2

In problems such as this, where motion takes place along a single line, it is not necessary to use vectors but we must be careful to assign positive and negative directions for both velocities and momenta. Thus we may write $u = +20$ and $v = -12$ and obtain

impulse = change in momentum
$$= mv - mu$$
$$= (\tfrac{1}{2} \times -12) - (\tfrac{1}{2} \times 20) = -16 \text{ N s}$$

The minus shows that the impulse is in the negative direction. Since this impulse is provided by the action of a force which acts for 0.02 s we have

impulse = Ft
$16 = 0.02F$
force $= 16 \div 0.02 = 800$ N

Exercise 11(a)

1. Write down the momentum of
    (i)   A man of mass 75 kg running at 6 m s^{-1}
    (ii) A tennis ball of mass 60 g moving at 25 m s^{-1}
    (iii) A trunk of mass 15 kg sliding at 20 cm s^{-1}
    (iv) A car of mass 3/4 tonne moving at 72 km h^{-1}
2. Which of the following provides the larger impulse?
    (i) $70\mathbf{i} + 240\mathbf{j}$ N for 0.2 s
    (ii) $0.3\mathbf{i} + 0.4\mathbf{j}$ N for $1\tfrac{1}{2}$ minutes.
3. A wooden block of mass 800 g at rest on a rough horizontal surface is given a horizontal impulse of 6 N s. With what speed does the block begin to move? If the block slides for $2\tfrac{1}{2}$ seconds before coming to rest, find the friction force acting and hence deduce the co-efficient of friction.
4. A force $\mathbf{F} = 14\mathbf{i} - 20\mathbf{j}$ N acts for 6 seconds on a body of mass 8 kg. What impulse does the body receive? If its initial velocity was $-3\mathbf{i} + 2\mathbf{j} \text{ m s}^{-1}$ what will be its velocity at the instant the force ceases? Find also the displacement during this time.
5. A cricket ball of mass 150 g strikes the bat with velocity $25\mathbf{i} - \mathbf{j} \text{ m s}^{-1}$ and leaves the bat with velocity $-23\mathbf{i} + 15\mathbf{j} \text{ m s}^{-1}$. What impulse does the ball receive? If bat and ball are in contact for 1/20 second, estimate the magnitude of the force on the ball, assumed constant. ($\mathbf{i}$ and $\mathbf{j}$ are in horizontal and upward vertical directions.)
6. A car of mass 0.8 tonne is travelling at 30 m s^{-1}. What braking force is required to reduce its speed by one third in a time of 2 seconds? If the same braking force is maintained, after what further time will the car be brought to rest?

7. What force is required to change the velocity of a 50 kg body from $-\mathbf{i} + 2\mathbf{j}$ m s^{-1} to $3\mathbf{i} + 4\mathbf{j}$ m s^{-1} in a time of 10 seconds? What force would then be required to bring the body to rest in a further 5 seconds? Find the position vector of the point of rest relative to the starting point.

8. Two forces $\mathbf{F}_1 = 3\mathbf{i} - 12\mathbf{j}$ N and $\mathbf{F}_2 = 10\mathbf{i} + 3\mathbf{j}$ N act on a stationary body for times 2 seconds and 3 seconds respectively. What is the momentum vector of the body when both forces have ceased? If the body has mass 6 kg, with what speed will it be moving?

9. A ball falls vertically from a height of 2.5 m and rebounds to a height of 0.9 metre. If the mass of the ball is 300 g, find the magnitude of the impulse it receives on striking the ground.

10. A body moving with momentum $7\mathbf{i} + \mathbf{j}$ N s is acted on by a force of $-\mathbf{i} + 2\mathbf{j}$ N. Show that after 2 seconds have elapsed the speed of the body is the same as at the start. Prove that the angle through which the direction of motion has turned in this time is arctan (3/4).

11. Three people push a car of mass 1.2 tonnes, each with a force of 170 N. What impulse has the car received after 5 seconds? If the speed of the car increases by 2 m s^{-1} during this time, find the magnitude of the resistance to motion.

12. A locomotive is shunting a truck. The truck, which is initially at rest, is pushed with a force of 3000 N for 15 seconds before being released. If the truck rolls for a further 35 seconds before coming to rest, find the magnitude of the resisting force, assuming this to remain constant throughout the motion. Find also the momentum of the truck at the instant of release.

13. A body of mass m is travelling due north at speed u. What is the magnitude of the least impulse required to change the direction of motion to N $\theta°$ E, and in which direction should this impulse be applied? What will be the new speed of the body?

*14. A hose delivers a jet of water at 12 m s^{-1} through a nozzle of cross-sectional area 4 cm^2. Find the mass of water discharged each second and also its momentum. What force, acting for 1 s, is required to bring a body with this momentum to rest? If the jet is played directly onto a wall at a short distance from the nozzle, estimate the force exerted by the jet on the wall.

*15. In a packaging plant a conveyor belt moving at 1.4 m s^{-1} picks up a dozen 500 g cartons each second. The cartons are not initially moving in the direction of the belt. Calculate the momentum acquired each second by the cartons which are picked up and hence estimate the resisting force they exert on the belt.

11.2 Conservation of Momentum in an Impact

Suppose that there is a collision between two bodies m_1 and m_2 moving with velocities $\mathbf{u}_1$ and $\mathbf{u}_2$. The effect of the collision will normally be to alter the velocities of the balls, in both magnitude and direction. Let the new velocities be $\mathbf{v}_1$ and $\mathbf{v}_2$ respectively.

We are now able to prove an important result concerning the momenta of the balls before and after the impact. The result we shall obtain is really a consequence of Newton's Third Law which tells us that the forces the balls exert on one another during the duration of the impact are equal and opposite. (Fig. 3.)

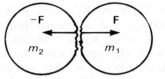

Fig. 3

If contact lasts for a small interval of time t, then the impulses received by the two balls are $\mathbf{F}t$ and $-\mathbf{F}t$ respectively. Using 'impulse = change in momentum' we therefore obtain

for mass m_1 $\quad \mathbf{F}t = m_1\mathbf{v}_1 - m_1\mathbf{u}_1$

for mass m_2 $\quad -\mathbf{F}t = m_2\mathbf{v}_2 - m_2\mathbf{u}_2$

adding $\quad\quad\quad 0 = m_1\mathbf{v}_1 - m_1\mathbf{u}_1 + m_2\mathbf{v}_2 - m_2\mathbf{u}_2$

$\Rightarrow m_1\mathbf{u}_1 + m_2\mathbf{u}_2 = m_1\mathbf{v}_1 + m_2\mathbf{v}_2$

i.e total momentum before impact = total momentum after impact

Thus in an impact between two bodies the total momentum of the two bodies remains the same. The *individual* momenta may change but in such a way that if one body loses momentum then the other body will gain an equal amount.

This is in fact a particular case of a more general result known as the **principle of conservation of momentum**.

> IF NO EXTERNAL FORCE ACTS ON A SYSTEM OF BODIES THEN THE TOTAL MOMENTUM OF THE SYSTEM WILL REMAIN UNCHANGED.

In the impact considered above, the 'system' consists of two bodies, and by an 'external force' we mean a force exerted on one or both of the bodies by some outside agency. The forces between the bodies on impact are not in this category. They are forces 'internal' to the system, i.e. caused by the action of one member of the system on another. Since there is no 'external' force, the principle predicts that momentum is conserved. In fact a system consisting of any number of bodies moving freely and colliding with one another will retain the same total momentum, providing that no outside or external force is brought to act on any part of the system.

Example 72

A particle A of mass 2 units moving with velocity $3\mathbf{i} + 5\mathbf{j}$ m s^{-1} collides with a stationary particle B of mass 3 units. The velocity of B after the impact is $3\mathbf{i} + 2\mathbf{j}$ m s^{-1}. Find the velocity of A after the impact and also the magnitude of the impulse between the particles.

Denoting the new velocity of A by **v** and using the result that the total momentum must be the same before and after impact, we have

$$2(3i + 5j) + 3(0) = 2v + 3(3i + 2j)$$
$$6i + 10j = 2v + 9i + 6j$$
$$2v = -3i + 4j$$
$$\Rightarrow \text{new velocity of A is } v = -1\tfrac{1}{2}i + 2j$$

On impact the particles receive equal and opposite impulses. These may be found by considering the change in momentum of either particle:

impulse experienced by B = change in momentum of B
$$= 3(3i + 2j) - 0$$
$$= 9i + 6j$$

the magnitude of this impulse is $\sqrt{9^2 + 6^2} = 3\sqrt{13}$ units

(The units are not necessarily N s since we are not told the units of mass used.)

Example 73

A 5 tonne truck rolling at 7 m s^{-1} is catching up on a 10 tonne truck rolling at 3 m s^{-1} along the same track and in the same direction. If the trucks couple on impact, with what speed will they continue?
The total momentum before impact

$$= (5 \times 7) + (3 \times 10) = 65 \text{ units}$$

After impact we have, in effect, a single body of mass 15 tonnes moving with a speed we shall call v. By conservation of momentum we have

$$15v = 65$$
$$\Rightarrow \text{speed after coupling} = 4\tfrac{1}{3} \text{ m s}^{-1}$$

Note: Since all terms in a conservation of momentum equation are of the form – mass × velocity – the units in which the masses and the velocities are measured are of no importance, providing consistency is observed.

Example 74

If the trucks of Example 73 are moving in opposite directions and if they do not couple on impact, find the subsequent motion of the 5 tonne truck, given that the 10 tonne truck rolls back with speed 1 m s^{-1} after impact.

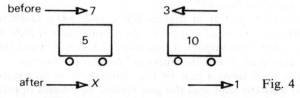

If, in Fig. 4, we let positive velocities and momenta be to the right, then the total momentum before impact is $(5 \times 7) - (10 \times 3) = 5$ units.

It is desirable in questions of this sort to mark the velocities after impact in the same direction, as in Fig. 4. We then obtain

$$5X + 10(1) = 5$$
$$5X = -5 \quad X = -1$$

Thus the motion of both trucks is reversed by the impact, each in fact rolling back with speed 1 m s^{-1}.

Exercise 11(b)

1. A marble of mass 12 g moving at 6 m s^{-1} strikes a second marble of mass 15 g which is at rest. Find the speed imparted to the second marble if the 12 g marble moves after impact
   (i) with speed 1 m s^{-1} in the same direction
   (ii) with speed $1/2 \text{ m s}^{-1}$ in the opposite direction

*2. A man throws a suitcase of mass 12 kg onto a stationary trolley of mass 48 kg. If the suitcase lands on the trolley with horizontal velocity 3 m s^{-1} and does not slip, find the speed with which the trolley begins to move. Would slipping alter the final situation? Justify your answer.

3. Two equal billiard balls collide when moving with velocities $-\mathbf{i} + \mathbf{j}$ m s^{-1} and $2\mathbf{i} \text{ m s}^{-1}$. If the first ball is brought to rest, find the velocity of the second ball after the impact and the angle through which its direction of motion is deflected.

*4. A 25 g bullet travelling at 240 m s^{-1} has its speed reduced by one half in passing through a wooden block of mass 2 kg which is initially at rest. Explain why momentum is conserved in this situation and find the speed gained by the block if it is free to move in the direction of the shot. (Neglect any loss of mass due to the hole made by the bullet.)

5. Particles with masses of 3 units and 2 units collide when moving with velocities 14 m s^{-1} south and 15 m s^{-1} N $\theta°$ E where $\theta = \arctan (4/3)$. Write the velocity vectors in terms of unit vectors east and north. Hence find the resulting speed and direction of motion if the particles coalesce on impact.

6. A body of mass 5 kg moving with velocity $12\mathbf{i} \text{ m s}^{-1}$ is brought to rest by a collision with a second body moving with velocity $-8\mathbf{i} \text{ m s}^{-1}$. If the speed of the second body is doubled as a result of the impact, find its mass.

7. A line of empty trucks with total mass 20 tonnes is rolling at speed 1 m s^{-1}. The line passes below a coal hopper from which 40 tonnes of coal is delivered (vertically) into the trucks. With what speed do the trucks leave the hopper?

8. Two bodies A and B of masses 500 g and 300 g respectively collide when moving in exactly opposite directions with speeds 3 m s^{-1} and 2 m s^{-1}. After the impact B has speed 3.5 m s^{-1}. Find the new speed and direction of A and the impulse between the bodies.

*9. A shot is fired from a gun by the detonation of an explosive charge. Explain why the shot and the gun receive equal and opposite impulses as a result of the explosion. If both are initially at rest, what will be the total momentum after the bullet has been fired? Hence find the recoil velocity of a gun of mass 300 kg when a 5 kg shot is fired horizontally at 450 m s^{-1}. What constant force is required to bring the gun to rest in $1\frac{1}{2}$ seconds?

10. A truck of mass 5 tonnes rolling at 7 m s^{-1} runs into a second stationary truck. The two trucks couple and move together after the impact. What braking force is required to bring them to rest in 10 seconds?

11. Two stunt drivers tie their cars together with a long piece of rope, which is initially slack, and then drive off in opposite directions. The masses of the cars are 0.75 and 0.9 tonnes and their speeds when the rope tightens are 40 km h^{-1} and 36 km h^{-1} respectively. The rope breaks but the speed of the heavier car is reduced to 26 km h^{-1}. Find the new speed of the other car and also the impulse transmitted by the rope before it breaks.

*12. (i) A rifle fires a bullet of mass 20 g with muzzle velocity 480 m s^{-1}. The person firing the rifle prevents it from recoiling by steadying it against his shoulder. What impulse does he feel in his shoulder?

(ii) If a machine gun fires 50 such bullets in a 10 second burst, what average force is exerted on the mountings of the gun?

13. (i) Masses m_1 and m_2 (where $m_1 > m_2$) are supported by a light string passing over a smooth light pulley. Motion is allowed to take place, starting from rest. By considering the impulses given by the weights of the two bodies, show that the speed they reach after t seconds is

$$\frac{m_1 - m_2}{m_1 + m_2}gt$$

(ii) When moving downwards at speed v, the mass m_1 lands on a horizontal surface from which it does not rebound. Find the speed with which it is subsequently jerked back into motion and also the impulse it receives at this instant.

14. A body moving with initial speed 8 m s^{-1} is deflected by 60° and has its speed reduced to 5 m s^{-1} as a result of an impact with a stationary body of equal mass. Find the speed with which the second body moves after impact. (Take unit vectors along and perpendicular to the initial direction of motion.)

15. Two bodies A and B of masses 3 kg and 4 kg respectively collide when moving with velocities $4\mathbf{i} + 3\mathbf{j}$ m s^{-1} and $-5\mathbf{i} + \mathbf{j}$ m s^{-1}. After the impact they move in directions parallel to the vectors $\mathbf{j}$ and $4\mathbf{i} + \mathbf{j}$ respectively. Find the speeds of the bodies after impact and the vector representing the impulse received by A.

11.3 Work and Kinetic Energy (K.E.)

We have seen that the product, force × time, (i.e. impulse) is of use in a number of situations. We now consider the product, force × distance, which is of similar importance.

When a force acting on a body moves it into a new position, then the 'point of application' of the force moves and we say the body does **work**.

(Fig. 5.) The amount of work done is measured by the product, force ×
distance, providing that the force remains constant.

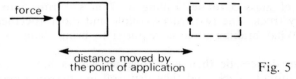

We are therefore defining **work** as follows

A FORCE IS SAID TO DO WORK WHEN IT MOVES ITS
POINT OF APPLICATION IN ITS OWN DIRECTION, AND
WORK DONE = FORCE × DISTANCE.

(For the work done by a changing force see section 18.5.) Notice that under
this definition a man pushing hard against a solid wall is not doing any
work, since the distance moved by his 'point of application' is zero.
Although clearly tiring himself, his effort is being wasted since he achieves
nothing.

The unit of work could be called the newton metre or Nm (in the same
way as the unit of impulse is called the newton second), but it is generally
called the **joule**. 1 joule may be defined as the work done when a force of 1
newton moves its point of application through 1 metre.

An important concept in applied mathematics and science in general is
that of **energy**. Basically a body is said to possess energy if it has the capacity
for doing work. (The underlying assumption behind the concept being that it
is possible for energy to be converted into work and vice-versa.) There are
many different sources of energy: to give one example, certain chemicals
possess energy which may be released on detonation and utilised in doing
work accelerating a gunshot or opening the door of a safe.

The first type of energy we shall be concerned with is that known as
kinetic energy. This may be defined as the energy a body possesses due to
movement. There are many situations in which the movement of a body is
used to do work. For example: to drive a nail into a block of wood, work
must be done against the resistance offered by the wood. This work is obtained from the kinetic energy of the moving hammer head.

We shall now derive a link between work and kinetic energy. Consider
Fig. 6 in which a horizontal force F accelerates a body from initial speed u to
final speed v. If the force is constant the acceleration will be uniform and
such that $F = ma$. We may therefore write

$$v^2 - u^2 = 2as$$

Multiplying by m $\quad mv^2 - mu^2 = 2(ma)s = 2Fs$

$$\Rightarrow \quad Fs = \tfrac{1}{2}mv^2 - \tfrac{1}{2}mu^2$$

If we use the quantity $\tfrac{1}{2}mv^2$ as a measure of kinetic energy then this equation
may be interpreted as

work done = change in K.E.

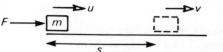

Fig. 6

Note: the unit of K.E. is the same as that of work, i.e. the joule. Thus a body of mass 5 kg moving at 4 m s^{-1} has K.E. $= 1/2 \times 5 \times 16 = 40$ joules.

Example 75

A body of mass 8 kg moves a distance of 10 metres under the action of a force of 16 N. How much kinetic energy does the body gain? If it was moving initially with speed 3 m s^{-1}, what will be its new speed?

The force does work $16 \times 10 = 160$ joules and this will increase the K.E. of the body by the same amount

that is   increase in K.E. $= 160$ joules

the initial K.E. of the body is $1/2 \times 8 \times 9 = \quad 36$ joules
the final K.E. is therefore $\qquad 36 + 160 = 196$ joules

$$\tfrac{1}{2}mv^2 = 196$$
$$4v^2 = 196$$

final speed $= 7$ m s^{-1}

Example 76

A block of 1/2 kg, initially at rest, is moved 5 metres across a rough horizontal surface by a force of 3.2 N. If the speed reached is 6 m s^{-1}, find the co-efficient of friction.

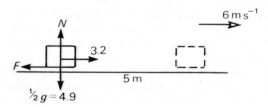

Fig. 7

In this question the friction force F does work *against* the motion. This work will reduce the K.E. of the block. We may therefore write

change in K.E. $= (5 \times 3.2) -$ work done by F
$1/2 \times 1/2 \times 36 = 16 - 5\,F$
$\Rightarrow$ friction $= 1.4$ N

Since the normal reaction N will equal 4.9 N the co-efficient of friction

$$\mu = \frac{1.4}{4.9} = \frac{2}{7}$$

Exercise 11(c)

1. Find the kinetic energy of the following:
   (i)   A rock of mass 12 kg falling at 20 m s^{-1}
   (ii) A table tennis ball of mass 2.6 g moving with speed 10 m s^{-1}
   (iii) A lorry of mass 8 tonnes moving at 45 km h^{-1}
   (iv) A particle of mass 100 g moving with velocity $5\mathbf{i} - 7\mathbf{j}$ m s^{-1}.
2. What will be the kinetic energy of a body of mass 6 kg initially at rest, after it has been accelerated through a distance of 15 m by a force of 12 N? With what speed will it now be moving?
3. A force of 15 newtons moves a body of mass 4 kg through a distance of 60 cm. How much work is done? What will be the speed of the body (i) if it was initially at rest (ii) if it was moving initially with speed 2 m s^{-1} in the same direction as the force?
4. What force is required to accelerate a car of mass 0.8 tonnes from 10 m s^{-1} to 15 m s^{-1} over a distance of 40 metres (neglect resistances). If the same force is maintained through what further distance will the car travel before its speed in increased to 20 m s^{-1}?
5. A body moving under the action of a force of 25 N is accelerated from 5 m s^{-1} to 7 m s^{-1} in a distance of 3 metres. Find the mass of the body.
6. What constant braking force is required to bring a bus of mass 18 tonnes moving at a speed of 30 km h^{-1} to rest in a distance of 15 metres?
7. A stone of mass m slides on a rough horizontal surface. If the co-efficient of friction is μ how much kinetic energy does it lose whilst sliding a distance d? How far does it travel in the time that its speed is reduced from v to $v/2$?
8. A block of mass 400 g initially at rest on a rough horizontal surface is moved through a distance of 90 cm by a force of 3 N. If the co-efficient of friction is 1/4 what speed does the block acquire?
9. A car of mass 0.8 tonnes is pushed from rest by two people each of whom exerts a force of 55 N. If after 30 metres the speed of the car is $5/2$ m s^{-1}, find the resistance to motion (assumed constant).
10. What force is required to accelerate a body of mass 40 kg from 12 m s^{-1} to 16 m s^{-1} in a distance of 8 metres when there is a resistance to motion of 70 N? If this force then ceases, find how far the body travels before it is again moving at 12 m s^{-1}.
11. A cyclist starting from rest exerts an average force of 80 N over a distance of 15 metres and then free-wheels. If he travels a further 45 metres before coming to rest, find the total force resisting motion. What is the greatest kinetic energy of the cyclist during the motion?
12. With its engine producing a thrust of 300 newtons, a motorboat doubles its initial speed in a distance d. The engine is then switched off. If the boat comes to rest in a further distance $2d$, find the resistance to motion offered by the water.

11.4 Potential Energy (P.E.)

The reader may have noticed that in all the exercises of the previous section motion took place on a given horizontal level. This is because a complication is introduced when we consider the possibility of bodies being at different levels or heights.

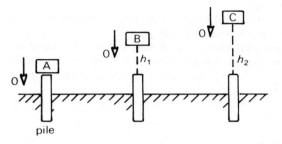

pile   Fig. 8

Imagine that a 'pile' is being driven into the ground at a building site. Consider 'pile-drivers' A, B and C held stationary in the positions shown in Fig. 8. As all three are at rest, none possesses kinetic energy. Unless the ground is exceptionally soft, A will not be able to drive in the pile. We would expect B, however, to drive in the pile if it is dropped from its higher position. B may therefore be said to possess energy, since it has the capacity for doing work. This type of energy, which is due solely to the extra height of B's position, is called **potential energy**.

The pile-driver C will have greater potential energy than B, since it may be expected to drive the pile further into the ground. Thus the higher the position of a body, the greater will be its potential energy.

If we wish to maintain our idea that work and energy are interchangeable, it is logical to measure the potential energy of a body in terms of the work which must be done to raise the body to its higher position.

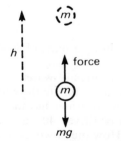

Fig. 9

If the mass of the body is m, the least force needed to lift the body is equal to its weight mg, and the work done in raising it to height h is therefore

force mg × distance $h = mgh$ (Fig. 9)

We may therefore make the following definition:

POTENTIAL ENERGY IS THE ENERGY POSSESSED BY A BODY BY VIRTUE OF BEING AT A GREATER HEIGHT THAN ITS SURROUNDINGS. IT IS MEASURED BY THE QUANTITY mgh.

The height h may be measured from any convenient level (referred to as the 'zero level for potential energy'). This is normally, but not necessarily, chosen as ground level.

We now have three quantities which are interchangeable. To return to our initial example, the **work** needed to lift pile-driver B to height h_1 above the pile is stored as **potential energy**. As B falls it loses its **potential energy** but gains instead **kinetic energy**. Finally this is converted back to **work** driving in the pile, (although we shall see in section 11.6 that some energy is lost in the impact).

Example 77

How much work must be done by a crane in order to lift a 200 kg packing case to a height of 6 m above the ground? If the case is dropped from this position, with what speed will it strike the ground?

The work done by the crane will be equal to the P.E. acquired by the packing case:

i.e $mgh = 200 \times 9.8 \times 6 = 11,760$ joules

When the case strikes the ground all of this potential energy will have been converted into K.E. We therefore have

$$\tfrac{1}{2}mv^2 = 11\ 760$$
$$v^2 = 117.6 \qquad \text{speed} = 10.85 \text{ m s}^{-1}$$

The second part could, of course, be solved by using the uniform acceleration equations.

Exercise 11(d)

1. How much work is done in lifting a mass of 80 kg through a height of 5 metres?

2. A dam contains 8000 million litres of water. If the water descends 150 metres to the generating station, estimate the energy which the dam may be considered to store. (1 litre of water has mass 1 kg.)

*3. A stake of mass 500 g is to be driven 40 cm into a sloping bank which offers a resistance of 20 N. How much work must be done to drive it in (i) horizontally, (ii) vertically downwards? Explain briefly why these answers differ.

*4. (i) A falling body accelerates at rate g. Use the uniform acceleration equations to obtain an expression for the square of the velocity attained in falling through a vertical distance h from the rest. Hence show that the kinetic energy gained by the body is equal to the potential energy it has lost.

　(ii) How much kinetic energy is gained by a falling body of mass 5 kg during each metre of its descent?

5. After falling vertically through 20 metres from rest, a stone has kinetic energy 5 joules. Find the mass of the stone. What further distance will the stone fall before its velocity has doubled?

6. A body of mass m kg is at rest on horizontal ground. W joules of work are done in lifting the body to a certain height above the ground. The body is then allowed to fall. With what speed will it strike the ground? If the body does not rebound, find also the impulse which it receives on impact.

7. The potential energy of a large body may be found by considering all of its mass to be concentrated at the centre of gravity. A paving stone lying flat on the ground has mass 12 kg and dimensions 80 cm × 50 cm. How much work must be done in order to rotate the stone about one of its shorter edges into an upright position? (Neglect the thickness of the stone.)

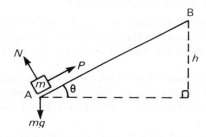

Fig. 10

*8. (i) In Fig. 10, what must be the magnitude of the force P in order that the mass m is just moved up the incline, which is smooth. Show that the work done by P in moving the mass from A to B is mgh, i.e. equal to the potential energy gained by the mass.

(ii) How much work must be done by a conveyor belt ascending at an angle of 13° to the horizontal in order to carry a 300 g carton through a distance of 4 metres?

*9. (i) If the mass m of question 8 is released from rest at B, find its acceleration down the incline (assumed smooth). Hence show that the kinetic energy it possesses on its return to A is mgh, i.e. equal to the loss in potential energy.

(ii) A container of mass 200 kg slides a distance of 20 m down a smooth ramp inclined at 18° to the horizontal. What speed does it acquire?

10. How much work must be done to drag a 50 kg container 20 metres up an incline of 20° against a frictional resistance of 120 N?

11. A pendulum consists of a point mass attached to the end of a light string of length 50 cm. The mass is pulled aside until the string is an angle of arcsin 3/5 with the downward vertical and then released. Assuming that any potential energy lost is converted into kinetic energy, find the maximum speed of the mass in the subsequent motion.

12. The cross-section of a prism of mass 1/2 kg is a right-angled triangle whose shorter sides are 9 cm and 12 cm. The prism rests with the face containing the 12 cm edges in contact with a horizontal surface. It is then turned over onto the face containing the 9 cm edges. Find the highest position of the centre of gravity in this motion and hence find the work which must be done. How much work must be done to reverse the process?

11.5 The Work-Energy Principle

(In this section the abbreviations K.E. and P.E. will be used for kinetic energy and potential energy respectively.)

In section 11.3, where we restricted ourselves to the consideration of bodies moving on a given horizontal level, we found that

work done by force = change in K.E.

We have now seen, however, that the work done by a force can be utilised in lifting a body to a higher level, i.e. in increasing the P.E. of the body. It is therefore logical to extend the above result to

work done by force = change in total energy

where by 'total energy' is meant the sum of the K.E. and the P.E. of the body concerned. (This is sometimes called the mechanical energy of the body.)

In applying this new result to the study of motion there are two important cases to consider:

(i) **Cases where no external force does work.** If no force does work on a body, then its total (mechanical) energy will remain constant throughout its motion. (This is sometimes called the **principle of conservation of mechanical energy.**)

Some examples of this type of motion were encountered in exercise 11(d). Thus the falling body of question 4 moves in such a way that the potential energy it loses as it falls is converted into an equal quantity of kinetic energy. The total energy of the falling body therefore remains constant. In question 9 the same result was found to be true for a body sliding down a smooth incline. This is because the normal reaction N in Fig. 11a does no work on the body – its point of application is never moved in the same direction as the force N.

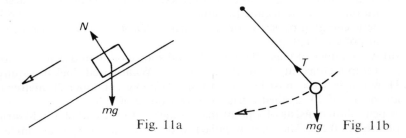

Fig. 11a   Fig. 11b

A similar example is that of the pendulum. (Fig. 11b.) As motion is always perpendicular to the line of the string, the tension force T never does any work and the pendulum must therefore move in such a way that its total energy is conserved.

Note: We need not concern ourselves with work done by the weight of the body, since this is essentially what is measured by potential energy.

(ii) **Cases where external forces do work.** In general any such forces may be divided into two categories:

'driving forces' those forces which tend to accelerate or help the motion
'resistances' those forces which act against the motion
Forces of the first kind will increase the energy of the moving body, whereas those of the second kind progressively eat away the energy. In fact we may write

$$\frac{\text{original}}{\text{energy}} + \frac{\text{work done by}}{\text{driving forces}} - \frac{\text{work done}}{\text{by resistances}} = \frac{\text{final}}{\text{energy}}$$

This is called the **work-energy principle**. The application of this principle is illustrated by the following two examples.

Example 78

A body slides down a rough plane of inclination arcsin (3/5). If the co-efficient of friction is 0.25, find the distance covered by the body in increasing its speed from 5 m s^{-1} to 7 m s^{-1}.

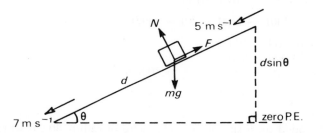

Fig. 12

In this motion energy is lost doing work against the frictional resistance F. Letting the distance covered by the body be d, and taking a zero P.E. level as shown in Fig. 12 we have

original energy − work done by F = final energy

that is $(\frac{1}{2}m5^2 + mgd \sin \theta) - Fd = \frac{1}{2}m7^2$ (1)

But $F = \mu N = \frac{1}{4}(mg \cos \theta) = \frac{1}{4}\left(\frac{4mg}{5}\right) = \frac{mg}{5}$ so that

equation (1) becomes

$(\frac{1}{2}m5^2 + \frac{3}{5}mgd) - \frac{1}{5}mgd = \frac{1}{2}m7^2$

$\Rightarrow \frac{2}{5}mgd = \frac{1}{2}m(49 - 25) = 12m$

cancelling m $d = \dfrac{30}{g} = 3.06$

Example 79

In Fig. 13 a cyclist, whose mass together with his machine is 80 kg, starts from rest at A and free-wheels downhill to B and along the flat to C. If there is a constant frictional resistance of 20 N, what average force must he now exert over the section of road CD in order just to reach the hilltop D?

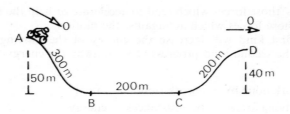

Fig. 13

There is no need to divide a motion such as this into stages. We may solve this problem by comparing the total energy of the cyclist in positions A and D. If the cyclist just reaches D as his velocity becomes zero then in both positions he possesses only potential energy.

Letting the driving force exerted by the cyclist over the section CD be P N, we have

$$\text{initial energy} + \text{work done by cyclist} - \text{work done by friction} = \text{final energy}$$

$$mg\,50 + 200P - (700 \times 20) = mg40$$

$$200P = 14\,000 - 10\,mg$$
$$= 14\,000 - 800g$$
$$\text{hence} \quad P = 70 - 4g = 30.8 \text{ N}$$

Exercise 11(e)

1. A bead is threaded on a smooth circular wire of radius 40 cm which is fixed in a vertical plane. The bead is given a small displacement from equilibrium at the highest point of the wire. Explain why mechanical energy is conserved in the ensuing motion and find the greatest speed attained by the bead.

2. 500 joules of work are done on a body of mass 8 kg. In the process the body is lifted vertically through 5 m. What speed must the body acquire if it was originally at rest?

3. A particle of mass 20 g is allowed to fall vertically through a fluid which offers a resisting force of 0.1 N. Find the speed attained by the particle after falling 50 cm from rest.

*4. A projectile is fired at 20 m s^{-1} from a point 15 metres above horizontal ground. Find the speed with which the projectile hits the ground and explain why this is independent of the angle of projection.

5. A body is projected up an incline of 30° at speed 10 m s^{-1}. Find the speed of the body after it has travelled 5 m
   (i) if the incline is smooth
   (ii) if the incline is rough and $\mu = 0.2$.

6. A truck of mass 15 tonnes begins to roll down an incline of arcsin (1/120). After 200 metres the track becomes level. How far from the foot of the incline will the truck come to rest if there is a constant resistance to motion of 900 N?

7. A point mass M attached by a light string to a fixed point O is released from rest in a position where OM is at 60° to the downward vertical. If

there is a peg at a distance $\frac{1}{4}$ OM vertically below O, find the angle between the lower part of the string and the vertical when the mass is next instantaneously at rest.

8. A body of mass 2 kg lies 30 cm from the edge of a rough horizontal table. The co-efficient of friction is 1/3. The body is connected by a light string running perpendicular to the edge of the table to a second body of mass 1.5 kg which hangs freely. Motion is allowed to take place from rest. Use the work-energy principle to find the speed with which the first body leaves the table.

9. A boy on a push-cart, with total mass 25 kg, is pushed for 13 metres up an incline of arcsin (1/35) by a friend who exerts an average force of 20 N over this distance. Find the total distance which the cart travels up the incline before it is again at rest, given that there is a constant frictional resistance of 6 N. Find also the greatest speed reached during the motion.

10. At a fairground the carriages of a big-dipper are hauled at a speed of 1 m s^{-1} to the top of the first rise, which is 15 metres above ground level, and then released. There are 40 metres of track before the top of the next rise which is 11 metres above the ground. If the speed of the carriages at this point is 5 m s^{-1}, find the frictional resistance per tonne, assuming this to remain constant. If the run finishes at ground level, what is the greatest possible length of track which may be used? Find also the highest rise which may be crossed at the point where 100 metres of track have been run.

11. A particle fired up a rough plane inclined at arctan (3/4) to the horizontal is found to return subsequently through the point of projection with half of its original speed. Find the co-efficient of friction.

11.6 Energy Loss in an Impact.

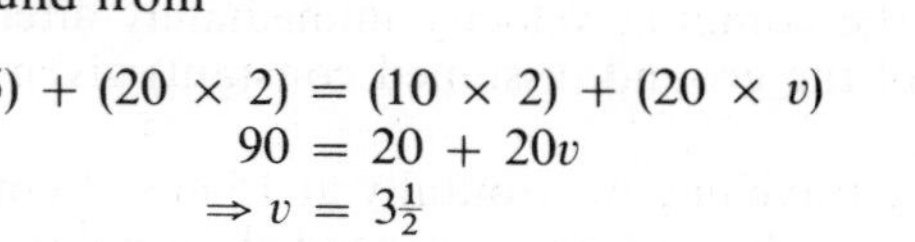

Fig. 14

In Section 11.2 we saw that momentum is conserved in an impact between two bodies. Thus in Fig. 14 the velocity v m s^{-1} of the 20 kg mass after the impact is found from

$$(10 \times 5) + (20 \times 2) = (10 \times 2) + (20 \times v)$$
$$90 = 20 + 20v$$
$$\Rightarrow v = 3\tfrac{1}{2}$$

If we now calculate the total kinetic energy of the two bodies before and after the impact we find

total K.E. before impact $= (1/2 \times 10 \times 25) + (1/2 \times 20 \times 4)$
$\qquad\qquad\qquad\qquad = 165$ joules

total K.E. after impact $= (1/2 \times 10 \times 4) + (1/2 \times 20 \times 12.25)$
$\qquad\qquad\qquad\qquad = 142.5$ joules

i.e. 22.5 joules of energy have been lost in the impact. (More correctly we should say that they have been converted into non-mechanical forms of energy such as heat and sound, and also in doing work deforming the bodies – see section 14.4.)

It is true to say that mechanical energy is lost in almost all impacts. In problems involving an impact we must be careful that the moment of impact is dealt with separately in accordance with the laws of momentum. Energy may be conserved in the motion prior to impact, or in that after impact, but it will not be conserved across the impact.

Note: In certain other situations where momentum is conserved, the bodies concerned may *gain* mechanical energy, e.g. the firing of a gun (where both the shot and the recoiling gun acquire kinetic energy from the detonation of the chemical charge).

Exercise 11 (f)

1. A 3 tonne truck rolling at 4 m s^{-1} overtakes a 5 tonne truck rolling at 2 m s^{-1} in the same direction. The trucks couple and move together after impact. Find the loss of energy at the impact.

2. Bodies of masses 3 kg and 2 kg collide when travelling with velocities $5\mathbf{i}$ and $-3\mathbf{i} \text{ m s}^{-1}$ respectively. The velocity of the 2 kg mass is exactly reversed by the impact. Find the new velocity of the 3 kg mass and the energy lost in the impact.

3. Two equal masses moving with velocities $3\mathbf{i} - 5\mathbf{j}$ and $5\mathbf{i} + \mathbf{j} \text{ m s}^{-1}$ coalesce on impact. Find the velocity vector of the resulting body and show that one-third of the total kinetic energy of the masses is lost in the impact.

4. A pistol of mass 500 g fires a bullet of mass 10 g with a speed of 200 m s^{-1}. Find the energy created by the detonation of the charge. How much work must be done to arrest the recoil of the pistol?

5. A 'perfectly elastic' collision is one in which no energy is lost. If such a collision occurs between masses of 2 kg and 5 kg moving with speeds 9 m s^{-1} and 2 m s^{-1} in the same direction, find the velocities of the masses after the impact.

6. A pile-driver of mass 600 kg falls from a height of 5 metres onto a pile of mass 100 kg. Find the common velocity immediately after impact and also the resistance of the ground (assumed constant) given that the pile penetrates by 25 cm.

7. A pellet of mass 10 g travelling horizontally at 15 m s^{-1} embeds itself in a lump of putty of mass 40 g which is suspended on a string of length 1 metre. Through what angle will the string turn before it is next momentarily at rest?

8. A nail of mass m is being driven horizontally into a wall. It is struck by a hammer head of mass M which is moving horizontally with speed v. If the hammer does not rebound on impact and if the nail is driven in a distance d by the blow, find an expression for the resisting force offered by the wall.

9. Two equal pans of mass M hang at rest on the ends of a light cord which passes over a smooth beam. A body of mass m falls vertically into one of the pans striking it with speed v and not rebounding.
    (i) Use momentum to find the speed with which the pans begin to move.
    (ii) Use energy to find the distance moved by the pans before their speed has doubled.

10. A shot of mass m is fired from a gun of mass M which is free to recoil in the opposite direction. If the detonation of the charge releases energy E, find the initial kinetic energy of the shot and explain why this may be expected to be considerably larger than the kinetic energy of the recoiling gun.

*11. A bullet of mass m travelling horizontally with speed v penetrates a fixed wooden block and is brought to rest. The energy lost by the bullet is $E = \frac{1}{2}mv^2$. If the block had been free to move on a smooth horizontal surface, find the common velocity which would be reached by the block and the bullet and show that the energy lost by the system in this case is $ME/(M + m)$ where M is the mass of the block. On the assumption that all of this energy is used in doing work against the resistance of the wood (assumed constant) show that the ratio of the penetrations in the two cases is $(M + m):M$.

12

Power

12.1 Power

The **power** of a machine measures the rate at which it can do work, i.e. the number of joules of work it is capable of doing each second. The unit used is the **watt** which is a rate of working of 1 joule per second. Most commonly encountered machines, however, are rated in terms of the **kilowatt** (or kW) which is equivalent to 1000 watts, or a rate of working of 1000 joules per second.

Thus a machine of power 2 kW would take 5 seconds to complete a task requiring 10 000 joules of work. A more 'powerful' machine could do the job more quickly since it would be able to get through more of the work each second. A $2\frac{1}{2}$ kW machine, for example, would complete the task in 4 seconds.

A machine does not have to work to its full capacity. It is therefore customary to talk of the power being *developed* by a machine in a given situation, as opposed to the maximum power output of which it is capable. The power developed by a machine is best found by considerations of energy, as the following example illustrates.

Example 80

Find the power developed by each of the following machines:
(i) A crane lifting a load of 200 kg at a steady speed of 2.5 m s^{-1}.
(ii) A lorry of mass 10 tonnes accelerating from 8 m s^{-1} to 12 m s^{-1} in a time of 5 seconds.
(iii) A pump lifting 50 litres of water through 6 metres in 8 seconds and discharging it through a hose at 6 m s^{-1}.

(i) During each second the 200 kg load is lifted through 2.5 m and therefore gains potential energy $200 \times 9.8 \times 2.5 = 4900$ joules. The crane must therefore be working at the rate of 4900 joules per second, which is 4.9 kW.
(ii) The kinetic energy of the lorry increases by

$$\frac{10\,000(144 - 64)}{2} = 5000 \times 80 = 400\,000 \text{ joules}$$

Since this happens in 5 seconds the average rate at which the engine must be working is 80 000 J s^{-1}, that is 80 kW.
(iii) Here we must consider both the potential energy and the kinetic energy gained by the water. Since 1 litre of water has mass 1 kg we have

P.E. gained by water $50 \times 9.8 \times 6 = 2940$ joules
K.E. gained by water $1/2 \times 50 \times 36 = 900$ joules

total work done in 8 seconds $= 3840$ joules

Thus the power developed by the pump is 480 J s^{-1}, that is 480 watts.

Exercise 12(a)

(1 litre of water has mass 1 kg.)

1. A winch raises a load of 25 kg through 20 metres in 7 seconds. What power does this require?
2. A car of mass 840 kg accelerates from rest to a speed of 25 m s^{-1} in 12 seconds. Find, to the nearest kW, the average power developed by the engine.
3. A man of mass 70 kg runs up stairs at the rate of 5 steps per second. At what rate is he working if each step is 16 cm high?
4. A crane working at 7 kW lifts a container at a steady speed of 0.6 m s^{-1}. What is the mass of the container?
5. 50 cubic metres of water pass each minute over a waterfall 15 metres high. If the energy of the water could be harnessed, what power would be available? (Consider P.E. only.)
6. A cyclist who, together with his machine, has mass 80 kg is travelling at 7 m s^{-1} on a horizontal track. If he sprints for 10 seconds, maintaining a work rate of 500 watts over this period, what speed will he reach? (Ignore resistances.)
7. (i) A pump delivers water at 12 m s^{-1} through a nozzle of internal cross-section 6 cm^2. What mass of water is discharged each second? Hence find the power at which the pump is working.
   (ii) The same pump is now used to raise water to a higher level. If the speed at which the water issues from the nozzle is now 10 m s^{-1}, find the vertical height through which it is being raised. (Assume the pump is working at the same rate as before.)
8. A car of mass 1 tonne ascending an incline of arcsin(1/20) accelerates uniformly from 10 m s^{-1} to 15 m s^{-1} in a distance of 50 metres. If there is a resistance to motion of 70 N, calculate the total work done by the engine during this period and hence deduce the average power developed.
9. (i) Show that the power needed to deliver a jet of water through a nozzle of given diameter is proportional to the cube of the velocity with which the jet is discharged.
   (ii) A pump working at 10 kW delivers water to a fire-hose. If the diameter of the nozzle is 3 cm at what speed does the jet issue and what is the furthest distance that the water may be thrown?

12.2 Power Developed by a Car or Train

Fig. 1

Consider a car travelling at speed v with its engine producing a forward thrust or 'driving force' D (Fig. 1). In one second the point of application of the force D will move forward by v units of distance, so that the work done by the engine is $D \times v$ units per second, that is,

power developed $= Dv$

If the driving force, D, is greater or less than the resistance to motion, R, then the velocity will in fact be changing. The above result, however, is still correct for the power developed at an instant, v being taken as the velocity at that instant.

12.3 Power Needed to Maintain a Steady Speed

In order to maintain a steady speed the driving force need only balance the resistance, i.e. $D = R$. Thus if a car is travelling against a constant resisting force of 500 N we have

Power needed to maintain 15 m s^{-1} $500 \times 15 = 7\,500$ watts
Power needed to maintain 20 m s^{-1} $500 \times 20 = 10\,000$ watts
Power needed to maintain 25 m s^{-1} $500 \times 25 = 12\,500$ watts

The greater the speed of the car the greater is the power required. There will therefore be a maximum speed at which the engine is developing its full power. In the example considered, if the power of the engine is 18 kW then the top-speed v against a resistance of 500 N is such that $500 \times v = 18\,000$, i.e. 36 m s^{-1}. We notice that this is independent of the mass of the car (though this will affect acceleration and hence the time taken for this speed to be reached).

Note: In practice the resisting force will not remain constant as the speed increases. It is generally the sum of two parts; a frictional resistance which is fairly constant, and air resistance which increases roughly as the square of the speed.

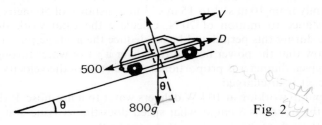

500
800g
Fig. 2

The maximum speed a car can maintain is clearly affected by a gradient in the road. In ascending an incline the engine will have to overcome an additional 'resisting force' due to the component of the car's weight which acts down the incline. Thus if the car in our example has mass 800 kg and the incline is 1 in 20 [$\arcsin(1/20)$] we have

total resistance $= 500 + 800g \sin \theta$
$= 500 + 40g = 892$ N

At top-speed, $D = 892$ N also, and $Dv = 18\ 000$. Hence the maximum speed on this incline is

$$v = \frac{18\ 000}{892} = 20.2 \text{ m s}^{-1}$$

When running down an incline the component of the car's weight will help the engine by *reducing* the effective resistance to motion.

Exercise 12(b)

1. What power must a cyclist develop in order to maintain a speed of 24 km h^{-1} against a resistance of 15 N?
2. At its top-speed of 100 km h^{-1} the engine of a lorry is developing 40 kW of power. What is the resistance to motion at this speed?
3. A motorbike is travelling at 24 m s^{-1} against a resistance of 320 N. What power is being developed? If the resistance is proportional to the square of the speed, what power would be required at 30 m s^{-1}?
4. A car of mass 750 kg is ascending an incline of arcsin(1/25) against resistances of 200 N. What power is required to maintain a speed of 60 km h^{-1}?
5. A 3-tonne lorry travelling at 54 km h^{-1} on the level is working at 12 kW. What power must it develop in order to maintain the same speed on an incline of arcsin(1/20), resistances remaining the same?
6. A cyclist has to dismount when his speed is reduced to 2 m s^{-1}, at which speed the resistance to motion is 10 N. If the total mass of the cyclist and his machine is 90 kg, show that the steepest hill he can ascend when working at 240 watts is approximately 1 in 8.
7. A train of mass 250 tonnes is ascending an incline of 1 in 200 at 20 m s^{-1}. If the engine is working at 565 kW, find the resistance to motion at this speed. At what rate would the engine be working when the train is travelling at the same speed down the incline?
8. The total force resisting the motion of a small car is of the form $(a + bv^2)$ N, where v m s^{-1} is the speed of the car and a and b are constants. At 10 m s^{-1} the car develops 5/2 kW of power and at 20 m s^{-1} it develops 8 kW. Find the values of a and b. If the maximum speed of the car is 26 m s^{-1}, what is the greatest power the engine can develop?
9. A cyclist working at 200 watts can maintain a speed of 5 m s^{-1} up an incline of 1 in 28 and 10 m s^{-1} down the same incline. If the resistance to motion is proportional to the square of the speed, find the total mass of the cyclist and his machine and also the resistance opposing his motion at 5 m s^{-1}. At what rate would he need to work in order to maintain 10 m s^{-1} on the flat?
10. A lorry of mass M is travelling against a uniform resistance. The maximum speed of the lorry up an incline of angle θ is v and the maximum speed down the same incline is $2v$. If the engine develops the same power P in each case, show that $\sin \theta = P/(4Mgv)$ and find the maximum speed on the level.

11. The power required to maintain a steady speed v against a resistance of the form $a + bv^2$ (where a and b are constants) is P. The power required to maintain speed $2v$ is $3P$. Find the power required to maintain speed $3v$.

12.4 Power and Acceleration

If an engine can produce power P, then the maximum drive force available at a given speed v will be given by $D = P/v$ (in accordance with the result power $= Dv$). So for the car of power $18\ \text{kW}$ considered in section 12.3 we would have

at $10\ \text{m s}^{-1}$ maximum drive force $= 18\ 000/10 = 1800\ \text{N}$
$20\ \text{m s}^{-1}$ maximum drive force $= 18\ 000/20 = \ \ 900\ \text{N}$
$30\ \text{m s}^{-1}$ maximum drive force $= 18\ 000/30 = \ \ 600\ \text{N}$

In practice the power available will not be the same at all speeds, and will depend also on which gear is engaged, but the basic point illustrated by these figures, i.e. that the drive force available decreases as the speed increases, will still apply.

In order to calculate the maximum acceleration possible in a given case we must first subtract the total resisting force in order to obtain the overall forward force on the car. If the car considered above has mass $800\ \text{kg}$ and is travelling against a resistance of $500\ \text{N}$, the following results are obtained.

speed	overall forward force	acceleration
$10\ \text{m s}^{-1}$	$1800 - 500 = 1300\ \text{N}$	$1.625\ \text{m s}^{-2}$
$20\ \text{m s}^{-2}$	$900 - 500 = \ \ 400\ \text{N}$	$0.500\ \text{m s}^{-2}$
$30\ \text{m s}^{-1}$	$600 - 500 = \ \ 100\ \text{N}$	$0.125\ \text{m s}^{-2}$

Since, as has been mentioned, the resistance normally increases with speed, this 'tailing off' of acceleration will normally be even more pronounced than these figures suggest. As the top-speed of the car is approached, acceleration becomes very slow indeed.

Example 81

A car of mass $750\ \text{kg}$ can develop a power of $9\ \text{kW}$. When ascending an incline of 1 in 50 the top-speed of the car is $30\ \text{m s}^{-1}$. Assuming that the resistance to motion is proportional to the square of the speed, find the maximum acceleration the car can achieve when ascending the same incline at $20\ \text{m s}^{-1}$.

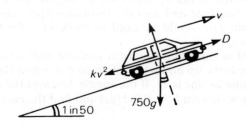

Fig. 3

The component of the weight down the incline is

$$\frac{1}{50} \times 750g = 15g = 147 \text{ N}$$

Using power $= DV$ the drive force available is $9000/30 = 300$ N at the top-speed of 30 m s^{-1} and $9000/20 = 450$ N at 20 m s^{-1}.

At top-speed $\quad D = $ total resistance
$$300 = 147 + K(30)^2 \quad\quad (K \text{ constant})$$
$$\Rightarrow \quad 900K = 153$$

At 20 m s^{-1} $\quad$ total resistance
$$= 147 + K(20)^2$$
$$= 147 + 4/9 \times 153 = 215 \text{ N}$$

The overall force produced at 20 m s^{-1} is therefore $450 - 215 = 235$ N and the acceleration, from $F = ma$, will be

$$\frac{235}{750} = 0.31 \text{ m s}^{-2}$$

Exercise 12(c)

1. At 12 m s^{-1} the resistance to motion experienced by a 3 tonne lorry is 400 N. If the engine can develop 30 kW, find the maximum acceleration which is possible at this speed (i) on the level (ii) when ascending an incline of arcsin$(1/20)$.
2. The resistance to motion experienced by a 5 tonne motor coach is $(700 + 2v^2)$ N where v is the speed of the coach in m s^{-1}. If the engine can develop 75 kW, find the maximum acceleration of the coach when travelling on a level road at (i) 15 m s^{-1} (ii) 25 m s^{-1}.
3. A railway engine has mass 90 tonnes and can work at 640 kW. Find the maximum acceleration it can achieve when pulling six 25 tonne coaches up a gradient of 1 in 200 at 80 km h^{-1}, given that resistances amount to 50 N per tonne. Find also the greatest number of such coaches with which the engine could maintain this speed on the incline.
4. A lorry of mass 3 tonnes is travelling at 60 km h^{-1} on a level road. If the engine is working at 30 kW, what is the resistance to motion at this speed? The road begins to rise with gradient 1 in 15. If the maximum power of the lorry is 45 kW, show that it cannot maintain its speed and find the least possible retardation at the start of the incline.
5. The top-speed of a car when ascending an incline of angle θ is v. Show that the maximum acceleration possible when the car travels at speed v on the level is $g \sin \theta$, assuming the resistance to motion at this speed to be unchanged. Find also the maximum acceleration possible when the car descends the same incline at speed v.
6. A car of mass 800 kg can develop a maximum power of $7\frac{1}{2}$ kW. When travelling on the level at 20 m s^{-1} the maximum acceleration of the car is 0.25 m s^{-2}. At a speed of 30 m s^{-1} the maximum acceleration is 0.0625 m s^{-2}. If the resistance to motion is of the form $(a + bv^2)$ N, where

v is the speed in m s^{-1}, find the values of the constants a and b. Show also that the top-speed of the car is between 34 and 35 m s^{-1}.

7. The resistance to the motion of a small car of mass 500 kg is $(135 + 3v/2)$ newtons, where v is the speed in m s^{-1}. If the power of the engine is 5.4 kW, find the maximum speed of the car and its maximum acceleration when travelling at 18 m s^{-1}.

13
Probability

13.1 Introduction

When a coin is tossed there is no reason to suppose that a 'head' is more likely or less likely to occur than a 'tail'. We say that the probability of obtaining a head is 1/2 and that the probability of obtaining a tail is also 1/2. This may be abbreviated as

$$p(\text{head}) = 1/2 \qquad p(\text{tail}) = 1/2$$

It is important to understand exactly what is meant by this. It does *not* mean that in every two tosses of the coin we will obtain one head and one tail. A more accurate interpretation is that in a large number of tosses we would expect about one-half to be heads and one-half to be tails. Experimentally we find that the larger the number of 'trials' the more closely our results agree with this. Consider, for example, the following experimental results in which the proportions of heads and tails obtained are measured by their 'relative frequencies' (i.e. number of occurrences ÷ number of trials).

number of trials	occurrences		relative frequencies	
	heads	tails	heads	tails
20	12	8	0.6	0.4
100	53	47	0.53	0.47
500	246	254	0.492	0.508

A further simple example is that of drawing a card from a well-shuffled pack of 52 playing cards. Here there are 52 possible 'outcomes' and again, there is no reason for supposing that any one of these is more likely to occur than another. In cases such as this, where all outcomes are equally likely, we may define the probability of a particular 'event' occurring as

$$\text{probability} = \frac{\text{number of successful outcomes}}{\text{total number of outcomes}}$$

where a 'successful' outcome is one in which the event concerned takes place.

Thus $p(\text{card is a diamond}) = \dfrac{13}{52} = \dfrac{1}{4}$

$$p(\text{card is a king or queen}) = \frac{8}{52} = \frac{2}{13}$$

$$p(\text{card is not an ace}) = \frac{48}{52} = \frac{12}{13}$$

The above definition only applies when all possible outcomes are equally likely. There are a number of situations in which the outcomes may appear, at first glance, to be equally likely but, in fact, are not so at all. For example, when adding the numbers thrown on two dice we may obtain eleven different results (from 2 to 12). It is wrong to say, however, that the probability of scoring 2 is 1/11, since these eleven different outcomes are not equally likely. We may see this by representing the number thrown on the first dice and that thrown on the second dice as an ordered pair. The following table shows that a score of 2 may only be obtained in 1 way, whereas a score of 3 is possible in 2 ways, and a score of 4 in 3 ways, etc.

score	ordered pairs			
2	(1, 1)			
3	(1, 2)	(2, 1)		
4	(1, 3)	(2, 2)	(3, 1)	
5	(1, 4)	(2, 3)	(3, 2)	(4, 1)

For each number which may occur on the first dice there are six possible numbers which may be thrown on the second. There are therefore thirty-six different ordered pairs and these are all equally likely. Thus, for example,

$$p(\text{score of 2}) = \frac{1}{36}$$

$$p(\text{score of 4}) = \frac{3}{36} \text{ or } \frac{1}{12}$$

$$p(\text{score of 5 or less}) = \frac{10}{36} \text{ or } \frac{5}{18}$$

Exercise 13(a)

1. With a single throw of a dice what is the probability of obtaining:
   (i)   a six
   (ii) a number greater than 2
   (iii) an even number?
2. In 'Russian roulette' one bullet is placed in a revolver which may take six bullets, the magazine is spun and the revolver held to the head and fired. What is the probability of survival?
3. In a year chosen at random, what is the probability that Christmas Day will fall at a week-end?
4. If a card is drawn from a standard pack of 52 playing cards, what is the probability that it is
   (i) a black card
   (ii) a picture card (king, queen or jack)

(iii) a black picture card

(iv) neither a black card nor a picture card?

5. If two pupils are selected at random from a class, what is the probability that both were born in the same month? (Assume that the chances of being born in each month are equal.)

6. A card is drawn from a pack and found to be the king of spades. If this card is not replaced, what is the probability that the next card drawn is

   (i) another king

   (ii) another spade?

7. If two dice are thrown, what is the probability that

   (i)   the two numbers add up to 6

   (ii) the two numbers add up to 9 or more

   (iii) the two numbers are equal

   (iv) there is no six

   (v)   there is at least one six?

8. List the possible outcomes when three coins are tossed and hence write down the probabilities of throwing

   (i)   two heads

   (ii) at least two heads

   (iii) all three coins the same

9. A domino is marked with two numbers from 0 to 6. If no two dominoes bear the same combination of numbers, how many are there in a complete set? What is the probability that a domino selected at random will

   (i)   contain a six

   (ii) have two equal numbers

   (iii) have a value of five (i.e. the total of the two numbers must be five)?

10. Manchester United and Liverpool are 2 of 16 teams remaining in the F.A. Cup. What is the probability that they will be drawn to play against one another in the next round?

11. Six people are to be seated at a round table. What is the probability that Mr. A is placed

    (i) opposite to Mr. B

    (ii) next to Mr. B? (Assume that the places are allocated at random.)

12. A colour-blind electrician is wiring a plug. The 'earth' lead must be connected to the correct terminal but, for the particular appliance concerned, it does not matter if the 'live' and 'neutral' leads are the wrong way round. What is the probability that the appliance will operate?

13.2 Permutations and Combinations

Eight sprinters are having a race. In how many ways can the first three places be filled? Since 8 different sprinters may finish first and, in each case, this leaves 7 who may come second and 6 who may come third, the answer is

$$8 \times 7 \times 6 \text{ or } \frac{8!}{5!}$$

This is the number of possible *orders* (or **permutations**) of 3 items chosen from 8. It is sometimes written $^8P_3$.

A slightly different situation arises if the race is a heat in which the first three to finish qualify for the next round. Here we may wish to know how many different sets of 3 sprinters can qualify. The order of the first 3 places is now immaterial; thus if A, B and C are three particular sprinters, the finishing orders

$$
\begin{array}{cccc}
A & B & C & \dots \\
B & C & A & \dots \\
B & A & C & \dots \text{ etc.}
\end{array}
$$

all lead to the same three sprinters qualifying. There are $3 \times 2 \times 1$ or 3! such orders in which the first three places may be filled by A, B and C. Since the same must be true for *every* possible set of three qualifiers and since, as we have seen, the total number of orders possible for the first three places is $8 \times 7 \times 6$, we deduce that the number of distinct sets of qualifiers must be ...

$$
\frac{8 \times 7 \times 6}{3 \times 2 \times 1} \text{ or } \frac{8!}{5! \, 3!}
$$

This is known as the number of **combinations** of 3 which may be chosen from 8 and is written $^8C_3$ for short.

Combinations are of particular importance in work on probability as the next two examples will illustrate. The following results will be needed

(i) $^nC_r = \dfrac{n!}{(n-r)! \, r!}$ e.g. $^{11}C_4 = \dfrac{11!}{7! \, 4!}$ or $\dfrac{11 \times 10 \times 9 \times 8}{4 \times 3 \times 2 \times 1}$

(ii) $^nC_r = {}^nC_{n-r}$ e.g. $^8C_5 = {}^8C_3$

The second result should be clear intuitively since, for example, each time a selection of 3 items is made from 8 there is automatically a simultaneous selection of 5 – those items which are rejected.

Example 82

In a Tombola there are 15 tickets left 3 of which win prizes. If I buy 4 tickets, what is the probability that I will win a prize?

The number of possible combinations of 4 tickets which I may receive is

$$
^{15}C_4 \text{ or } \frac{15 \times 14 \times 13 \times 12}{4 \times 3 \times 2 \times 1}
$$

If I am *not* to win a prize these 4 tickets must all have been selected from the 12 non-winning tickets. The number of ways in which this may be done is

$$
^{12}C_4 \text{ or } \frac{12 \times 11 \times 10 \times 9}{4 \times 3 \times 2 \times 1}
$$

Thus my probability of not winning is

$$^{12}C_4 \div {}^{15}C_4 = \frac{12 \times 11 \times 10 \times 9}{15 \times 14 \times 13 \times 12} = \frac{33}{91}$$

So p(winning) $= 1 - \dfrac{33}{91} = \dfrac{58}{91}$

Note: The probability required here is that of winning at least one prize (i.e. one prize or possibly more than one). The method used is the most direct way of calculating this.

Example 83

Of the 12 registered electors in Heath Close, 6 are Labour voters, 5 are Conservative and 1 is Liberal. A pollster speaks to 3 of these electors. What is the probability that
(i) the Liberal is interviewed
(ii) those interviewed are all Conservatives
(iii) one of each party is interviewed?

The number of distinct sets of 3 electors whom the pollster may call on is

$$^{12}C_3 = \frac{12 \times 11 \times 10}{3 \times 2 \times 1} = 220$$

(i) If the Liberal is one of the 3 interviewed, then the remaining 2 must be selected from the 11 Labour and Conservative voters. The number of ways in which this may be done is

$$^{11}C_2 = \frac{11 \times 10}{2 \times 1} = 55$$

thus required probability $= \dfrac{55}{220} = \dfrac{1}{4}$

(ii) The number of sets of 3 electors who are all Conservative is

$$^5C_3 = {}^5C_2 = \frac{5 \times 4}{2 \times 1} = 10$$

required probability $= \dfrac{10}{220} = \dfrac{1}{22}$

(iii) There are 6 different Labour supporters who may be interviewed, 5 different Conservatives but only 1 Liberal. Thus one of each party may be selected in $6 \times 5 \times 1 = 30$ ways.

required probability $= \dfrac{30}{220} = \dfrac{3}{22}$

Exercise 13(b)

1. A housewife selects 3 eggs at random from a box of 6. If 2 of the eggs in the box are bad, what is the probability that the eggs selected

(i) are all good

(ii) include one bad egg?

2. A transistor radio runs on two batteries. I have eight batteries in a box but three have already been used. If I select two batteries at random, what is the probability that the radio will operate?

3. Six places are available on a school outing. The names of the ten pupils who wish to go are placed in a hat and six names are drawn. What is the probability that

(i) Mary and her best friend are both chosen

(ii) only one of the two is chosen?

4. Six of the eighteen housewives in Grime Street use Fomo in preference to any other detergent. A market researcher interviews four of the house-wives. What is the probability that

(i) none of those interviewed uses Fomo

(ii) a majority of those interviewed uses Fomo?

5. A cut-price tyre-merchant has ten tyres of a particular size in stock, of which three are defective. He selects four tyres at random for a customer's car. What is the probability that

(i) exactly one is defective

(ii) at least one is defective?

6. A second survey, this time of 4 electors, is made in Heath Close (see example 83). Find the probability that of those interviewed

(i)   all are Labour voters

(ii) none are Conservative voters

(iii) a majority (i.e. 3 or 4) are Conservative voters.

7. In a game of Bridge, what is the probability of a player being dealt a hand containing

(i)   all four aces

(ii) three aces

(iii) all red cards

(iv) no ace nor picture card?

(Answers may be left in terms of combinations.)

8. A doctor treats 7 of 14 patients suffering from a certain disease with a new drug. The remaining 7 patients are given the old treatment. He finds that of 6 patients recovering, 4 are in the first group. On the assumption that there is no significant difference in the two treatments, calculate the pro-bability that 4 or more of the 6 patients recovering will have been given the new drug. Do you think the doctor is justified in claiming that the new treatment is more effective than the old?

13.3 Use of Set Notation

Set notation provides a convenient shorthand in the setting out of work on probability. In this section the main ideas are illustrated by reference to a simple example but the general results quoted always apply.

A single card is to be drawn from a pack. Considering the 52 playing cards to be our universal set $\mathscr{E}$ we may define subsets of $\mathscr{E}$ such as

$D = \{\text{diamonds}\}$
$A = \{\text{aces}\}$
$P = \{\text{picture cards, i.e. kings, queens, jacks}\}$
$B = \{\text{black cards}\}$

Given a particular set X we shall use $n(X)$ to denote the number of cards (or 'elements') within that set; thus $n(D) = 13$ and $n(A) = 4$, etc. By $p(X)$ we shall mean the probability that the single card drawn belongs to set X. For example

$$p(D) = \frac{1}{4} \quad p(A) = \frac{1}{13} \quad \text{etc.}$$

In general, where X is a subset of the set $\mathscr{E}$ of all possible outcomes, we may say (providing these outcomes are equally likely) that

$$p(X) = \frac{n(X)}{n(\mathscr{E})}$$

e.g. $p(D) = \dfrac{n(D)}{n(\mathscr{E})} = \dfrac{13}{52} = \dfrac{1}{4}$

Complement. If $D = \{\text{diamonds}\}$ then the **complement** of set D, denoted by D′, is defined as

$D' = \{\text{cards which are not diamonds}\}$
similarly $A' = \{\text{cards which are not aces.}\}$

The probability of drawing a card which is not a diamond may therefore be written as

$$p(D') = \frac{39}{52} = \frac{3}{4}$$

The relation between the sets D and D′ is illustrated by Fig. 1. (This type of diagram is known as a Venn diagram.)

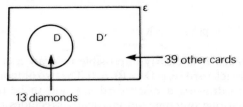

Fig. 1

Intersection. If the set $A = \{\text{aces}\}$ is added to Fig. 1, then since the ace of diamonds is within set D and the remaining three aces are within D′, we obtain Fig. 2a. The **intersection** (or overlap) of sets A and D (denoted $A \cap D$) is defined as the set of cards which belong in both A and D, i.e. which are both aces and diamonds. (There is only one card satisfying both these conditions.) Similarly $A \cap D'$ denotes the set of cards which belong in both A and D′, i.e. which are aces but which are *not* diamonds. Thus

$$A \cap D = \left\{ \text{ace} \diamondsuit \right\}$$
$$A \cap D' = \left\{ \text{ace} \heartsuit, \ \text{ace} \clubsuit, \ \text{ace} \spadesuit \right\}$$

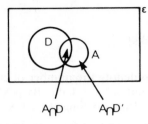 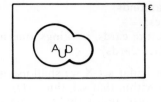

A∩P   A∩P'   Fig. 2

Using this notation the probability of drawing a card which is an ace but not a diamond could be written p(A ∩ D'). In the same way p(B ∩ P) would mean the probability of drawing a black picture card.

In fact $p(A \cap D') = \dfrac{3}{52}$ $p(B \cap P) = \dfrac{6}{52}$ or $\dfrac{3}{26}$

Union. The **union** of sets A and D (denoted A ∪ D) is the set obtained when the two sets A and D are combined together, (Fig. 2b). This set, which contains all the aces and all the diamonds, comprises 16 cards. (Care must be taken not to count the ace of diamonds twice.)

In fact $n(A \cup D) = n(A) + n(D) - n(A \cap D)$
$$16 = 4 \quad + 13 \quad - 1$$

By p(A ∪ D) we would mean the probability of drawing a card which is *either* an ace *or* a diamond. This probability is 16/52 or 4/13.

In general it is true that if X and Y are any two subsets of $\mathscr{E}$ then

$$n(X \cup Y) = n(X) + n(Y) - n(X \cap Y)$$

from which it follows that

$$\frac{n(X \cup Y)}{n(\mathscr{E})} = \frac{n(X)}{n(\mathscr{E})} + \frac{n(Y)}{n(\mathscr{E})} - \frac{n(X \cap Y)}{n(\mathscr{E})}$$

that is

$$p(X \cup Y) = P(X) + p(Y) - p(X \cap Y) \qquad (1)$$

Mutually exclusive events. It is clearly impossible to draw a card which is both a diamond and a black card i.e. p(D ∩ B) = 0. The two outcomes (i) drawing a diamond and (ii) drawing a black card are said to be **mutually exclusive**. This means that one outcome automatically precludes the other.

On the Venn diagram (Fig. 3) the sets D = {diamonds} and B = {black cards} are quite distinct (or 'disjoint'). They possess no intersection – we

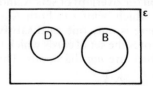

Fig. 3

sometimes write D ∩ B = φ, where φ is called the 'empty set'. (A set with nothing in it.)

In general two sets of outcomes X and Y are mutually exclusive if and only if $X \cap Y = \varphi$

i.e. $p(X \cap Y) = 0 \Leftrightarrow X \cap Y = \varphi$

When X and Y are mutually exclusive we see that equation (1) above reduces to

$$p(X \cup Y) = p(X) + p(Y)$$

Exercise 13(c)

1. The following are sets of outcomes when throwing 1 dice:

    P = {prime numbers}   O = {odd numbers}
    A = {4 or more}   B = {2 or less}

    Find p(P), p(P'), p(B'), p(O $\cap$ A), p(A $\cap$ P'), p(A $\cup$ B), p(A $\cap$ B), p(O' $\cap$ B).
2. The following are sets of outcomes when drawing 1 card from a standard pack of 52:

    H = {hearts}   C = {clubs}
    K = {kings}   P = {picture cards}

    Find p(H), p(C'), p(P'), p(H $\cap$ P), p(K $\cap$ H'), p(H $\cup$ C), p(C $\cup$ P), p(C $\cap$ K'), p(K $\cup$ P'), p(C' $\cap$ H').
3. (i) A and B are events such that p(A) = 0.3, p(A $\cap$ B) = 0.1 and p(A $\cup$ B) = 0.7. Find p(B), p(B'), p(A $\cap$ B') and p(A' $\cup$ B').
    (ii) If A and B are events such that p(A) = 1/3 and p(A $\cap$ B) = 1/12, find the greatest possible value of p(B) and the least possible value of p(A $\cup$ B).
4. (i) If A and B are mutually exclusive events, is it true that A' and B' are also mutually exclusive? Justify your answer by means of Venn diagrams.
    (ii) If A and B are mutually exclusive events and p(A) = 1/4 p(B) = 2/5, find p(A $\cup$ B) and p(A' $\cap$ B').
5. Justify the following results by means of Venn diagrams:
    (i)   p(A $\cup$ B) = p(A) + p(B) − p(A $\cap$ B)
    (ii) p(A $\cap$ B) + p(A $\cap$ B') = p(A)
    (iii) p(A' $\cap$ B') = 1 − p(A $\cup$ B)
6. The draw is about to take place for the quarter-finals of the F.A. Cup and the non-league team Chopham are one of the eight remaining teams.

    H = {Chopham are drawn at home}
    L = {Chopham are drawn against Leeds}

    Find p(H), p(L), p(H $\cap$ L), p(H $\cup$ L), p(H $\cup$ L').
7. Twelve athletes are divided into two groups of six for the preliminary heats in the 200 metres. The two competitors with the fastest times for the event are Mr. X and Mr. Y.

    X = {Mr. X drawn in the first heat}
    Y = {Mr. Y drawn in the first heat}

    Find p(X), p(X $\cap$ Y), p(X $\cup$ Y), p(X $\cap$ Y').

8. A further survey, this time of 4 electors, is made in Heath Close. (See example 83.)

> L = {at least one Labour voter is interviewed}
> C = {at least one Conservative voter is interviewed}

Find p(L′), p(C), p(L ∪ C), p(L ∩ C).

13.4 The Multiplication Law for Independent Events

Two events are said to be **independent** if the outcome of one cannot influence the outcome of the other in any way.

If two cards are drawn from a pack and the first card is replaced and the pack re-shuffled before the second is drawn, then the second card drawn cannot be affected by whichever card is drawn first. The results of the two draws would be independent.

In this situation, what would be the probability of drawing (i) 2 hearts (ii) 1 heart (iii) 0 heart? The different outcomes may conveniently be represented in what is termed a **tree-diagram**. (Fig. 4.)

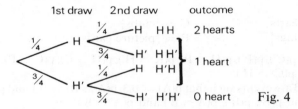

Fig. 4

The probabilities on each draw of obtaining a heart (H) or not a heart (H′) are 1/4 and 3/4 respectively. These are marked on the appropriate 'branches' of the tree diagram.

We shall use the notation HH, HH′ etc. to represent the outcomes {2 hearts}, {heart then not a heart} etc. Consider the occasions in which the first card drawn is a heart – to a good approximation this will be in one quarter of the cases if we consider a sufficiently large number of trials. In one quarter of these cases (i.e. in one-sixteenth of the original number of trials) we may expect to obtain a heart on the second draw, and in the remaining three-quarters (i.e. three-sixteenths of the original trials) a card which is not a heart. We therefore have

$$p(HH) = \frac{1}{16} \quad p(HH') = \frac{3}{16}$$

We notice immediately that these results may be obtained by multiplying the probabilities on the individual branches concerned in the tree diagram, i.e.

$$p(HH) = p(H)p(H) = \frac{1}{4} \times \frac{1}{4}$$

$$p(HH') = p(H)p(H') = \frac{1}{4} \times \frac{3}{4}$$

The probabilities of the remaining two outcomes are readily found in this way

$$p(H'H) = \frac{3}{4} \times \frac{1}{4} = \frac{3}{16}$$

$$p(H'H') = \frac{3}{4} \times \frac{3}{4} = \frac{9}{16}$$

In answer to the question we therefore have

$$p(2 \text{ hearts}) = \frac{1}{16} \qquad p(1 \text{ heart}) = \frac{6}{16} \qquad p(0 \text{ heart}) = \frac{9}{16}$$

In general if two events A and B are independent then $p(AB) = p(A).p(B)$ where we shall use $p(AB)$ to denote the probability of A occurring first and then B also occurring.

In some situations, however, it may be possible for two independent events A and B to occur *simultaneously*. In this case it is preferable to write $p(A \cap B) = p(A).p(B)$, where $p(A \cap B)$ is the probability of both A and B occurring together. As an example of this, consider a school of 300 children, of whom 100 are blond and 120 wear spectacles. Suppose one child is selected at random and let

B = {blond children}
S = {children with spectacles}

Thus $p(B) = 1/3$ and $p(S) = 2/5$. If we assume that there is no link between a child's eyesight and the colour of his hair, then events B and S are independent and we may write

$$p(B \cap S) = p(B).p(S) = \frac{2}{15}$$

that is the probability of selecting a blond child who wears spectacles is $\frac{2}{15}$.

Warning: The importance of the correct use of notation must be stressed. It would be wrong in the first example we have considered to write

$$p(H \cap H') = p(H)p(H')$$

since $p(H \cap H')$ would logically represent the probability of a *single draw* resulting in a card which is both a heart and not a heart. The notation $p(HH')$ is essential here.

Example 84

If two cards are drawn from a pack and the first card is *not* replaced, what is the probability of drawing (i) 2 hearts (ii) 1 heart?

Here the probabilities on the second draw are influenced by the outcome of the first draw. Thus the probability of obtaining a heart on the second draw is 12/51 if a heart has already been drawn, but 13/51 if one has not been

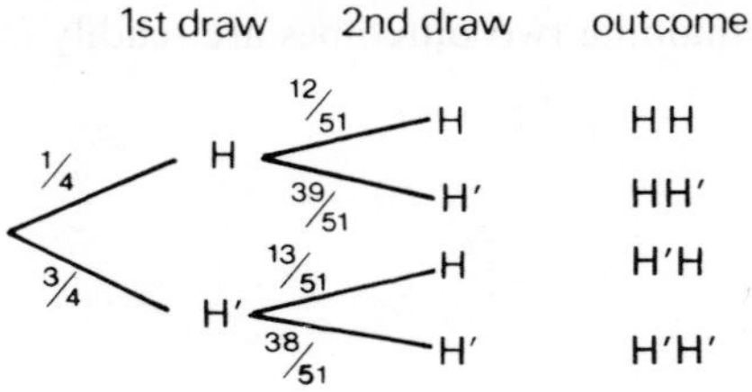

Fig. 5

drawn. After marking the various probabilities on the tree-diagram (Fig. 5) we obtain

$$p(HH) = \frac{1}{4} \times \frac{12}{51} = \frac{1}{17}$$

$$p(HH') = \frac{1}{4} \times \frac{39}{51} = \frac{13}{68}$$

$$p(H'H) = \frac{3}{4} \times \frac{13}{51} = \frac{13}{68}$$

hence $p(2 \text{ hearts}) = \frac{1}{17}$ $p(1 \text{ heart}) = \frac{26}{68} = \frac{13}{34}$

Example 85

In a large batch of seed 70% give red flowers, 20% yellow flowers and 10% white flowers. If 3 seeds are planted, what is the probability of obtaining (i) 3 red flowers (ii) 1 of each colour (iii) at least one white flower.

Here we need not draw the tree diagram. It is preferable instead to consider only the particular branches (or outcomes) which are relevant. Since the number of seeds in the batch is large, we may assume that the proportions of the different colours are not significantly altered by the removal of the first seed or by that of the second seed, i.e. that the 'colours' of the three seeds selected are independent. Thus

(i) $p(RRR) = p(R)p(R)p(R) = \dfrac{7}{10} \times \dfrac{7}{10} \times \dfrac{7}{10} = 0.343$

(ii) $p(RYW) = p(R)p(Y)p(W) = \dfrac{7}{10} \times \dfrac{2}{10} \times \dfrac{1}{10}$

$p(YWR) = p(Y)p(W)p(R) = \dfrac{2}{10} \times \dfrac{1}{10} \times \dfrac{7}{10}$

etc.

There are 3! or 6 orders in which one seed of each colour may be selected, and each of these has the same probability, i.e. 0.014

Thus $p(1 \text{ of each colour}) = 6 \times 0.014 = 0.084$

(iii) Here it is easiest to calculate first the probability of obtaining no white flowers.

$$p(W'W'W') = p(W')p(W')p(W') = \frac{9}{10} \times \frac{9}{10} \times \frac{9}{10} = 0.729$$

Then, since all other possibilities must contain at least 1 white flower, the required probability is

$$1 - 0.729 = 0.271$$

Exercise 13(d)

1. If two cards are drawn from a pack of 52 playing cards, find, by drawing tree-diagrams, the probabilities of obtaining 2 aces and exactly 1 ace
   (i) when the first card is replaced
   (ii) when the first card is not replaced.
2. I have 4 red socks and 2 blue socks in a drawer. Draw a tree-diagram to show the possible outcomes when two of the socks are removed at random. What is the probability of obtaining
   (i)   2 red socks
   (ii) 2 blue socks
   (iii) one of each colour?
3. I hold 3 diamonds and 4 clubs. Three cards are drawn at random and without replacement. Find the probability that they are all from the same suit.
4. What is the probability that two cards dealt from the top of a standard pack of playing cards will be a 'pontoon'? (A Pontoon consists of an ace together with a king, queen or jack.)
5. (i)   Two dice are thrown. What is the probability that at least one of the numbers is a six?
   (ii) Three dice are thrown. What is the probability of obtaining at least one six?
   (iii) How many dice must be thrown in order that the probability of at least one six appearing exceeds 0.8?
6. Of 24 pupils attending a mathematics lesson, 3 have forgotten their text-books, 4 their tables and 6 have 'forgotten' their homework. If these events may be considered independent, what is the probability that the first pupil spoken to by the teacher will have forgotten
   (i)   both his textbook and his tables
   (ii) his text-book but not his homework
   (iii) either his text-book or his homework
   (iv) at least one of the three items?
7. Each car in a second-hand car lot may suffer from one or more of the following defects, which may be considered to occur independently
   $R = \{rust\}$
   $M = \{mechanical\ faults\}$
   $T = \{tyres\ need\ replacement.\}$
   On a particular site 18 cars are on offer and $n(R) = 8, n(M) = 6, n(T) = 9$. A car is examined carefully. Find
   $$p(R \cap M),\ p(R \cup M),\ p(R' \cap M' \cap T),\ p(R \cup M \cup T).$$
8. Assuming that the probability of being born in any given month is 1/12, find the probability that 4 people selected at random will have
   (i) all their birthdays in different months
   (ii) two or more birthdays in the same month.

9. The semi-finals of the F.A. Cup are Arsenal vs Chopham and Liverpool vs Everton. The manager of Arsenal is confident that his team could beat Chopham in nine matches out of ten. In the final he feels the opponents are twice as likely to be Liverpool as Everton. If his opinions are correct, what is the probability that the final will be
    (i) Arsenal vs Liverpool
    (ii) Arsenal vs Everton?
    If the probability of Arsenal beating Everton is 2/3 and their chances against Liverpool are even, how would you rate Arsenal's chances of winning the cup? (Draw a tree-diagram.)
10. In a large batch of seed 50% give white flowers, 30% pink flowers and 20% blue flowers. If three seeds are planted, find the probability of obtaining
    (i)   3 white flowers
    (ii) 2 white flowers and 1 pink flower
    (iii) no pink flowers
    (iv) at least 1 blue flower.
11. In question 10, how many seeds must I plant in order to be 90% confident of obtaining at least one blue flower?
12. A bag contains 3 white balls and 5 red balls. Find the probability that the *second* ball removed from the bag is white. (The first ball removed is not replaced.)

13.5 The Binomial Probability Distribution

(A knowledge of the binomial expansion for positive integral index is assumed in this section.)

At first sight the binomial expansion

$$\left(\frac{5}{6} + \frac{1}{6}\right)^5 = \left(\frac{5}{6}\right)^5 + {}^5C_1\left(\frac{5}{6}\right)^4\left(\frac{1}{6}\right) + {}^5C_2\left(\frac{5}{6}\right)^3\left(\frac{1}{6}\right)^2 + \ldots.$$

may seem rather pointless since the left-hand side is clearly equivalent to $(1)^5$ or 1. Thus the terms of the expansion on the right-hand side must add up to 1.

Consider, however, a situation in which five dice are thrown and we are required to calculate the probabilities of obtaining (i) no six (ii) 1 six (iii) 2 sixes, etc. We shall represent the outcomes {throwing a six} and {not throwing a six}, on one dice, by 6 and N respectively. Thus $p(6) = \frac{1}{6}$ and $p(N) = \frac{5}{6}$.

(i)   No six is obtained only by the outcome:

    N N N N N

Since the numbers thrown on the five dice are independent, we have

$$p(\text{No six}) = \frac{5}{6} \times \frac{5}{6} \times \frac{5}{6} \times \frac{5}{6} \times \frac{5}{6} = \left(\frac{5}{6}\right)^5$$

(ii) One six is obtained in each of the outcomes:

```
N  N  N  N  6
N  N  N  6  N
N  N  6  N  N   etc.
```

There are 5 (or $^5C_1$) of these outcomes and each has probability

$\left(\dfrac{5}{6}\right)^4\left(\dfrac{1}{6}\right)$ so that

$$p(1 \text{ six}) = {}^5C_1 \left(\dfrac{5}{6}\right)^4\left(\dfrac{1}{6}\right)$$

(iii) Two sixes are obtained in the outcomes:

```
N  N  N  6  6
N  N  6  N  6
N  N  6  6  N   etc.
```

The number of these outcomes is equal to the number of ways in which the 2 positions of the sixes may be selected from 5 positions, i.e. $^5C_2$. Each outcome has probability $\left(\dfrac{5}{6}\right)^3\left(\dfrac{1}{6}\right)^2$

$$\text{thus } p(2 \text{ sixes}) = {}^5C_2 \left(\dfrac{5}{6}\right)^3\left(\dfrac{1}{6}\right)^2$$

It is now becoming clear that these probabilities are given by the successive terms of the binomial expansion considered. The relation between the quantities involved in the expansion and those of the physical situation concerned is made clear in Fig. 6

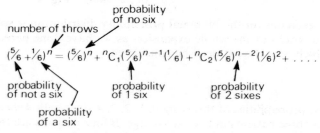

number of throws

probability of no six

probability of not a six

probability of a six

probability of 1 six

probability of 2 sixes

$$\left(\tfrac{5}{6} + \tfrac{1}{6}\right)^n = \left(\tfrac{5}{6}\right)^n + {}^nC_1\left(\tfrac{5}{6}\right)^{n-1}\left(\tfrac{1}{6}\right) + {}^nC_2\left(\tfrac{5}{6}\right)^{n-2}\left(\tfrac{1}{6}\right)^2 + \ldots$$

Fig. 6

Since the terms on the right-hand side will cover all the possible outcomes from 0 to n sixes, it is clear that they should add up to 1.

In general, if an event with probability p of 'success' and $q(= 1-p)$ of 'failure' is repeated n times, then the probabilities of obtaining 0, 1, 2, 3 ... successes are given by the terms of the binomial expansion $(q + p)^n$. (Fig. 7.)

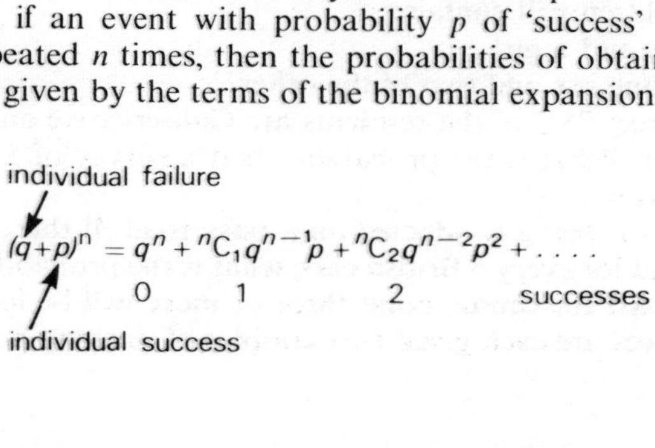

individual failure

individual success

$$(q+p)^n = q^n + {}^nC_1 q^{n-1}p + {}^nC_2 q^{n-2}p^2 + \ldots$$

0 1 2 successes

Fig. 7

Example 86

The probability of a particular operation succeeding is 1/3. In 4 such operations compare the probabilities of obtaining 0, 1, 2, 3, 4 successes.

Here we have $p = 1/3$, $q = 2/3$ and $n = 4$ so that the binomial expansion used is

$$\left(\frac{2}{3} + \frac{1}{3}\right)^4 = \left(\frac{2}{3}\right)^4 + {}^4C_1\left(\frac{2}{3}\right)^3\left(\frac{1}{3}\right) + {}^4C_2\left(\frac{2}{3}\right)^2\left(\frac{1}{3}\right)^2 + {}^4C_3\left(\frac{2}{3}\right)\left(\frac{1}{3}\right)^3 + \left(\frac{1}{3}\right)^4$$

$$= \frac{16}{81} \quad + \quad \frac{4.8}{81} \quad + \quad \frac{6.4}{81} \quad + \quad \frac{4.2}{81} \quad + \frac{1}{81}$$

The probabilities of obtaining 0, 1, 2, 3, 4 successes are therefore

$\dfrac{16}{81}, \dfrac{32}{81}, \dfrac{24}{81}, \dfrac{8}{81}, \dfrac{1}{81}$ respectively.

The relative likelihoods of these different outcomes are illustrated in Fig. 8.

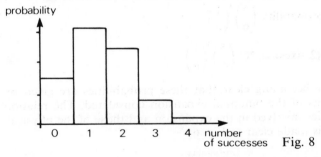

Fig. 8

Note: In most exercises on the binomial probability distribution it will not be necessary to write out the whole expansion as we have done here. Only those terms which are relevant need be considered.

Exercise 13(e)

1. Compare the probabilities of throwing 0, 1, 2, 3, 4 sixes with 4 dice.
2. A drug cures three patients in five on average. If four patients are treated, what is the probability that at least three will recover?
3. Taking the male : female birth ratio as 1 : 1, what is the probability that a family of 5 children will contain:
    (i) four boys and a girl
    (ii) three of one sex and two of the other?
4. In a certain street 75% of the residents are Conservative and the remainder are Labour. What is the probability that a survey of 5 residents will indicate a Labour win?
5. A traffic census is being conducted on a busy road. If there are 3 foreign cars on the road for every 5 British cars, what is the probability that of the first five cars past the census point three or more will be foreign?
6. Eight housewives are each given two samples of washing powder to try –

one a well-known brand and the other a new powder called Fizz. They are asked to say which gives the cleaner wash. On the assumption that there is no discernible difference between the powders and that the housewives select their preferences at random, what is the probability that six or more will express a preference for Fizz?

7. A four-engined aircraft is to make a flight of duration 2 hours. The probability of each engine failing during this time is 0.01. The aircraft can continue if one engine fails but if two engines fail then a forced landing must be made. Find the following probabilities, giving answers correct to 1 significant figure:

    (i) that at least one engine will fail

    (ii) that a forced landing will be necessary.

8. In a row of six telephone kiosks there are, on average, two free at any one time. If two people arrive simultaneously, what are the probabilities that

    (i) one of the two must wait (not both)

    (ii) both may call.

13.6 Conditional Probability

Example 87

(i) Mrs. Jones has two children. The elder is a boy. What is the probability that the other child is also a boy?

(ii) Mrs. Smith also has two children, one of whom is known to be a boy. What is the probability that the other child is also a boy?

The answer to part (i) of this question is clearly 1/2, since, when the second child is born, its sex cannot be influenced by the fact that the first child was a boy.

We are tempted to suppose that the answer to part (ii) is also 1/2 but in fact the situation is rather different. We are not told which of the two children (i.e. the elder or the younger) is known to be a boy. We must therefore consider all the possible outcomes for the sexes of two children. There are four of these (Fig. 9) and all are equally likely.

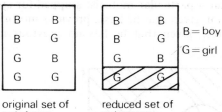

original set of outcomes   reduced set of outcomes   Fig. 9

However the outcome G G (or 2 girls) cannot apply if one of the children is known to be a boy. Our set of possible outcomes therefore reduces to three (Fig. 9), and these are still equally likely. In only one of these are *both* children boys, so the required probability must be 1/3.

This is an example of **conditional probability**. The effect of the 'condition' (in this case that one of the two children must be a boy) is to reduce the number of outcomes which would otherwise have been possible.

Consider two events A and B which may occur simultaneously. We shall use the notation p(B | A) to mean the probability that B occurs given that A has occurred. Using set notation the condition that A has occurred reduces the number of possible outcomes from $n(\mathscr{E})$ to $n(A)$. If B has also occurred then we have the event $B \cap A$, (see Fig. 10).

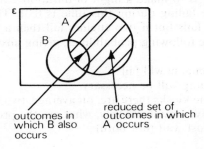

outcomes in which B also occurs

reduced set of outcomes in which A occurs

Fig. 10

We therefore have

$$p(B \mid A) = \frac{n(B \cap A)}{n(A)} = \frac{n(B \cap A)}{n(\mathscr{E})} \times \frac{n(\mathscr{E})}{n(A)}$$

that is

$$p(B \mid A) = \frac{p(B \cap A)}{p(A)}$$

Example 88

In a certain area the police find that 40% of motorists stopped for speeding have previous motoring convictions and 15% are in excess of the legal limit for blood-alcohol. 10% of those stopped fall within both categories. Find the probability that a particular motorist stopped for speeding will (i) have excess blood alcohol, given that he has a previous motoring conviction (ii) satisfy the alcohol test, given that he has no previous motoring conviction.

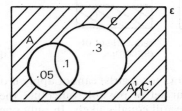

Fig. 11

Let C = {motorist has previous conviction}
   A = {motorist has excess blood-alcohol.}

Then we are given p(C) = 0.4 p(A) = 0.15 p(A ∩ C) = 0.1. From these we may draw the Venn diagram of Fig. 11. We notice in passing that the events

A and C cannot be considered independent since $p(A \cap C) \neq p(A) . p(C)$.
(i) In set notation we require $p(A \mid C)$

$$p(A \mid C) = \frac{p(A \cap C)}{p(C)} = \frac{0.1}{0.4} = \frac{1}{4}$$

(ii) Here we require $p(A' \mid C') = \dfrac{p(A' \cap C')}{p(C')}$

$A' \cap C'$ is the event that the motorist has neither a previous conviction nor excess blood-alcohol. This is represented by the outer shaded area in Fig. 11 and we see, by subtraction, that

$$p(A' \cap C') = 1 - (0.05 + 0.1 + 0.3) = 0.55$$

Also $\qquad p(C') = 1 - p(C) = 0.6$

Thus $\quad p(A' \mid C') = \dfrac{0.55}{0.6} = \dfrac{11}{12}$

Exercise 13(f)

1. List the 36 possible outcomes when throwing two dice. If one of the numbers thrown is a 2, find the probability that
   (i) the other is also a 2
   (ii) the total score is 7.
2. Of three children one is known to be a girl. What is the probability that
   (i) both the others are boys
   (ii) at least one of the others is a boy?
3. Three coins are tossed. What is the probability that exactly two heads occur, given
   (i) that the first coin tossed is a head
   (ii) that at least one of the coins is a head?
4. If two dice are thrown and the numbers obtained are different, what is the probability that the total score is (i) 5 (ii) 8?
5. Three small companies A, B and C share the same office premises. The three staff of Company A own a Ford, a Morris and a Rover. The four staff of Company B own two Morris's, a Ford and a Rover. The three staff of Company C are each provided with a Ford by their company.

   B = {the first person leaving is in Company B}
   M = {the first person leaving owns a Morris.}

   Find $p(B)$, $p(M)$, $p(M \cap B)$, $p(M \mid B)$, $p(B \mid M)$.

   (Assume that each person is equally likely to leave first.)
6. (i) Two events A and B may be defined as independent if $p(B \mid A) = p(B)$, i.e. if the occurrence of event A does not alter the probability of event B. Use this definition to prove that if A and B are independent events which may occur simultaneously then $p(A \cap B) = p(A).p(B)$.
   (ii) Prove that if $p(B \mid A) = p(B)$, then $p(A \mid B) = p(A)$.

7. A glider cannot be flown safely if either of the following events occur:

W = {windspeed above a certain level}
T = {air-temperature below a certain level.}

At a certain time of the year records show that $p(W) = 0.3$, $p(T) = 0.1$ and $p(W \cap T) = 0.05$.

(i) What is the probability that a glider may be flown on a given day at this time of the year?

(ii) Are the events W and T independent?

(iii) Describe each of the following probabilities in words and evaluate them.

$p(T \mid W)$　$p(W' \mid T')$.

*8. (i) Use a tree diagram to show that for two non-independent events A and B

$$p(B) = p(A)\,p(B \mid A) + p(A')\,p(B \mid A').$$

(ii) Two marksmen A and B take part in a shooting contest in which each has three shots at the target. The order of firing is determined by spinning a coin. In practice A hits the bull two times in three shots and B five times in six.

A = {A shoots first}
T = {the first marksman to shoot scores three bulls}

Find $p(T \mid A)$ and $p(T \mid A')$. Hence deduce $p(T)$. Find also $p(A \mid T)$.

9. A spins three coins and B spins two.

A = {A obtains more heads than B}

Find the following probabilities:

(i) $p(A \mid B$ obtains 2 heads)
(ii) $p(A \mid B$ obtains 1 heads)
(iii) $p(A \mid B$ obtains 0 heads)

Draw a tree-diagram and hence find $p(A)$.

14

Elasticity and Restitution

14.1 Hooke's Law

An *elastic* body is one which can recover its original form after being subjected to some form of deformation – frequently an extension or compression. All bodies are elastic to some degree though in many cases the change in dimension which can be produced by outside forces is so slight as to be barely appreciable and little error arises in ignoring it.

The most familiar examples of elastic bodies are springs and 'elastic strings' (e.g. rubber bands). For these it is easy to demonstrate that any extension produced is directly proportional to the load applied. Thus, in Fig. 1, if we double the attached mass m we find that the extension x is doubled as a result. The extension x is defined as the increase in length beyond the 'natural' or unstretched length of the spring.

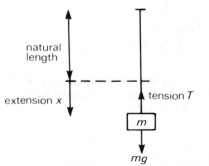

natural length

extension x

tension T

m

mg Fig. 1

For the equilibrium of the attached mass m we have $T = mg$, so that the tension in the spring (or string) may be taken as a measure of the extending force mg. It follows that the tension is itself proportional to the extension,

that is $T = kx$

This is **Hooke's Law** and experimentally it has been found to apply quite well to all bodies within certain limits of extension. (If the load is increased indefinitely there will come a point at which permanent deformation or damage is caused to the material of the body – the *elastic limit*.)

Re-arranging Hooke's Law as $k = T/x$ we see that the constant k may be interpreted physically as the force needed to produce unit extension. It is therefore a measure of the 'stiffness' of the body. For a spring it is frequently called the *spring rate*. The units of k are those of force per unit extension, i.e. $N\,m^{-1}$ or $N\,mm^{-1}$ etc.

So far we have considered only the *extension* of a body. In practice Hooke's Law applies far more frequently to cases of *compression*, for which the same result holds (again within certain limits). It is important to notice that if, in Fig. 1, we consider a compression to be defined by a negative value of x, then the formula $T = kx$ predicts a negative value of T. This indicates that the force in the spring will be reversed in direction, i.e. a force of thrust rather than of tension.

Example 89

Two elastic strings of string rates 5 N cm^{-1} and 3 N cm^{-1} are tied end to end. The first string is 2 cm longer in natural length than the second. Calculate the tension in each string when they are used jointly to support a mass of 4 kg.

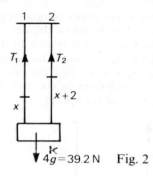

Fig. 2

In Fig. 2 the strings are separated for convenience. If the first string is extended by x cm then the second must be extended by $(x + 2)$ cm, as their total lengths must be equal. Thus we have

$$T_1 = k_1 x \qquad = 5x \qquad (1)$$
$$T_2 = k_2(x + 2) = 3(x + 2) \qquad (2)$$

but for equilibrium $T_1 + T_2 = 4g = 39.2$ hence

$$8x + 6 = 39.2$$
$$8x = 33.2 \quad \Rightarrow x = 4.15 \text{ cm}$$

Substituting back in 1 and 2 the tensions are

$$T_1 = 20.75 \text{ N}$$
$$T_2 = 18.45 \text{ N}$$

Exercise 14(a)

1. An elastic string of natural length 40 cm is stretched 8 cm by a force of 14 N. What will be the total length of the string when it is used to support hanging masses of (i) 5 kg (ii) 2 kg?
2. The length of a spring is 69 cm when supporting a mass of 4 kg and 76 cm when supporting a mass of 6 kg. Find the natural length of the spring and the force required to stretch it to a total length of 80 cm.

3. Two strings AB and CD each stretch 8 cm when supporting loads of 1/2 kg. The ends B and C are fastened together and the joint string is suspended from A. What is the total extension when the following masses are attached?

    (i) 1/2 kg at B   (ii) 1/2 kg at D

    (iii) 1/2 kg at both B and D   (iv) 1 kg at B

    (v) 1 kg at D.

4. When hanging vertically a certain mass m extends a spring by 10 cm. If the mass is now placed on a smooth plane of inclination arctan (3/4) and is attached by the spring to a point on the plane, what will be the extension of the spring when the mass rests in equilibrium?

5. When used separately to support a mass m, two elastic strings of equal length are stretched by 10 cm and by 15 cm respectively. If they are tied side by side, what will be the extension of the combined string when supporting the same mass?

6. The tension in an elastic string of natural length 1 m is 26 N when it is stretched between two points 1.2 m apart on the same horizontal level. What mass attached to the midpoint of the string will rest in equilibrium 0.25 m below the level of the end attachments?

7. Two strings of equal length are stretched an equal distance d when supporting hanging masses m_1 and m_2 respectively. If the two strings are fastened side by side, what mass would stretch the combined string by the same distance d? If the two strings were fastened end to end, what hanging mass would stretch this combination by a distance d?

8. An elastic string of natural length 20 cm and string rate 6 N cm^{-1} is threaded through the centre of a spring of natural length 30 cm and spring rate 24 N cm^{-1}. The string is then stretched and fastened to each end of the spring. Find the 'natural length' of the combined body thus formed. What force is necessary to

    (i) extend the body by 4 cm?

    (ii) compress it by 3 cm?

9. An elastic string of natural length 40 cm is attached at one end to a fixed point O. The other end is fastened to a small ring of mass m which is free to slide on a smooth vertical wire at a horizontal distance of 48 cm from O. When the ring is in equilibrium on the wire the length of the string is 50 cm. What would be the length of the string if the ring was suspended on it vertically beneath O?

10. An elastic string of natural length a is extended by $a/3$ when supporting a small heavy ring hanging freely. The ring is now threaded onto a smooth circular wire of radius a fixed in a vertical plane and the free end of the string is attached to the highest point of the wire. Find the possible lengths of the string for which the ring may rest in equilibrium on the wire.

14.2 Work Required to Stretch a Spring

In stretching a spring we must pull with a force which is always at least equal in magnitude to the opposing tension force in the spring. But as the length of the spring is increased so this tension increases. Thus the work needed is not a simple application of work = force × distance, since we must pull with an ever-increasing force.

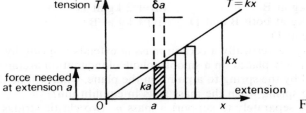

Fig. 3

Fig. 3 is a graph of tension against extension ($T = kx$). At extension a the tension is ka. If we consider this tension to remain unchanged over a small increase in extension δa, then the work done in increasing the extension from a to $(a + \delta a)$ is $(ka)\delta a$ – the area of the shaded strip in Fig. 3. Thus an estimate for the total work done in producing extension x is the sum of all such strips from 0 to x. But as the incremental value $\delta a \to 0$ our approximation is improved and, at the same time, the total area of the strips approaches more closely the area under the graph. Thus

Work required = area under graph
$$= \tfrac{1}{2} . x . kx = \tfrac{1}{2} kx^2$$
Alternatively, by calculus, the work required is

$$\int_0^x ka.da = \left[\frac{1}{2}ka^2\right]_0^x = \frac{1}{2}kx^2$$

Note: (i) This result may be written as $(\tfrac{1}{2}kx).x$ i.e. mean tension × extension. This frequently gives the simplest method of calculation.

(ii) The same results are true for the work required to compress a spring, x measuring the compression from the unstretched position.

Units. Providing we adhere to the standard units of force and distance then the result for the work required will be in the standard unit of work, i.e. the joule. This means that when using the formula $\tfrac{1}{2}kx^2$, k must be in N m^{-1} and x must be in metres.

Elastic energy. We regard the work done in stretching or compressing an elastic body as being stored as **elastic energy** by the body. Thus a stretched spring supporting a hanging load jumps wildly when the load is removed as this releases the elastic energy of the spring. In certain circumstances this energy may be retrieved. Simple examples are the catapult, where the energy is used to import kinetic energy to the pellet, and the clock-spring, where the energy is released gradually in driving the mechanism.

Example 90

An elastic string is stretched 15 cm by a force of 16 N. How much work must be done to double this extension?

Using work done = mean tension × extension and measuring force in newtons and extension in metres, the work already done in providing the initial 15 cm of extension is

$$\frac{1}{2} \times 16 \times \frac{15}{100} = 1.2 \text{ joules}$$

It is wrong to suppose that the same work will be needed to create a further 15 cm of extension. The correct result is found by comparing the amounts of work needed to produce extensions of 15 cm and 30 cm from the unstretched length (or, equivalently, the energies stored by the string in each of these two instances). When the extension is 30 cm the tension will be doubled, i.e. 32 N, so that the total work needed to produce 30 cm of extension is

$$\frac{1}{2} \times 32 \times \frac{30}{100} = 4.8 \text{ joules}$$

The work required to double the original extension of 15 cm is therefore 3.6 joules.

Example 91

An elastic string is stretched 10 cm by a certain mass hanging in equilibrium. The mass is pulled downwards by a further 20 cm and then released from rest. Find
(i) the speed with which it returns through its equilibrium position
(ii) the greatest height to which it rises.

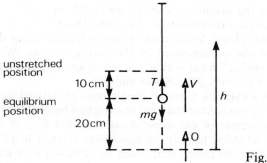

Fig. 4

At the equilibrium position (Fig. 4) we have

$$T = kx = mg$$
$$0.1\,k = mg \Rightarrow k = 10mg$$

(i) When the mass m has risen to its equilibrium level, some (but not all) of the elastic energy of the string will have been released. That which has been released has been converted partly into the kinetic energy of the mass and partly into the extra potential energy that the mass now possesses. We work from the energy equation:

$$\text{loss in elastic energy} = \text{K.E.} + \text{P.E.}$$
$$\tfrac{1}{2}k(0.3)^2 - \tfrac{1}{2}k(0.1)^2 = \tfrac{1}{2}mv^2 + mg(0.2)$$
$$5mg(0.09 - 0.01) = \tfrac{1}{2}mv^2 + 0.2mg$$
$$\Rightarrow \tfrac{1}{2}mv^2 = 0.2mg$$
$$v^2 = 0.4g$$
$$v = 1.98 \text{ m s}^{-1}$$

(ii) At the highest point reached the mass has no kinetic energy since it is instantaneously at rest. Assuming that the mass rises above the unstretched position of the string so that all the elastic energy of the string is released, we have

$$\text{initial elastic energy} = \text{P.E. gained by } m$$
$$\tfrac{1}{2}k(0.3)^2 = mgh$$
$$5mg(0.09) = mgh$$
$$\Rightarrow h = 0.45 \text{ metres}$$

The mass rises through a total height of 45 cm. Since the string is now slack the mass will start to fall and if energy is conserved completely it will return through 45 cm to its starting point. After this the cycle will be repeated. In practice some energy is lost so that the magnitude of the oscillations decreases progressively and the mass ultimately finishes at rest in its equilibrium position.

Exercise 14(b)

1. A 5 kg mass extends a spring by 14 cm when hanging in equilibrium. Find the work needed to
   (i)   extend the spring by 10 cm
   (ii) increase the extension from 10 cm to 14 cm
   (iii) increase the extension from 14 cm to 18 cm.
2. When a pinball player holds back a spring-loaded firing device with a force of 15 N, the compression of the spring is 2 cm. What energy is stored in the spring? What will be the initial speed of the ball, which has mass 25 g, if it receives 75% of this energy?
3. A boy makes a catapult from an elastic cord of natural length *l*. At the instant that a stone is fired the cord is stretched by 50% and its tension is 500 times the weight of the stone. Assuming that 60% of this energy is imparted to the stone find (i) the maximum vertical height and (ii) the maximum horizontal range, that could be achieved with this shot.
*4. An elastic string is stretched 12 cm by a 3 kg mass hanging in equilibrium. A boy pulls the mass slowly downwards until the total extension is 20 cm. Find the energy stored by the spring in each position and also the work done by the boy. (Leave your answers in terms of *g*.)
5. The boy of question 4 pulls the 3 kg mass down until the total extension of the string is 28 cm. By comparing the energy stored by the string with that needed to lift the mass through 28 cm, explain why the string must go slack in the motion following the release of the mass, (from rest). Find the greatest height to which the mass rises and its speed at the instant the string slackens.

6. In question 12 of exercise 2(c) it was assumed that the retardation provided by the climbing rope was uniform. Explain why this is not in fact the case and find more realistic estimates for the greatest tension the rope must withstand in both cases. What does this suggest about the results obtained by the earlier method?

7. An elastic string of length a is stretched by $a/4$ when used to suspend a body of mass m from a fixed point O. If the body is released from rest at O, what will be the greatest length of the string in the ensuing motion? Find also the speed of the body as it passes through its previous equilibrium position.

8. A small ring of mass m is threaded on a smooth circular wire of radius r which is fixed in a vertical plane. The ring is attached to the highest point of the wire by an elastic string of natural length a. When the ring is in equilibrium the string is stretched by $a/8$. By considering the force-triangle for the equilibrium of the ring, show that the string-rate (k) is $9mg/r$. If the ring is given a small displacement from rest at the highest point of the wire, show that it is next instantaneously at rest when the length of the string is $3a/2$ (irrespective of the value of r).

14.3 The Modulus of Elasticity

The constant k which we have called the 'spring rate' has the disadvantage that its value does not depend on the material and construction of the spring alone. It depends also on the length of the spring.

Consider a spring whose extension is a when supporting a load of weight W. We could consider each half of the spring to be stretched by $a/2$ or each third of the string to be stretched by $a/3$, (Fig. 5), etc.

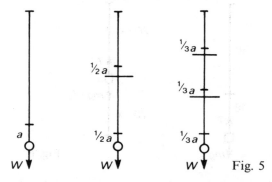

Fig. 5

But the tension is the same throughout the spring, i.e. equal in magnitude to W for the complete spring, a 'half-spring' or a 'third-spring'. Using $T = kx$ we therefore have

for the complete spring $W = ka$ $k = W/a$
for a half-spring $W = k(a/2)$ $k = 2W/a$
for a third-spring $W = k(a/3)$ $k = 3W/a$

i.e. if we reduce the natural length of the spring by one half (one third) the value of k is doubled (trebled).

In fact k is inversely proportional to the natural length l and we may write

$$k = \lambda\frac{1}{l}$$

where λ is a new constant. λ is known as the **modulus of elasticity** (or **elastic constant**) of the spring considered. It is a property of the material and construction of the spring alone, being independent of the length taken.

In terms of the modulus of elasticity λ the results of sections 14.1 and 14.2 may be re-written as follows

Hooke's law $T = kx$ or $T = \dfrac{\lambda x}{l}$

elastic energy $\frac{1}{2}kx^2$ or $\dfrac{\lambda x^2}{2l}$

We see by considering the dimensions of the Hooke's law result (i.e. force = $\lambda \times$ distance $\div$ distance) that the unit of λ will be equivalent to that of force, i.e. the newton. λ may be interpreted physically as the force required to double the length of the spring or string concerned.

Example 92

A string of natural length 30 cm stretches by 18 cm when supporting a mass m. If the string is stretched between two fixed points 48 cm apart in a vertical line and the mass is attached to the point two-thirds of the way down the string, find the length of the upper section when the mass is in equilibrium.

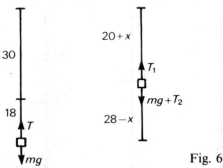

Fig. 6

We shall take all distances in cm in this example, since the formula $T = \lambda x/l$ involves the *ratio* of two distances so that the units employed are not important. (This is *not* true of the energy result $\lambda x^2/2l$.) Thus from the original equilibrium situation (Fig. 6) we have

$$mg = \frac{\lambda 18}{30} \Rightarrow \lambda = \frac{5mg}{3}$$

If, in the new situation, the upper section is stretched from 20 cm to (20 + x) cm then the total length of the lower section is (28 − x) cm, i.e. an extension of $(18 - x)$ cm, the natural length of this section being 10 cm. Thus in Fig. 6

$$T_1 = \frac{\lambda x}{20} \quad T_2 = \frac{\lambda(18 - x)}{10} \quad (x \leqslant 18)$$

(We are using at this point the fact that both sections of the string have the same modulus λ as the original string. This would not be true of the string-rate k.)

but for equilibrium $T_1 - T_2 = mg$

$$\frac{\lambda x}{20} - \frac{\lambda(18 - x)}{10} = mg$$

$$\frac{5mg}{3} \left\{ \frac{x - (36 - 2x)}{20} \right\} = mg$$

$$5(3x - 36) = 60$$
$$\Rightarrow x = 16 \text{ cm}$$

Thus the upper section has length 36 cm and the lower section 12 cm. (Both are stretched.)

Exercise 14(c)

1. An elastic spring of modulus 120 N has natural length 30 cm. Find
    (i) the tension in the spring when its length is 36 cm
    (ii) the thrust in the spring when its length is 26 cm.
   Find also the energy stored by the spring in each case.
2. An elastic string has modulus 40 N. Find the force needed to extend the string by 20% from its natural length. If the work needed to do this is 0.2 joule, find (i) the natural length of the string and (ii) the further work needed to increase the extension to a total of 30%.
3. An elastic string of natural length 60 cm stretches by 24 cm when supporting a mass of 2 kg. Find the modulus of elasticity.
    (i) The string is cut into equal halves both of which are attached at one end to a fixed point O. If the mass is suspended from O by both sections of string, find the extension in each.
    (ii) If in part (i) the two sections of string have natural lengths 25 cm and 35 cm, find the vertical distance below O at which the mass would rest in equilibrium. State also the tension in each string section.
4. A light elastic string of modulus 24 N and natural length 60 cm is stretched between two points 75 cm apart in a vertical line. A small body is attached to the midpoint of the string. Show that if the weight of the body is 12 N it will rest in equilibrium with the lower half of the string slack. Find the equilibrium positions of bodies of weight (i) 8 N, (ii) 14 N.
5. An elastic spring of natural length 0.6 m and modulus 120 N is stretched between two points A and B 0.7 m apart on a smooth horizontal surface. A particle of mass 0.2 kg is attached to the midpoint of the spring. The particle is displaced by 0.15 m towards B and then released from rest. Find (i) the speed (ii) the acceleration of the particle at the instant when it has travelled 0.1 m.

6. An elastic string of natural length 65 cm is attached to points A and B which are 60 cm apart horizontally and such that A is 15 cm higher than B. A smooth ring of weight 6 N threaded on the string rests in equilibrium at a level 15 cm lower than B. Find the modulus of the string.

7. A particle of weight 5 N is attached by a string of modulus 20 N and natural length 40 cm to a point O on a rough horizontal table top. The greatest distance from O at which the particle can remain in equilibrium on the table is 43 cm. Find the co-efficient of friction between the particle and the table. At what distance from O should the particle be released (from rest) if it is subsequently to come to rest again just as the string slackens?

8. If in question 7 the particle is projected from O with a speed of 2 m s^{-1} find (i) the greatest length of the string in the ensuing motion and (ii) the distance from O at which the particle finally comes to rest. (Take $g = 10 \text{ m s}^{-2}$.)

14.4 Direct Impact of Two Bodies

We discuss in this section the different outcomes which can result from an impact of two bodies moving in the same straight line. Such an impact is said to be *direct*. It is found that bodies of one material will behave differently on impact to bodies of another material and the reason for this is to be found in the different elastic properties of the materials concerned.

There are two stages in any impact. During the first stage (Fig. 7) the regions of the two bodies that are in contact are compressed. Work is required to do this (as it is when compressing a spring) so that some of the kinetic energy of the system is transferred to energy stored by the compressed regions.

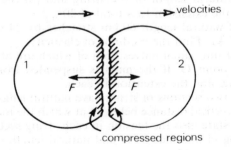

Fig. 7

What happens in the second stage depends on how '*elastic*' are the bodies concerned, i.e. how closely they approximate to springs in their ability (i) to recover their original forms and (ii) to store and subsequently release the energy of compression. The two extreme cases are as follows.

(i) **Perfectly elastic bodies.** The compressed regions spring back out completely, releasing all of the energy of compression and forcing the bodies apart again. Thus for a *perfectly elastic impact*
  the bodies recover their original forms

no kinetic energy is lost
the bodies separate with 'high' relative velocity.

(ii) Inelastic bodies. Here the compressed regions do not spring out at all. The energy of compression is not released and the bodies are not forced apart. For an *inelastic impact*
the bodies remain permanently dented
kinetic energy is lost providing the work of compression
the bodies do not separate (i.e. zero relative velocity after impact).

In practice the behaviour of almost all bodies is somewhere between these extremes, i.e. some but not all of the energy of compression is released. This means that (i) some kinetic energy is lost by the system, and (ii) the bodies separate after impact, but not with as high a relative velocity as perfectly elastic bodies.
Although kinetic energy is almost invariably lost in an impact, momentum is, in all cases, conserved. This is because the duration of the impact is necessarily the same for each body and at any instant the forces involved are equal and opposite. The two bodies must, therefore, experience equal and opposite impulses, i.e. any momentum lost by one will be gained by the other.

14.5 Newton's Law of Impact

Conservation of momentum alone is not sufficient to solve a problem on direct impact. As has been seen in the previous section, the outcome is dependent also on the elastic properties of the bodies concerned. Fig. 8, for example, illustrates two possible outcomes which might result from the impact of spheres of masses 2 and 1 units moving with velocities as shown. Both are consistent with conservation of momentum.

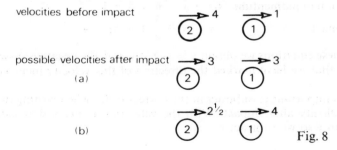

Fig. 8

The outcome (a) is that which would result from an inelastic impact (after which the bodies do not separate) whereas (b) might be obtained in an impact between spheres of a more elastic nature.
In experimental observation of impacts it has been found that for a given pair of bodies the relative velocity with which the bodies separate is a fixed fraction of the relative velocity with which they collide,

i.e. $\left(\begin{array}{c}\text{relative magnitude of velocity}\\\text{after impact}\end{array}\right) = e.\left(\begin{array}{c}\text{relative magnitude of velocity}\\\text{before impact}\end{array}\right)$

This is known as **Newton's Law of impact** and the fraction *e*, which is a constant for a given pair of bodies, is called the **co-efficient of restitution**. For inelastic bodies *e* = 0 so that the relative velocity after impact is zero. The other extreme value, that applying to perfectly elastic bodies, is *e* = 1, but this value is never attained in practice. Values of 0.9 and above, however, are found for hard resilient bodies such as steel ball bearings and glass marbles.

Returning to the example of Fig. 8 we see that the co-efficient of restitution which would lead to the outcome (b) is $1\frac{1}{2}/3$ or 1/2, the relative velocities before and after impact being 3 and $1\frac{1}{2}$ units respectively.

It is important to remember that Newton's law of impact, being an experimental law, is not exact and can only be expected to apply under certain circumstances; in particular the impact must occur in free space or on a smooth surface. Outside forces, such as friction, can greatly alter the situation, as billiard players will realise.

Example 93

The co-efficient of restitution between two spheres is 3/4. Their masses are 1 and 6 units. The spheres collide directly when moving with speeds 5 and 1 units respectively in opposite directions. Find the speeds and directions after impact.

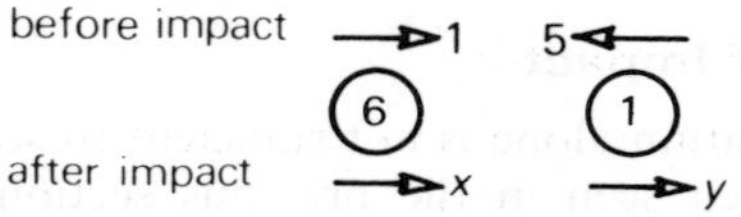

Fig. 9

In our diagram (Fig.9) it is best to mark the velocities after impact *in the same direction* even though this may not in fact be the case. Taking positive momentum to the right in Fig. 9, we have

conservation of momentum $\quad 6x + y = 6 - 5 = 1$

law of impact $\qquad\qquad\qquad y - x = \dfrac{3}{4}(1 + 5) = 4\frac{1}{2}$

Solving these equations we obtain $x = -1/2$, $y = 4$, the negative answer for *x* telling us that we have marked the direction of this velocity incorrectly.

Note: It is important to subtract in the correct order when writing down the relative velocity after impact. With the velocities as marked, *x* cannot be larger than *y* so we subtract $y - x$.

Example 94

Three spheres of masses 4*m*, 2*m* and *m* lie at rest in a straight line on a smooth horizontal surface. The co-efficient of restitution between all three spheres is *e*. The sphere of mass 4*m* is projected directly towards the other spheres. Show there will be at least three impacts if *e* < 1/2.

It is convenient to represent the velocities of the spheres during the different phases of the motion as in Fig. 10. The first impact is between 4*m* and 2*m*.

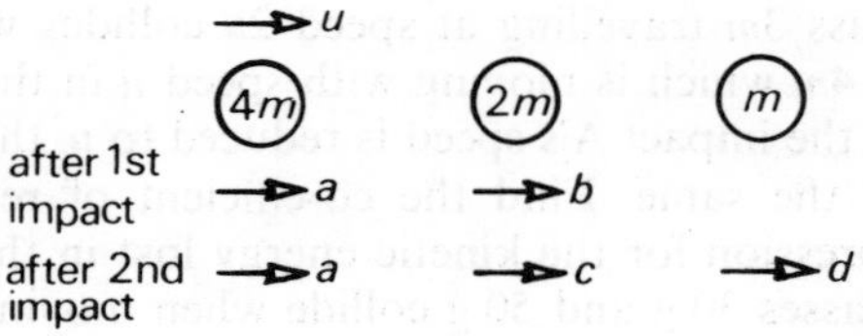

$$\xrightarrow{\quad u\quad}$$

(4m)　　(2m)　　(m)

after 1st
impact $\xrightarrow{\ a\ }$　$\xrightarrow{\ b\ }$

after 2nd $\xrightarrow{\ a\ }$　　$\xrightarrow{\ c\ }$　$\xrightarrow{\ d\ }$
impact

Fig. 10

momentum　　$4ma + 2mb = 4mu$ (or $2a + b = 2u$)

Law of impact　　　$b - a = eu$

$$\Rightarrow a = \frac{1}{3}(2 - e)u \quad b = \frac{2}{3}(1 + e)u$$

We can economise on working by noticing that the second impact is identical in all respects to the first (one sphere at rest, masses in ratio 2 : 1). Thus

$$c = \frac{1}{3}(2 - e)b \quad d = \frac{2}{3}(1 + e)b$$

$$\Rightarrow c = \frac{2}{9}(1 + e)(2 - e)u \quad d = \frac{4}{9}(1 + e)^2 u$$

If there is to be a third impact it must be between $4m$ and $2m$. The condition for this to occur is

$$a > c$$

$$\frac{1}{3}(2 - e)u > \frac{2}{9}(1 + e)(2 - e)u$$

Since $(2 - e)$ must be positive we can divide it out from this inequality, obtaining

$$3 > 2(1 + e)$$
$$3 > 2 + 2e$$
$$\Rightarrow e < 1/2 \text{ for a third impact}$$

Exercise 14(d)

(All impacts may be assumed to be direct.)

1. A marble of mass 20 g moving with speed 3 m s^{-1} strikes a stationary marble of mass 30 g. Find
   (i) the speeds after impact if $e = 0.9$
   (ii) the value of e if the first marble is brought to rest.
2. A sphere of mass 0.6 kg moving with velocity $6i$ m s^{-1} overtakes and collides with a sphere of mass 0.4 kg moving with velocity $3i$ m s^{-1}. If $e = 2/3$ find the velocities after the collision and also the kinetic energy lost in the impact.
3. Two ball bearings each of mass 50 g collide when travelling with velocities $12i$ m s^{-1} and $-8i$ m s^{-1} respectively. If $e = 0.8$ find their velocities after the collision and the magnitude of the impulse each receives on impact.

4. A particle A of mass $3m$ travelling at speed $2u$ collides with a second particle B of mass $4m$ which is moving with speed u in the same direction. As a result of the impact A's speed is reduced to u, the direction of motion remaining the same. Find the co-efficient of restitution and obtain also an expression for the kinetic energy lost in the impact.

5. Two marbles of masses 30 g and 50 g collide when moving in opposite directions with speeds 70 cm s^{-1} and 30 cm s^{-1} respectively. After the impact the marbles both move at the same speed but in opposite directions. Find the co-efficient of restitution.

6. Particles of masses m and km collide when moving in opposite directions with speeds $2u$ and u respectively. If the particle of mass m is brought to rest, find the co-efficient of restitution and show that $k > 1/2$.

7. A body of mass 2 kg collides with a stationary body of mass m kg. One-third of the original kinetic energy of the system is lost as a result of the impact. (i) If the impact is inelastic, find the value of m. (ii) If the 2 kg body is brought to rest, find the value of m and also the co-efficient of restitution.

8. Two particles A and B of masses $3m$ and $4m$ are at rest on a smooth horizontal table. A is projected towards B with velocity ui m s^{-1}.
   (i)   Show that the velocity of A is reversed in direction as a result of the impact if $e > 3/4$.
   (ii) Find the range of possible values in which B's velocity after impact may lie and state clearly the circumstances in which each of the two extreme values arises.
   (iii) Find the maximum possible kinetic energy loss and state the circumstances in which this occurs.

9. Find the energy loss in an inelastic impact between bodies of masses m_1 and m_2, one of which is initially at rest and the other moving at speed u.

10. Three identical small balls A, B and C lie at rest in a straight line on a smooth horizontal surface. The co-efficient of restitution between any pair of balls is e. If A is projected towards B with speed u, find the speeds of all three balls after two impacts have occurred and show that there must necessarily be a third impact.

11. Three small spheres A, B and C of masses $4m$, $6m$ and $9m$ respectively lie in a straight line on a smooth horizontal surface. If A is projected towards B with speed u, find the speeds of the spheres after the first two impacts. Show that if $e = 2/3$ then two of the spheres are brought to rest. Prove also that there is a third impact if $e < 2/3$.

12. Two particles A and B hang from a fixed point O on light inextensible strings of equal length. A is pulled aside through an angle θ and then released from rest. If A is brought to rest by the subsequent impact and B swings aside through an angle φ, prove that

$$e = \frac{\sin \frac{1}{2}\varphi}{\sin \frac{1}{2}\theta}$$

13. A particle A is allowed to fall freely from rest at the same instant as a second particle B of equal mass is projected upwards with speed v from a point vertically below. An impact occurs after which the particle A

just returns to its original position. Show that the impact occurs when both particles have been moving for a time $(1 + e)v/4g$ and find the ratio of the distances covered in this time. Prove also that B continues to rise after the impact if $e < 1/3$.

*14. (i) In an impact between two bodies of equal mass moving with speeds u and $v(u > v)$ in the same direction, show that the common velocity reached at the end of the compression stage of the impact is $(u + v)/2$. Hence show that the kinetic energy used in compression is $m(u - v)^2/4$.

(ii) If the bodies separate after impact with speeds x and y $(y > x)$, explain why $u + v = x + y$ and use this result to show that the energy of compression which is released again in the expansion stage of the impact is $m(y - x)^2/4$.

(iii) Hence show that the fraction of the energy of compression which is released is given by e^2.

14.6 Impact with a Fixed Plane

If a body strikes a fixed plane when moving with speed v in a direction normal to the plane, then it will rebound with speed ev, where e is the co-efficient of restitution between the body and the plane. (Fig. 11.) This is a

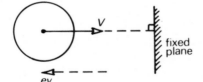

Fig. 11

consequence of Newton's law of impact, the relative velocities before and after impact being simply the velocities of the body as the plane is unable to move.

Notice that we cannot use conservation of momentum in this situation. Although it is true to say that the body and the plane receive equal and opposite impulses, that given to the plane is effectively shared with the earth (to which the plane is fixed), producing a change in velocity which is far too small to be measured.

Exercise 14(e)

1. A ball is released from rest at height h above horizontal ground. Show that if the co-efficient of restitution is e, the ball will bounce to height e^2h.

2. At what speed should a ball be thrown vertically downwards if it is just to return to its starting point after bouncing on horizontal ground 2.5 metres below, the co-efficient of restitution being 0.8?

3. A small ball A lies at rest on a smooth horizontal surface at a distance d from a fixed vertical wall. An identical ball B travelling towards the wall at speed u collides directly with A. If the co-efficient of restitution between A and B and between A and the wall is 0.6, find the distance from the wall at which the second impact between A and B occurs.

4. Two particles A and B of masses m and km respectively lie on a horizontal surface in a line perpendicular to a fixed vertical wall. The co-efficient of restitution between A and B and between B and the wall is e. A is projected directly towards B with speed u. If A is brought to rest by the first impact, show that $k = 1/e$. B rebounds from the wall and then strikes A again. If the final speeds of A and B are in the ratio $2 : 1$, find the value of e.

*5. Show that for a ball bouncing on a horizontal surface the times for successive bounces form a geometric progression with common ratio e. If the speed of the ball immediately *after* the first bounce is v, show that the further time which elapses before the ball is at rest is $2v/g(1 - e)$. Hence show that if the ball is initially released from a height h, then the total time for which the ball is bouncing is

$$\frac{1 + e}{1 - e} \sqrt{\frac{2h}{g}}$$

15

Circular Motion

15.1 Angular Velocity

There are two types of motion: Translation (or straight line motion) and Rotation. The rate at which a body moves along a straight line is measured by its speed, the rate at which it rotates about an axis by **angular speed**. This is simply a measure of the angle through which the body turns in a given interval of time, e.g. 10° per minute or 5 radians per second. The units usually employed are radians per second (rad s^{-1}) but there are alternatives in common usage, e.g. a long-playing record turns with an angular speed of $33\frac{1}{3}$ r.p.m (revolutions per minute). This would be equivalent to

$$\frac{100}{3} \times 2\pi \text{ radians per minute}$$

or $\quad \dfrac{100}{3} \times \dfrac{2\pi}{60} = \dfrac{10\pi}{9} \text{ rad s}^{-1}$

It should be mentioned at this point that the term **angular velocity** is widely used in preference to angular speed and we shall therefore use it in this book from this point. Technically angular velocity is a vector quantity but in our work we shall not be concerned with its directional aspect, only with its magnitude.

Speed of a rotating point

In Fig. 1 the point P is turning in a circle of radius r. The distance s which it covers in describing an angle of θ radians is given by

$$s = r\theta$$

differentiating $\quad \dfrac{ds}{dt} = r\dfrac{d\theta}{dt} \quad (r \text{ constant})$

i.e. $\quad v = rw$

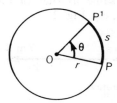

Fig. 1

where w is the angular velocity at any instant (given by the rate at which the angle θ is changing) and v is the speed of the moving point at that instant.

The result $v = rw$ is only valid when the angular velocity w is measured in radians per second. As an example consider a long-playing record of radius 15 cm. When turning at $33\frac{1}{3}$ r.p.m ($10\pi/9$ rad s^{-1}) the speed of a point on the outer rim is

$$v = \frac{15}{100} \times \frac{10\pi}{9} = \frac{\pi}{6}$$
$$= 0.524 \text{ m s}^{-1}$$

Exercise 15(a)

1. An 'E.P.' record has diameter $17\frac{1}{2}$ cm and turns at 45 r.p.m. Find its angular velocity in rad s^{-1} and the speed of a point on the rim of the record.
2. An electric fan rotates at 350 r.p.m. At what speed are the tips of the blades moving if the diameter of the fan is 20 cm?
3. A bicycle has wheels of diameter 60 cm. Find the total angle (in radians) through which the wheels turn in travelling 30 metres. If this distance is covered in 4 seconds, find the average angular velocity with which the wheels turn.
4. A belt moving at 4 m s^{-1} passes round a wheel of radius 28 cm. What is the angular velocity of the wheel in rad s^{-1} and how many turns does it make per minute?
5. What is the angular velocity in rad s^{-1} of (i) the second hand (ii) the minute hand of a clock. If the tip of the second hand moves 66 times faster than that of the minute hand, find the ratio of their radii.
*6. The point of contact of a bicycle wheel with the ground is instantaneously at rest (otherwise the bicycle would be skidding) and the wheel may be considered to rotate instantaneously about the stationary point of contact. Explain why the highest point of the wheel is always moving twice as fast as the bicycle itself. Explain also why there are always points on the wheel of a railway locomotive which are moving backwards (no matter how fast the locomotive is travelling).

15.2 Uniform Circular Motion

In chapter 5 we saw that acceleration is a vector quantity which defines the rate at which the velocity vector of a body is changing. If the direction of the acceleration vector is the same as that of the velocity vector, then straight line motion must result, e.g. Fig. 2.

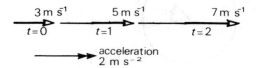

Fig. 2

If, however, the direction of the acceleration is different to that of the velocity, then the body follows a curved path. The simplest example of this is a projectile thrown horizontally but subject to a downward acceleration due to gravity, e.g. Fig. 3. The path of the projectile is parabolic.

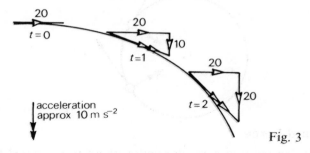

Fig. 3

We now ask the question: what sort of acceleration will result in a body travelling in a circular path at a steady speed? The most convenient way to approach this problem is to use the results for the differentiation of vectors which were established in section 5.8. Consider a body moving with uniform angular velocity ω in a circular path of radius r, (Fig. 4). The speed of the body is given by $v = r\omega$.

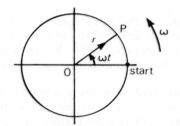

Fig. 4

If the body starts at the position indicated and reaches point P after time t, then the angle through which it will have turned in this time is ωt. The position vector OP in terms of unit vectors $\mathbf{i}$ and $\mathbf{j}$ along the axes shown is therefore

$$\mathbf{r} = r \cos \omega t \, \mathbf{i} + r \sin \omega t \, \mathbf{j}$$

Thus
$$\mathbf{v} = \frac{d\mathbf{r}}{dt} = -\omega r \sin \omega t \, \mathbf{i} + \omega r \cos \omega t \, \mathbf{j}$$

$$\mathbf{a} = \frac{d\mathbf{v}}{dt} = -\omega^2 r \cos \omega t \, \mathbf{i} - \omega^2 r \sin \omega t \, \mathbf{j}$$

i.e.
$$\mathbf{a} = -\omega^2 \mathbf{r}$$

The acceleration of the point P is therefore opposite in direction to the position vector $\mathbf{r}$, i.e inwards towards the centre of the circle. The magnitude of this acceleration is $\omega^2 r$ (or v^2/r, using the result $v = r\omega$).

Summary. A body moving in a circular path at steady speed is subject to an acceleration which is fixed in magnitude (v^2/r or $\omega^2 r$) but continually changing in direction since, at any instant, it must be directed towards the centre of the path, (Fig. 5).

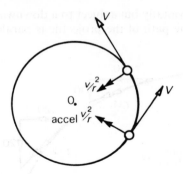

Fig. 5

15.3 Inward Force

No body can move in a circular path without being caused to do so by some outside force. (In the absence of such a force the body will move in a straight line path in accordance with Newton's First Law.)

Using the equation of motion $\mathbf{F} = m\mathbf{a}$, we see that in order to provide the required acceleration for circular motion (i.e. $\mathbf{a} = -\omega^2\mathbf{r}$) we must have a force

$$\mathbf{F} = -m\omega^2\mathbf{r}$$

This force, being necessarily in the same direction as the acceleration (Newton's Second Law), must always be directed towards the centre of the circular path. Its magnitude is $m\omega^2r$ or mv^2/r. We shall call this force the *inward force* needed for circular motion. It is sometimes called centripetal force.

Such a force must be provided in a given situation by some known agency, e.g. friction in the case of a car cornering (Fig. 6), tension in a string as, for example, when a conker is twirled on a string, or gravitational attraction in the case of a satellite orbiting the earth. If for some reason the inward force ceases to act, then the body concerned will cease to describe a circular path. Thus if the string of the conker snaps the conker flies off – reverting for that instant to straight line motion along the tangent to its previous path. A similar thing happens to the cornering car if it encounters a patch of ice.

Example 95

Find the greatest speed at which a car can negotiate a corner of radius 50 m on a horizontal track without skidding, if the co-efficient of friction between the tyres and the track is 0.4.

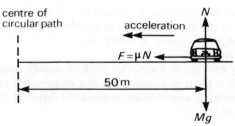

As the dimensions of the car will be small compared with the radius of the corner we are justified in treating the car as a point mass in this problem. The total of the contact forces at the four wheels is therefore marked as a single force N. We consider the case where the maximum available friction μN is needed to provide the inward force.

R($\leftarrow$) inward force $\qquad \dfrac{Mv^2}{r} = \mu N$

R($\uparrow$) no acceleration $\quad Mg = N$

Hence, dividing, $\qquad\qquad \dfrac{v^2}{rg} = \mu$

that is $\qquad\qquad\qquad\quad v^2 = 0.4 \times 50 \times 9.8$

$\qquad\qquad\qquad \Rightarrow \quad v = 14 \, \text{m s}^{-1}$

To negotiate this corner at a faster speed would require a larger inward force than the friction is capable of providing. The car would skid (or else follow a path of larger radius).

Exercise 15(b)

1. A particle of mass 250 g is attached to a point O on a smooth horizontal surface by a string of length 50 cm. What is the tension in the string when the particle describes a horizontal circle about O with angular velocity 12 rad s^{-1}? If the maximum tension the string can withstand is 50 N, find the greatest possible angular velocity of the particle.

2. What co-efficient of friction is required in order that a car travelling on a horizontal track at 54 km h^{-1} may negotiate a corner of radius 75 m without skidding?

3. A boy swings a conker of mass 35 g in a horizontal circle of radius 70 cm. The string may be assumed to remain horizontal. If the string snaps when its tension is 5 N, at what speed will the conker fly off and after what interval of time will it be 2.5 metres horizontally from the centre of its circular path?

4. The maximum safe speed of a car on a corner of radius 45 m is 12 m s^{-1}. What is the maximum speed of the car on a corner of radius 60 m, assuming the road surface to be the same as before?

5. A particle is placed gently at a distance d from the centre of a record player turntable rotating at $33\frac{1}{3}$ r.p.m. Is the particle more likely to slip near the centre or near the edge of the turntable? If the co-efficient of friction is 0.15, find the range of values of d for which slipping would occur.

6. A cylinder of radius r rotates about its axis, which is vertical, with angular velocity ω. Show that a particle in contact with its inner surface will not slip providing $\omega^2 \geqslant g/\mu r$, where μ is the co-efficient of friction at the contact.

7. A particle of mass 0.4 kg is attached to a point P on a smooth horizontal surface by an elastic string of natural length 0.5 m and modulus 120 N. Find the length of the string when the particle describes horizontal circles about P with an angular velocity of 15 rad s^{-1}.

8. Two equal masses of 2 kg are attached to the ends A and B of a light rod of length 1 m. The rod rotates in a horizontal plane at 5 rad s^{-1} about a point P on its length where AP = 0.6 m. Find the tension in each section of the rod and deduce the strain on the pivot, stating its direction.

9. Two equal particles are attached to the midpoint and to one end of an inextensible string. The other end of the string is attached to a point on a smooth horizontal plane and the system is made to describe horizontal circles about this point. Find the ratio of the tensions in the two parts of the string, assuming it to remain straight.

10. A particle of mass m describes a horizontal circle on an elastic string of natural length l and modulus λ, the string remaining horizontal. Find the extension in the string when the particle moves with angular velocity ω and show that the string must snap if $\omega^2 \geqslant \lambda/ml$.

*11. The gravitational attraction exerted by the earth on a body is inversely proportional to the square of the distance of the body from the centre of the earth. Taking the earth to be a sphere of radius 6400 km, find the speed of a satellite orbiting the earth at a height of 300 km, and find to the nearest minute the time taken for one circuit of the earth.

15.4 Banked Tracks and The Conical Pendulum

Banking the road on a bend enables a car to corner without needing friction, for the inward force needed can be provided by the inward component of the normal reaction, (Fig. 6).

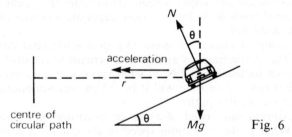

Fig. 6

If there is no friction between the tyres and the road, then we have

R($\leftarrow$)   inward force $\dfrac{Mv^2}{r} = N \sin \theta$

R($\uparrow$) no acceleration $Mg = N \cos \theta$

dividing $\dfrac{v^2}{rg} = \tan \theta$

This equation enables the correct angle of banking θ to be calculated if the corner is to be designed for a particular speed v. The corner may of course be negotiated at higher speeds than v, providing sufficient friction is available. The best method for solving problems of this nature is illustrated in example 96.

A similar configuration of forces to that of Fig. 6 is encountered with the *conical pendulum.* Here a particle suspended on a light string describes horizontal circles, the line of the string tracing out the surface of a cone, (Fig. 7).

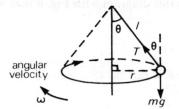

angular velocity

ω

mg Fig. 7

If the string is fixed in length, l, then the radius of the circular path followed by the particle is given by $r = l \sin \theta$

$$R(\leftarrow) \quad \text{inward force} \quad m\omega^2(l \sin \theta) = T \sin \theta$$
$$\Rightarrow \qquad T = m\omega^2 l$$
$$R(\uparrow) \text{ no acceleration} \qquad T \cos \theta = mg$$
$$\text{dividing} \qquad \sec \theta = \frac{\omega^2 l}{g}$$

For a given length pendulum rotating at a given angular velocity ω this equation will determine the inclination θ of the string to the vertical. Notice that this is independent of the mass of the particle. Since $\sec \theta \geqslant 1$ there is a minimum angular rate at which the pendulum may rotate; in fact $\omega^2 \geqslant l/g$.

Example 96

A corner of radius 150 m is banked at 15°.
(i) At what speed will a car have no tendency to side-slip?
(ii) If the co-efficient of friction between tyres and road is 0.4, find the greatest possible speed at which the corner may be taken without skidding.

(i) Any tendency of a car to side-slip is opposed by friction. We are required, therefore, to find the speed at which a car can corner without friction. Using the result obtained in the above section for a banked track

$$\text{i.e.} \quad \frac{v^2}{rg} = \tan \theta$$
$$v^2 = 150 \times 9.8 \times \tan 15° = 393.8$$
$$\Rightarrow \text{speed } v = 19.8 \text{ m s}^{-1}$$

(ii) At the greatest possible speed friction will be limiting. We may therefore replace the normal and frictional forces by a total reaction (section 9.5) at

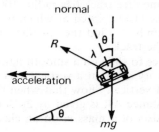

normal

R

λ

θ

acceleration

θ

mg Fig. 8

angle λ to the normal, where tan $\lambda = 0.4$, i.e. $\lambda = 21° 48'$. This gives the force diagram of Fig. 8, where $\theta = 15°$ and $\lambda = 21° 48'$.

It is clear by comparing this diagram with Fig. 6 that we will now obtain the result

$$\frac{v^2}{rg} = \tan(\theta + \lambda)$$

$$v^2 = 150 \times 9.8 \times \tan 36° 48'$$

$$\Rightarrow \text{speed } v = 33.2 \text{ m s}^{-1}$$

Exercise 15(c)

1. At what angle should a road be banked on a corner of radius 120 m if cars travelling at 20 m s^{-1} are to have no tendency to side-slip?

2. In level flight the weight of an aircraft is supported by upward lift forces created by the passage of the wings through the air. These forces may be taken as normal to the upper surfaces of the wings. Explain how a pilot can turn the aircraft in a horizontal circle by banking. If an aircraft moving at 150 m s^{-1} is banked at an angle of 20°, what will be the radius of the turn effected?

3. A conical pendulum consisting of a particle of mass 20 g on an inextensible string of length 30 cm rotates at 7 rad s^{-1}. Find (i) the tension in the string (ii) the angle between the string and the vertical (iii) the speed of the particle.

4. A hemisphere of radius r is fixed with its rim uppermost and in a horizontal plane. A particle of mass m moves in a horizontal circle on its smooth inner surface with angular velocity ω. Show that the depth, d, of the circle below the centre of the hemisphere is independent of r and find the value of d if $\omega = 14$ rad s^{-1}.

5. A conical pendulum consists of a particle of mass m on an elastic string of natural length a and modulus $6mg$. The pendulum rotates with the string inclined at 60° to the vertical. Find the tension in the string and show that its length is $4a/3$. Hence find the angular velocity of the particle.

6. A race track corner of radius 180 m is banked at $22\frac{1}{2}°$. If a certain car can just remain stationary on this corner without slipping, what is the co-efficient of friction between its tyres and the track? Find also the fastest speed at which the car can negotiate the corner without skidding.

7. Another corner on the same race track has radius 100 m and is banked at 30°. A driver finds that the fastest speed at which he can take the corner without skidding is 120 km h^{-1}. Find the co-efficient of friction between the tyres of the car and the track.

8. A small heavy ring R is free to slide on a smooth light rod AB. The rod is rotated with angular velocity ω about a vertical axis through A, with AB held at 60° to the upward vertical. Show that when the ring is stationary relative to the rod the distance AR is given by $2g/3\omega^2$.

9. A conical pendulum consists of a mass m on an elastic string of natural

length a. When rotating at ω rad s^{-1} the length of the string is l. Prove that $m\omega^2 a = \lambda(l - a)/l$ where λ is the modulus of the string. On such a pendulum a string of length 16 cm is stretched to 20 cm at a certain angular velocity. If the angular velocity is increased by 50% show that the length will increase to nearly 30 cm.

15.5 Harder Problems

The following worked example is typical of problems involving motion in a horizontal circle under several forces, of which two or more have components contributing towards the necessary inward force. In general a satisfactory method will be the division of the two equations found by (i) overall inward force $= m\omega^2 r$ (ii) vertical forces balance (no vertical acceleration).

Example 97

A light rod AB of length 0.6 m is freely pivoted at A and supports a load at B. The rod is maintained in a horizontal position by an inextensible string joining B to a point C 0.8 m vertically above A. The system rotates about the line AC. Show that the rod will be under thrust if the angular velocity is less than $\omega = \sqrt{5g/4}$ and find the ratio of the forces in AB and CB when the angular velocity is 2ω.

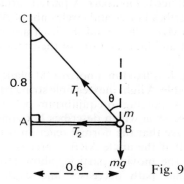

Fig. 9

We shall begin by assuming that both the string and the rod are under tension. These forces, as they act on the load at B, are marked T_1 and T_2 in Fig. 9. By Pythagoras, $\sin \theta = 3/5$ and $\cos \theta = 4/5$, so that

$$R(\leftarrow) \quad \text{inward force} \qquad \frac{3T_1}{5} + T_2 = m\omega^2 \frac{3}{5}$$

$$R(\uparrow) \quad \text{no acceleration} \qquad \frac{4T_1}{5} = mg$$

$$\text{dividing} \qquad \frac{3T_1 + 5T_2}{4T_1} = \frac{3\omega^2}{5g} \tag{1}$$

The rod AB is in thrust when $T_2 < 0$. If this is the case, then from equation (1) we have

$$\frac{3\omega^2}{5g} < \frac{3T_1}{4T_1} \text{ or } \frac{3}{4}$$

$$\Rightarrow \omega^2 < \frac{5g}{4}$$

When the angular velocity is twice this critical value, then $\omega^2 = 5g$ and equation (1) gives

$$\frac{3T_1 + 5T_2}{4T_1} = 3$$
$$3T_1 + 5T_2 = 12T_1$$
$$9T_1 = 5T_2$$
$$\Rightarrow T_1 : T_2 = 5 : 9$$

Note: With this type of question it is very often better to treat each part of the problem as a particular case of a more general result (equation (1) in this example) rather than to deal with each separately.

Exercise 15(d)

1. The ends of a light inextensible string are attached to points A and B in a vertical line at a distance 0.9 m apart. A particle attached to the midpoint, M, of the string describes horizontal circles about AB. When both strings are taut the angle AMB = 90°. Find the least angular velocity for which both strings are taut and find the ratio of their tensions when the angular velocity is 14 rad s^{-1}.

2. A small smooth ring R is fixed in a horizontal plane at a height h above a smooth horizontal table. A light inextensible string passing through the ring connects a particle A hanging in equilibrium below the ring to a second particle B of equal mass m which describes horizontal circles on the surface of the table. Prove that the normal reaction between B and the table is $mg - m\omega^2 h$ and that the angle ARB is arccos $(\omega^2 h/g)$, where ω is the angular velocity of the moving particle. Show that as ω increases, the radius of the circular path decreases and explain what happens as $\omega^2 \to g/h$. (Assume that the particle A is not brought into contact with either the table or the ring.)

3. A small smooth ring R of mass 0.1 kg is free to slide on an inextensible string of length 0.85 m, the ends of which are attached to points A and B a distance 0.65 m apart with A vertically above B. The ring rotates in a horizontal circle about AB with AR = 0.6 m. Show that the speed v m s^{-1} of the ring is given by $v^2 = 51g/91$ and find the tension in the string.

4. Two equal light rods AB and BC, freely jointed at B, carry a mass m at B and a ring of mass m is attached to C. The ring is free to slide on a smooth rod fixed in a vertical line beneath A. Prove that when the system rotates at angular velocity ω about AC, the depth of the ring below A is $6g/\omega^2$.

5. A smooth light rod is free to rotate in a horizontal plane about its mid-point M. A small heavy ring R of mass m is threaded onto the rod and

attached to a point P vertically above M, where MP $= a$, by an elastic string of natural length a. Prove that the contact force between the rod and the ring vanishes when $\omega^2 = g/a$, if in this situation the distance MR $= 3a/4$ find the modulus of the string. Find also the contact force and the distance MR when $\omega^2 = 2g/a$.

6. Two small smooth rings of masses m and $2m$ are threaded on a smooth circular wire of radius 0.5 m and connected by a light rod of length 0.8 m. The wire is made to rotate about a fixed vertical diameter. Find the angular velocity at which the rod remains at rest relative to the wire in a vertical position and find the force in the rod in this situation.

15.6 Motion in a Vertical Circle

Consider a small car of mass 500 kg crossing the brow of a hill at 10 m s^{-1}, (Fig. 10). We shall suppose that the highest part of the hill is circular

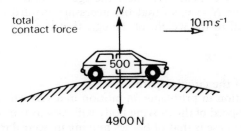

Fig. 10

in section with radius 25 m. The car is then travelling in a circular path of radius 25 m and a force of

$$\frac{mv^2}{r} = \frac{500 \times 100}{25} = 2000 \text{ N}$$

Considering the vertical forces acting on the car (Fig. 10) we have

$4900 - N = 2000$
contact force $N = 2900$ N

i.e. considerably less than that occurring during level motion.

If the car is driven sufficiently fast it will leave the road. When this happens $N = 0$ as contact is broken. The limiting case is therefore when the required inward force is exactly equal to the weight of the car, that is

$$\frac{mv^2}{r} = 4900$$
$\Rightarrow$ speed $v = 15.7$ m s^{-1}

The car will therefore leave the road if travelling at a speed greater than 15.7 m s^{-1}.

A similar situation, though one which is not so simple to understand, is that of an egg in a basket which is swung in a vertical circle. Providing the basket is swung round quickly enough the egg does not fall, but what prevents it from doing so? The answer to this is that the egg has no real wish to fall! Consider the highest point of the circle, (Fig. 11). If free to move independently the egg would not fall vertically but fly off instead along the tangent to its circular path – just as a cricket ball does when released by the bowler.

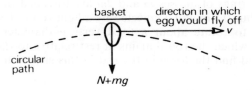

Fig. 11

The contact force from the basket, (which actually presses down on the egg) together with the weight of the egg, provides a downward force which prevents the egg from following this tangential path and forces it instead into a circular one. In the critical case where the egg is about to lose contact with the basket we have $N = 0$, so that the necessary inward force for the circular motion is equal to the weight of the egg, that is

$$\frac{mv^2}{r} = mg \quad \Rightarrow v^2 = rg$$

where r is the radius of the circular path.

A frequent complication in problems on motion in a vertical circle is that in many situations the speed of the moving body will vary as it moves around the circle. An important case is that of bodies moving in accordance with the principle of conservation of mechanical energy. Example 98 considers a problem of this type.

Example 98

A particle of mass 30 g hangs from a fixed point O on an inelastic string of length 40 cm. Find the least horizontal velocity with which the particle may be projected if it is to describe complete circles about O. Find also the tension in the string (i) at the lowest point of the path, (ii) when the string is horizontal.

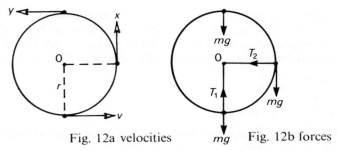

Fig. 12a velocities   Fig. 12b forces

In problems of this nature it is often easier to work in terms of symbols and substitute values only at the end. We shall therefore call the mass m and the radius of the circular path r.

Since no external force does work on the particle (the tension always being perpendicular to the motion), Mechanical Energy is conserved and the velocities shown in Fig. 12a are related as follows

$$\text{loss in K.E} = \text{gain in P.E}$$
$$\tfrac{1}{2}mv^2 - \tfrac{1}{2}my^2 = mg \times 2r \Rightarrow v^2 = y^2 + 4gr \tag{1}$$
$$\tfrac{1}{2}mv^2 - \tfrac{1}{2}mx^2 = mg \times r \qquad v^2 = x^2 + 2gr \tag{2}$$

When the particle is projected with the least possible speed v, the string will just slacken at the highest point of the circle, (Fig. 12b). Thus

$$\text{inward force} \quad \frac{my^2}{r} = mg \Rightarrow y^2 = gr$$

from (1) $\qquad v^2 = 5gr = 5 \times 9.8 \times 0.4$

$\Rightarrow$ least speed $\qquad v = 4.43 \text{ m s}^{-1}$

(i) At the lowest point of the path

$$\text{inward force} \quad \frac{mv^2}{r} = T_1 - mg \quad \text{where } v^2 = 5gr$$

$$\Rightarrow T_1 = 6\,mg = 1.76 \text{ N}$$

(ii) When the string is horizontal

$$\text{inward force} \quad \frac{mx^2}{r} = T_2 \quad \text{where } x^2 = 3gr \text{ from (2)}$$

$$\Rightarrow T_2 = 3mg = 0.88 \text{ N}$$

We notice in passing that when the string is horizontal the particle is subject to overall forces of $T_2 = 3mg$ horizontally and mg vertically downwards. At this instant it is therefore subject to accelerations of $3g$ horizontally and g vertically downwards.

Exercise 15(e)

1. A motocross rider and his machine, of total mass 160 kg, cross the highest point of a small hillock at 12 m s^{-1}. Find the total contact force between the wheels and the ground if the highest part of the hillock may be taken as a circular arc of radius 20 m. At what speed would the machine leave the ground?

2. A light aircraft loops the loop. At the highest point of the loop the speed of the aircraft is 75 m s^{-1} and the radius of the path followed is 180 m. Find the magnitude of the contact force between the pilot, whose mass is 80 kg, and his seat at this moment.

3. A man swings a basket containing an egg of mass 60 g in a vertical circle, the egg moving in a circle of radius 80 cm. Find the least angular velocity which must be maintained if the egg is not to fall from the basket. If the man maintains a steady angular velocity of 5 rad s^{-1}, find the greatest and least values of the contact force between the egg and the basket. (Assume that there is sufficient friction to prevent the egg slipping on the basket.)

4. When the bob of a simple pendulum passes through its lowest position,

the tension in the string is $2W$, where W is the weight of the bob. Find the total angle through which the pendulum swings and the tension in the string at the extreme positions.

5. A swing is free to move in a circular arc of radius 2.5 m. A child of mass 20 kg seated on the swing moves in an arc which rises on both sides to 0.5 m above the lowest point. Find the force exerted by the child on the seat of the swing (i) at the lowest point of the path (ii) at the extreme points of the path. State also the magnitude and direction of his acceleration in both cases.

6. A particle of mass 50 g is attached to a fixed point O by an inextensible string of length 30 cm. The particle is held at the same level as O with the string taut. Find the least velocity with which the particle must be projected vertically downwards if it is to complete vertical circles about O. Find also the greatest and least tensions in the string if the particle is projected with twice this speed. (Take $g = 10 \text{ m s}^{-2}$.)

7. A tobogganist travelling across snow-covered horizontal ground is unable to avoid a bank of drifted snow 2 m high. The section of the upper part of the bank is a circular arc of radius 6 m and the sides run smoothly onto the horizontal ground. Ignoring any resistances, find the limits between which the toboggan's speed must lie if it is to cross the bank without leaving the snow.

8. A point mass m is attached by a string of length l to a fixed point O. The mass is released from rest with the string horizontal and taut. Find the tension in the string as the mass passes through the lowest point of its path. At this moment the string encounters a small peg P fixed vertically below O. Show that the mass will describe complete circles about P if OP $\geqslant 3l/5$.

9. A particle of mass m attached to a fixed point O by an inextensible string of length l describes complete vertical circles about O. If the greatest tension in the string is four times the least, find the speed of the particle at the lowest point of the circle. Find also the tension in the string when it is horizontal.

15.7 Harder Problems

In this section we consider problems of motion in a vertical circle in which a contact or tension force must be found at a general point on the circle, or in which the particle leaves its circular path at some unknown point.

Example 99

A particle is at rest at the highest point of a fixed smooth sphere of radius r. If the particle is projected at speed v along the surface of the sphere, where $v^2 = \frac{1}{2}gr$, find an expression for the contact force between the particle and the sphere when the radius to the particle has turned through an angle θ. Find also the depth of the particle below its starting point at the instant it leaves the sphere.

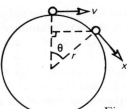

Fig. 13a velocities

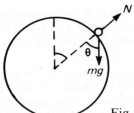

Fig. 13b forces

Let the speed of the particle at the instant required be x (Fig. 13a). Then by conservation of mechanical energy

$$\tfrac{1}{2}mx^2 = \tfrac{1}{2}mv^2 + mgr(1 - \cos \theta)$$

From this formula we can easily obtain an expression for the quantity mx^2/r, which will be the magnitude of the inward force required at the point considered. We obtain

$$\frac{mx^2}{r} = \frac{mv^2}{r} + 2mg(1 - \cos \theta)$$
$$= \tfrac{1}{2}mg + 2mg - 2mg \cos \theta \quad (v^2 = \tfrac{1}{2}rg)$$

But from the force diagram of Fig. 13b we see that the inward force is $mg \cos \theta - N$

that is $\quad mg \cos \theta - N = 5mg/2 - 2mg \cos \theta$
$$\Rightarrow N = mg(3 \cos \theta - 5/2)$$

The particle leaves the sphere when $N = 0$, i.e. when $\cos \theta = 5/6$. Its depth below the starting point is therefore

$$r - r\cos \theta = r/6$$

Exercise 15(f)

1. A particle P of mass m is released from rest at a point on the inner rim of a smooth hemispherical bowl of centre O fixed with its rim uppermost and in a horizontal plane. Find the contact force between the particle and the hemisphere when the radius OP has turned through (i) 30°, (ii) 60°.

2. A particle P is displaced from rest at the highest point of a smooth cylinder of radius r fixed with its axis horizontal. Find an expression for the normal reaction between the particle and the cylinder when the radius to P is inclined at angle θ to the upward vertical. Hence find the speed and direction of P's velocity at the instant it leaves the cylinder.

3. A particle of mass m attached by an inextensible string of length l to a fixed point O is projected vertically downwards with speed $\sqrt{4gl}$ from a position in which the particle is level with O and the string is taut. If the greatest tension that the string can withstand is $6mg$, find the angle through which the string turns before it breaks.

4. A pendulum carrying a bob of mass m swings through a total angle of 2α. Find an expression for the tension in the string when its inclination to

the vertical is θ. If the greatest tension is twice the least, find the value of α. For this value of α find also the components of the acceleration of the bob (i) along the string (ii) perpendicular to the string when $\theta = $ arc cos (4/5).

5. The particle of question 3 is projected horizontally at speed $\sqrt{3gl}$ from the position in which it hangs vertically below O. Find the height of the particle above its initial position at the instant the string goes slack and the further vertical height to which the particle rises.

6. A light rod OA of length 25 cm is freely pivoted at O and carries a small body of mass 1/2 kg at A. The end A is projected horizontally at 2.5 m s^{-1} from its lowest possible position. Find the tension in the rod when OA has turned through an angle θ and show that the tension changes to thrust when $\theta = \arccos(-1/6)$. What further vertical height does A gain before it comes instantaneously to rest. (Take $g = 10$ m s^{-2}.)

7. A smooth cylinder is fixed with its axis horizontal and a string passing over the top of the cylinder connects two equal particles A and B which are at rest in contact with opposite ends of a horizontal diameter of the cylinder. A is given a slight downward displacement. Show that the speed of B when it leaves the surface of the cylinder is $\sqrt{gd/2}$ where d is the total distance A has descended at that instant.

8. A skier starts to slide down an icy slope which at first descends at a uniform angle α but after a distance d runs smoothly into a convex circular slope of radius r, whose centre is $2d$ vertically below the skier's starting point. Find the values of α and r. If the skier starts from rest and if there is no friction, show that he has descended through a vertical height. $2d/3$ when he leaves the slope and find his speed at this instant.

*9. A cylindrical drum of radius r rotates at uniform angular velocity ω about its axis which is horizontal. A particle of mass m in contact with its rough inner surface remains at rest relative to the drum. If $\omega^2 = 2g/r$, find expressions for the normal and frictional forces exerted by the drum on the particle when its angular displacement from the lowest point of the cylinder is θ. Hence show that the particle is most likely to slip when $\theta = 120°$ and find the least co-efficient of friction necessary to prevent slipping.

16
Vectors in Three-Dimensions

16.1 Cartesian Components

Any vector in three-dimensions may be expressed in terms of unit vectors **i**, **j** and **k** taken in the directions of the Ox, Oy and Oz axes of a Cartesian reference system. Considering any vector **OP** (Fig. 1), we have

$$\mathbf{OP} = \mathbf{OM} + \mathbf{MN} + \mathbf{NP}$$
$$= c\mathbf{k} + a\mathbf{i} + b\mathbf{j}$$

that is $\mathbf{OP} = a\mathbf{i} + b\mathbf{j} + c\mathbf{k}$

where the magnitudes a, b and c of the three components are most easily visualised as the edges of a three-dimensional rectangular box enclosing the vector concerned.

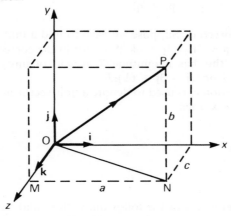

Fig. 1

Addition, subtraction and scalar multiplication. These operations are performed as easily in three-dimensions as they were in two dimensions (section 5.2). For example

if $\quad \mathbf{p} = \quad 2\mathbf{i} - 3\mathbf{j} + 6\mathbf{k}$
$\quad\quad \mathbf{q} = -2\mathbf{i} + 6\mathbf{j} - 2\mathbf{k}$

then $\mathbf{p} + \mathbf{q} = \quad\quad 3\mathbf{j} + 4\mathbf{k}$ (add components)
$\quad \mathbf{p} - \mathbf{q} = 4\mathbf{i} - 9\mathbf{j} + 8\mathbf{k}$ (subtract components)
$\quad 2\mathbf{p} \quad = 4\mathbf{i} - 6\mathbf{j} + 12\mathbf{k}$ (multiply components)

Vectors in parallel directions. A scalar multiple of a given vector **x** (e.g. 2**x** or −3**x**) is, by definition, a vector in the same direction as **x** (or −**x**). It follows that two vectors **x** and **y** will be in like parallel directions if there exists a positive scalar λ such that $\mathbf{x} = \lambda\mathbf{y}$. To illustrate this consider the vectors

$$\mathbf{r} = 6\mathbf{i} - 9\mathbf{j} + 18\mathbf{k}$$
and $$\mathbf{s} = \mathbf{i} - 3\mathbf{j} + \mathbf{k}$$

We notice that $\mathbf{r} = 3\mathbf{p}$ so that **r** and **p** are in like parallel directions. Furthermore, since $\mathbf{s} = -\mathbf{q}/2$, **s** and **q** are in unlike parallel directions, (the result implying that **s** is in the same direction as the vector $-\mathbf{q}$).

Magnitude of a vector. Applying Pythagoras' theorem to Fig. 1 we have

$$OP^2 = ON^2 + NP^2$$
$$= (a^2 + c^2) + b^2$$

that is if $\mathbf{OP} = a\mathbf{i} + b\mathbf{j} + c\mathbf{k}$ then $|\mathbf{OP}| = \sqrt{a^2 + b^2 + c^2}$

Using the vectors defined above as examples

$$\mathbf{p} = 2\mathbf{i} - 3\mathbf{j} + 6\mathbf{k} \quad \Rightarrow \quad |\mathbf{p}| = \sqrt{4 + 9 + 36} = 7 \text{ units}$$
$$\mathbf{q} = -2\mathbf{i} + 6\mathbf{j} - 2\mathbf{k} \quad\quad |\mathbf{q}| = \sqrt{4 + 36 + 4} = 2\sqrt{11} \text{ units}$$
$$\mathbf{p} + \mathbf{q} = \quad\quad 3\mathbf{j} + 4\mathbf{k} \quad |\mathbf{p} + \mathbf{q}| = \sqrt{9 + 16} \quad\quad = 5 \text{ units}$$

Notice again, as in section 5.2, that these results are in accordance with the 'Triangle Inequality' $|\mathbf{p} + \mathbf{q}| \leqslant |\mathbf{p}| + |\mathbf{q}|$

Unit vector in a given direction. Suppose we wish to find a unit vector in the direction of the vector $\mathbf{p} = 2\mathbf{i} - 3\mathbf{j} + 6\mathbf{k}$. A vector in the correct direction is the vector **p** itself but this has magnitude 7 instead of unity. The vector required is therefore $\mathbf{p}/7$ or $(2\mathbf{i} - 3\mathbf{j} + 6\mathbf{k})/7$.

In general, if the notation $\mathbf{e}_x$ is used to denote a unit vector in the direction of some specified vector **x**, then

$$\mathbf{e}_x = \frac{1}{|\mathbf{x}|}\,\mathbf{x}$$

Exercise 16(a)

1. Write down the magnitudes of the following vectors and hence find unit vectors in the directions concerned
   (i) $\mathbf{i} + 2\mathbf{j} - 2\mathbf{k}$ (ii) $-2\mathbf{i} + 6\mathbf{j} - 9\mathbf{k}$ (iii) $5\mathbf{i} - \mathbf{j} + 7\mathbf{k}$
2. Given $\mathbf{a} = 3\mathbf{i} + 5\mathbf{j} - \mathbf{k}$, $\mathbf{b} = 3\mathbf{i} - \mathbf{j} - 4\mathbf{k}$ and $\mathbf{c} = 4\mathbf{j} + 2\mathbf{k}$ write down the vectors $\mathbf{a} + \mathbf{b}$, $\mathbf{b} - \mathbf{a}$, $-2\mathbf{c}$ and $2\mathbf{b} + \mathbf{c}$.
   Which of the four vectors you have found is largest in magnitude and which two are parallel?
3. If $\mathbf{p} + \mathbf{q} = 6\mathbf{i} - 10\mathbf{j} + 4\mathbf{k}$ and $\mathbf{p} - \mathbf{q} = 3\mathbf{i} + 2\mathbf{j} + 8\mathbf{k}$, find the magnitudes of the vectors **p** and **q**.
4. If $\mathbf{OA} = 2\mathbf{i} - 3\mathbf{j} + 2\mathbf{k}$ and $\mathbf{OB} = 3\mathbf{i} - 7\mathbf{j} + 10\mathbf{k}$, find a unit vector in the direction of **AB**.
5. The co-ordinates of three points are P(3, −1, 1), Q(4, 2, −1) and R(7, 11, −7). By writing down the vectors **PQ** and **QR** show that the points are collinear. In which ratio does Q divide PR?

6. Forces $\mathbf{F}_1 = 2\mathbf{i} - 2\mathbf{j} - 4\mathbf{k}$, $\mathbf{F}_2 = 5\mathbf{i} - \mathbf{j}$ and $\mathbf{F}_3 = -3\mathbf{i} + 3\mathbf{j} + \mathbf{k}$ Newtons act on a point mass of 3 kg initially at rest. Find the magnitude of the acceleration of the mass.

7. Show that the points A(4, 3, 0), B(5, 2, 3). C(2, 1, −3) and D(4, −1, 3) form a trapezium, and state the ratio of the parallel sides.

8. If $\mathbf{r} = 3\mathbf{i} + 3\mathbf{j} - 6\mathbf{k}$, $\mathbf{s} = \mathbf{i} - 7\mathbf{j} + 6\mathbf{k}$ and $\mathbf{t} = -2\mathbf{i} - 5\mathbf{j} + 2\mathbf{k}$, find the values of λ and μ such that the vector $\mathbf{r} + \lambda\mathbf{s} + \mu\mathbf{t}$ is parallel to the x axis.

16.2 The Scalar Product

If two vectors **a** and **b** are written in Cartesian components as

$$\mathbf{a} = a_1\mathbf{i} + a_2\mathbf{j} + a_3\mathbf{k}$$
$$\mathbf{b} = b_1\mathbf{i} + b_2\mathbf{j} + b_3\mathbf{k}$$

then we define the **scalar product** of these two vectors, **a.b**, by

$$\boxed{\mathbf{a.b} = a_1b_1 + a_2b_2 + a_3b_3}$$

The result obtained from this 'product' is always a plain number or scalar – hence the name scalar product. For example

if $\quad\mathbf{x} = 2\mathbf{i} - 3\mathbf{j} + 4\mathbf{k}$
$\quad\quad\mathbf{y} = -\mathbf{i} - 3\mathbf{j} + 2\mathbf{k}$

then $\quad\mathbf{x.y} = -2 + 9 + 8 = 15$

At first sight this may seem a rather meaningless definition to make. The scalar product, however, has a number of important uses due largely to the following result, which will be proved shortly,

$$\boxed{\mathbf{a.b} = |\mathbf{a}|\,|\mathbf{b}|\cos\theta}$$

where θ is the angle between the positive directions of the vectors **a** and **b**, (Fig. 2)

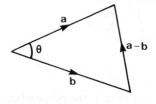

Fig. 2

In order to establish this result, let

$$\mathbf{a} = a_1\mathbf{i} + a_2\mathbf{j} + a_3\mathbf{k}$$
$$\mathbf{b} = b_1\mathbf{i} + b_2\mathbf{j} + b_3\mathbf{k}$$

then $\quad\mathbf{a} - \mathbf{b} = (a_1 - b_1)\mathbf{i} + (a_2 - b_2)\mathbf{j} + (a_3 - b_3)\mathbf{k}$

Working from the cosine rule in Fig. 2, we have

$$|\mathbf{a} - \mathbf{b}|^2 = |\mathbf{a}|^2 + |\mathbf{b}|^2 - 2|\mathbf{a}| |\mathbf{b}| \cos \theta$$
$$\Rightarrow (a_1 - b_1)^2 + (a_2 - b_2)^2 + (a_3 - b_3)^2$$
$$= (a_1^2 + a_2^2 + a_3^2) + (b_1^2 + b_2^2 + b_3^2) - 2|\mathbf{a}| |\mathbf{b}| \cos \theta$$

Removing all the square terms reduces this to

$$-2a_1b_1 - 2a_2b_2 - 2a_3b_3 = -2|\mathbf{a}| |\mathbf{b}| \cos \theta$$
$$\Rightarrow \quad a_1b_1 + a_2b_2 + a_3b_3 = |\mathbf{a}| |\mathbf{b}| \cos \theta$$
$$\text{i.e.} \quad \mathbf{a}.\mathbf{b} = |\mathbf{a}| |\mathbf{b}| \cos \theta$$

Note: Many textbooks prefer to *define* the scalar product by $\mathbf{a}.\mathbf{b} = |\mathbf{a}| |\mathbf{b}| \cos \theta$. Although this has advantages the author feels that the definition $\mathbf{a}.\mathbf{b} = a_1b_1 + a_2b_2 + a_3b_3$ is more suitable at this level, since it is considerably easier to grasp conceptually.

Angle between two vectors. This is readily found using the scalar product. As an example consider the vectors $\mathbf{a} = 4\mathbf{i} - 8\mathbf{k}$ and $\mathbf{b} = 2\mathbf{i} - 4\mathbf{j} + 4\mathbf{k}$

$$|\mathbf{a}| = \sqrt{16 + 64} = \sqrt{80} = 4\sqrt{5}$$
$$|\mathbf{b}| = \sqrt{4 + 16 + 16} = 6$$
$$\mathbf{a}.\mathbf{b} = \quad 8 + 0 - 32 = -24$$

Thus, working from the result $\mathbf{a}.\mathbf{b} = |\mathbf{a}| |\mathbf{b}| \cos \theta$ we have

$$-24 = 24\sqrt{5} \cos \theta$$
$$\cos \theta = \frac{-1}{\sqrt{5}} \simeq -0.4472$$
$$\Rightarrow \theta = 116° \; 34'$$

Perpendicular vectors. If two vectors are perpendicular then their scalar product must be zero (since $\cos \theta = 0$ when $\theta = 90°$). When vectors are given in Cartesian components this gives a very simple test for perpendicularity.

Exercise 16(b)

1. Evaluate the following scalar products:
    (i) $(3\mathbf{i} - 2\mathbf{j} + 3\mathbf{k}).(2\mathbf{i} - 5\mathbf{j} - 4\mathbf{k})$
    (ii) $(2\mathbf{i} + 4\mathbf{j} - \mathbf{k}).(-\mathbf{i} - \mathbf{j} - 6\mathbf{k})$
    (iii) $(\mathbf{i} - 2\mathbf{j}).(-\mathbf{i} + 3\mathbf{j} - 2\mathbf{k})$
    (iv) $\mathbf{i}.\mathbf{i}$
    (v) $\mathbf{j}.\mathbf{k}$
    (vi) $(\mathbf{i} + \mathbf{k}).\mathbf{j}$
2. Which pairs of vectors in question 1 are perpendicular?
3. (i) If $\mathbf{a} = -2\mathbf{i} + \mathbf{j} + 3\mathbf{k}$, $\mathbf{b} = 4\mathbf{i} - 3\mathbf{j} + 2\mathbf{k}$ and $\mathbf{c} = 3\mathbf{i} - 7\mathbf{j} - \mathbf{k}$, find the vector $\mathbf{a} + \mathbf{b}$ and evaluate the scalar products $\mathbf{a}.\mathbf{c}$, $\mathbf{b}.\mathbf{c}$ and $(\mathbf{a} + \mathbf{b}).\mathbf{c}$. Verify that $(\mathbf{a} + \mathbf{b}).\mathbf{c} = \mathbf{a}.\mathbf{c} + \mathbf{b}.\mathbf{c}$.
    (ii) Is the following statement also true?

$$\mathbf{a}.(\mathbf{b} + \mathbf{c}) = \mathbf{a}.\mathbf{b} + \mathbf{a}.\mathbf{c}$$

4. Find the angle between each pair of vectors:
   (i) $4\mathbf{i} - 4\mathbf{j} + 7\mathbf{k}$ and $-\mathbf{i} + 4\mathbf{j} + 8\mathbf{k}$
   (ii) $6\mathbf{i} - 8\mathbf{j}$ and $4\mathbf{i} - 12\mathbf{j} + 3\mathbf{k}$
   (iii) $-2\mathbf{i} + 3\mathbf{j} - \mathbf{k}$ and $-4\mathbf{i} - 6\mathbf{j} + 2\mathbf{k}$
5. Show that the lines joining the points A(4, -2, -3) and B(7, -1, 6) to the point C(1, 0, 2) are perpendicular.
6. A triangle has vertices L(8, 4, -3), M(6, 3, -4) and N(7, 5, -5). Find the angle LMN.
7. If $\mathbf{a} = 2\mathbf{i} - \mathbf{j} + 6\mathbf{k}$ and $\mathbf{b} = \mathbf{i} - \mathbf{j} - \mathbf{k}$ show that $\mathbf{a} + \mathbf{b}$ is perpendicular to $\mathbf{b}$ and find the angle between the vectors $\mathbf{a} + \mathbf{b}$ and $\mathbf{a} - \mathbf{b}$.
*8. (i) Find λ and μ such that the vector $\mathbf{i} + \lambda\mathbf{j} + \mu\mathbf{k}$ is perpendicular to both $\mathbf{x}$ and $\mathbf{y}$ where $\mathbf{x} = 2\mathbf{i} - 3\mathbf{j} + \mathbf{k}$ and $\mathbf{y} = 6\mathbf{i} + \mathbf{j} - 2\mathbf{k}$.
   (ii) Hence state a vector normal to the plane containing $\mathbf{x}$ and $\mathbf{y}$.
   (iii) State which of the following vectors are coplanar with $\mathbf{x}$ and $\mathbf{y}$

$$\mathbf{p} = 2\mathbf{i} - 5\mathbf{j} + 2\mathbf{k}, \quad \mathbf{q} = 3\mathbf{i} - \mathbf{k}, \quad \mathbf{r} = 2\mathbf{j} - \mathbf{k}.$$

*9. (i) If $\mathbf{x} = a\mathbf{i} + b\mathbf{j} + c\mathbf{k}$ makes angles α, β and γ with the three co-ordinate axes, use the scalar product $\mathbf{x}.\mathbf{i}$ to establish that

$$\cos \alpha = \frac{a}{\sqrt{a^2 + b^2 + c^2}}$$

   and write down similar results for $\cos \beta$ and $\cos \gamma$. (These are called the **direction cosines** of the vector $\mathbf{x}$.)
   (ii) Show that the unit vector $\mathbf{e}_x$ may be written in the form $\cos \alpha\, \mathbf{i} + \cos \beta\, \mathbf{j} + \cos \gamma\, \mathbf{k}$. Hence or otherwise prove that $\cos^2 \alpha + \cos^2 \beta + \cos^2 \gamma = 1$.
10. (i) Write down the direction cosines of each vector in question 1 of exercise 16(a).
    (ii) Calculate the angles which the following vectors make with each of the three co-ordinate axes

$$2\mathbf{i} - 3\mathbf{j} + 6\mathbf{k}, \quad \mathbf{i} + 4\mathbf{j} - 8\mathbf{k}$$

16.3 Some Questions on Earlier Work

The vector work earlier in this book was restricted to two-dimensions. The results established, however, are equally valid in three-dimensions and the following exercise gives a short selection of three-dimensional problems on earlier work. In general the methods used are identical to those employed previously.

Exercise 16(c)

1. Bodies of masses 3 kg and 5 kg collide when moving with velocities $3\mathbf{i} - 4\mathbf{j} + \mathbf{k}$ m s^{-1} and $-\mathbf{i} + 5\mathbf{k}$ m s^{-1} respectively. If the bodies coalesce find the velocity of the joint mass after the impact, the loss of kinetic energy and the magnitude of the impulse between the bodies.
2. (i) If $\mathbf{OP} = 4\mathbf{i} - 3\mathbf{j} + 5\mathbf{k}$ and $\mathbf{OQ} = 10\mathbf{i} + \mathbf{j} - 5\mathbf{k}$ find the position

vectors of the midpoint of PQ and the point dividing PQ in the ratio
5 : 3.

(ii) Prove that if two forces m **OA** and n **OB** act at the origin then their
resultant is given by $(m + n)$ **OR**, where R divides AB in the ratio
$n : m$.

3. Particles A and B of masses 2 and 3 units are moving with uniform
velocities $3\mathbf{i} + \mathbf{j} - 4\mathbf{k}$ m s^{-1} and $-\mathbf{i} + 3\mathbf{j}$ m s^{-1} respectively. Their positions at time $t = 0$ are $2\mathbf{j} + 5\mathbf{k}$ and $4\mathbf{i} - 3\mathbf{j} - 2\mathbf{k}$ (metres) respectively.
Write down the position vector of each particle at time t s and hence find
the position vector of the centre of mass at time t s. With what velocity
does the centre of mass move?

4. A body starts with velocity $-4\mathbf{i} + 3\mathbf{j} - 5\mathbf{k}$ m s^{-1} and moves with uniform acceleration $\mathbf{i} - 2\mathbf{j} + \mathbf{k}$ m s^{-2}. Show that after 5 s the speed of the
body is momentarily the same as its initial speed and find the angle
through which the direction of motion has turned during this time. Find
also the instant at which the body is moving perpendicular to its initial
direction of motion.

5. Two equal smooth spheres A and B collide when moving with velocities
$-3\mathbf{i} - \mathbf{k}$ m s^{-1} and $\mathbf{i} + 4\mathbf{j} + 5\mathbf{k}$ m s^{-1} respectively. After impact sphere
A has velocity $6\mathbf{j} + 2\mathbf{k}$ m s^{-1}. Find the angle between the paths of the two
spheres immediately after the impact. Show also that B is deflected
through 90° and that the impact is perfectly elastic.

6. A body of mass 4 kg moving initially through the origin with velocity
$2\mathbf{i} - 4\mathbf{j} + 2\mathbf{k}$ m s^{-1} is acted on by a varying force $\mathbf{F} = 8t\mathbf{i} + 16\mathbf{j}$ N. Find
the velocity of the body at time t s and deduce the times at which the
velocity of the body is perpendicular to its original direction of motion.
Find also the position vector of the body at each of these times.

7. A light framework in the form of a tetrahedron has vertices at the origin
O and at A(3, -1, 2), B(2, 4, 1) and C(-2, 0, -2). Point masses of 1, 2, 3
and 4 units respectively are attached at these points. Find the co-ordinates
of the centre of mass. If the tetrahedron hangs in equilibrium from O, show
that the edge OA is horizontal.

8. Two bodies A and B move with uniform velocities $3\mathbf{i} - 2\mathbf{j}$ and $\mathbf{i} + 4\mathbf{j} -$
$2\mathbf{k}$ from initial positions $2\mathbf{i} + 11\mathbf{j} - 3\mathbf{k}$ and $9\mathbf{i} - 10\mathbf{j} + 4\mathbf{k}$ respectively.
Show that the bodies will collide and find the position vector of the point
of collision.

16.4 Commutative and Distributive Laws for the Scalar Product

Commutative law. A commutative operation is one for which the order of
operation does not influence the result. Thus ordinary arithmetic addition is
commutative, (e.g. $4 + 7 = 7 + 4 = 11$), but subtraction is not, (e.g. $4 - 7$
$\neq 7 - 4$).

The scalar product of two vectors is commutative since if $\mathbf{a} = a_1\mathbf{i} + a_2\mathbf{j}$
$+ a_3\mathbf{k}$ and $\mathbf{b} = b_1\mathbf{i} + b_2\mathbf{j} + b_3\mathbf{k}$ then we have from our definition of the
scalar product

$$\mathbf{a}.\mathbf{b} = a_1b_1 + a_2b_2 + a_3b_3$$
$$\mathbf{b}.\mathbf{a} = b_1a_1 + b_2a_2 + b_3a_3$$

These two quantities are clearly equal.

Distributive laws. Broadly speaking, distributive laws are said to apply when brackets may be removed or inserted in accordance with the customary algebraic rules. In question 3 of exercise 16(b) rules of this nature were demonstrated with particular vectors **a**, **b** and **c**,

i.e. $(\mathbf{a} + \mathbf{b}).\mathbf{c} = \mathbf{a}.\mathbf{c} + \mathbf{b}.\mathbf{c}$

$\mathbf{a}.(\mathbf{b} + \mathbf{c}) = \mathbf{a}.\mathbf{b} + \mathbf{a}.\mathbf{c}$

The general truth of these laws is easily proved. For example, using the same notation as above,

$$\mathbf{a} + \mathbf{b} = (a_1 + b_1)\mathbf{i} + (a_2 + b_2)\mathbf{j} + (a_3 + b_3)\mathbf{k}$$

Thus $(\mathbf{a} + \mathbf{b}).\mathbf{c} = (a_1 + b_1)c_1 + (a_2 + b_2)c_2 + (a_3 + b_3)c_3$

$= (a_1 c_1 + a_2 c_2 + a_3 c_3) + (b_1 c_1 + b_2 c_2 + b_3 c_3)$

$= \mathbf{a}.\mathbf{c} + \mathbf{b}.\mathbf{c}$

In practice the above laws permit us to simplify complicated scalar products in much the same way as ordinary algebraic products. For example, the scalar product $(\mathbf{b} + \mathbf{a}).(\mathbf{b} - \mathbf{a})$ is equivalent to $\mathbf{b}.\mathbf{b} - \mathbf{a}.\mathbf{a}$. Quantities such as $\mathbf{b}.\mathbf{b}$ and $\mathbf{a}.\mathbf{a}$ are usually abbreviated to $\mathbf{b}^2$ and $\mathbf{a}^2$. This enables us to write the above statement in a form which is directly analogous to the well-known algebraic 'difference of two squares' i.e. $(\mathbf{b} + \mathbf{a}).(\mathbf{b} - \mathbf{a}) = \mathbf{b}^2 - \mathbf{a}^2$.

Notes: (i) The justification of this result is as follows:

$(\mathbf{b} + \mathbf{a}).(\mathbf{b} - \mathbf{a}) = \mathbf{b}.(\mathbf{b} - \mathbf{a}) + \mathbf{a}.(\mathbf{b} - \mathbf{a})$

$= \mathbf{b}.\mathbf{b} - \mathbf{b}.\mathbf{a} + \mathbf{a}.\mathbf{b} - \mathbf{a}.\mathbf{a}$

$= \mathbf{b}.\mathbf{b} - \mathbf{a}.\mathbf{a}$

the first two steps using the distributive laws and the third step the commutative law.

(ii) A moment's thought should convince the reader that $\mathbf{b}.\mathbf{b}$ (or $\mathbf{b}^2$) is equal to the square of the magnitude of **b**.

Example 100

Prove that the diagonals of a rhombus intersect at right angles.

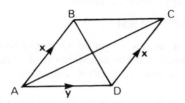

Fig. 3

Let the rhombus be labelled ABCD (Fig. 3) and let $\mathbf{AB} = \mathbf{DC} = \mathbf{x}$ and $\mathbf{AD} = \mathbf{y}$. The diagonals AC and **BD** are then given by

$\mathbf{AC} = \mathbf{y} + \mathbf{x}$

$\mathbf{BD} = \mathbf{y} - \mathbf{x}$

To establish that the diagonals are at right angles we show that **AC.BD** = 0

$$\textbf{AC.BD} = (\textbf{y} + \textbf{x}).(\textbf{y} - \textbf{x})$$
$$= \textbf{y}^2 - \textbf{x}^2$$
$$= 0$$

since for a rhombus the vectors **x** and **y** are necessarily equal in magnitude.

Exercise 16(d)

1. Expand $(\textbf{a} + \textbf{b}).(\textbf{a} + \textbf{b})$ and $(\textbf{a} - \textbf{b}).(\textbf{a} - \textbf{b})$. Hence prove that **a** + **b** and **a** − **b** are equal in magnitude only if **a** and **b** are perpendicular.

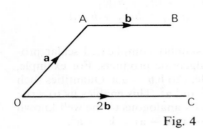

Fig. 4

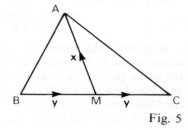

Fig. 5

2. Write down expressions for the vectors **OB** and **BC** in Fig. 4. Prove that if OA = AB then OB is perpendicular to BC.
3. If **a.b** = **a.c** which (if any) of the following are true?
    (i) **b** = **c**   (ii) |**b**| = |**c**|
    (iii) **a** makes equal angles with **b** and **c**.
   OACB is a rhombus. **OA** = **a** and **OB** = **b**. Write down **OC** in terms of **a** and **b** and hence show that **OA.OC** = **OB.OC**. Which geometrical property of the rhombus follows from this?
4. Use vectors to prove that the angle in a semi-circle is a right angle.
5. In a tetrahedron OABC the position vectors of A, B and C relative to O are **a**, **b**, and **c** respectively. If AB is perpendicular to OC and AC is perpendicular to OB, prove that **a.b** = **b.c** = **c.a** and hence show that BC must be perpendicular to OA.
6. In Fig. 5 M is the midpoint of BC. Expand **BA²** and **CA²** in terms of **x** and **y** and hence prove Appolonius's Theorem which states that

$$BA^2 + CA^2 = 2.AM^2 + 2.BM^2$$

7. The equations $\textbf{v} = \textbf{u} + \textbf{a}t$ and $\textbf{s} = \frac{1}{2}(\textbf{u} + \textbf{v})t$ apply to uniformly accelerated motion. By re-arranging these equations and using the scalar product $(\textbf{v} + \textbf{u}).(\textbf{v} - \textbf{u})$ obtain a further equation valid for uniform acceleration.
8. Prove that in a parallelogram the sum of the squares of the diagonals is twice the sum of the squares of two adjacent sides.

16.5 Resolved Parts

The resolved part of a vector **x** in the direction taken by another vector **d**

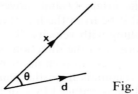

Fig. 6

is $|\mathbf{x}| \cos \theta$, (Fig. 6). This may easily be obtained from the scalar product of the two vectors, since

$$|\mathbf{x}| \cos \theta = \frac{|\mathbf{x}| |\mathbf{d}| \cos \theta}{|\mathbf{d}|} = \frac{\mathbf{x}.\mathbf{d}}{|\mathbf{d}|}$$

i.e. take the scalar product and divide out the magnitude of the 'direction' vector. When the direction is specified by a unit vector, so that $|\mathbf{d}| = 1$, then the resolved part is given directly by the scalar product with this unit vector.

Example 101

Replace the force $\mathbf{F} = \mathbf{i} - 7\mathbf{j} + 2\mathbf{k}$ by two components $\mathbf{F}_1$ and $\mathbf{F}_2$ which are along and perpendicular to the direction of the vector $\mathbf{d} = 4\mathbf{i} + 2\mathbf{j} - 4\mathbf{k}$.

We have $\quad \mathbf{F}.\mathbf{d} = |\mathbf{F}| |\mathbf{d}| \cos \theta = -18$
$$|\mathbf{d}| = \sqrt{16 + 4 + 16} = 6$$

The resolved part $|\mathbf{F}| \cos \theta$ in the direction of the vector $\mathbf{d}$ is therefore (-18) $\div 6 = -3$. The component vector $\mathbf{F}_1$ must therefore have magnitude 3 and be *opposite* in direction to $\mathbf{d}$. Thus

$$\mathbf{F}_1 = -\tfrac{1}{2}\mathbf{d} = -2\mathbf{i} - \mathbf{j} + 2\mathbf{k}$$

Since the two component vectors must satisfy the relation $\mathbf{F}_1 + \mathbf{F}_2 = \mathbf{F}$ the second component is now easily found:

$$\mathbf{F}_2 = \mathbf{F} - \mathbf{F}_1 = 3\mathbf{i} - 6\mathbf{j}$$

Note: Since $\mathbf{F}_1$ and $\mathbf{F}_2$ are intended to be in perpendicular directions, it is sensible to check that $\mathbf{F}_1.\mathbf{F}_2 = 0$. This is found to be the case.

Exercise 16(e)

1. Find the resolved part of the vector $\mathbf{a} = -2\mathbf{i} + 6\mathbf{j} - 4\mathbf{k}$ in the direction of each of the following vectors:
   (i) $6\mathbf{i} + 3\mathbf{j} - 2\mathbf{k}$ (ii) $-2\mathbf{i} + \mathbf{j} + 4\mathbf{k}$ (iii) $-5\mathbf{i} - 3\mathbf{j} - 2\mathbf{k}$
2. Forces $\mathbf{F}_1 = -2\mathbf{i} + 4\mathbf{j}$, $\mathbf{F}_2 = 6\mathbf{i} - \mathbf{j} + 3\mathbf{k}$ and $\mathbf{F}_3 = 2\mathbf{j} - 5\mathbf{k}$ units act at a point. Find the resultant force and verify that the sum of the re-solved parts of the forces in the direction of the vector $9\mathbf{i} + 8\mathbf{j} - 12\mathbf{k}$ is equal to the resolved part of the resultant in this direction.
3. (i) Replace the vector $\mathbf{v} = 3\mathbf{i} + 4\mathbf{j} - \mathbf{k}$ by two component vectors parallel and perpendicular to the direction of the vector $\mathbf{OA}$ where $\mathbf{A}$ has co-ordinates (14, 2, 5)

(ii) A particle leaves the origin O and moves with uniform velocity **v** m s^{-1}. How far will it be from the line through O and A after 5 s?

4. A smooth sphere travelling with velocity $7\mathbf{i} - \mathbf{j} - 6\mathbf{k}$ strikes a smooth fixed plane which is normal to the direction of the vector $2\mathbf{i} + 2\mathbf{j} - \mathbf{k}$. Split the velocity of the sphere into components parallel and normal to the plane. The sphere rebounds from the plane in such a way that its speed normal to the plane is reduced by half but its velocity parallel to the plane is not altered. Find the velocity of the sphere after impact.

5. A force $\mathbf{F} = \mathbf{i} - \mathbf{j} - 2\mathbf{k}$ N is applied to a ring of mass 0.2 kg threaded on a smooth straight wire whose direction is parallel to the vector $6\mathbf{i} + 2\mathbf{j} - 9\mathbf{k}$. Determine the acceleration of the ring and the reaction of the ring on the wire.

*6. (i) If $\mathbf{a} = 10\mathbf{i} - 5\mathbf{j} + 3\mathbf{k}$ find λ_1, λ_2 and λ_3 the resolved parts of $\mathbf{a}$ in the directions of the unit vectors $\mathbf{e}_1$ $\mathbf{e}_2$ and $\mathbf{e}_3$ respectively, where

$$\mathbf{e}_1 = \frac{1}{5}(3\mathbf{i} + 4\mathbf{j}), \mathbf{e}_2 = \frac{1}{5}(-4\mathbf{i} + 3\mathbf{j}), \mathbf{e}_3 = \mathbf{k}.$$

Verify that $\mathbf{a} = \lambda_1\mathbf{e}_1 + \lambda_2\mathbf{e}_2 + \lambda_3\mathbf{e}_3$

(ii) Find also μ_1 μ_2 and μ_3 the resolved parts of $\mathbf{a}$ in the directions of the unit vectors $\mathbf{f}_1$ $\mathbf{f}_2$ and $\mathbf{f}_3$ where $\mathbf{f}_1 = \frac{1}{5}(3\mathbf{i} + 4\mathbf{k})$, $\mathbf{f}_2 = \frac{1}{5}(-4\mathbf{i} + 3\mathbf{j})$, $\mathbf{f}_3 = \mathbf{j}$

Show that $\mathbf{a} \neq \mu_1\mathbf{f}_1 + \mu_2\mathbf{f}_2 + \mu_3\mathbf{f}_3$

(iii) Explain the difference between these two cases.

*7. Show that the unit vectors $\mathbf{e}_1$ $\mathbf{e}_2$ and $\mathbf{e}_3$ are mutually perpendicular where

$$\mathbf{e}_1 = \mathbf{j}, \mathbf{e}_2 = \frac{1}{13}(5\mathbf{i} + 12\mathbf{k}), \mathbf{e}_3 = \frac{1}{13}(12\mathbf{i} - 5\mathbf{k})$$

Hence express the following vectors in the form $\lambda_1\mathbf{e}_1 + \lambda_2\mathbf{e}_2 + \lambda_3\mathbf{e}_3$
(i) $\mathbf{a} = 3\mathbf{i} - 3\mathbf{j} + 2\mathbf{k}$ (ii) the vector **i**.

16.6 The Work done by a Force

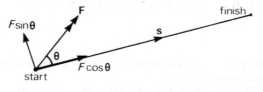

Fig. 7

Suppose that under the action of a constant force **F** a body undergoes displacement **s** (not necessarily in the same direction as the force). Since the force-component $F \sin \theta$ (Fig. 7) does no work, the work done is $F \cos \theta \times s$ or $|\mathbf{F}|\,|\mathbf{s}| \cos \theta$. This can therefore be found by the scalar product **F.s**.

that is | Work done = **F.s** |

When several forces $\mathbf{F}_1$ $\mathbf{F}_2$ $\mathbf{F}_3$ etc. act, then adding the work done by the forces individually we may write

$$
\begin{aligned}
\text{total work done} &= \mathbf{F}_1.\mathbf{s} + \mathbf{F}_2.\mathbf{s} + \mathbf{F}_3.\mathbf{s} + \ldots \\
&= (\mathbf{F}_1 + \mathbf{F}_2 + \mathbf{F}_3 \ldots).\mathbf{s} \\
&= \mathbf{R}.\mathbf{s}
\end{aligned}
$$

where $\mathbf{R}$ is the resultant force.

An interesting application of the scalar product was indicated in question 7 of exercise 16(d). A constant force $\mathbf{F}$ will produce a uniform acceleration $\mathbf{a}$ (in accordance with $\mathbf{F} = m\mathbf{a}$) and the uniform acceleration equations of section 5.6 will govern the motion. These may be re-arranged as follows:

$$
\mathbf{v} + \mathbf{u} = \frac{2}{t}\mathbf{s} \quad [\mathbf{s} = \tfrac{1}{2}(\mathbf{u} + \mathbf{v})t]
$$

$$
\mathbf{v} - \mathbf{u} = t\mathbf{a} \quad [\mathbf{v} = \mathbf{u} + \mathbf{a}t]
$$

Thus $\quad (\mathbf{v} + \mathbf{u}).(\mathbf{v} - \mathbf{u}) = (\frac{2}{t}\mathbf{s}).(t\mathbf{a})$

$$
\Rightarrow \quad v^2 - u^2 = 2\mathbf{a}.\mathbf{s}
$$

Furthermore, multiplying both sides by $\tfrac{1}{2}m$ gives

$$
\tfrac{1}{2}mv^2 - \tfrac{1}{2}mu^2 = m\mathbf{a}.\mathbf{s}
$$
$$
\Rightarrow \tfrac{1}{2}mv^2 - \tfrac{1}{2}mu^2 = \mathbf{F}.\mathbf{s}
$$

This last result is clearly interpreted as work done = change in kinetic energy.

Note: The scalar product $\mathbf{F}.\mathbf{S}$ may of course be negative in sign. We see from the above result that this will be associated with a decrease in kinetic energy so that $\mathbf{F}$ is by nature a 'resisting' force. In Fig. 7 a negative scalar product occurs when the angle θ is obtuse so that $\mathbf{F}$ has a component opposing the displacement $\mathbf{S}$.

Exercise 16(f)

1. A particle of mass 8 units acted on by two forces $\mathbf{F}_1 = -\mathbf{i} - 2\mathbf{j} + 2\mathbf{k}$ and $\mathbf{F}_2 = 3\mathbf{i} + \mathbf{k}$ moves from point A(1, 2, −1) to point B(4, 0, 4). Find the work done on the particle. If the particle is initially at rest, with what speed does it reach B?
2. (i) A body of mass 2 kg moving with initial velocity $3\mathbf{i} + \mathbf{j} - 2\mathbf{k}$ m s^{-1} is acted on by a constant force $\mathbf{F} = -6\mathbf{i} + 10\mathbf{j}$ N. Find the displacement undergone by the body during the next four seconds and the work done by the force $\mathbf{F}$ in this time.
   (ii) If a body of mass m moving with initial velocity $\mathbf{u}$ is subject to a uniform force $\mathbf{F}$ for time t, prove that the work done by the force is

$$
(\mathbf{u}.\mathbf{F})t + \frac{t^2}{2m} \mathbf{F}^2
$$

   Use this result to verify your answer to part (i).

3. A force of magnitude 12 units is applied in the direction of the vector $2\mathbf{i} - 2\mathbf{j} + \mathbf{k}$ to a particle of mass 2 units movng initially with speed 10 units in the direction of the vector $4\mathbf{j} + 3\mathbf{k}$. Show that the work done by the force during the next t units of time is $36t^2 - 40t$. Hence find the time at which the speed of the particle is

 (i) again 10 units   (ii) 18 units.

4. (i) Two forces $\mathbf{F}_1 = 5\mathbf{i} + 3\mathbf{j} - 12\mathbf{k}$ and $\mathbf{F}_2 = \mathbf{i} - 15\mathbf{j} - 6\mathbf{k}$ act for five seconds on a body of mass 3 units. During this time the body moves from point $A(-2, 5, 20)$ to point $B(8, -10, -10)$. Find the change in the K.E. of the body.

 (ii) Find the velocity vectors of the body as it passes through A and B. (Hint: find the vectors $\mathbf{v} + \mathbf{u}$ and $\mathbf{v} - \mathbf{u}$.) Hence verify your answer to part (i).

17

Variable Force and Differential Equations

17.1 Separating the Variables

In the first three sections of this chapter we shall be concerned with motion in a straight line under the action of forces varying in accordance with some known formula or law.

To begin with, consider a body of mass 5 kg moving initially at 10m s^{-1} and acted on by a force F N whose magnitude at time t s is given by $F = 100/(t + 5)^2$. We notice that this force decreases with time, being 4 N at $t = 0$, 1 N at $t = 5$, and so on.

Using $F = ma$ we find that the acceleration of the body is $20/(t + 5)^2$ m s^{-2}. When this is a function of time we may integrate directly, as in section 1.7, to obtain an expression for the velocity at time t

$$\text{Thus} \quad a = \frac{dv}{dt} = \frac{20}{(t + 5)^2}$$

$$\Rightarrow v = \frac{-20}{t + 5} + c$$

The constant of integration c must be evaluated before proceeding with a second integration to find the displacement at time t. Here, since $v = 10$ when $t = 0$ we find $c = 14$

$$\text{i.e.} \quad v = \frac{ds}{dt} = 14 - \frac{20}{t + 5}$$

$$\Rightarrow s = 14t - 20\ln(t + 5) + d$$

where d is a second constant. A rather more convenient method of approach, which to a certain extent avoids the rather tedious evaluation of constants of integration, is that known as **separating the variables**. This method, which will be needed for the more difficult work of sections 17.2 onwards, is illustrated by the following worked example. It is recommended that exercise 17(a) should be worked in this way so that some practice in this method is gained before section 17.2 is tackled.

Example 102

A body of mass 5 kg, moving initially at 10 m s^{-1}, is acted on by a force $F = 100/(t + 5)^2$ newtons. Find the speed reached after 10 s and the distance travelled in this time.

The equation of motion $F = ma$ gives

$$\frac{dv}{dt} = \frac{20}{(t + 5)^2}$$

We now separate the two variables v and t in this equation, at the same time turning both sides of the equation into definite integrals on which *the limits must correspond*. Thus, for the lower limits, we have $v = 10$ (velocity integral) when $t = 0$ (time integral), and for the upper limits v will denote the velocity corresponding to time t,

that is

$$\int_{10}^{v} dv = \int_{0}^{t} \frac{20}{(t + 5)^2} dt$$

$$\left[v \right]_{10}^{v} = \left[\frac{-20}{t + 5} \right]_{0}^{t}$$

$$v - 10 = \frac{-20}{t + 5} + 4$$

$$\Rightarrow v = 14 - \frac{20}{t + 5}$$

The speed after 10 seconds is therefore $12\frac{2}{3}$ m s^{-1}. Notice that the 'constant of integration' is found automatically when the limits are evaluated.

In the second part of this question we have no need for a general formula giving displacement at time t. We therefore choose limits of $t = 0$ and $t = 10$ on the time integral in order to obtain directly the distance travelled during this time. Thus

$$v = \frac{ds}{dt} = 14 - \frac{20}{t + 5}$$

$$\Rightarrow \int_{0}^{s} ds = \int_{0}^{10} 14 - \frac{20}{t + 5} dt$$

$$s - 0 = \left[14t - 20\ln(t + 5) \right]_{0}^{10}$$

$$s = (140 - 20\ln 15) - (-20\ln 5)$$

$$\Rightarrow \text{distance} = 140 - 20\ln 3 \text{ metres}$$

Exercise 17(a)

1. A body of mass 4 kg, initially at rest, is acted on by a force $F = (6 - t)^2$ newtons where $0 \leqslant t \leqslant 6$ (seconds). Find the speed of the body after 6 s and the distance travelled.
2. A particle of unit mass is acted on by a force of magnitude $1 - \sin \frac{1}{2}t$ ($0 \leqslant t \leqslant \pi$). If the particle is initially at rest, find an expression for the distance covered at time t.
3. A body of mass 5 kg moving initially at 2 m s^{-1} is accelerated by a force whose magnitude at time t s is $20/(4 + t)$ newtons. Find the speed of the

body at time (i) 8 s, ((ii) t s. How long is taken to double the initial speed of the body?

4. The thrust developed by a rocket of mass 80 kg at time t s is $4000t/(1 + t^2)$ newtons (after subtraction of the weight and resistance).
   (i) Find the maximum thrust and sketch the graph of thrust against time.
   (ii) Find the maximum acceleration experienced by the rocket.
   (iii) If the rocket burns out after 7 s, find the speed reached from rest.

5. The braking force on a car of mass 750 kg increases uniformly from 2000 to 4000 newtons in the first second of braking and then remains constant.
   (i) Write down an expression for the braking force which is valid for $0 \leqslant t \leqslant 1$.
   (ii) If the car is moving initially at 20 m s^{-1} find the speed after 1 s and the further time needed to bring the car to rest.
   (iii) Calculate the total stopping distance.

6. A body of mass 20 kg, initially at rest, is accelerated by a force $800/(t + 2)^2$ newtons.
   (i) Find the limiting speed which the body approaches.
   (ii) Find the distance covered when 90% of this speed has been acquired.
   (iii) Show that for small values of t the distance covered is approximately $5t^2$ metres.

7. A body of mass 10 units is accelerated from rest by a force F whose magnitude at time t is given by

$$F = 14 - 2t \quad (0 \leqslant t \leqslant 5)$$
$$F = 100/t^2 \quad (t > 5)$$

Find the speed of the body at time $t = 10$ and the distance covered in this time.

8. A body of mass m, initially at rest, is acted on by a force $F = mk(1 - e^{-kt})$ for T s. Find the speed reached and the distance covered in this time. Show also that when t is small the speed is approximately proportional to t^2 and the distance to t^3.

9. A body of mass 1 kg travelling initially at 1 m s^{-1} is brought to rest by a force $F = 72t/(t + 4)^3$ N. Find the time at which the body comes to rest and the distance travelled before this occurs.

17.2 Force as a Function of Velocity

There are many situations in which the forces acting on a body vary with the speed of the body. An example of this is that of a vehicle working at constant power. Here the drive force created will decrease as the vehicle gains speed, in accordance with the result $P = Dv$ or $D = P/v$ (section 12.2). A further important example is provided by forces such as air-resistance which are caused by the motion of a body through a resisting medium. Such forces are often found to be approximately proportional to the square of the body's speed.

The solution of problems of this nature is illustrated by the following two examples. It is important to remember that when solving for distance the equation of motion $F = ma$ is usually re-written in the form $F = mv \cdot \dfrac{dv}{ds}$, (see example 104) using the result

$$a = \frac{dv}{dt} = \frac{dv}{ds} \cdot \frac{ds}{dt} = v \cdot \frac{dv}{ds}$$

Example 103

A lorry of mass 3 tonnes develops a steady power of 72 kw whilst accelerating from 10 m s^{-1} to 15 m s^{-1}. If the resistance to motion is constant at 3000 N, find the time taken.

Using $P = Dv$ we have $72\,000 = Dv$ so that the forward (drive) force exerted by the engine is $72\,000/v$ N. Remembering to subtract the resisting force, the equation of motion $F = ma$ becomes

$$\frac{72\,000}{v} - 3000 = 3000 \frac{dv}{dt}$$

or $\qquad \dfrac{dv}{dt} = \dfrac{24}{v} - 1 = \dfrac{24 - v}{v}$

(This is a simple example of a **differential equation**, i.e. an equation involving the derivative(s) of an unknown variable. By solving the differential equation we mean the process by which an expression or formula for this variable is found.)

To solve this problem we separate the variables v and t, as in the previous section, take limits of 10 and 15 (m s^{-1}) on the velocity integral and set $t = 0$ when $v = 10$,

$$\int_0^t dt = \int_{10}^{15} \frac{v}{24 - v} dv = \int_{10}^{15} \frac{24}{24 - v} - 1 \, dv$$

$$\Rightarrow t = [-24 \ln(24 - v) - v]_{10}^{15}$$

$$= [+24 \ln(24 - v) + v]_{15}^{10}$$

$$= 24 \ln \frac{14}{9} - 5$$

$$\simeq 5.6 \text{ s}$$

Example 104

A body of mass 1 kg falls vertically through a fluid which exerts a resistance of $\frac{1}{10}v^2$ N when the speed of the body is v m s^{-1}. Taking $g = 10 \text{ m s}^{-2}$ find

(i)   the 'terminal' velocity of the body
(ii) the time taken to reach half this velocity from rest
(iii) the distance covered in this time.

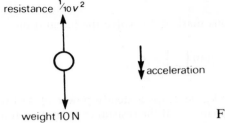

resistance $\frac{1}{10}v^2$

acceleration

weight 10 N

Fig. 1

(i) The forces acting on the body are shown in Fig. 1. The resistance increases with the speed of the body until eventually it becomes equal to the weight of the body and no further acceleration is possible. Thus the speed of the body approaches a limiting or terminal value v which is such that $v^2/10 = 10$

$\Rightarrow$ terminal velocity $= 10 \text{ m s}^{-1}$

(ii) The equation of motion may be written as

$$10 - \frac{1}{10}v^2 = 1 \cdot \frac{dv}{dt}$$

$$\text{or } 100 - v^2 = 10\frac{dv}{dt} \tag{1}$$

To find the time taken to reach a speed of 5 m s^{-1} separate the variables and choose appropriate limits as follows:

$$\int_0^t dt = 10\int_0^5 \frac{1}{100 - v^2}\,dv = \frac{1}{2}\int_0^5 \frac{1}{10 + v} + \frac{1}{10 - v}\,dv$$

$$t = \frac{1}{2}\Big[\ln(10 + v) - \ln(10 - v)\Big]_0^5$$

$$= \frac{1}{2}\Big[\ln\frac{10 + v}{10 - v}\Big]_0^5 = \frac{1}{2}(\ln3 - \ln1)$$

$$\text{time taken} = \frac{1}{2}\ln3 \simeq 0.55 \text{ s}$$

(iii) Using $\dfrac{dv}{dt} = v \cdot \dfrac{dv}{ds}$ re-write the equation of motion (1) as

$$100 - v^2 = 10v \cdot \frac{dv}{ds}$$

$$\Rightarrow \int_0^s ds = \int_0^5 \frac{10v}{100 - v^2}\,dv$$

$$s = [-5\ln(100 - v^2)]_0^5$$

$$= -5\ln75 + 5\ln100$$

$$\text{distance fallen} = 5\ln\tfrac{4}{3} \simeq 1.44 \text{ m}$$

Exercise 17(b)

In this exercise questions marked * involve the integration

$$\int \frac{1}{a^2 + x^2} dx = \frac{1}{a} \arctan\left(\frac{x}{a}\right) + c$$

1. A car of mass 750 kg develops a steady power of 45 kw while accelerating from 20 to 25 m s^{-1}. If the resistance to motion remains constant at 1500 N, find how long this takes. State also the maximum speed at this power and against the same resistance.

2. A body of mass 2 kg moves horizontally in a medium which exerts a resisting force proportional to the square of the speed of the body. Initially the speed of the body is 10 m s^{-1} and the resistance is 20 N. Find the speed after 2 s and the distance covered in this time.

3. A cyclist starting from rest maintains a steady forward force of 65 N. If there is a constant frictional resistance of 16 N and if the air resistance at speed v m s^{-1} is v^2 N, find the maximum speed he can attain. If the mass of the cyclist together with his machine is 84 kg, find the time taken to reach a speed of 5 m s^{-1} and the distance covered in this time.

*4. If the cyclist of question 3 stops pedalling when he reaches a speed of 5 m s^{-1}, show that he can expect to free-wheel for roughly 20 s, and find the distance he will travel before coming to rest.

5. A body is thrown vertically upwards with speed u. If the air-resistance encountered by the body at speed v is kv^2 per unit mass, find an expression for the greatest height reached and verify that if k is small your answer approximates to $u^2/2g$.

6. A model boat of mass 2 kg is powered by an electric motor which works at a steady power of 50 watts. At speed v m s^{-1} the resistance encountered by the boat due to its movement through the water is $2v$ newtons. Find the time taken by the boat to reach a speed of 4 m s^{-1} from rest and the distance travelled in this time.

7. A body of mass 1/2 kg is projected vertically downwards at 5 m s^{-1} in a medium which offers a resistance to motion of $v^2/80$ N at speed v m s^{-1}. What is the terminal speed of the body? Show that the times taken to accelerate from 5 to 10 m s^{-1} and from 10 to 15 m s^{-1} are in the ratio $\ln(9/5) : \ln(7/3)$ and find the ratio of the distances covered in these two times. (Take $g = 10$ m s^{-2}.)

8. The body of question 7 is allowed to fall vertically from rest. Show that its speed at time t s is $20(e^t - 1)/(e^t + 1)$ m s^{-1}. (Take $g = 10$ m s^{-2}.) Find also an expression for the speed of the body when it has fallen through a distance d.

9. A body of mass m moves on a horizontal plane. The resistance to motion at speed v is given by $c + kv$ where c and k are constants. If the body is projected with initial speed u, find expressions for the time taken for the body to come to rest and for the distance then travelled. Verify that when k is small these results agree with those obtained by momentum and energy respectively for motion against a constant resistance c.

*10. A body falling vertically against air resistance has terminal velocity u. The body is projected vertically upwards at this same speed u. If the air resistance is taken to be proportional to the square of the body's speed, find the time taken before the body is instantaneously at rest and the height gained in this time. Find also the speed of the body as it passes again through its original position.

11. Find to the nearest metre the distance travelled by the lorry of example 103 in accelerating from 10 m s^{-1} to 15 m s^{-1}.

12. A body is allowed to fall vertically from rest in a medium offering a resistance proportional to the square of the body's speed. If the terminal speed of the body is $2u$, show

(i) that the time taken to reach speed u is $\dfrac{u}{g} \ln 3$ and find the speed when twice this time has elapsed.

(ii) that the distance covered while reaching speed u is $\dfrac{2u^2}{g} \ln (4/3)$ and find the speed when twice this distance has been covered.

13. Whilst accelerating from 10 m s^{-1} to 15 m s^{-1} a motorcycle maintains a steady power of 8 kw and the total resistance to motion, which is of the form $a + bv$ where $v \text{ m s}^{-1}$ is the speed of the motorcycle and a and b are constants, increases from 300 to 350 N. If the total mass of the machine and its rider is 150 kg find the time taken.

17.3 Force as a Function of Displacement

Perhaps the two most familiar examples of forces which vary according to the displacement of a body are that exerted on a body by an elastic string and that due to gravitational attraction.

Gravitational force is considered in the next section. For the moment we shall deal with problems of a more hypothetical nature, designed to illustrate the general method of approach with forces of this type. As will be seen in the following example, it is usual to write $v \cdot \dfrac{dv}{ds}$ for the acceleration and begin by solving the resulting differential equation for velocity v in terms of displacement s.

Example 105

A body of mass 5 kg is attracted towards a fixed point 0 by a force $20s^{-3/2}$ N, where s metres is the distance of the body from 0 $(s > 0)$. If the body passes initially through a point 1 m from 0 with velocity 4 m s^{-1} away from 0, find how far it travels before its speed is reduced to 2 m s^{-1}. Find also the time that this takes.

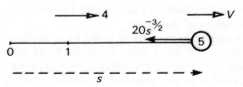

Fig. 2

It is vital to realise in this problem that the force appears as a negative quantity in the equation of motion, since it is opposite in direction to increasing displacement (Fig. 2). We therefore have

$$-20s^{-3/2} = 5a = 5v \cdot \frac{dv}{ds}$$

$$\Rightarrow \int_4^v v\,dv = \int_1^s -4s^{-3/2}\,ds$$

$$\left[\frac{1}{2}v^2\right]_4^v = \left[8s^{-1/2}\right]_1^s$$

$$\tfrac{1}{2}v^2 - 8 = 8s^{-1/2} - 8 \tag{1}$$

Thus $v^2 = 16s^{-1/2}$ or $16/\sqrt{s}$. When $v = 2\sqrt{s} = 4$, so that $s = 16$. This means that the body has travelled 15 metres. To find the time taken we take the square root of the result for v^2 and proceed as follows:

$$v = \frac{ds}{dt} = 4s^{-1/4}$$

$$\Rightarrow \int_1^{16} s^{1/4}\,ds = 4\int_0^t dt$$

$$4t = \left[\frac{4}{5}s^{5/4}\right]_1^{16} = \frac{4}{5}(32 - 1)$$

$$t = \frac{31}{5} = 6.2 \text{ s}$$

Notes: (i) The second stage of this solution is possible only because the constant terms disappear from equation (1). Had this not been the case we would have obtained $v = \sqrt{16s^{-1/2} + c}$ leading to an integration beyond the scope of this book.

(ii) If, as in this example, the square root of v^2 may be written down exactly, it is necessary to consider whether the positive or negative root is appropriate. In many cases the negative root must be taken.

Exercise 17(c)

1. A body of mass 1 kg is attracted towards a fixed point O by a force $s^2/12$ newtons, where s metres is the distance of the body from O. If the body is released from rest at a distance of 6 m from O, find the speed with which it reaches O.

2. A body of mass 2 kg is attracted towards a fixed point O by a force $36/s^2$ newtons, where s metres is the distance of the body from O ($s > 0$). The body is projected from a point 4 m from O with velocity 3 m s^{-1} away from O. Find how far the body travels before its speed is reduced to 2 m s^{-1} and the time taken in doing so.

3. When at distance s metres from a fixed point O, a body of mass 3 kg is subject to a force of $4s^{1/2}$ N away from O. If the body is displaced from rest at O, show that the distance travelled is proportional to the fourth power of the time. Find also the speed of the body after 2 s.

4. A body of mass 4 kg initially at rest 10 m from a fixed point O, is subject to a force directed away from O and of magnitude $2500/s^3$ N, where s metres is the distance of the body from O. Show that the speed of the body approaches a limiting value and state this limiting value. Find also the distance travelled by the body before its speed is 2 m s^{-1} and the time taken in doing so.

5. A particle of mass 1/2 kg is moving initially with speed 6 m s^{-1} through a fixed point O. When at distance s metres from O, the body is subject to a force of $8s$ newtons away from O and there is a uniform resistance to motion of 12 newtons. Find the speed of the body after moving 1 m and the time taken. Show also that the particle will ultimately approach a position of rest $1\frac{1}{2}$ m from O.

6. When at distance s metres from a fixed point O, a body of mass 1 kg is subject to forces $2s^3$ newtons away from O and $8s$ newtons towards O. If initially the body is moving through O with speed 4 m s^{-1}, find how far it travels before coming to rest and the time taken in travelling the first half of this distance.

17.4 Gravitation

In proposing his theory of gravitation in the seventeenth century Newton suggested that any two bodies attracted one another with equal and opposite forces F, such that

$$F \propto \frac{m_1 m_2}{r^2}$$

m_1 and m_2 being the masses of the two bodies and r the distance between them. This theory helped to explain such phenomena as

(i) The near circular orbit of the Moon around the Earth. Newton realised that this could only occur if the Moon were subject to a force directed towards the Earth. The orbit of the Earth around the Sun was explained in the same way.

(ii) Bodies falling to Earth, e.g. stones released from the top of a tower. The stone is subject to a gravitational force (normally termed its weight) directed towards the centre of the Earth. The Earth in fact experiences an equal force towards the stone, but as the Earth has such vast mass this force has no measurable effect.

With large bodies such as the Earth, the distance r is the distance between the centres of the bodies, not that between their surfaces. Thus the gravitational force on a stone falling from a tower does not change significantly as there is little change (comparatively) in the distance of the stone from the centre of the Earth. We are therefore justified, in situations of this type, in taking the acceleration due to gravity as uniform. But in considering, for example, the motion of a rocket rising to a considerable height above the Earth's surface, we must take into account the decrease in the gravitational attraction as the rocket gets further from the Earth.

Example 106

Taking the Earth to be a sphere of radius R, show that the 'escape velocity', with which a rocket fired vertically from the Earth's surface may escape the Earth's gravitational field, is given by $\sqrt{2gR}$, where g is the acceleration due to gravity at the surface of the Earth.

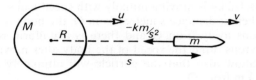

Fig. 3

Letting the masses of the Earth and the rocket be M and m respectively, the gravitational pull on the rocket is proportional to Mm/s^2 where s is the displacement of the rocket from the centre of the Earth. (Fig. 3.) For convenience we may therefore take the magnitude of the force to be km/s^2 where k is a constant. The equation of motion is then

$$-\frac{km}{s^2} = ma = mv \cdot \frac{dv}{ds}$$

$$\Rightarrow \int -\frac{k}{s^2}\,ds = \int v\,dv$$

To 'escape' the rocket must be capable of reaching any required distance from the Earth, i.e. an infinite distance. In the limiting case the rocket will be brought to rest as it achieves this. The limits chosen on the integrations are therefore as follows:

$$\int_R^\infty -\frac{k}{s^2}\,ds = \int_u^0 v\,dv$$

$$\Rightarrow 0 - \frac{1}{2}u^2 \quad = \left[\frac{k}{s}\right]_R^\infty = 0 - \frac{k}{R}$$

$$\Rightarrow u^2 = \frac{2k}{R}$$

To find the constant k we remember that the force km/s^2 will be equal to what is usually taken as the weight of the rocket (i.e. mg) when the rocket is at the surface of the Earth, that is

$$\frac{km}{R^2} = mg \Rightarrow k = gR^2$$

Hence $u^2 = 2gR$ and the result is established.

Note: Taking $g = 9.8$ m s^{-2} and $R = 6400$ km this escape velocity is evaluated as

$$\sqrt{2 \times 9.8 \times 6400 \times 1000}$$
$$= \sqrt{196 \times 64 \times 10^4}$$
$$= 14 \times 8 \times 100$$
$$= 11\,200 \text{ m s}^{-1}$$

Exercise 17(d)

In this exercise R denotes the radius of the Earth and g the acceleration due to gravity at the surface of the Earth.

1. If the 'weight' of a body at the surface of the Earth is mg, what will it be at distance (i) $2R$ (ii) $5R$ from the centre of the Earth? What will be the initial acceleration of a body released from rest at height (i) $R/5$ (ii) $R/2$ above the Earth's surface?

2. Write down in terms of g and R the magnitude of the gravitational force on a body of mass m (i) at distance r from the centre of the Earth (ii) at height h above the Earth's surface. Show that the speed of a satellite in circular orbit at height h above the Earth is $R\sqrt{g/(R + h)}$.

3. A meteor of mass m travelling directly towards the centre of the Earth enters the Earth's gravitational field at speed u. At what speed will it strike the Earth and how much work is done on the meteor by the Earth's gravitational field? (Give answers in terms of g and R.)

4. (i)   Show that the work done in lifting a body of mass m to height h above the surface of the Earth is $mgRh/(R + h)$ and show that this approximates to the usual result for potential energy when h is small in comparison to R.

(ii) Use the result of question 2 to show that the total work which must be done to put a satellite of mass m in orbit at height $R/15$ is $17\,mgR/32$.

(iii) If, due to the resistance of the atmosphere the height of the satellite is slowly reduced to $R/19$, find the energy lost by the satellite. Show, however, that its kinetic energy is in fact increased.

5. A rocket is fired vertically from the surface of the Earth with speed u, less than the 'escape speed' needed to leave the Earth's gravitational field. What is the greatest distance it reaches from the centre of the Earth? From your result, deduce the formula for the 'escape speed'. (Give answers in terms of g and R.)

6. Two identical spheres of radius a and mass m are held with their centres a distance $2b$ apart and then released. If the gravitational attraction between masses m_1 and m_2 is Gm_1m_2/r^2, where r is the distance between their centres, find the speeds of the spheres on impact. (You may assume that no other forces act on the spheres.)

17.5 Exponential Growth and Decay

The exponential functions e^{kt} and e^{-kt}, where k is a positive constant and t denotes time, have the property that their rates of change (ke^{kt} and $-ke^{-kt}$ respectively) are always proportional to the values of the functions themselves, that is

$$\text{if} \qquad A = e^{kt} \qquad\quad B = e^{-kt}$$

$$\text{then} \quad \frac{dA}{dt} = kA \qquad \frac{dB}{dt} = -kB$$

We therefore expect these functions to provide solutions to scientific situations where the rate at which a quantity Q changes with time is always proportional to the value of that quantity. If Q is increasing then the solution is of the form $Q = Q_0 e^{kt}$, where Q_0 is the initial value of the quantity Q ($e^{kt} = 1$ when $t = 0$), whereas if Q is decreasing the solution $Q = Q_0 e^{-kt}$ will apply. Situations of this type are frequently described as **exponential growth** and **decay** respectively.

A good example of exponential growth is afforded by the multiplication of bacteria in a culture. Here it is reasonable to suppose that at any instant the number of new bacteria being formed is proportional to the number n of bacteria actually present, that is

$$\frac{dn}{dt} = kn \quad (k > 0)$$

A solution of the form $n = n_0 e^{kt}$ may therefore be expected to give a prediction of actual behaviour, (n_0 being the number of bacteria present initially). Fig. 4a is a sketch of this solution.

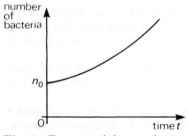
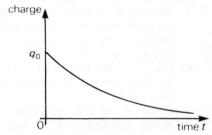

Fig. 4a Exponential growth   Fig. 4b Exponential decay

An example of exponential decay is the rate at which electrical charge leaks from a capacitor. This is known to be proportional to the charge q remaining on the capacitor, that is

$$\frac{dq}{dt} = -kq \quad (k > 0)$$

The solution is $q = q_0 e^{-kt}$ where q_0 is the initial charge on the capacitor. This solution is illustrated in Fig. 4b.

Although it is usual to write down these solutions directly they may be obtained by the methods used earlier in this chapter. With the electrical capacitor we have, for example

$$\frac{dq}{dt} = -kq$$

$$\Rightarrow \int_{q_0}^{q} \frac{1}{q} \, dq = -k \int_{0}^{t} dt$$

$$\Rightarrow \ln\left(\frac{q}{q_0}\right) = -kt \tag{1}$$

$$\Rightarrow \frac{q}{q_0} = e^{-kt}$$

The logarithmic equation (1) is frequently of more use in the handling of numerical problems than the solution itself. This is shown in the following worked example.

Example 107

The rate at which a body cools is proportional to the excess temperature of the body above that of its surroundings (Newton's law of cooling). A body heated to 55°C in a room whose temperature is constant at 15°C is found to have cooled to 40°C after five minutes. How long will the body take to cool to 20°C? Find also an expression for the temperature after t minutes.

If we use T to denote *excess* temperature (i.e. true temperature $-15°$) then $dT/dt = -kT$ so that the solution is of the form

$$T = T_0 e^{-kt} \tag{2}$$

where $T_0 = 55 - 15 = 40$. The logarithmic form of this is

$$\ln\left(\frac{T}{T_0}\right) = -kt \text{ or } \ln\left(\frac{T_0}{T}\right) = +kt$$

We have $T = 40 - 15 = 25$ when $t = 5$, and we wish to know when $T = 20 - 15 = 5$. Substituting

$$\ln\left(\frac{40}{25}\right) = 5k \quad \text{and} \quad \ln\left(\frac{40}{5}\right) = kt \tag{3}$$

$$\text{dividing } \frac{t}{5} = \frac{\ln 8}{\ln 1.6} = \frac{2.0794}{0.4700}$$

$$\Rightarrow t \simeq 22 \text{ (minutes)}$$

Notice that the value of k is not needed in solving this part of the question. It may be found, however, from line (3) if required

$$k = \frac{1}{5}\ln\left(\frac{40}{25}\right) = \frac{1}{5}\ln 1.6 = 0.094$$

From line (2) the excess temperature is $T = 40e^{-0.094t}$ so that the true temperature after t minutes is given by

$$\text{temperature} = 40\,e^{-0.094t} + 15 \quad (°C)$$

This result may be used to predict the temperature of the body at any specified time.

Exercise 17(e)

1. The number of bacteria in a culture increases at a rate which is proportional at any instant to the number of bacteria present. Initially there were 80 and this increases to 200 in 10 minutes. Find the number of bacteria present after a further 10 minutes and the total time which elapses before the number reaches 1000.
2. The rate at which electrical charge leaks from a capacitor is proportional

to the charge remaining on the capacitor. If the charge is Q_0 at time $t = 0$ and $3Q_0/4$ after $1/10$ s, find an expression for the charge remaining after t s. Find also the times at which the charge remaining is (i) $Q_0/2$ (ii) $Q_0/10$.

3. A body is heated to 80°C and allowed to cool in surroundings kept at a constant temperature of 20°C. After two minutes the body has cooled to 68°C. Assuming Newton's law of cooling (example 107) what will be the temperature after ten minutes and how long will the body take to cool to 25°C?

*4. The rate of decay of a radio-active substance is proportional at any instant to the mass of the substance remaining. If the initial mass m decays to $m/2$ in time t, find the mass of radio-active substance remaining after time $2t$ and after time $3t$. Explain the meaning of the term 'half-life'.

5. The intensity of a beam of light decreases as it passes through glass. The rate of decrease of intensity I with distance x is directly proportional to x. If glass 5 cm thick absorbs 16% of a beam of light, what percentage is absorbed by similar glass 8 cm thick?

6. The number of bacteria in a culture is increasing at the rate of n bacteria per second for every 100 bacteria present. After how long is the number of bacteria doubled? Estimate the value of n for a culture in which the number of bacteria increases from 90 to 200 in 15 minutes.

*7. A capacitor carrying an initial charge of q_0 has charge q_1 remaining after one minute. Find the charge remaining after two minutes and after three minutes. Show that the values of the charge remaining after successive intervals of one minute form a geometric progression and state the common ratio of this progression.

8. A body is heated to an excess temperature $T_0°$ above the temperature of its surroundings. When the excess temperature has fallen to $T_1°$ the body is cooling at a per second. Show that the temperature after t seconds is given by

$$T_0 e^{-at/T_1}$$

Find also (i) the time for which the body has been cooling when the excess temperature has fallen to T_1 (ii) the time at which the fall in temperature (from T_0 to T_1) has been doubled ($T_1 > T_0/2$).

17.6 Some Further Differential Equations

Example 108

An immersion heater supplies heat to the water in a tank at a steady rate sufficient to raise the temperature of the water by $a°$ each minute if no heat is lost. At the same time, however, the water cools at $kT°$ per minute where $T°$ is the difference in temperature between the water and its surroundings. Find an expression for T when the heater has been on for t minutes, given that $T = 0$ initially.

After t minutes the temperature difference T is subject to an increase at rate $a°$ per minute and also a decrease at rate $kT°$ per minute, i.e. the overall rate of increase of temperature with time, dT/dt, is given by

$$\frac{dT}{dt} = a - kT$$

Hence
$$\int_0^T \frac{dT}{a - kT} = \int_0^t dt$$

$$-\frac{1}{k}\left[\ln(a - kT)\right]_0^T = t$$

$$\ln\left(\frac{a - kT}{a}\right) = -kt$$

This is equivalent to

$$\frac{a - kT}{a} = e^{-kt}$$

from which the solution for T is found to be

$$T = \frac{a}{k}[1 - e^{-kt}]$$

Note: As t increases the exponential e^{-kt} will tend to zero so that T tends to a limiting value of a/k. (This limiting value may be obtained by noticing the value of T which makes $dT/dt = 0$.) A sketch of the solution is shown in Fig. 5.

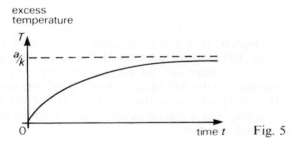

Fig. 5

Example 109

In a certain chemical reaction two substances A and B react in equal quantities to produce a new chemical. The rate at which the reaction proceeds at any instant is proportional to the product of the amounts of A and B remaining. Initially A and B are present in the ratio $2 : 1$. If after a certain time T one-half of substance B has reacted, find what fraction will have reacted after time $2T$.

Let the initial amounts of A and B present be $2a$ and a respectively and suppose that after time t an equal quantity x of each has reacted. The rate at which the reaction proceeds may be measured by the rate at which x is increasing with time, so that we may write the following differential equation

$$\frac{dx}{dt} = k(2a - x)(a - x)$$

where k is a constant. From this we obtain

$$\int_0^x \frac{dx}{(2a - x)(a - x)} = k \int_0^t dt$$

$$\frac{1}{a} \int_0^x \frac{1}{(a - x)} - \frac{1}{(2a - x)} dx = kt$$

$$\Rightarrow \ln\left(\frac{2a - x}{a - x}\right) - \ln 2 = akt \tag{1}$$

the ln2 appearing when the lower limit $x = 0$ is substituted. At time T we have $x = a/2$ and line (1) becomes

$$akT = \ln 3 - \ln 2 = \ln(3/2)$$

Now considering time $2T$ we obtain

$$\ln\left(\frac{2a - x}{a - x}\right) - \ln 2 = 2akT = 2 \ln (3/2)$$

$$\Rightarrow \frac{2a - x}{2a - 2x} = (3/2)^2 = 9/4$$

From this $x = 5a/7$ so that the fraction of substance B which has now reacted is 5/7.

Exercise 17(f)

1. The number of bacteria in a culture increases at the rate of 4 bacteria per minute for every 100 bacteria present. At the same time an antibiotic introduced into the culture kills off bacteria at a steady rate of 10 per minute. If there are initially 200 bacteria, find the number remaining after 10 minutes. How long will the antibiotic take to kill all the bacteria?
2. The current i at time t in a certain electrical circuit varies in accordance with the differential equation

$$\frac{1}{L}\frac{di}{dt} + Ri = E.$$

If $i = 0$ when $t = 0$, find the current at time t, and sketch the nature of your solution.
3. In a certain industrial process the rate of production of a particular substance is proportional to the quantity already produced. The quantity produced doubles in 1 hour. When an amount Q units has been produced, the process is allowed to continue but m units of the substance are removed each minute. Find the amount of substance present after a further hour. Comment briefly on the case $m = Q\ln 2/60$.
4. If the process of question 3 is to be designed so that the amount of

substance present is exhausted 5 hours after the first products are removed, show that the amount removed during each hour should be $(32/31)Q$ ln2/60.

5. In a certain chemical reaction a quantity q of a reagent is being transformed into a new substance and the rate at which the reaction proceeds is proportional to the amount of reagent remaining. Show that the amount transformed after time t is $q(1 - e^{-kt})$ where k is a constant.

6. A water tank of uniform cross-sectional area A is being filled by a pipe which supplies V units of water every minute. The tank has a small hole in its base through which water leaks at a rate kh units per minute, where h is the depth of water in the tank. Initially the depth of water is h_0. If $V > kh_0$ show that the level of water will rise and find the depth of water after t minutes. Show, however, that the depth cannot increase beyond a certain value. If this value is $2h_0$, prove that the time taken for the depth to reach $3h_0/2$ is $2h_0 A\ln2/V$.

7. In another chemical reaction one molecule of a substance X is produced by the reaction of one molecule each of two reagents A and B. The rate at which the reaction proceeds is proportional to the product of the concentrations, (i.e. molecules per unit volume) of A and B. The initial concentration of both A and B is a. Show that if the concentration of X at time t is x then

$$\frac{dx}{dt} = k(a - x)^2$$

where k is a constant and solve this for x given that $x = 0$ when $t = 0$. If the concentrations of A and B are reduced to $a/2$ in time T, find the concentrations at times $2T$, $3T$ and $4T$.

8. The water in a hot water tank cools at a rate which is proportional to the excess temperature $T°C$ of the water above its surroundings. When $T = 60$ the water is cooling at $1°C$ per minute. When switched on the heater supplies sufficient heat to raise the temperature of the water by $1\frac{1}{2}°C$ each minute (neglecting heat loss by cooling). If $T = 0$ when the heater is switched on, show that t minutes later

$$\frac{dT}{dt} = (90 - T)/60$$

Hence find the number of degrees by which the temperature of the water has risen half an hour after switching on. Show also that if room temperature is a steady $15°C$ then the water will boil in a little under 3 hours.

9. A town of population N (which may be assumed constant) is hit by an epidemic of an incurable but not fatal illness. The rate at which the illness spreads is considered to be proportional to the product of the number x of those who have contracted the illness and the number of those who have not. Write down a differential equation involving N and x. If during a certain week the percentage of the population who are suffering from the illness increases from 10% to 20%, estimate what the percentage figure will be after a further 1 week, 2 weeks.

18

Integration Methods

18.1 Integration as a Summation Process

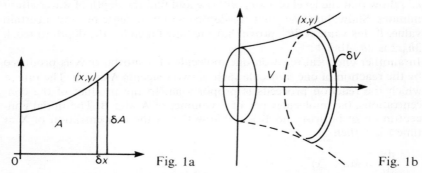

Fig. 1a

Fig. 1b

The student is almost certainly familiar with the integration results for the area under a curve and for the volume of a solid revolution. These are usually derived by a method which may be outlined as follows. Letting A be the area under the curve from the origin as far as x co-ordinate x (Fig. 1a) and δA the small increase in area caused by an increase δx in the x co-ordinate, then

$$\delta A \simeq y \,.\, \delta x \quad \Rightarrow \frac{\delta A}{\delta x} \simeq y$$

$$\text{letting } \delta x \to 0 \quad \frac{dA}{dx} = y$$

$$\Rightarrow A = \int y \, dx$$

For the volume of revolution

$$\delta V \simeq \pi y^2 \delta x \quad \Rightarrow \frac{\delta V}{\delta x} \simeq \pi y^2$$

$$\text{letting } \delta x \to 0 \quad \frac{dV}{dx} = \pi y^2$$

$$\Rightarrow V = \pi \int y^2 dx$$

In each case, the integration is performed between limits corresponding to the limits of the area or volume required. Thus to find the area under a curve from $x = a$ to $x = b$ we evaluate the definite integral

$$\int_a^b y \, dx$$

We shall now see that there is a more convenient way of interpreting these results.

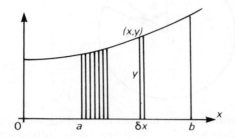

Fig. 2

If we imagine the area from $x = a$ to $x = b$ to be split into a number of narrow strips, each of width δx, then the area of a typical strip (Fig. 2) is approximately $y \cdot \delta x$. An estimate for the area required is provided by the sum of all such strips from $x = a$ to $x = b$.

that is   area $\simeq \displaystyle\sum_{x=a}^{x=b} y \cdot \delta x$

As the strip-width $\delta x \to 0$ the accuracy of the estimate is improved and the result obtained from this sum will therefore approach the definite integral

$\displaystyle\int_a^b y\, dx$ which as we have seen, gives the true area

It is therefore convenient to regard this integration as being a method for summing the individual areas $y.\delta x$ from $x = a$ to $x = b$. Similarly if a solid of revolution is divided into a number of discs of thickness δx, then a typical disc has volume $\pi y^2 \delta x$ and the result

$$\text{volume} = \int_a^b \pi y^2\, dx$$

may be regarded as a summation of all such discs from $x = a$ to $x = b$.

As a further example of this idea of summation we shall recall the work done in stretching an elastic string to extension x. Imagine that this is achieved by a succession of very small extensions, each of magnitude δy. When the stretch in the string is y, the work required to produce the next small extension is approximately $T.\delta y$ or $(ky)\delta y$. The total work done is the sum of all such contributions from $y = 0$ (string slack) to $y = x$ (final extension). This summation is performed by the integral

$$\int_{y=0}^x ky\, dy = \tfrac{1}{2} kx^2$$

Example 110

Prove that the area of a circle is πr^2.

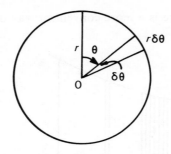

Fig. 3

The area may be divided into a number of small sectors each of angle $\delta\theta$. One such sector is shown in Fig. 3. When $\delta\theta$ is sufficiently small these sectors are almost triangular and have area approximately equal to $(r.\delta\theta)r/2$ $= r^2.\delta\theta/2$ (using $\frac{1}{2}$ base × height). The area of the circle is the sum of all such sectors from $\theta = 0$ to $\theta = 2\pi$

i.e. $$\int_0^{2\pi} \frac{1}{2}r^2 \, d\theta = \frac{1}{2}r^2 \int_0^{2\pi} d\theta = \pi r^2$$

Exercise 18(a)

1. Show by integration that the volume of a cone is $\pi r^2 h/3$.
2. The tension in a certain device is proportional to the square of the distance x by which the device is extended. If the constant of proportionality is k, find an expression for the total work needed to produce an extension x.
3. Show that the area beneath the curve $y = 1/x$ for $x \geqslant 1$ is infinite but the corresponding volume of revolution about the x-axis is finite. If the volume of this solid is defined as 1 unit, does this mean that 1 unit in volume of paint can be made to cover an infinite area?
4. A cap of thickness h is sliced off from a sphere of radius r. Prove that the volume of the cap is $\pi h^2(3r - h)/3$.

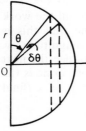

Fig. 4

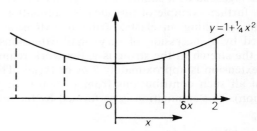

$y = 1 + \frac{1}{4}x^2$

Fig. 5

*5. Fig. 4 shows a hemispherical shell of radius r. Show that the surface area of the shaded ring is approximately $2\pi r^2 \cos\theta.\delta\theta$. Hence prove that the surface area of a sphere is $4\pi r^2$.
*6. A solid is formed by rotating the area between $y = 1 + x^2/4$, the x-axis and the lines $x = 1$, $x = 2$ about the y-axis. (Fig. 5.) Show that the volume

formed by rotating the strip shown is approximately $2\pi xy.\ \delta x$. Hence find the volume of the solid.

18.2 C.G. of Laminae and Solids of Revolution

We now turn our attention to some further problems on centre of gravity, in which we shall be using integration to perform the summations of the Cartesian equations derived in section 8.1, i.e.

$$M\bar{x} = \Sigma\ mx \quad M\bar{y} = \Sigma\ my$$

Example 111

Find the centre of gravity of a uniform solid formed by rotating about the x-axis the section of the curve $y = x^2$ which lies between $x = 0$ and $x = 3$.

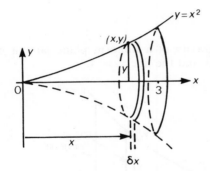

Fig. 6

By symmetry the centre of gravity of this solid lies on the x-axis, i.e. $\bar{y} = 0$.
To find $\bar{x}$ we shall use the formula $M\bar{x} = \sum mx$.
Considering the solid to be split into a large number of discs each of thickness δx, the mass of a typical disc (Fig. 6) is proportional to its volume, i.e. $k(\pi y^2\ \delta x)$, where k is the mass per unit volume, and the centre of gravity of the disc is at position x on the x-axis. Thus

$$M\bar{x} = \sum mx = \sum(k\pi y^2\delta x)\ x$$
$$= k\pi\sum y^2x.\delta x$$

The summation, which is over all such discs from $x = 0$ to $x = 3$, is performed by the following integration

$$M\bar{x} = k\pi \int_0^3 y^2x\ \mathrm{d}x$$

$$= k\pi \int_0^3 x^5\ \mathrm{d}x \quad \text{since } y = x^2$$

$$= \frac{k\pi}{6}(3)^6 \tag{1}$$

To complete the calculation we need to find the total mass M. This will be the volume of the solid multiplied by k and requires a further integration, i.e. $M = k \displaystyle\int_0^3 y^2 \, \mathrm{d}x$

$= k\pi \displaystyle\int_0^3 x^4 \, \mathrm{d}x$ since $y = x^2$

$= \dfrac{k\pi}{5}(3)^5$ (2)

Hence from (1) and (2)

$$\bar{x} = \frac{(3)^6}{6} \div \frac{(3)^5}{5} = \frac{15}{6} \text{ or } 2.5$$

The position of the centre of gravity is (2.5, 0)

Note: The powers of 3 in lines (1) and (2) should not be evaluated since they cancel easily.

Example 112

Find the centre of gravity of a uniform plane lamina bounded by the curve $y = x^3$, the x-axis and the line $x = 4$.

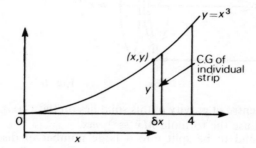

Fig. 7

This lamina has no axis of symmetry so both $\bar{x}$ and $\bar{y}$ need to be established. If the lamina is split into a large number of narrow strips each of thickness δx then the typical strip shown in Fig. 7 has mass $k(y.\delta x)$, where k is the mass per unit area, and centre of gravity at position $(x, y/2)$. It is important not to overlook the 1/2 multiplying the y-co-ordinate. We continue as follows:

$M\bar{x} = \sum mx$ $M\bar{y} = \sum my$

$\phantom{M\bar{x}} = \sum(ky.\delta x)x$ $\phantom{M\bar{y}} = \sum(ky.\delta x)y/2$

$\phantom{M\bar{x}} = k\displaystyle\int_0^4 yx \, \mathrm{d}x$ $\phantom{M\bar{y}} = \dfrac{k}{2}\displaystyle\int_0^4 y^2 \, \mathrm{d}x$

$\phantom{M\bar{x}} = k\displaystyle\int_0^4 x^4 \, \mathrm{d}x$ $\phantom{M\bar{y}} = \dfrac{k}{2}\displaystyle\int_0^4 x^6 \, \mathrm{d}x$

$\phantom{M\bar{x}} = \dfrac{k(4)^5}{5}$ $\phantom{M\bar{y}} = \dfrac{k(4)^7}{14}$

Finally we need the total mass M which is the total area of the lamina multiplied by k

i.e. $M = k \int_0^4 y \, dx$

$= k \int_0^4 x^3 \, dx = \dfrac{k(4)^4}{4}$

Hence $\bar{x} = \dfrac{4}{5} \div \dfrac{1}{4} = \dfrac{16}{5}$ $\bar{y} = \dfrac{(4)^3}{14} \div \dfrac{1}{4} = \dfrac{128}{7}$

The position of the centre of gravity is (16/5, 128/7)

Exercise 18(b)

In questions 1–4 find the centres of gravity of the given solids of revolution.

1. $y = \sqrt{x}$ about the x axis for $0 \leqslant x \leqslant 3$
2. $y = 1/x^2$ about the x axis for $x \geqslant 1$
3. $y = x^2$ about the y axis for $0 \leqslant y \leqslant 4$
4. $y = 1 + x^2$ about the x axis for $0 \leqslant x \leqslant 1$

In questions 5–8 find the centres of gravity of uniform plane laminae bounded by the given lines:

5. $y = x^2$, the x axis and $x = 5$
6. $y = 4 - x^2$ and the positive axes
7. $y = \cos x$ and the x axis for $-\pi/2 \leqslant x \leqslant \pi/2$
8. $y = e^x$, the x axis, $x = 0$ and $x = \ln 2$.

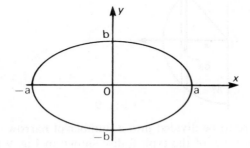

Fig. 8

9. Fig. 8 shows the ellipse $\dfrac{x^2}{a^2} + \dfrac{y^2}{b^2} = 1$.

   (i) Show that the volume of the 'ellipsoid' formed by rotating the ellipse about the x axis is $4\pi ab^2/3$.
   (ii) Does the ellipsoid formed by rotation about the y axis have equal volume?
   (iii) A uniform solid is in the form of the half of the ellipsoid of part (i) for

which $x \geqslant 0$. Show that the centre of gravity of this solid is at $x = 3a/8$.

10. The section of the curve $y = \cos x$ for which $-\pi/2, \leqslant x \leqslant \pi/2$ is rotated about the y axis. Find the position of the centre of gravity of the resulting solid of revolution. (Hint: rotate 'vertical' strips about the y axis as in exercise 18(a), question 6. The integrations must be evaluated 'by parts'.)

18.3 Standard Centre of Gravity Results

In section 8.3 a number of important centre of gravity results were quoted without proof. A proof is now given for the result of the solid hemisphere. Hints for the remaining proofs are given in exercise 18(c).

The student should notice in particular that when a formula exists for the total volume or area of the body considered, it is often more convenient to find the mass of the typical disc or strip considered as a fraction of the total mass M by using

$$\text{mass of element} = \frac{\text{area/volume of element}}{\text{total area/volume of body}} \times M$$

This is illustrated in the following worked example.

Example 113

Prove that the centre of gravity of a uniform solid hemisphere is at distance $3r/8$ from its centre.

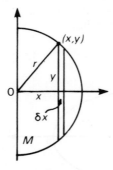

Fig. 9

Imagine the hemisphere to be divided into a number of narrow discs, each of thickness δx. The volume of the typical disc shown in Fig. 9 is approximately $\pi y^2 . \delta x$. Comparing this with the total volume of the hemisphere, $2\pi r^3/3$, we may write

$$\text{mass of disc} \simeq \frac{\pi y^2 . \delta x}{2\pi r^3/3} M \quad \text{or} \quad \frac{3My^2}{2r^3} . \delta x$$

Then $\quad M\bar{x} = \sum mx$

$$= \sum \left(\frac{3My^2}{2r^3} . \delta x \right) x$$

$$\Rightarrow \bar{x} = \frac{3}{2r^3} \int_0^r y^2 x \, dx$$

$$= \frac{3}{2r^3} \int_0^r r^2 x - x^3 \, dx \quad \text{since } y^2 = r^2 - x^2$$

$$= \frac{3}{2r^3} \left[\frac{r^2 x^2}{2} - \frac{x^4}{4} \right]_0^r$$

$$= \frac{3}{2r^3} \cdot \frac{r^4}{4} \quad \text{or} \quad \frac{3r}{8}$$

Exercise 18(c)

1. A cone of radius r and height h may be formed by the rotation of a straight line about the x axis as in Fig. 10. What is the equation of this straight line? Hence show that the mass of the typical disc shown in Fig. 10 is approximately $3Mx^2.\delta x/h^3$ where M is the total mass of the cone. Prove that the centre of gravity of a cone is distant $h/4$ from its base.

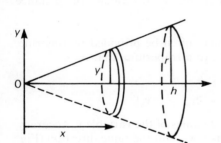

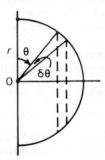

Fig. 10   Fig.11

*2. Prove that the centre of gravity of a uniform semi-circular lamina is at distance $4r/3\pi$ from its centre. (Hint: divide the semi-circle into narrow sectors as in example 110. Work in terms of r and θ.)

3. Show that the centre of gravity of a uniform semi-circular wire is at distance $2r/\pi$ from its centre. (Work in terms of r and θ.)

4. Fig. 11 shows a hemi-spherical shell of radius r. Show that the mass of the shaded ring is approximately $M \cos \theta. \delta\theta$ where M is the total mass of the shell. Deduce that

$$\bar{x} = r \int_{0-}^{\pi/2} \sin \theta.\cos \theta \, d\theta$$

and show that the result obtained from this is $r/2$.

5. Use the method of question 2 to show that the centre of gravity of a uniform plane lamina in the form of a sector of a circle of angle 2α is at distance $2r\sin\alpha/3\alpha$ from the centre. Such a lamina, when suspended from one end of its curved boundary, is found to rest with its axis of symmetry horizontal. Show that α satisfies the equation $3\alpha = 2 \tan \alpha$.

6. Taking Fig. 9 to represent a uniform semi-circular lamina, show that the mass of the shaded strip is approximately $4My.\delta x/\pi r^2$. Hence obtain

the result of question 2 by a different method. Compare the difficulty of the two methods.

18.4 Approximate Integration. Simpson's Rule

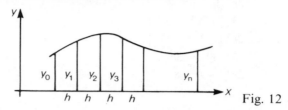

A variable y changes with respect to x and values $y_0 \; y_1 \; y_2 \; \ldots \; y_n$ of this variable are known at equally spaced intervals of x. (Fig. 12.) A recurrent problem is that of estimating the area beneath the graph of y, (i.e. $\int y \, dx$) from the known values $y_0 \; y_1 \; y_2 \; \ldots \; y_n$ and the interval width h. If, for example, we are concerned with the velocity of a moving body and values of this velocity are measured at equally spaced intervals of time, then an estimate for the area under the velocity-time graph will enable us to estimate the distance travelled by the body.

Trapezium rule. A reasonable estimate may often be provided by this rule, which approximates each strip in Fig. 12 to a trapezium, that is

$$\text{area} \tfrac{1}{2}(y_0 + y_1)h + \tfrac{1}{2}(y_1 + y_2)h + \tfrac{1}{2}(y_2 + y_3)h + \ldots$$

$$\text{or } \frac{h}{2}\{y_0 + 2y_1 + 2y_2 + 2y_3 \ldots + 2y_{n-1} + y_n\}$$

This rule may be used with any number of values of the variable y. Accuracy is poor when the curvature of the graph is always in the same direction (Fig. 13) since in one case every trapezium is an over-estimate and in the other case an under-estimate.

Fig. 13

Simpson's rule. This rule, which is established by fitting quadratic curves through successive sets of three points, may be stated as follows:

$$\text{area} \simeq \frac{h}{3}\{y_0 + 4y_1 + 2y_2 + 4y_3 \ldots + 2y_{n-2} + 4y_{n-1} + y_n\}$$

The proof of this result may be found in most Pure Mathematics texts. Only an odd number of values may be used,

with 3 values $A \simeq \tfrac{1}{3}h\{y_0 + 4y_1 + y_2\}$
5 values $A \simeq \tfrac{1}{3}h\{y_0 + 4y_1 + 2y_2 + 4y_3 + y_4\}$
7 values $A \simeq \tfrac{1}{3}h\{y_0 + 4y_1 + 2y_2 + 4y_3 + 2y_4 + 4y_5 + y_6\}$

As an indication of the accuracy that may be achieved with Simpson's rule, imagine that we wish to estimate the area under the curve $y = \sin x$ between $x = 0$ and $x = \pi/3$. We shall compare our answer with the exact result obtained by integration, that is

$$\int_0^{\pi/3} \sin x \, dx = \left[-\cos x \right]_0^{\pi/3} = -1/2 + 1 = 1/2$$

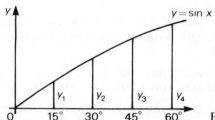

Fig. 14

Taking five values then the spacing interval is 15° or $\pi/12$ radians, (Fig. 14). The values themselves are

$y_0 = \sin 0° = 0$
$y_1 = \sin 15° = 0.2588$
$y_2 = \sin 30° = 0.5000$
$y_3 = \sin 45° = 0.7071$
$y_4 = \sin 60° = 0.8660$

Working from Simpson's rule for 5 values (above) we obtain

$$\text{area} \simeq \frac{\pi}{36}\{0 + 4(0.2588) + 2(0.5) + 4(0.7071) + 0.866\}$$

$$= \frac{\pi}{36} \times 5.7296 = 0.5001 \text{ (taking } \pi = 3.142)$$

This is correct to three figures. (Greater accuracy cannot be expected since the sine values are taken from four-figure tables.) The value given by the trapezium rule is 0.497, a lower degree of accuracy being expected, since every trapezium is an under-estimate.

Exercise 18(d)

1. Estimate the value of $\int_2^5 y \, dx$ from the following data:

y	1.9	2.7	2.8	2.5	2.3	2.2	2.2
x	2	2.5	3	3.5	4	4.5	5

2. Use Simpson's rule (7 values) to obtain an estimate for the area bounded by $y = e^{-x}$, the x axis and the lines $x = 0.1$, $x = 0.4$. Compare your result with that obtained by direct integration.
3. Obtain a value for ln3 by using Simpson's rule (9 value.) to estimate the area beneath the curve $y = 1/x$ in the range $1 \leqslant x \leqslant 3$.
4. (i) Use Simpson's rule (5 values) to estimate the value of:

$$\int_0^1 \frac{dx}{1 + x^2}$$

(ii) Use the result $\int \dfrac{dx}{1 + x^2} = \arctan x$ to obtain a value for π.

5. Estimate the distance moved by the body of question 12, exercise 1(d) during the 6 seconds given.

6. The cross-sectional area of the hull of a 6 metre boat is measured at intervals along its length. From the following results estimate the cubic capacity of the hull.

distance from bow	(m)	0	1	2	3	4	5	6
cross-sectional area	(m²)	0	2.1	3.5	3.8	3.7	3.0	0

*7. Use Simpson's rule (5 values) to estimate the volume of the solid of revolution formed by rotating $y^4 = 1 + x^2$ about the x axis in the range $0 \leqslant x \leqslant 2$.

8. Estimate the distance travelled by the aircraft of question 11, exercise 1(d) during the 40 seconds of motion given.

18.5 Impulse and Work Done by a Variable Force

In chapter 11 the following results were derived for motion in a straight line under a constant force F:

impulse/momentum $\quad Ft = mv - mu$
work/kinetic energy $\quad Fs = \frac{1}{2}mv^2 - \frac{1}{2}mu^2$

We shall now see how these results need to be modified in the case of a changing force F. We start, in each case, from the equation of motion $F = ma$ which determines the acceleration at any instant of the motion from the magnitude of the force acting

(i) $\qquad F = \dfrac{mdv}{dt} \Rightarrow \displaystyle\int_{t_1}^{t_2} F\, dt = \int_u^v m\, dv$

$\qquad \Rightarrow \int F\, dt = mv - mu$

that is, $\quad$ impulse = change in momentum

(ii) $F = \dfrac{mdv}{dt} = mv\dfrac{ds}{ds} \Rightarrow \displaystyle\int_{s_1}^{s_2} F\, ds = \int_u^v mv\, dv$

$\qquad \Rightarrow \displaystyle\int F\, ds = \frac{1}{2}mv^2 - \frac{1}{2}mu^2$

that is, work done = change in K.E.

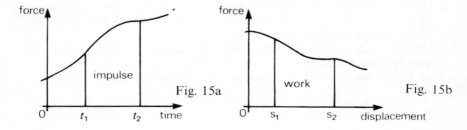

Fig. 15a

Fig. 15b

Impulse is therefore given by the area under the force-time graph (Fig. 15a) and work by the area under the force-displacement graph, (Fig. 15b). In a number of situations these areas are conveniently estimated by Simpson's rule.

Example 114

A body of mass 6 kg, moving initially at 3 m s^{-1}, is accelerated by a force whose magnitude F newtons changes with the distance s metres travelled by the body in accordance with the following table:

s	0	2	4	6	8	10	12
F	26	37	46	53	58	60	57

If there is a uniform resistance to motion of 12 N, estimate the speed of the body when it has moved 12 metres.

(In solving this question we need to assume that the force F always acts in the direction of the body's initial motion.) We begin by using Simpson's rule to estimate the work done on the body by the *overall* force acting, i.e. we use the following values:

distance (metres)	0	2	4	6	8	10	12
overall force (newtons)	14	25	34	41	46	48	45

work done $\simeq \frac{1}{3}h\{14 + 4(25) + 2(34) + 4(41) + 2(46) + 4(48) + 45\}$

$\quad\quad\quad\quad = \frac{2}{3} \times 675 = 450$ joules

Finally we equate this work to the change in kinetic energy of the body, i.e.

$$\frac{1}{2}6.v^2 - \frac{1}{2}6.(3)^2 = 450$$
$$\Rightarrow 3v^2 = 450 + 27 = 477$$

From this the speed of the body is found to be approximately 12.6 m s^{-1}.

Exercise 18(e)

1. A car of mass 700 kg starts from rest. The pull exerted by the engine decreases with time in accordance with the following table:

time (seconds)	0	1	2	3	4	5	6
pull (newtons)	2720	2160	1880	1680	1540	1400	1320

Find the total impulse received by the car during the 6 seconds and hence estimate the speed gained. (Ignore resistances.)

2. A body of mass 10 kg is accelerated from rest by a force whose magnitude is given by the following table:

force (newtons)	32	39	45	50	54	57	59	60	60
distance (metres)	0	5	10	15	20	25	30	35	40

Find the total work done by the force when the body has travelled (i) 20 m (ii) 40 m. Find also the speed of the body and the rate of working of the force at these instants.

3. A crate of mass 50 kg is being lowered vertically on a cable. The tension in the cable varies as follows:

tension (newtons)	500	528	550	567	582	595	605
time (seconds)	0	0.5	1	1.5	2	2.5	3

Initially the crate is moving downwards at 5 m s^{-1}. Estimate its speed when the 3 seconds have elapsed.

4. A cyclist and his machine together have mass 100 kg. The cyclist increases speed from 5 m s^{-1} to 7 m s^{-1} in a distance of 36 metres and the force he exerts decreases over this distance in accordance with the following table:

force (newtons)	82	73	66	60	55	52	50
distance (metres)	0	6	12	18	24	30	36

Find the work done by the cyclist and hence estimate the resistance to motion (assumed constant) which he experiences.

*5. A body of mass 30 kg is accelerated by a constant force of 100 N. The resistance to motion, which varies with the speed of the body, is given by the following table:

speed (m s^{-1})	10	12	14	16	18
resistance (newtons)	18	26	35	46	59

(i) Use the equation of motion to show that the distance covered by the body is

$$m \int \frac{v}{F} \, dv$$

where F is the overall force acting. Hence estimate the distance covered by the body in accelerating from 10 m s^{-1} to 18 m s^{-1}.

(ii) Find also the time which this takes and the average speed of the body during this time.

6. The speed of a body varies over a distance of 60 metres as follows:

distance (metres)	0	15	30	45	60
speed (m s^{-1})	12.5	13.1	13.5	13.8	14.0

Estimate the time taken by the body over this distance.

19
Simple Harmonic Motion (S.H.M.)

19.1 The Simple Harmonic Oscillation

The displacement-time formula $x = a \sin \omega t$ represents an oscillation about the origin O between $x = a$ and $x = -a$. Consider the following values:

$$
\begin{aligned}
\text{time } t = 0 \qquad & \text{displacement } a \sin\omega t = 0 \\
= \pi/2\omega \qquad & = a \\
= \pi/\omega \qquad & = 0 \\
= 3\pi/2\omega \qquad & = -a \\
= 2\pi/\omega \qquad & = 0
\end{aligned}
$$

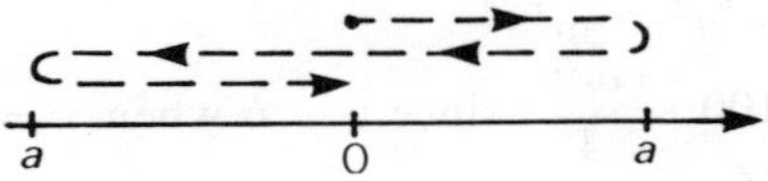

Fig. 1

A body performing such an oscillation moves from the origin to maximum positive displacement, returns through the origin and continues to maximum negative displacement before finally returning to the origin for a second time, (see Fig. 1). After this the cycle is repeated, since the values $\sin 2\pi \rightarrow \sin 4\pi$, $\sin 4\pi \rightarrow \sin 6\pi$, etc. ... are identical to those for $\sin 0 \rightarrow \sin 2\pi$. The motion is therefore **periodic** (one which repeats itself in a fixed interval of time) and the time for one complete oscillation is $2\pi/\omega$. The following terms are of importance:

amplitude (a)	the distance from the centre of the oscillation to an extreme point
angular velocity (ω)	the reason for this name will be apparent in section 19.3
period $(2\pi/\omega)$	the time of 1 complete oscillation
frequency $(\omega/2\pi)$	the number of oscillations in unit time (1/period).

19.2 Velocity and Acceleration

If we differentiate the displacement-time formula of section 19.1 the following results are obtained for the velocity and for the acceleration of a body undergoing such a motion:

$$\text{displacement} \qquad x = a \sin\omega t$$

$$\text{velocity} \qquad \frac{\mathrm{d}x}{\mathrm{d}t} = a\omega \cos\omega t = \omega\sqrt{a^2 - x^2} \qquad (1)$$

$$\text{acceleration} \quad \frac{d^2x}{dt^2} = -a\omega^2 \sin\omega t = -\omega^2 x \tag{2}$$

Notes: (i) From (1) the maximum velocity is $a\omega$ and this occurs when $x = 0$, i.e. at the centre of the oscillation.

(ii) From (2) the acceleration is proportional to the displacement but opposite in direction (i.e. always towards the centre of the oscillation).

(iii) The maximum acceleration is $\omega^2 a$ (in magnitude) and occurs at the extremes of the oscillation.

Example 115

A body oscillating about a fixed point O reaches a maximum speed of 10 m s^{-1} and has speed 6 m s^{-1} when at a distance 0.5 m from O. Find (i) the amplitude and frequency of the oscillation (ii) the average speed of the body over one oscillation.

(i) With the usual notation the maximum speed is $a\omega$. Thus $a\omega = 10$. We now work from the velocity result, (1) above,

$$v = \omega\sqrt{a^2 - x^2}$$
$$\Rightarrow v^2 = \omega^2 a^2 - \omega^2 x^2$$
$$36 = 100 - \frac{\omega^2}{4} \quad \text{since } v = 6 \text{ when } x = 1/2$$
$$\Rightarrow \omega = 16$$

$$\text{amplitude} = \frac{a\omega}{\omega} = \frac{10}{16} = 0.625 \text{ m}$$

$$\text{frequency} = \frac{\omega}{2\pi} = \frac{8}{\pi} = 2.55 \text{ cycles per second}$$

(ii) The average speed is *not* one-half of the maximum speed. It is calculated by dividing the total distance covered in one oscillation by the time taken (i.e. the period of the oscillation), i.e.

$$\text{average speed} = \frac{4a}{2\pi/\omega} = \frac{2.5}{\pi/8} = \frac{20}{\pi}$$
$$\text{average speed} = 6.36 \text{ m s}^{-1}$$

Note: The average *velocity* over one oscillation is zero since the net displacement in this time is 0.

Exercise 19(a)

All oscillations may be taken as simple harmonic

1. The displacement x metres of a particle at time t is given by the formula $x = 0.4 \sin10t$. Write down the amplitude and period of the oscillation. Find also the maximum speed and the maximum acceleration of the particle.

2. A body oscillating 15 times per second has maximum acceleration 24 m s^{-2}. Find its maximum speed and the distance between two consecutive

positions of rest. Find also the average speed of the body over this distance.

3. A particle starts at the origin O and makes 5 oscillations per second of amplitude 25 cm centred on O. Write down the displacement-time formula and calculate the speed and acceleration of the particle when it is (i) 15 cm (ii) 24 cm from O.

4. A piston oscillates in a cylinder of length 15 cm. Find the greatest number of oscillations per second that can be made without the speed of the piston exceeding 9 m s^{-1}.

5. A body is oscillating with amplitude 1.7 m. After travelling 0.1 m from a position of rest, the body has speed 2 m s^{-1}. How much further does the body travel before its speed reaches 4 m s^{-1} and what is the greatest speed that it achieves?

6. A particle is oscillating with amplitude $1/2$ m. At a certain instant its speed is 10 m s^{-1} and the magnitude of its acceleration is 75 m s^{-2}. Find
    (i)   the displacement at this instant (from the centre)
    (ii) the frequency of the oscillation
    (iii) the speed of the particle when the magnitude of its acceleration is 150 m s^{-2}.

*7. A horizontal plate oscillates vertically up and down with amplitude a and frequency f. A small body is placed on the plate.
    (i) Show that the body will leave the plate if $4\pi^2 f^2 a > g$. Will this happen when the plate is moving up or down?
    (ii) If the amplitude is 15 mm what is the greatest frequency of oscillation for which the body can remain on the plate?

8. If, in question 7, the amplitude is 15 mm and the frequency is 6 cycles per second, find the distance from the centre of the oscillation at which the body leaves the plate. Find also the speed of the body at this instant.

19.3 The Circular Representation

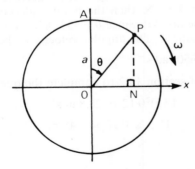

Fig. 2

In Fig. 2 the point P describes a circular path of radius a at uniform angular rate ω radians/sec. As it does so the point N, which is the projection of P on the x-axis, oscillates along the diameter from $x = a$ to $x = -a$. We can easily demonstrate that the oscillations of N are, in fact, simple harmonic. For if P starts at position A on the circle, then after t seconds angle AOP $= \theta = \omega t$ radians

$\Rightarrow$ ON $= a \sin \theta = a \sin \omega t$

Any simple harmonic motion may be regarded as the projection of a uniform circular motion upon a diameter (though the point P describing the circle need not always start at the position corresponding to A). This is sometimes referred to as the circular representation of S.H.M. and it is a device which is of frequent use in problem solving.

The student should notice that the period of the S.H. oscillation $(2\pi/\omega)$ may be interpreted as the time taken by P to complete one circle, (i.e. 2π radians) at an angular rate of ω radians/sec. This is why ω is sometimes called the 'angular velocity' of the oscillation.

Example 116

A particle is performing a simple harmonic oscillation of amplitude 20 cm. After leaving an extreme point of the oscillation the particle travels 32 cm in 1/7 s and is still moving in the same direction. Find its speed and the magnitude of its acceleration at this instant.

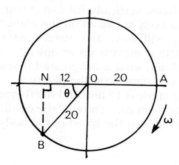

Fig. 3

Consider the circular representation of Fig. 3. If the particle moves along the horizontal diameter from A to N, then the point undergoing uniform circular motion describes the arc AB. Since $\theta = 53° \ 8'$ ($\cos \theta = 0.6$) this is an arc of $126° \ 52'$ or 2.214 radians. The angular velocity is therefore

$$\omega = 7 \times 2.214 = 15.50 \text{ rad s}^{-1}$$

We now use the results of section 19.2 to complete the question:

acceleration $= \omega^2 x = (15.5)^2 0.12 = 28.8 \text{ m s}^{-2}$

speed $= \omega\sqrt{a^2 - x^2} = 15.5 \times 0.16 = 2.48 \text{ m s}^{-1}$

Exercise 19(b)

All oscillations are simple harmonic.

1. A body is performing an oscillation of amplitude 1.5 m. After being instantaneously at rest, the body travels 0.5 m in 0.1 sec. Find the speed of the body at this instant and the further time that elapses before the body is again at rest.

2. A body is oscillating with amplitude 8 cm. At a certain instant the body is at a point P 4 cm from the centre of oscillation O and has velocity 0.6 m s⁻¹ away from O. Find the time that elapses before the particle (i) first returns to P, (ii) first returns to O.

3. An oscillating particle passes a certain point P on its path at successive intervals of 0.2 s and 0.6 s. If its speed at this point is 5 m s⁻¹, find the amplitude of the oscillation and the distance of P from the centre.

4. A particle moving away from the centre O of its oscillation has speed 48 cm s⁻¹ when 7 cm from O and speed 30 cm s⁻¹ when 20 cm from O. Find the amplitude of the oscillation and the time taken between the two points. Show also that when the same time has elapsed again, the particle will be momentarily at rest.

5. A body is performing simple harmonic oscillations in a long narrow tube. A 20 cm section of the tube is made of glass and the body is visible in this section for intervals of 0.3 s, disappearing at either side for 0.2 s and 0.4 s respectively. Find the distance between the points of rest of the body and the greatest distance it reaches from the visible section of the tube.

6. Show that in a simple harmonic oscillation the speed exceeds 60% of the maximum speed for 80% of the travel and approximately 59% of the time.

19.4 Other Displacement–Time Formulae

In this section we consider some further displacement-time formulae which give rise to simple harmonic motion. The student should understand that there is no difference between the actual characteristics of the motions governed by these various formulae – the difference lies only in the point on the oscillation at which each motion commences.

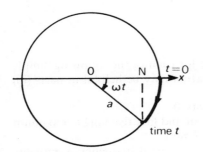

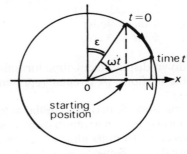

Fig. 4a $ON = a \cos \omega t$ Fig. 4b $ON = a \sin(\omega t + \varepsilon)$

(i) $x = a \sin \omega t$ This formula is considered in section 19.1. This is a motion in which the particle starts at the centre of the oscillation.

(ii) $x = a \cos \omega t$ When $t = 0$ $x = a$. Motion begins from an extreme point of the oscillation. The circular representation is shown in Fig. 4a.

(iii) $x = \sin(\omega t + \varepsilon)$ This is the most general case, when $t = 0$ $x = a \sin \varepsilon$ (see Fig. 4b) so that motion may start at any position on the oscillation depending on the value of the angle ε (the **phase angle**).

Note: In fig. 4b, as it is drawn, the particle will move outwards from its starting position. If we require a motion in which the initial motion is inwards, from the same position, then the phase angle ε will need to be the corresponding second quadrant angle.

Alternative form for the general S.H.M. The formula $x = a\sin(\omega t + \varepsilon)$ may be expanded as follows:

$$x = a\sin(\omega t + \varepsilon)$$
$$= a\sin \omega t.\cos \varepsilon + a\cos \omega t.\sin \varepsilon$$
$$= A\sin \omega t + B\cos \omega t$$

where $A = a\cos \varepsilon$ and $B = a\sin \varepsilon$ are constants. Thus any linear combination of the formulae (i) and (ii) above will also define a simple harmonic motion. In this form, however, the amplitude and phase angle are not so apparent. In fact

$$\text{amplitude } a = \sqrt{a^2(\cos^2 \varepsilon + \sin^2 \varepsilon)} = \sqrt{A^2 + B^2}$$
$$\text{phase-angle } \tan \varepsilon = \frac{a\sin \varepsilon}{a\cos \varepsilon} = \frac{B}{A} \text{ that is } \varepsilon = \arctan (B/A)$$

The initial displacement is $x = B$. Thus the motion $x = 6\sin\omega t - 8\cos\omega t$ would have amplitude 10 units and start at $x = -8$.

Exercise 19(c)

1. State the amplitude, period, initial displacement and initial direction of motion (i.e. out or in) for each of the following motions:
   (i) $x = 3\sin 4\pi t$
   (ii) $x = 10\cos 5t$
   (iii) $x = 5\sin [\pi(2t + 1)/6]$
   (iv) $x = 5\sin [\pi(2t - 1)/6]$
   (v) $x = 4\sin t + 3\cos t$
   (vi) $x = 4\sin t - 3\cos t$

2. Write down displacement-time formulae for each of the following simple harmonic motions. (A circular representation may be helpful in parts (iii) and (iv).)
   (i)   amplitude 5, period 2, initial velocity 0
   (ii) starting from maximum displacement and first reaching a maximum speed of 16 units after a time of 1/8 unit
   (iii) oscillating between $x = 2$ and $x = -2$ with frequency 5, moving initially towards O from displacement $+ \sqrt{2}$
   (iv) amplitude 6, starting from displacement $+ 3$ with velocity $+ 9$ (i.e. away from O)

3. Obtain displacement-time formulae in the form $A\sin\omega t + B\cos\omega t$ for each of the following motions:
   (i) amplitude 5, initial displacement $+ 3$, initial velocity $+ 16$
   (ii) period 8, starting with velocity $+ 5\pi/4$ from displacement $- 12$. State also the amplitude of this oscillation and find the position and velocity after 2 s.

19.5 The S.H.M. Differential Equation

The student may easily verify, by differentiation, that the velocity and acceleration results of section 19.2 apply to all the displacement-time forms considered in the previous section. We shall now define simple harmonic motion in terms of the acceleration property.

> ANY LINEAR MOTION IN WHICH THE ACCELERATION IS PROPORTIONAL TO THE DISPLACEMENT FROM A FIXED POINT, BUT IN THE OPPOSITE DIRECTION, IS SAID TO BE SIMPLE HARMONIC.

That is a simple harmonic motion is one governed by the differential equation

$$\frac{d^2 x}{dt^2} = -\omega^2 x$$

The importance of the acceleration being in the opposite direction (signified by the minus sign in the differential equation) cannot be over-stressed. If this were not the case quite a different motion would result, as a moment's thought should suggest.

Solution of the S.H.M. differential equation. We may now obtain the general displacement-time form of section 19.4 by direct solution of the above equation. We shall assume that there is a maximum displacement (or amplitude) a and that the body concerned is at rest when in such a position. The differential equation may be written

$$\frac{dv}{dt} = -\omega^2 x \text{ or } v\frac{dv}{dx} = -\omega^2 x$$

$$\Rightarrow \int_0^v v\,dv = -\omega^2 \int_a^x x\,dx \quad (v = 0 \text{ when } x = a)$$

$$\Rightarrow \tfrac{1}{2}v^2 = -\tfrac{1}{2}\omega^2(x^2 - a^2)$$

$$\Rightarrow v = \frac{dx}{dt} = \omega\sqrt{a^2 - x^2} \quad \text{where } |x| \leqslant |a|$$

We have now established the velocity result of section 19.2 as a consequence of our definition. Separating the variables again we obtain

$$\int \frac{dx}{\sqrt{a^2 - x^2}} = \int \omega\,dt$$

The standard method of solving the integral on the left-hand side is to make the substitution $x = a \sin \theta$. The equation then reduces to

$$\int 1 \cdot d\theta = \int \omega\,dt$$

$$\Rightarrow \theta = \omega t + \varepsilon \quad (\varepsilon \text{ constant})$$

Thus $x = a \sin \theta = a \sin(\omega t + \varepsilon)$

Note: In problems where the S.H.M. differential equation is encountered, it is customary to write down the most appropriate form of the solution directly, rather than to repeat this rather awkward derivation.

Example 117

The displacement x metres of a body at time t s is governed by the differential equation $\ddot{x} = -x/4$. Obtain the displacement-time formula for the motion given that $x = 4$ and $\dot{x} = -1$ when $t = 0$. Find also the speed of the body when $x = 2$.

We recognise the differential equation as being of the form $\ddot{x} = -\omega^2 x$. The motion is therefore simple-harmonic with $\omega = 1/2$. We try a solution of the form $x = A \sin\omega t + B \cos\omega t$, that is

$$x = A \sin \tfrac{1}{2}t + B \cos \tfrac{1}{2}t \tag{1}$$
$$\Rightarrow v = \dot{x} = \tfrac{1}{2}A \cos \tfrac{1}{2}t - \tfrac{1}{2}B \sin \tfrac{1}{2}t \tag{2}$$

From (1) the initial displacement is B and from (2) the initial velocity is $A/2$. Using the initial conditions given in the question, it follows that $B = 4$ and $A = -2$, so that the solution is

$$x = -2 \sin \tfrac{1}{2}t + 4 \cos \tfrac{1}{2}t$$

The amplitude of this oscillation is $\sqrt{A^2 + B^2} = \sqrt{20}$ metres. The speed of the body when $x = 2$ can therefore be found as follows:

$$v = \omega\sqrt{a^2 - x^2} = \tfrac{1}{2}\sqrt{20 - 4}$$
$$\Rightarrow \text{speed} = 2 \text{ m s}^{-1}$$

Exercise 19(d)

1. Write down solutions for each of the following differential equations:
   (i) $\ddot{x} = -16x$ given that $x = 0$ and $\dot{x} = 8$ when $t = 0$
   (ii) $\ddot{x} = -0.01x$ given that $x = 5$ and $\dot{x} = 0$ when $t = 0$.
2. Solve the differential equation $\ddot{x} = -4x$ given that $x = -5$ and $v = +24$ when $t = 0$. State the maximum values of displacement, velocity and acceleration under this motion.
3. The displacement x metres of a body from a fixed point O is related to the time t s by the equation

   $$\frac{d^2x}{dt^2} = -\frac{x}{25}$$

   When $x = 0$ the speed of the body is 0.5 m s^{-1}. Find the greatest displacement of the body from O during the motion and the speed of the body when $x = 2$.
4. The displacement x of a body from a certain point varies in accordance with the equation

   $$\frac{d^2x}{dt^2} = -\frac{\pi^2 x}{9}$$

When $t = 3/2$ the body is instantaneously at rest at $x = 6$. Find the displacement and velocity of the body when $t = 2$.

5. The level of water x metres in a certain harbour is found to vary in approximate accordance with

$$\frac{d^2x}{dt^2} = -\frac{x}{4}$$

where t is the time in hours. If the difference between high and low water is 4 metres, find approximate answers for:

(i)   the time between successive high tides
(ii) the rise in the water level during the first hour after low water
(iii) the rate at which the level is falling two hours after high water.

19.6 Oscillations of a Stretched Spring

In section 14.2 we saw how conservation of energy may be used to determine the levels between which a particle on a stretched spring will oscillate. We shall now prove that such oscillations are simple-harmonic in nature.

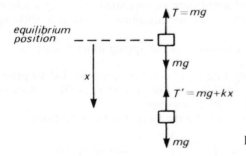

Fig. 5

Consider the particle first at its equilibrium position. Here the tension T in the spring must be equal to the weight mg of the particle. Imagine now that the particle is oscillating on the spring and at a certain instant is at displacement x below the *equilibrium position*, (Fig. 5). The tension is now increased from its previous value (mg) by an amount proportional to x; in fact $T' = mg + kx$ (where k is the spring rate) so that the particle is subject to an overall force of kx upwards. Its acceleration is therefore kx/m in the opposite direction to the displacement, i.e.,

$$\frac{d^2x}{dt^2} = -\frac{k}{m}x$$

This is the simple-harmonic differential equation with $\omega^2 = k/m$. From the properties of S.H.M. the following facts are now established for any oscillation of a particle on a spring:

1. The centre of the oscillation ($x = 0$) is the *equilibrium position*, and this is where the particle will be moving fastest.

2. The particle will oscillate through *equal distances above and below the equilibrium position.*

3. Since $\omega^2 = k/m$ (or λ/ml where λ is the modulus and l the natural length of the spring) the period of oscillation is:

$$\frac{2\pi}{\omega} = 2\pi\sqrt{\frac{m}{k}} \quad \text{or} \quad 2\pi\sqrt{\frac{ml}{\lambda}}$$

(Note that this period will be the same for all oscillations of a given particle on a given spring – irrespective of the amplitude.)

The same results will apply to oscillations on an elastic string, provided the string does not go slack at any stage of the motion.

Example 118

A mass of 50 g hanging freely extends a spring by 2 cm.

(i) Find the period of oscillation and the greatest speed reached by the particle if it is pulled down a further 1 cm and then released.

(ii) Find the period and amplitude of oscillation if the particle is struck vertically downwards from its equilibrium position with speed 10 cm s^{-1}.

(iii) State also the least extension of the spring in each motion.

We first need the spring rate k. This is the force needed to produce unit extension (i.e. 1 metre) – in this case the weight of a 50×50 g or $5/2$ kg body, i.e. $k = 5/2 \times 9.8 = 49/2$ newtons/m.

The period of oscillation will be the same for both motions:

$$\omega = \sqrt{\frac{k}{m}} = \sqrt{\frac{49}{2 \times 0.05}} = \sqrt{490} \text{ or } 7\sqrt{10}$$

$$\Rightarrow \text{period } \frac{2\pi}{\omega} = \frac{2\pi}{7\sqrt{10}} \simeq 0.28 \text{ s}$$

To complete the question:

(i) The amplitude of the oscillation will be 1 cm or 0.01 m. Thus

$$\text{greatest speed } = a\omega = \frac{7\sqrt{10}}{100} \simeq 0.22 \text{ m s}^{-1}$$

(ii) This is really part (i) in reverse, since the mass starts at the centre of the oscillation so that 10 cm s^{-1} must be its greatest speed, that is $a\omega = 0.1$

$$\Rightarrow \text{amplitude } = \frac{1}{70\sqrt{10}} \text{ m or } \frac{\sqrt{10}}{7} (0.45) \text{ cm}$$

(iii) The answers to this part follow, without further calculation, from note 2 above. The least extension will be:

first motion $2 - 1$ $= 1$ cm
second motion $2 - 0.45 = 1.55$ cm

Exercise 19(e)

1. A 400 g mass is suspended from one end of an elastic string. In equilibrium the string is stretched by 8 cm. The mass is lifted vertically until the string is just slack and then released from rest. How far does the mass fall before next coming to rest and how long does this take?

2. A body of mass 1/7 kg is attached to a 75 cm spring of modulus 21 newtons. The body is pulled down until the length of the spring is 90 cm and then released from rest. Find the shortest length of the spring in the subsequent motion, the greatest speed of the body and the period of oscillation.

3. A body of mass 250 g is attached to the end of a 50 cm elastic string of modulus 24.5 newtons. Find the extension of the string when the body hangs in equilibrium. If the body is now given a downward impulse of 0.14 N s, find the greatest and least extension of the string in the subsequent motion and the period of oscillation.

4. In question 3, what is the magnitude of the largest impulse which may be given to the 250 g mass if the string is not to go slack during the subsequent motion? Find in this case the speed and acceleration of the body when it has travelled a distance of 3 cm.

5. (i) Show that the period of vertical oscillation for a body on a spring is

$$2\pi \sqrt{\frac{x}{g}}$$

where x is the extension of the spring when the body hangs in equilibrium.

(ii) A certain mass extends a spring by 2 cm when hanging in equilibrium. How many oscillations will it make per minute if set in motion?

6. A scale pan of mass m extends a spring by a distance d when hanging in equilibrium. Find the amplitude and period of oscillation in each of the following cases

(i) A mass $m/2$ is placed gently in the scale pan as it rests in equilibrium.

(ii) The scale pan and the $m/2$ mass are allowed to take their new position of equilibrium and the $m/2$ mass is then carefully removed.

State in each case the greatest tension in the spring during the motion.

*7. Two springs, whose spring rates are k_1 and k_2 are fastened end to end and stretched between two fixed points on a smooth horizontal table. A small body of mass m is attached to their join.

(i) By considering the overall force on the body when it is displaced by a distance x from its equilibrium position, show that any motion of the body in the line of the springs is simple harmonic and find its period.

(ii) Are the same results true if the springs are stretched between two points in a vertical line?

8. Two springs of equal length l and moduli λ and 2λ respectively are tied end to end and stretched between points a distance $3l$ apart on a smooth

horizontal table. A particle of mass m attached to their join is pulled along the line of the springs until the second spring is just slack and then released from rest. Find the greatest speed reached by the particle in the ensuing motion and the time which elapses before it is next at rest.

9. (i) A small body is placed in a scale pan hanging on a spring and the system is allowed to take up its position of equilibrium, the total stretch in the spring then being a. The scale pan is then pulled downwards through distance d and released from rest. Prove that the body will leave the scale pan if $d > a$ and that, in this case, contact is broken at the instant the spring slackens.

   (ii) Show that if $d = 2a$, the body remains in contact with the pan for time

$$\frac{2\pi}{3}\sqrt{\frac{a}{g}}$$

10. An elastic string is stretched by 5 cm by a certain body hanging in equilibrium. The body is pulled vertically downwards until the total stretch in the spring is 20 cm and then released from rest. Find the time which elapses before the string goes slack and the speed of the body at this instant. Find also the further height to which the body rises.

19.7 The Simple Pendulum

A particle swinging in a plane on a light string is called a **simple pendulum** (see also conical pendulum: section 15.4). The particle itself is often called the bob. Consider an instant in such a swing when the angular displacement of the string from the vertical (its equilibrium position) is θ radians. If θ is

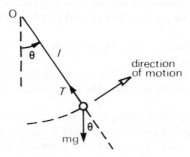

Fig. 6

increasing then the direction of motion of the bob is as shown in Fig. 6 and we have $v = l\omega$ where l is the length of the string and ω its angular velocity, (see section 15.1), i.e.

$$v = l\frac{d\theta}{dt}$$

differentiating $\begin{array}{l}\text{tangential} \\ \text{acceleration}\end{array} = l \cdot \dfrac{d^2\theta}{dt^2}$

The force acting along this line, however, is $mg \sin \theta$ in the opposite direction. Thus from the equation of motion $F = ma$

$$-mg \sin \theta = ml\frac{d^2\theta}{dt^2}$$

$$\Rightarrow \frac{d^2\theta}{dt^2} = \frac{-g}{l}\sin \theta$$

If θ is always small (i.e. providing the angle of swing is less than about $10°$ from the vertical) then $\sin \theta \simeq \theta$ and we may write

$$\frac{d^2\theta}{dt^2} \simeq \frac{-g}{l}.\theta$$

So for small oscillations the angle θ varies in accordance with the S.H.M. differential equation. The motion may therefore be regarded as (approximately) simple harmonic with $\omega^2 = g/l$. The period of each complete swing is

$$\frac{2\pi}{\omega} \text{ or } 2\pi\sqrt{\frac{l}{g}}$$

This is independent of the mass of the bob.

Exercise 19(f)

1. In a simple experiment to determine g, twenty complete swings of a simple pendulum of length 0.5 m are timed and found to take 28.4 seconds. Taking $\pi = 3.142$, what answer should be obtained for g?
2. (i) A 'seconds pendulum' is one which swings from rest to rest (i.e. half a complete oscillation) in 1 second. Taking $g = 9.81 \text{ m s}^{-2}$ and $\pi = 3.142$, calculate the length of such a pendulum.
   (ii) Calculate the percentage error in taking a pendulum of length 1 metre as being a seconds pendulum.
3. A simple pendulum of length l is performing small oscillations of α radians (from the vertical). Show that the average speed of the bob is

$$\frac{2\alpha}{\pi}\sqrt{lg}$$

4. The angle θ radians between the string of a pendulum and the vertical is related to the time t seconds by the equation

$$\frac{d^2\theta}{dt^2} \simeq -64\,\theta$$

Calculate the time of 1 complete swing. If the pendulum is released initially from a position in which the string is inclined at a small angle θ_0 radians to the vertical, write down an expression for θ in terms of t. Hence find the first value of t for which
   (i) $\theta = \theta_0/2$
   (ii) the angular speed $(d\theta/dt)$ of the pendulum reaches half its greatest value.

Answers to Exercises

Accuracy is generally to 3 significant figures. Angles are given to the nearest $1/10°$, except where a lower degree of accuracy is appropriate.

Exercise 1(a)

1. 27 m s^{-1}, 84 m
2. 20 s, 700 m
3. 120 m, $1\frac{2}{3} \text{ m s}^{-2}$
4. 1.5 km, 2100 km h^{-2}, 57 km h^{-1}
5. 0.0025 s
6. (i) 32 m, (ii) $1\frac{1}{3}$ s
7. 3.2 m s^{-2}, $22\frac{1}{2}$ cm
8. $3\frac{1}{3}$ s, 14.4 m s^{-1}
9. 2400 km h^{-2}, $\frac{1}{2}$ min, 80.6 km h^{-1}
10. 3 min, 40 km h^{-1}
11. 1.6 m s^{-2}, 2 m s^{-1}, $2\frac{1}{2}$ s, 5 s
12. retardation 1.2 m s^{-2}, 32.4 km h^{-1} (9 m s^{-1})
13. 72.9 km h^{-1}, $5/21 \text{ m s}^{-2}$

Exercise 1(b)

1. (i) Yes (ii) No (iii) Yes
2. 3.75 s, $-28\frac{1}{8}$ m
3. $1\frac{2}{3}$ s, -14 m s^{-1}
4. 20 s, 60 s
5. (i) -12, -8, $+12$ m (ii) -2, $+6$, $+14 \text{ m s}^{-1}$ (iii) -12.5 m
6. 1/2 s, 7 s, 25 m east
7. -6 m s^{-2}, $+13 \text{ m s}^{-1}$, $4\frac{1}{3}$ s

Exercise 1(c)

1. 4.9 m, 14.7 m, 24.5 m
2. 10.6 m s^{-1}, -9 m s^{-1}, 75.9 m, 77.5 m
3. 20.4 s, 2040 m
4. 30.6 m, 24.5 m s^{-1}
5. 3.64 s, 35.7 m s^{-1}
6. 5.3 m s^{-1}
7. 86.4 m
8. 1/7 s
9. 2 s, 12.8 m s^{-1}

10. 44.1 m
11. 1.2 s, 10.9 m from foot

Exercise 1(d)

2. 1 : 3
4. 1 : 2 : 2
6. B
7. 10 m, 30 m, 50 m, 5 m
8. (i) 5 m s^{-1} (ii) +2.5 m s^{-1}
9. (i) 2$\frac{1}{2}$ mins   (ii) 6$\frac{1}{3}$ km
10. (i) 5.1 ⩽ t ⩽ 15.4   (ii) 2.4, 0.5, −4.4 m s^{-1} (iii) 6.2 m s^{-1}
11. (i) 2.5, 1.0 m s^{-2} (ii) 1310/1320 m
12. (i) 3.25 m s^{-1} (ii) 0.8 m s^{-2} (iii) 2.8 m s^{-1}

Exercise 1(e)

1. 2$\frac{1}{2}$ m s^{-2}, 80 m
2. 120 km h^{-1}
3. 24 km h^{-1}, 2 km
4. 14.1 m s^{-1}
5. 9.1 s, 11 m s^{-1}

Exercise 1(f)

1. 1$\frac{1}{2}$ s, −1$\frac{1}{2}$ m s^{-1}
2. 14$\frac{2}{3}$ m, 14$\frac{2}{3}$ m s^{-1}
3. 38 m s^{-1}, 82$\frac{1}{2}$ m
4. 144 m, 18 m s^{-1}
5. (i) 0, 12 m s^{-2} (ii) 32 m
    (iii) 64 m   (iv) 10$\frac{2}{3}$ m s^{-1}, 0
6. 3 m s^{-1}, 4 m s^{-2}, 2$\frac{1}{2}$ s, 13 m s^{-1}

Exercise 2(b)

1. 2600 N
2. 40 m s^{-2}
3. 4.186 × 10^{-15} N
4. 3.75 m s^{-1}
6. 30 N
7. 150 N
8. 186 N
9. 360 kg
10. 2000 N
11. 0.105 N, 411 m
12. 1250 m, 7200 N
13. 8$\frac{1}{2}$ m
14. 4 s, 2$\frac{1}{2}$ m
15. 1$\frac{1}{2}$ D, 1/5

Exercise 2(c)

1. (i) 29.4 N   (ii) 24 500 N   (iii) 0.588 N
2. (i) 11.4 N   (ii) 9500 N   (iii) 0.228 N
3. 245 N
4. 29 400 N
5. 30 060 N
6. 600 N
8. retardation 1.2 m s^{-2}
9. 0.364 N
10. 5.8 s
11. 8 kg
12.a (i) 12.5 m s^{-1} (ii) 10g   (iii) 7000 N
    b 5700 N (tensions to 2 sig. figs.)

Exercise 2(d)

1. 117.6 N
2. (i) 67.6 N   (ii) 17.6 N   (iii) N = 0, acceleration
                                                    2.7 m s^{-2}
3. 117.6 N, 0
4. (i) 686 N   (ii) 777 N
5. 6170 N
6. 3.2 m s^{-2}
7. 115 N
8. (i) 49, 98 N   (ii) 59, 118 N

Exercise 2(e)

1. g/7 (1.4 m s^{-2}), 16.8 N, 0.707 s
2. g/8, 15.4 N, 3.43 N
3. 3.21 kg, 27 N
4. 2.04 kg
5. 1.56(5) s
6. $35\frac{1}{3}$ kg, 636 N
7. 0.8 m s^{-2}
8. (i) 1.4 m s^{-1} (ii) 2/7 s
9. 4 $Mmg/(M + m)$

Exercise 2(f)

2. (a) 16 kN, 6.4 kN (b) 26 kN, 10.4 kN
3. 7/6 m s^{-2}, 1020 N
4. 135.6 N, 56.5 N
5. 0.267 m s^{-2}, 150 N
6. 3.75 kN

Exercise 3(a)

1. (i) 7 m east   (ii) 13 m N 22.6°W   (iii) 13 m N 67.6°W
2. 10 km S 60°W

3. (i) 20 newtons N 53.1°E   (ii) 20 newtons S 53.1°W
4. 12.37 m s^{-1}, N 14°W
5. 85.9 newtons S 15.5°E, 1.70 m s^{-2}
6. (i) 4.47 km h^{-1} N 26.6°E   (ii) N 30°W   (iii) part (i)

Exercise 3(b)

1. 5.22 knots S 73.2° W
2. 4.20 knots N 65.9 E
3. 4.2°, 668 km h^{-1}
4. 3.1 knots, N 73.9° E
5. $2dv/(v^2 - u^2)$
6. (i) N 72.5° W   (ii) N 36.71° E
7. N 48.5° W, 36 min
8. N 61.1° W, 37 min
9. $d(t_1 + t_2)/2t_1t_2$
10. (i) 1.09 p.m.   (ii) 1.15 n.m
11. (i) 35.3 km h^{-1} (ii) N 66° E

Exercise 3(c)

1. 11.4 newtons N 37.6° E
2. 3.32 m s^{-2} S 45.7° E
3. N 36.4° W
4. 7.79 N
5. 3.08 m s^{-2} S 11.2° E

Exercise 3(d)

2. 10.4 N south
3. 22°, 5.29 N
4. 25g (245) N
5. 2.53 N
6. 512 N, 689 N
7. AL tension 5g/4 N BL thrust 3g/4 N
8. 1.6 N, 1.0 N
9. AB thrust 150g N, BC tension 120g N
10. 6.70 N, perpendicular to string
11. (i) 1470 N, 761 N   (ii) 1470 N, 1470 N, Yes
12. 28 N

Exercise 3(e)

1. 9 north, 2 west, 5 N 53.1° E, 5 S 53.1° E, 3.61 N 33.7° W, 17 N 28.1° E
2. 2 S 60° W, 8 south, 5.29 N 79.1° W, 8.72 N 36.6° E, 4.36 N 36.6° E, 12 N 60° W
6. (i) $2\sqrt{2}, 2\sqrt{2}$ (ii) $4\sqrt{2}, 4$ (iii) 2.31, 2.31
7. (i) $3\sqrt{3}, 3$ (ii) 5.80, 1.55   (iii) 6, 6
9. 1.94 m s^{-1}

Exercise 4(a)

1. (i) 6.78, 4.24   (ii) 20.8, 118   (iii) -2.27, 4.46
2. (i) 4.83   (ii) 27.0
3. 13.6 m s^{-2}
4. 1.92 N, 1.23 N
5. 715 N, 16.2 N
6. 2.93 N

Exercise 4(b)

1. (i) 28.4, 7.61 N   (ii) acceleration 0.87 m s^{-2}
2. $\sqrt{2d/g\sin\theta}$
3. 25°, 16.6 N
4. (i) 294 N   (ii) 294 N   (iii) 324 N
5. 1630 N
6. 108 N

Exercise 4(c)

1. (i) 8.30 Newtons N 32.9° W   (ii) 6.43 Newtons N 40.7 E
2. 3.82 Newtons S 21.8° W   (ii) 1.39 Newtons S 31° W
3. 3.86 newtons NE
4. (i) 6.02 N   (ii) -4.99 N
5. 0.51 m s^{-2}
6. (i) 2.83 m s^{-2}, 42.5 N   (ii) 0.46 m s^{-2}, 47.3 N
   (iii) 0.29(5) m s^{-2}, 40.9 N   (iv) 0.29(5) m s^{-2}, 53.8 N
7. (i) 200, 2600 N   (ii) 334 N
8. 1.14 m s^{-2}
9. 93.3 kN, 721 kN
10. -49.8 kN (stalls)
11. 306 N
12. (i) 16.2 N   (ii) 32.7 N
13. 17.6 N
14. 2.65 kg

Exercise 4(d)

1. (i) 34.3 N   (ii) 44.8 N   (iii) 23.8 N
2. (i) 9.8 N   (ii) 24.5 N   (iii) 41.7 N
3. 0.45
4. 13.25 m, 4.77 m
5. 0.38, 2/3 m
6. 0.042
8. 3.14 m s^{-2}
9. 0.184
10. 1.47 m s^{-2}, 0.66 m
11. 10 cm
12. 4.9 m s^{-2}, 1/7 s, 5 cm

13. 0.51
14. 2.94 m s^{-2}, 2.01 m

Exercise 4(e)

1. 2.07 m s^{-2}
2. (i) 170 N   (ii) 231 N
3. 0.455 m s^{-2}
4. 22.51 N
6. (i) 49 N   (ii) 533 N
7. (ii) 18.4°   (iii) 0.404, 1.47 m s^{-2}
9. 2 $Mg\sin\theta$

Exercise 5(a)

1. 2 **AD**   (ii) 2 **SQ**
5. (i) P, T coincident   (ii) Q, R coincident
7. (i) **AC**   (ii) $1\frac{1}{2}$ **AC**   (iii) $2\frac{1}{2}$ **AB**
8. (i) 3 **AY**   (ii) 2 **BY**   (iii) **AY**

Exercise 5(b)

1. (i) $2\mathbf{j}$, $-3\mathbf{i}$, $\mathbf{i} + 2\mathbf{j}$, $3\mathbf{i} - \mathbf{j}$, $-2\mathbf{i} + 2\mathbf{j}$, $-\mathbf{i} - \mathbf{j}$
   (ii) 2, 3, $\sqrt{5}$, $\sqrt{10}$, $2\sqrt{2}$, $\sqrt{2}$
2. $5\mathbf{i} + 12\mathbf{j}$ metres, 13 metres
3. (i) $\mathbf{F}_2$ (ii) $\sqrt{17}$ newtons S 76° E
4. (i) 5   (ii) $\sqrt{29}$ (iii) 13
5. (i) 4   (ii) -9
6. N 18.4°W at 9.49 knots, $2\mathbf{i} + 9\mathbf{j}$ N 12.5° E, 30.9°
7. $-\mathbf{i} + 4\mathbf{j}$ newtons
8. 5, 25, 41
   Unit vectors $\frac{1}{5}(3\mathbf{i} - 4\mathbf{j})$, $\frac{1}{25}(7\mathbf{i} + 24\mathbf{j})$, $-\frac{1}{41}(9\mathbf{i} + 40\mathbf{j})$
9. (i) $a = 1$ $b = 2$
   (ii) $3(\mathbf{i} + \mathbf{j}) - 1(\mathbf{i} - \mathbf{j})$, $-1(\mathbf{i} + \mathbf{j}) - (\mathbf{i} - \mathbf{j})$, $2(\mathbf{i} - \mathbf{j})$
10. $240\mathbf{i} - 320\mathbf{j}$ km h^{-1}, $(60, -80)$, 44.7 km h^{-1} N 26.6° E

Exercise 5(c)

1. $-5\mathbf{i} + 2\mathbf{j}$, $\mathbf{i} - \mathbf{j}$, $3\mathbf{i} + 9\mathbf{j}$, $\mathbf{i} - 10\mathbf{j}$
2. (i) $\mathbf{i} - 3\mathbf{j}$, $-5\mathbf{i} + 4\mathbf{j}$ (ii) $-\mathbf{i} - 6\mathbf{j}$, $-7\mathbf{i} + \mathbf{j}$
4. 3 : 2
5. (12, 16)
6. $\mathbf{a} + \mathbf{c} - \mathbf{b}$
7. (i) $20\mathbf{i} + \mathbf{j}$ n.m   (ii) $18\mathbf{i} - \mathbf{j}$ n.m, $2\sqrt{2}$ n.m
8. $\mathbf{r}$, $\mathbf{r} + \mathbf{s}$, $2\mathbf{s}$, $2\mathbf{s} - \mathbf{r}$, $\mathbf{s} - \mathbf{r}$
9. $3\mathbf{i} - 1\frac{1}{2}\mathbf{j}$, $4\frac{1}{2}\mathbf{i} + 2\mathbf{j}$
10. (i) $3\frac{1}{2}\mathbf{j}$ (ii) $2.8\mathbf{i} + 4.2\mathbf{j}$ (iii) $\mathbf{i} + 3\frac{3}{4}\mathbf{j}$
12. (i) $\frac{1}{2}(\mathbf{b} + \mathbf{c})$, $\frac{1}{2}(\mathbf{a} + \mathbf{c})$ (ii) $\frac{1}{3}(\mathbf{a} + \mathbf{b} + \mathbf{c})$ (iii) $\frac{1}{3}(\mathbf{a} + \mathbf{b} + \mathbf{c})$

13. $\frac{2}{3}\mathbf{i} + \frac{2}{3}\mathbf{j}$

14. (i) $\frac{1}{2}(\mathbf{c} - \mathbf{a})$ (ii) $\frac{1}{2}(\mathbf{c} - \mathbf{a})$

Exercise 5(d)

1. (i) $5\mathbf{i} + 3\mathbf{j}$ (ii) $7\mathbf{i} - 2\mathbf{j}$ (iii) $(3 + 2t)\mathbf{i} + (8 - 5t)\mathbf{j}$, 11.4 m

2. (i) $-\mathbf{i} + 5\mathbf{j}$ (ii) $7\mathbf{i} + 9\mathbf{j}$ (iii) $(4t - 3)\mathbf{i} + (2t + 4)\mathbf{j}$, 3/4 s, 13 m

3. 4 p.m., $\frac{3}{5}(7\mathbf{i} + 24\mathbf{j})$ knots
4. 0.4 s, 4 s
5. 4.18 p.m., 0.707 n.m
6. $33\mathbf{i} + 20\mathbf{j}$

Exercise 5(e)

1. $\frac{1}{4}\mathbf{i} - \frac{3}{4}\mathbf{j}$ m s^{-2}, $3\frac{1}{2}\mathbf{i} - \frac{1}{2}\mathbf{j}$ m s^{-1}, $4\frac{1}{2}\mathbf{i} - 3\frac{1}{2}\mathbf{j}$ m s^{-1}
2. $7\mathbf{i} + 5\mathbf{j}$ m s^{-1}, $11\mathbf{i} - 3\mathbf{j}$ m s^{-1}, $(3 + 4t)\mathbf{i} + (7 - 2t)\mathbf{j}$ m s^{-1}
   (i) $3\frac{1}{2}$ s, (ii) 2/3 s
3. 0.49 m s^{-2}, N 76.4° E
4. 7.68 m s^{-2}

Exercise 5(f)

1. $\mathbf{r} = (6t - t^2)\mathbf{i} + 2t\,\mathbf{j}$
2. $\mathbf{r} = 10t\,\mathbf{i} + (21t - 4.9t^2)\mathbf{j}$, 43 m, 8°, $-40°$
3. $4\frac{2}{3}$ s
4. $14\mathbf{i} - 2\mathbf{j}$, $32\mathbf{i} - 16\mathbf{j}$
5. $-0.88\mathbf{i} + 1.36\mathbf{j}$ newtons, $110\mathbf{i} - 170\mathbf{j}$ m
6. $7\mathbf{i} - \mathbf{j}$ m, 6.32 m s^{-1}
7. $3\mathbf{i} - 9\mathbf{j}$ newtons, $6\mathbf{i} - 11\mathbf{j}$ m s^{-1}
8. $4\mathbf{i} + 10\mathbf{j}$ m, $-\mathbf{i} - 2\mathbf{j}$ m s^{-1}, $\mathbf{F}_2 = 1.25\mathbf{i} + 2.5\mathbf{j}$ newtons, $2\mathbf{i} + 6\mathbf{j}$ m

Exercise 5(g)

1. $-4\mathbf{i}$, $8\mathbf{i} - 4\mathbf{j}$, $20\mathbf{i} - 8\mathbf{j}$ m s^{-1}, $2\sqrt{10}$ m s^{-2}
2. (i) $9\mathbf{i} + 6\mathbf{j}$, 36 (ii) $-3\mathbf{i} + 6\mathbf{j}$
3. $\frac{2}{3}\mathbf{i} - \frac{1}{3}\mathbf{j}$, $\frac{4}{9}\mathbf{i} + \frac{4}{9}\mathbf{j}$
4. 13, $(5\mathbf{i} + 12\mathbf{j})/13$, 8.54
5. $2\mathbf{i} - 3.3\mathbf{j}$, $2\mathbf{i} - 1.65\mathbf{j}$, $2\mathbf{i} + 1.65\mathbf{j}$, $2\mathbf{i} + 3.3\mathbf{j}$ newtons
7. $67\mathbf{i} + 63\mathbf{j}$, 126.5 units
8. $\mathbf{r} = 2t.\mathbf{i} + t^3\mathbf{j}$
9. $\mathbf{r} = (t - 2)^2\mathbf{i} + (t - 4 + 4/t)\mathbf{j}$
10. $54\mathbf{i} - 28\mathbf{j}$ m s^{-1}, $72\mathbf{i} - 66\mathbf{j}$ m

Exercise 6(b)

1. $_X\mathbf{v}_Y = -_Y\mathbf{v}_X$
2. $_C\mathbf{v}_B = -4\mathbf{i} + 4\mathbf{j}$

4. (i) $\mathbf{i} + 2\mathbf{j}$ (ii) $-\mathbf{i} - 2\mathbf{j}$ (iii) $5\mathbf{i} - 2\mathbf{j}$ (iv) $-6\mathbf{i}$
5. (i) $4\mathbf{i} + 2\mathbf{j}$ (ii) $5\mathbf{i} + 4\mathbf{j}$ (iii) $(3 + t)\mathbf{i} + 2t\,\mathbf{j}$, 1.8 s
6. $-2\mathbf{i} + 6\mathbf{j}$, $3\mathbf{i} - 2\mathbf{j}$, $-12\mathbf{i} + 5\mathbf{j}$
7. (i) $-2\mathbf{i} - \mathbf{j}$ (ii) $8\mathbf{i} + 4\mathbf{j}$, $6\mathbf{i} + 3\mathbf{j}$ (iii) $45\mathbf{i} - 10\mathbf{j}$
8. (i) $3\mathbf{j}$ m, $-\mathbf{i} + \mathbf{j}$ m s^{-1} (ii) $2\mathbf{i} + 5\mathbf{j}$ m, $3\mathbf{i} + \mathbf{j}$ m s^{-1}
   (iii) $\mathbf{r} = (t^2 - t)\mathbf{i} + (t + 3)\mathbf{j}$ $\mathbf{v} = (2t - 1)\mathbf{i} + \mathbf{j}$
9. $\mathbf{v} = (5 - 3t^2)\mathbf{i} + (3 - 2t)\mathbf{j}$, $9\mathbf{i} - \mathbf{j}$

Exercise 6(c)

1. 9.17 m s^{-1} N 71° W
2. (i) 25 km h^{-1} east   (ii) 5 km h^{-1} east
   (iii) 15 km h^{-1} east   (iv) 23.2 km h^{-1} S 72° E
3. 9.65 knots N 28° W
4. 642 km h^{-1} S 19.6° W
5. N $67\frac{1}{2}$ W, 0.765 U
6. N 16° E or S 16° E
7. 6 km h^{-1}
8. 13.2 m s^{-1} N 49° E
9. 40 km h^{-1}, No

Exercise 6(d)

1. 0.75 n.m, $15\frac{1}{2}$ min
2. (i) 25 m, (ii) 15.7 m
3. 2.47 km, 60 s
4. 5.7 m
5. 4 n.m, $12.26\frac{1}{2}$ p.m.
6. 17.2 knots, N 43.4° W
7. $10t^2 - 78t + 153$, 0.95, $t = 3.9$
8. 0.89, $25.6\mathbf{i} - 9.3\mathbf{j}$ and $24.8\mathbf{i} - 8.9\mathbf{j}$

Exercise 6(e)

1. (i) S 38.7° W, 13.4 s   (ii) 2.5 m s^{-1}, west
2. 40 s, N 73.4° W
3. (i) 11.5 knots   (ii) S 68° E, S 12° E, 38 min
4. 21.3 knots
5. 1.42 n.m, S 48.2° E
6. (i) Yes (ii) No (iii) No

Exercise 7(a)

1. (i) 3, 13   (ii) $4\frac{1}{2}$, $12\frac{1}{2}$
2. 235 N, 353 N
3. 220.5 N 367.5 N, 661.5 N 318.5 N
4. $16\frac{2}{3}$ cms from A
5. $2\frac{1}{4}$ m past edge of ship
6. 29.4 N, 117.6 N, 1010 N, 1690 N

7. 350 N, 3 : 4
8. (i) 255 N, 137 N   (ii) $1\frac{3}{4}$ m   (iii) $4\frac{1}{4}$ m
9. (ii) $\sqrt{M_1 M_2}$
10. (i) 22 N   (ii) 26, 18 N   (iii) 22 N, No, Yes
11. 0.51 cm

Exercise 7(b)

1. (i)   10 N m anti-clockwise   (ii) 13 N m clockwise
   (iii) 13 N m anti-clockwise   (iv) 25 N m anti-clockwise
2. 4.9 N
3. 5W/3
4. (i) 69.1 N (ii) 240 N
5. $\frac{1}{2}$ W cosec θ
6. $\frac{1}{2}$ W cos θ perp. to AC
7. (i) 3.4 N (ii) 6.7 N
8. 3930 N, 3400 N
9. (i) 122.5 N (ii) 81.7 N

Exercise 7(c)

1. 10 N north 2 m from A
2. 4 N north 5.625 m from A
3. 17.8 N, N 51.7° E, 0.90 m from A
4. 3200 N, 69.9° to AB, $5\frac{2}{3}$ m from A
5. 1860 N, 53.8° to AB, $1\frac{1}{3}$ m from A
6. 7.62 N at 66.8° with AB, 40 cm from A
7. 11.2 N at 63.4° with AB, 30 cm from A
8. 14.4 N at 33.7° with BA, 110 cm from A
9. 6.40 N at 38.7° with AB, 75 cm from A
10. 11 N BC, 8 N BA, 5 N CA
11. 663 N, 55 cm from left-hand side
12. Distance $3a$ from B
13. $\mathbf{i} - \mathbf{j}$ N, $\mathbf{r} = 2a\,\mathbf{i}$

Exercise 7(d)

1. No   (ii) No   (iii) Yes, 14 units clockwise
2. (i) couple $2a$ anti-clockwise
                   (ii) resultant $4\mathbf{i} - 3\mathbf{j}$ (iii) couple $5a$ clockwise
4. (i) couple 2.ABCD   (ii) not couple   (iii) couple 1.ABCD
6. 25 N
7. (i) 2.94 N m   (ii) 2.94 N m   (iii) No
8. (i)   force 10 N north, couple 5 N m clockwise
   (ii)   7.62 N at 66.8° with AB, couple 0.9 N m sense ABCD
   (iii) 11.2 N at 63.4° with AB, couple 0.5 N m sense ABCD
   (iv) force $\mathbf{i} - \mathbf{j}$ N, couple a N m sense OABC

Exercise 8(a)

1. $\frac{1}{2}\mathbf{i} + 2\mathbf{j}$
2. (i) $1\frac{2}{3}\mathbf{i} + 3\mathbf{j}$ (ii) $-\frac{1}{2}\mathbf{i} + 3\mathbf{j}$
3. (i) $\bar{x} = 3\frac{1}{2}$ (ii) 9 units
4. (i) $-3\mathbf{i} + 1\frac{1}{2}\mathbf{j}$ (ii) 2 units, $y = 2$
5. $(m\mathbf{x} + n\mathbf{y})/(m + n)$
7. (i) $(\mathbf{b} + \mathbf{c})/2$ (ii) $(\mathbf{a} + \mathbf{b} + \mathbf{c})/3$
8. $\bar{x} = 2$

Exercise 8(b)

1. $(7\frac{1}{2}, 5)$ referred to right angled corner
2. $(30, 17)$
3. (i) $(2\frac{5}{6}, 3\frac{5}{6})$ (ii) $(3\frac{1}{36}, 4\frac{1}{36})$ referred to bottom left corner
4. (ii) $(4\frac{11}{12}, 3\frac{11}{12})$ referred to bottom left corner
5. 4.15 cm
6. $(\frac{5}{12}a, \frac{5}{12}b), (\frac{3}{8}a, \frac{3}{8}b)$
7. 91 cm
8. $1\frac{1}{8}$ cm from centre of larger circle
9. (i) 2/3 cm (ii) 5/7 cm (iii) 0
10. $R(\sqrt{5} - 1)/2$

Exercise 8(c)

1. $8\frac{6}{7}$ cm
2. $4\frac{1}{6}$ cm
3. $7d/15$
4. $9\frac{2}{3}$ cm
5. on AC 7.84 cm from A
6. 2.63 cm
7. 2.17 cm
8. 41.54 cm
9. $11d/28$
10. (i) $4r/3(4 + \pi)$ (ii) $\sqrt{2}\,r$
11. 15.3 cm
12. $(10 - 3\pi)\, a/3(4 - \pi)$

Exercise 8(d)

1. $19.2(5)°$
2. $20.5°, 3W/16$
3. (i) $33.7°$
4. (i) $26.6°$ (ii) $45°$
6. $W/40$ perp. to CD
7. $8\sqrt{2}\,r$
8. $46.3°$
9. 3 cm
11. (i) $W/9$ (ii) $a(\sqrt{3} - 1)/2$
12. $126/(16 + \pi), \pi/(16 + \pi)$, arctan $8/63\ (7.2°)$

Exercise 9(a)

1. $5W/6$, $2W/3$, $W/2$
2. $W/2$, $W/4$
3. $20g\sqrt{3}$ N, $10\sqrt{3}/38(0.46)$
5. $W\sqrt{5/3}$, arctan $1/2$ with vertical
6. $72g\sqrt{3}$ N, $6\sqrt{3}/17$ (0.61)
7. 8.52 tonnes, $12.5g$ kN at $16.2°$ with horizontal
8. arccos $(27\pi/260)$ $(71°)$
9. $W - P\cot\beta$

Exercise 9(b)

1. 11.2 N, 16.1 N
2. $6\frac{1}{4}$ N, $1\frac{3}{4}$ N
5. vertical, $3W\tan\theta/8$
6. $10°$
7. $W\cot 2\theta$, horizontal
8. $18.8°$
10. (i) 40 cm　(ii) 50 cm　(iii) $26.6°$　(iv) 2.74 N
11. $W\tan\theta$

Exercise 9(c)

1. $1/3$
2. arctan $a/(h + a\mu)$
3. $30°$, 13.1 N
4. $3W/16$, $3/16$
5. m, $1/\sqrt{3}$ (0.577)
7. $(a + b)/(a\cot\theta - h)$
8. $3/5$, $5W/3$

Exercise 9(d)

1. 134 N
2. (i) 11.74 N　　　　　　　　　　(ii) 2.32 N
3. 0.315
4. $\frac{1}{10}W\sqrt{2}$, $\frac{1}{2}W\sqrt{2}$

Exercise 10(a)

1. 51 m
2. 63 m, 3.1(5) s
3. (i) 11 m　　　　　　　　　　(ii) $27°$ below horizontal
4. 300 m, 900 m, 170 m s^{-1}
5. (ii) $2\frac{1}{2}$ s

Exercise 10(b)

1. 2.45 s, 490 m
2. 30.6 m, 28.7 m s^{-1}

3. 790 m
4. 27 m s^{-1}, about 14°
5. 14, 4.5 m
6. $x = 14t$, $y = -4.9t^2$, $y = -x^2/40$
7. (i) $h/4$ (ii) $d/\sqrt{2}$
8. 0.8 m, 0.35 m

Exercise 10(c)

1. 9 s, 101 m, 540 m
2. 40 m, 49.7 m, + 37 (above horizontal)
3. 4.8 s, 140 m, 26 m, $30\mathbf{i} + 8\mathbf{j}$ m s^{-1}
4. 8.3 m, $-7°$ (below horizontal)
5. 2020 m
6. 748 m, $-39°$
7. 21 m s^{-1}, 19.6 m
8. (i) 12.1 m s^{-1}, +60   (ii) 7.5 m s^{-1}, $-37°$
10. 1.75 m, 1.83 m, 1.22 m
12. 4 s, 87 m
13. $59\frac{1}{2}°$, 5.2 m
14. 15 m s^{-1}, $+37°$, 8.7(5) m
15. 16 m, 5 m, 13.5 m s^{-1}
16. $y = \frac{3}{4}x - x^2/320$, (224, 11.2), 5.6 s
17. 18.2 m s^{-1}, $+9°$

Exercise 10(d)

1. 2250 m
2. 140 m s^{-1}
3. 27° or 63°, 4940 m
4. 35 – 55°
5. 53.1°
6. 19.6 m s^{-1}
7. arccos (1/3) (70.5°)
9. arccos (2/3) (48.2°)

Exercise 10(e)

1. (i) $y = x - x^2/20$, $y = 2x - x^2/8$
      $y = 3x - x^2/4$, $y = 7x - 5x^2/4$
2. (i) 45° or arctan (5/3)   (ii) arctan (1/3) or arctan (17/9)
3. 18.2 m s^{-1}
4. 45°
5. 1000 m, arctan (3)
6. arctan (1/3) or arctan (11/3)
7. $(u^4 - g^2d^2)/2gu^2$, arctan (u^2/gd)

Exercise 11(a)

1. (i) 450 N s   (ii) 1.5 N s   (iii) 3 N s   (iv) 15 000 N s
2. Part (i)
3. $7\frac{1}{2}$ m s^{-1}, 2.4 N, 0.306
4. $84\mathbf{i} - 120\mathbf{j}$ N s, $7\frac{1}{2}\mathbf{i} - 13\mathbf{j}$ m s^{-1}, $13\frac{1}{2}\mathbf{i} - 33\mathbf{j}$ m
5. $-7.2\mathbf{i} + 2.4\mathbf{j}$ N s, 152 N
6. 4000 N, 4 s
7. $20\mathbf{i} + 10\mathbf{j}$ N, $-30\mathbf{i} - 40\mathbf{j}$ N, $17\frac{1}{2}\mathbf{i} + 40\mathbf{j}$ m
8. $36\mathbf{i} - 15\mathbf{j}$ N s, $6\frac{1}{2}$ m s^{-1}
9. 3.36 N s
11. 2550 N s, 30 N
12. 900 N, 31 500 N s
13. $mu\sin\theta$, $\theta°$ S of E, $u\cos\theta$
14. 4.8 kg, 57.6 N s, 57.6 N
15. 8.4 N s, 8.4 N

Exercise 11(b)

1. (i) 4 m s^{-1} (ii) 5.2 m s^{-1}
2. 0.6 m s^{-1}, No
3. $\mathbf{i} + \mathbf{j}$ m s^{-1}, 45°
4. 1.5 m s^{-1}
5. 6.79 m s^{-1} SE
6. $2\frac{1}{2}$ kg
7. 1/3 m s^{-1}
8. 0.3 m s^{-1} (changes direction), 1.65 N s
9. 0, $7\frac{1}{2}$ m s^{-1}, 1500 N
10. 3500 N
11. 28 km h^{-1}, 2500 N s
12. (i) 9.6 N s   (ii) 48 N
13. (ii) $m_2v/(m_1 + m_2)$ $m_1m_2v/(m_1 + m_2)$
14. 7 m s^{-1}
15. 5 m s^{-1}, $\frac{1}{2}\sqrt{17}$ m s^{-1}, $-12\mathbf{i} + 6\mathbf{j}$ N s

Exercise 11(c)

1. (i) 2400 J   (ii) 0.13 J   (iii) 625 000 J   (iv) 3.7 J
2. 180 J, 7.75 m s^{-1}
                    (i) 2.12 m s^{-1} (ii) 2.92 m s^{-1}
4. 1250 N, 56 m
5. $6\frac{1}{4}$ kg
6. $41\frac{2}{3}$ kN
7. μmgd, $3v^2/8\mu g$
8. 3.01 m s^{-1}
9. $26\frac{2}{3}$ N
10. 350 N, 32 m
11. 20 N, 900 J
12. 120 N

Exercise 11(d)

1. 3920 J
2. 1.2×10^{13} J
3. (i) 8 J   (ii) 6.04 J
4. (ii) 49 J
5. 25.5 g, 60 m
6. $\sqrt{2W/m}$, $\sqrt{2mW}$
7. 47.0 J
8. (ii) 2.65 J
9. (ii) 11.0 m s^{-1}
10. 5750 J
11. 1.4 m s^{-1}
12. 5 cm, 0.098 J, 0.049 J

Exercise 11(e)

1. 3.96 m s^{-1}
2. 5.20 m s^{-1}
3. 2.19 m s^{-1}
4. 26.3 m s^{-1}
5. (i) 7.14 m s^{-1} (ii) 5.83 m s^{-1}
6. 72.2 m
7. 70.5°
8. 1.18 m s^{-1}
9. 20 m, 2.70 m s^{-1}
10. 680 N, 217 m, 8.11 m
11. 9/20

Exercise 11(f)

1. 3750 J
2. $\mathbf{i}$ m s^{-1}, 36 J
3. $4\mathbf{i} - 2\mathbf{j}$ m s^{-1}
4. 204 J, 4 J
5. -1 m s^{-1}, 6 m s^{-1}
6. $6\sqrt{2}$ m s^{-1}, 107.7 kN
7. 57.3°
8. $M^2V^2/2d(m + M)$
9. (i) $mV/2M + m)$ (ii) $3mv^2/2g(2M + m)$
10. $ME/(M + m)$

Exercise 12(a)

1. 700 W
2. 22 kW
3. 549 W
4. 1190 kg
5. 122.5 kW
6. 13.2 m s^{-1}

7. (i) 7.2 kg, 518 W   (ii) 3.71 m
8. 90 500 J, 22.6 kW
9. (ii) 30.4(5) m s⁻¹, 94.6 m

Exercise 12(b)

1. 0.1 kW
2. 1440 N
3. 7.68 kW, 15 kW
4. 8.23 kW
5. 34.05 kW
7. 16 kN, 75 kW
8. $a = 200$, $b = 1/2$, 14 kW
9. 80 kg, 12 N, 480 W
10. $4v/3$
11. 7 P

Exercise 12(c)

1. (i) 0.7 m s⁻²   (ii) 0.21 m s⁻²
2. (i) 0.77 m s⁻²   (ii) 0.21 m s⁻²
3. 0.021 m s⁻², 8
4. 1800 N, 0.35 m s⁻²
5. $2g\sin\theta$
6. $a = 155$ $b = 1/20$
7. 30 m s⁻¹, 0.276 m s⁻²

Exercise 13(a)

1. (i) 1/6   (ii) 2/3   (iii) 1/2
2. 5/6
3. 2/7
4. (i) 1/2   (ii) 3/13   (iii) 3/26   (iv) 5/13
5. 1/12
6. (i) 1/17   (ii) 4/17
7. (i) 5/36   (ii) 5/18   (iii) 1/6   (iv) 25/36   (v) 11/36
8. (i) 3/8   (ii) 1/2   (iii) 1/4
9. 28   (i) 1/4   (ii) 1/4   (iii) 3/28
10. 1/15
11. (i) 1/5   (ii) 2/5
12. 1/3

Exercise 13(b)

1. (i) 1/5   (ii) 3/5
2. 5/14
3. (i) 1/3   (ii) 8/15
4. (i) 11/68   (ii) 1/12
5. (i) 1/2   (ii) 5/6

6. (i) 1/33   (ii) 7/99   (iii) 5/33
7. (i) $^{48}C_9/^{52}C_{13}$ (.0026)   (ii) $4 \times {}^{48}C_{10}/^{52}C_{13}$ (.041)
   (iii) $^{26}C_{13}/^{52}C_{13}$ (.000 016)   (iv) $^{36}C_{13}/^{52}C_{13}$ (.0036)
8. 127/429 (0.296), No

Exercise 13(c)

1. 2/3, 1/3, 2/3, 1/6, 1/3, 5/6, 0, 1/6
2. 1/4, 3/4, 10/13, 3/52, 3/52, 1/2, 11/26, 3/13, 11/13, 1/2
3. (i) 0.5, 0.5, 0.2, 0.9   (ii) 3/4, 1/3
4. (i) No   (ii) 13/20, 7/20
6. 1/2, 1/7, 1/14, 4/7, 13/14
7. 1/2, 5/22, 17/22, 3/11
8. 1/33, 92/99, 1, 89/99

Exercise 13(d)

1. (i) 1/169, 24/169   (ii) 1/221, 32/221
2. (i) 2/5   (ii) 1/15   (iii) 8/15
3. 1/7
4. 8/221
5. (i) 11/36   (ii) 91/216   (iii) 9
6. (i) 1/48   (ii) 3/32   (iii) 11/32   (iv) 29/64
7. (i) 4/27   (ii) 17/27   (iii) 5/27   (iv) 22/27
8. (i) 55/96   (ii) 41/96
9. (i) 3/5   (ii) 3/10, 1/2
10. (i) 0.125   (ii) 0.225   (iii) 0.343   (iv) 0.488
11. 11
12. 3/8

Exercise 13(e)

1. (625, 500, 150, 20, 1)/1296
2. 297/625
3. (i) 5/32   (ii) 5/8
4. 53/512
5. 0.275
6. 37/256 (0.145)
7. (i) 0.04 (.0394)   (ii) 0.0006 (.03940 − .038 81)
8. (i) 192/729 (0.263)   (ii) 473/729 (0.649)

Exercise 13(f)

1. 1/11   (ii) 2/11
2. (i) 3/7   (ii) 6/7
3. (i) 1/2   (ii) 3/7
4. (i) 2/15   (ii) 2/15
5. 2/5, 3/10, 1/5, 1/2, 2/3
7. (i) 0.65   (ii) No   (iii) 1/6, 13/18

8. (ii) 8/27, 125/216, 7/16, 64/189
9. (i) 1/8   (ii) 1/2   (iii) 7/8, 1/2

Exercise 14(a)

1. (i) 68 cm   (ii) 51.2 cm
2. 55 cm, 70 N
3. (i) 8 cm   (ii) 16 cm   (iii) 24 cm   (iv) 16 cm   (v) 32 cm
4. 6 cm
5. 6 cm
6. 3.06 kg
7. $m_1 + m_2$, $m_1 m_2/(m_1 + m_2)$
8. 28 cm   (i) 120 N   (ii) 90 N
9. 42.8 cm
10. $3a/2$ and $2a$

Exercise 14(b)

1. (i) 1.75 J   (ii) 1.68 J   (iii) 2.24 J
2. 0.15 J, 3 m s^{-1}
3. (i) 75l (ii) 150l
4. 0.18g, 0.50g, work done $= 0.08g$
5. 32.7 cm, 0.96 m s^{-1}
6. (i) 14 000 N   (ii) 11 500 N
7. $2a$, $3\sqrt{ag}/2$

Exercise 14(c)

1. (i) 24 N, 0.72 J   (ii) 16 N, 0.32 J
2. 8 N   (i) 0.25 m   (ii) 0.25 J
3. 49 N   (i) 6 cm   (ii) 35 cm, 19.6 and 0 N
4. Upper half stretched by (i) $12\frac{1}{2}$ cm (ii) $17\frac{1}{2}$cm
5. (i) $4\sqrt{5}$ m s^{-1} (ii) 200 m s^{-2}
6. 32.5 N
7. 0.3, 46 cm
8. (i) 1/2 m   (ii) 1/3 m

Exercise 14(d)

1. (i) $(-)0.42$, 2.28 m s^{-1} (ii) 2/3
2. 4i and 6i m s^{-1}, 0.6 J
3. -6i and 10i m s^{-1}, 0.9 N s
4. 3/4, $3mu^2/8$
5. 0.6
6. $(2 - k)/3k$
7. (i) 1   (ii) 3, 2/3
8. (ii) $(3u/7)$i to $(6u/7)$i   (iii) $6mu^2/7$
9. $m_1 m_2 u^2/2(m_1 + m_2)$

10. $(1 - e)u/2$, $(1 - e^2)u/4$, $(1 + e)^2u/4$
11. $(2 - 3e)u/5$, $2(1 + e)(2 - 3e)u/25$, $4(1 + e)^2u/25$
13. $1 + e : 7 - e$

Exercise 14(e)

2. 5.25 m s^{-1}
3. $9d/17$
4. $1/2$

Exercise 15(a)

1. 4.71 rad s^{-1}, 0.41 m s^{-1}
2. 3.67 m s^{-1}
3. 100 rad, 25 rad s^{-1}
4. 14.3 rad s^{-1}, 136
5. (i) $\pi/30$ (ii) $\pi/1800$, $11 : 10$

Exercise 15(b)

1. 18 N, 20 rad s^{-1}
2. $3/g$
3. 10 m s^{-1}, 0.24 s
4. 13.9 m s^{-1}
5. edge, $d > \,'12$ cm
7. 0.8 m
8. 30 N, 20 N, 10 N towards A
9. $3 : 2$
10. $mw^2l^2/(\lambda - mw^2l)$
11. 7.74 km s^{-1}, 91 min

Exercise 15(c)

1. $18.8°$
2. 6.3 km
3. 0.294 N, $48.2°$, 1.57 m s^{-1}
4. $d = g/w^2$, 5 cm
5. $2mg$, $\sqrt{3g/2a}$
6. 0.414, 42 m s^{-1}
7. 0.336

Exercise 15(d)

1. $14/3$ rad s^{-1}, $5 : 4$
3. 1.82 N
5. $5mg$, mg downwards, $4a/3$
6. 8.57 rad s^{-1}, thrust $4mg$

Exercise 15(e)

1. 416 N, 14 m s^{-1}
2. 1720 N
3. $3\frac{1}{2}$ rad s^{-1}, 1.79 N, 0.61 N
4. 120°, W/2
5. (i) 274 N, 2g/5 upwards   (ii) 157 N, 3g/5 along tangent
6. 3 m s^{-1}, $7\frac{1}{2}$ N, $4\frac{1}{2}$ N
7. 6.26 to 9.90 m s^{-1}
8. 3mg
9. $\sqrt{7gl}$, 5mg

Exercise 15(f)

1. (i) 3mg/2   (ii) $3\sqrt{3}mg/2$
2. $mg(3\cos\theta - 2)$, $\sqrt{2gr/3}$ at arccos (2/3) to horizontal
3. arcsin (2/3)
4. $mg(3\cos\theta - 2\cos\alpha)$, arccos (3/4), g/10, 3g/5
5. 4l/3, 4l/27
6. $2\frac{1}{2} + 15\cos\theta$, 25/12 cm
8. 30°, $\sqrt{3}\,d$, $\sqrt{4gd/3}$
9. $mg(2 + \cos\theta)$, $mg\sin\theta$, $1/\sqrt{3}$

Exercise 16(a)

1. (i) 3   (ii) 11   (iii) $5\sqrt{3}$
2. $-2\mathbf{c}$, $\mathbf{b} - \mathbf{a}$ and $-2\mathbf{c}$
3. $8\frac{1}{2}$, $6\frac{1}{2}$
4. $(\mathbf{i} - 4\mathbf{j} + 8\mathbf{k})/9$
5. 1 : 3
6. 5/3 m s^{-2}
7. 2 : 1
8. $\lambda = 1\frac{1}{2}$, $\mu = -1\frac{1}{2}$

Exercise 16(b)

1. (i) 4 (ii) 0 (iii) -7 (iv) 1 (v) 0 (vi) 0
2. Parts (ii), (v) and (vi)
3. (i) -16, 31, 15   (ii) Yes
4. (i) 63.6°   (ii) 22.6°   (iii) 115.4°
6. 60°
7. 29.3°
8. (i) $\lambda = 2$ $\mu = 4$ (ii) $\mathbf{i} + 2\mathbf{j} + 4\mathbf{k}$ (iii) $\mathbf{p}$ and $\mathbf{r}$
10. (i) 1/3, 2/3, $-2/3$; $-2/11$, 6/11, $-9/11$; $1/\sqrt{3}$, $-1/5\sqrt{3}$, $7/5\sqrt{3}$
    (ii) 73.4°, 115.4°, 31.0°; 83.6°, 63.6°, 152.7°

Exercise 16(c)

1. $\frac{1}{2}(\mathbf{i} - 3\mathbf{j} + 7\mathbf{k})$, 45 J, $15\sqrt{3/2}$ N s
2. (i) $7\mathbf{i} - \mathbf{j}$, $7\frac{3}{4}\mathbf{i} - \frac{1}{2}\mathbf{j} - 1\frac{1}{4}\mathbf{k}$
3. $(3\mathbf{i} + 11\mathbf{j} - 8\mathbf{k})/5$
4. $120°$, $t = 10/3$
5. $111.4°$
6. $t = 2$ and $t = 6$, $6\frac{2}{3}\mathbf{i} + 4\mathbf{k}$, $84\mathbf{i} + 48\mathbf{j} + 12\mathbf{k}$
7. $(0.4, 1, -0.1)$
8. $12\frac{1}{2}\mathbf{i} + 4\mathbf{j} - 3\mathbf{k}$

Exercise 16(d)

2. $\mathbf{OB} = \mathbf{a} + \mathbf{b}$, $\mathbf{BC} = \mathbf{b} - \mathbf{a}$
3. none are true   diagonal bisects angle
7. $\mathbf{v}^2 - \mathbf{u}^2 = 2\mathbf{a}.\mathbf{s}$

Exercise 16(e)

1. (i) 2   (ii) $-6/\sqrt{21}$ (iii) 0
2. $\mathbf{R} = 4\mathbf{i} + 5\mathbf{j} - 2\mathbf{k}$, sum of resolved parts $52/17$
3. (i) $2.8\mathbf{i} + 0.4\mathbf{j} + \mathbf{k}$, $0.2\mathbf{i} + 3.6\mathbf{j} - 2\mathbf{k}$ (ii) $5\sqrt{17}$ m
4. $4\mathbf{i} + 4\mathbf{j} - 2\mathbf{k}$, $3\mathbf{i} - 5\mathbf{j} - 4\mathbf{k}$, $\mathbf{i} - 7\mathbf{j} - 3\mathbf{k}$
5. 10 m s^{-2}, $(-\mathbf{i} - 15\mathbf{j} + 4\mathbf{k})/11$ N
6. (i) $2, -11, 3$ (ii) $8.4, -11, -5$
7. (i) $-3\mathbf{e}_1 + 3\mathbf{e}_2 + 2\mathbf{e}_3$ (ii) $(5\mathbf{e}_2 + 12\mathbf{e}_3)/13$

Exercise 16(f)

1. 25 units, $2\frac{1}{2}$ units
2. (i) 512 J, $-12\mathbf{i} + 44\mathbf{j} - 8\mathbf{k}$
3. (i) $10/9$ (ii) $28/9$
4. (i) 780 units   (ii) $\mathbf{u} = -3\mathbf{i} + 7\mathbf{j} + 9\mathbf{k}$,
                                   $\mathbf{v} = 7\mathbf{i} - 13\mathbf{j} - 21\mathbf{k}$

Exercise 17(a)

1. 18 m s^{-1}, 81 m
2. $\frac{1}{2}t^2 - 2t + 4\sin\frac{1}{2}t$
3. (i) $2 + 4\ln 3$ (ii) $2 + 4\ln(1 + \frac{1}{4}t)$, $4(\sqrt{e} - 1)$
4. (i) 2000 N   (ii) 25 m s^{-2} (iii) $25\ln 50$ m s^{-1}
5. (i) $2000(1 + t)$ (ii) 16 m s^{-1}, 3 s   (iii) $42\frac{2}{9}$ m
6. (i) 20 m s^{-1} (ii) $360 - 40\ln 10$ m
7. (i) $5\frac{1}{2}$ (ii) $45\frac{5}{6} - 10\ln 2$
8. $kT + e^{-kT} - 1$, $\frac{1}{2}kT^2 - T + (1 - e^{-kT})/k$
9. 2 s, $72\ln(3/2) - 28$ m

Exercise 17(b)

1. 7.9 s, 30 m s^{-1}
2. $3\frac{1}{3}$ m s^{-1}, 10 ln3 or 11.0 m
3. 7 m s^{-1}, 10.8 s, 30.0 m
4. 18.8 s, 39.5 m
5. $\dfrac{1}{2k}\ln\left(1 + \dfrac{ku^2}{g}\right)$
6. 0.52 s, 1.49 m
7. 20 m s^{-1}, ln(5/4) : ln(12/7)
8. $20(1 - e^{-d/20})^{1/2}$
9. $\dfrac{m}{k}\ln\left(1 + \dfrac{ku}{c}\right), \dfrac{m}{k}\left[u - \dfrac{c}{k}\ln\left(1 + \dfrac{ku}{c}\right)\right]$
10. $\pi u/4g$, $(u^2/2g)$ ln 2, $u/\sqrt{2}$
11. 72 m
12. (i) $8u/5$ (ii) $\sqrt{7}u/2$
13. 5 ln(200/121) = 2.51 s

Exercise 17(c)

1. $2\sqrt{3}$ m s^{-1}
2. 5 m, 19/9 s
3. 32/81 m s^{-1}
4. $2\frac{1}{2}$ m s^{-1}, 20/3 m, 16/3 s
5. 2 m s^{-1}, $\frac{1}{4}$ ln 3 = 0.275 s
6. 2 m, $\frac{1}{4}$ ln 3 = 0.275 s

Exercise 17(d)

1. (i) $mg/4$ (ii) $mg/25$ (i) $25g/36$ (ii) $4g/9$
2. (i) mgR^2/r^2 (ii) $mgR^2/(R + h)^2$
3. $(u^2 + 2gR)^{1/2}$, mgR
4. (iii) $mgR/160$
5. $2gR^2/(2gR - u^2)$
6. $[Gm(b - a)/2ab]^{1/2}$

Exercise 17(e)

1. 500, 27.6 min
2. $Q_0e^{-2.87t}$ (i) 0.24 s   (ii) 0.80 s
3. 39.7°, 22.3 min
4. $m/4$, $m/8$
5. 41%
6. 100 ln 2/n, 0.0887
7. $q_1{}^2/q_0$, $q_1{}^3/q_0{}^2$, q_1/q_0
8. $\dfrac{T_1}{a}\ln\left(\dfrac{T_0}{T_1}\right), \dfrac{T_1}{a}\ln\left(\dfrac{T_0}{2T_1 - T_0}\right)$

Exercise 17(f)

1. 175, 40.2 min
2. $E(1 - e^{-RLt})/R$
3. $2Q - (60m/\ln 2)$
6. $\dfrac{V}{k} - \left(\dfrac{V}{k} - h_0\right)e^{\frac{-kt}{4}}$
7. $x = kta^2/(kta + 1)$, $a/3$, $a/4$, $a/5$
8. 35.4°
9. 36%, 56%

Exercise 18(a)

2. $kx^3/3$
6. $39\pi/8$ cu units

Exercise 18(b)

1. (2, 0)
2. $(1\frac{1}{2}, 0)$
3. (0, 8/3)
4. (5/8, 0)
5. (3.75, 7.5)
6. (0.75, 1.6)
7. (0, $\pi/8$)
8. (2 ln2 − 1, 3/4)
10. $\left(0, \dfrac{\pi + 2}{16}\right)$

Exercise 18(d)

1. 7.32
2. 0.234(5)
3. 1.098(7)
4. (i) 0.785(4)   (ii) 3.14(16)
5. 16.7 m
6. 16.7 m³
7. 9.29(4)
8. 1845 m

Exercise 18(e)

1. 10 610 N s, 15.2 m s⁻¹
2. (i) 887 J, 13.3 m s⁻¹, 719 W   (ii) 2053 J, 20.3 m s⁻¹, 1220 W
3. 0.64 m s⁻¹
4. 2230 J, 28.6 N
5. (i) 56.5 m   (ii) 3.91 s, 14.4(5) m s⁻¹
6. 4.47 s

Exercise 19(a)

1. 0.4 m, 0.628 s, 4 m s^{-1}, 40 m s^{-2}
2. 0.255 m s^{-1}, 5.4 mm, 0.162 m s^{-1}
3. $x = 0.25 \sin 10\pi t$ (i) 6.28 m s^{-1}, 148 m s^{-1}, (ii) 2.20 m s^{-1}, 237 m s^{-2}
4. 19.1 c.p.s
5. 0.35 m, 5.92 m s^{-1}
6. (i) 1/6 m (ii) 3.38 c.p.s (iii) 7.91 m s^{-1}
7. (ii) 4.07 c.p.s
8. 6.9 mm, 0.50 m s^{-1}

Exercise 19(b)

1. 9.40 m s^{-1}, 0.274 s
2. (i) 0.242 s   (ii) 0.302 s
3. 90 cm, 63.7 cm
4. 25 cm, 0.322 s
5. 29.3 cm, 7.3cm

Exercise 19(c)

1.

	Amplitude	Period	Start	Direction
(i)	3	$\frac{1}{2}$	0	out
(ii)	10	$2\pi/5$	10	in
(iii)	5	6	$2\frac{1}{2}$	out
(iv)	5	6	$-2\frac{1}{2}$	in
(v)	5	2π	3	out
(vi)	5	2π	-3	in

2. (i) $x = 5 \cos\pi t$ (ii) $x = (4/\pi) \cos 4\pi t$
   (iii) $x = 2 \sin(10\pi t + 3\pi/4)$
                                         (iv) $x = 6 \sin (\sqrt{3}t + \pi/6)$
3. (i) $x = 4 \sin 4t + 3 \cos 4t$

   (ii) $x = 5 \sin \dfrac{\pi t}{4} - 12 \cos \dfrac{\pi t}{4}$, 13, $+5$, $+3\pi$

Exercise 19(d)

1. (i) $x = 2 \sin 4t$ (ii) $x = 5 \cos (t/10)$
2. $x = 12 \sin 2t - 5 \cos 2t$, 13, 26, 52
3. 2.5 m, 0.3 m s^{-1}
4. $3\sqrt{3}$, $-\pi$
5. (i) 12.6 h (ii) 0.24 m (iii) 0.84 m h^{-1}

Exercise 19(e)

1. 16 cm, 0.28 s
2. 70 cm, 1.4 m s^{-1}, $\pi/7$ s
3. 5 cm, 9 cm and 1 cm, $\pi/7$ s
4. 0.175 N s, 0.56 m s^{-1}, -5.88 m s^{-2}
5. 211

6. (i) $d/2$, $2\pi\sqrt{3d/2g}$, $2mg$
   (ii) $d/2$, $2\pi\sqrt{d/g}$, $3mg/2$
7. (i) $2\pi\sqrt{m/(k_1 + k_2)}$ (ii) Yes
8. $\sqrt{\lambda l/3m}$ $\pi\sqrt{ml/3\lambda}$
10. 0.136 s, $7\sqrt{2}/5$ m s^{-1}, 20 cm

Exercise 19(f)

1. 9.79 m s^{-2}
2. (i) 99.4 cm (ii) 0.3%
4. $\pi/4$ s, (i) $\pi/24$ s (ii) $\pi/48$ s

Index

Index